Endorsements

Yoga Crisis offers a unique and fascinating window into the per-spectives and experiences of the plaintiffs in the most highly pub-licized yoga trial of all time. Readers will discover a very different side of the story than the one portrayed by the media.

– Candy Gunther Brown,
Harvard Ph.D. and Author of
Debating Yoga and Mindfulness in Public Schools -
Reforming Secular Education or Reestablishing Religion?

What can one do when a school district makes decisions that blind-side parents mandating yoga as the new Physical Education cur-riculum in elementary schools? The answer is to do what Jennifer Sedlock was forced to do—uncover and expose the truth no matter the cost! This book tells the story of her and other's relentless pur-suit and tenacious efforts to preserve and protect the minds and hearts of children in public schools.

– Clark Gilbert,
Former Superintendent, Tri City Christian Schools, Wheaton
Graduate (Wheaton Law - Review of trial titled:
How the CA Judge got it Wrong).

India banned yoga in their schools shortly after this trial. Having traveled to India, the Hindu people cannot comprehend why Americans think yoga is *just exercise*. I am deeply concerned that yoga is being taught in our public schools. *Yoga Crisis* addresses why students should not be led to pray and meditate in a yoga format.

– Bob Botsford,
Pastor and Author, Horizon Church,
Rancho Santa Fe, CA.

THE YOGA CRISIS IN AMERICA

JENNIFER SEDLOCK

THE YOGA
CRISIS
in
AMERICA

A WAKE-UP CALL TO PROTECT THE CHILDREN

Laura —
What a Journey!
Thank you for all
the support &
prayers!
love
[signature]

Xulon Press Elite

Xulon Press Elite
2301 Lucien Way #415
Maitland, FL 32751
407.339.4217
www.xulonpress.com

Unless otherwise indicated, Scripture quotations taken from the Holy Bible, New International Version (NIV). Copyright © 1973, 1978, 1984, 2011 by Biblica, Inc.™. Used by permission. All rights reserved.

Edited by Xulon Press.

Printed in the United States of America.

ISBN-13: 978-1-5456-2333-6

Foreword
by Rebecca Melton

J ennifer Sedlock is uniquely qualified to write this book. For the nearly thirty years of our acquaintance, three things stand out most: her integrity, her faith, and her boundless energy. In combination, the three are a force for good in this challenging world.

First consider her integrity. She is an educated woman with a Bachelor's degree in Business from University of California Berkeley and a Master's Degree in Organization Development from University of San Francisco. Her education along with her business experience (we met in management), have built a foundation of law, wisdom and critical thinking skills. Jennifer knows what ethical dealings involve and has been trained to spot deception, manipulation, and illegal activity (including bribery and use of gifts against policy).

As for faith, she has consistently operated to do the right thing, even when it has been difficult: from leaving a treasured church when led by the Lord to do so; to choosing to set aside a lucrative career to dedicate herself to the mission of raising a family; and to pursuing the yoga in schools problem. She speaks truth and has communicated difficult things in love, in this book, and to me throughout the years. We all need at least one friend who we can trust to do that. For 30 years, she has been that one for me.

Next, consider the energy required to add taking on a school system to an already full plate. Jennifer has served multiple boards and positions over the years aiding various causes for the schools, such as budgets, fundraisers, and volunteering in math, English and PE. In addition, her volunteering at church has included both leadership and children's programs. These service activities all occurred while raising her family, working part time coaching high school sports, and of course, her professional job! There's that boundless energy I mentioned.

Her composure was impressive throughout the process. Despite the difficulty of this situation as it grew into a lawsuit, and now exposing it with this book, she didn't "get upset" and "act crazy." She researched, asked questions, asked others their opinions, and shared what she learned with school officials and politely asked for her children's rights.

When met with opposition as tall as a mountain, she and her husband were the only two with the courage, the integrity and the faith to "stay the course." Imagine all the calls from reporters intruding in your life. Imagine the nights her children came to her about being picked on at school, and having to move schools impacting friendships for her little girl and the entire family. Consider putting hundreds of hours and thousands of dollars of your own, to seek protection for other children and to be forced to seek safety for your own family.

In truth, we cannot imagine what she faced – but you can read about it here. Further, if there is danger in yoga being in schools, wouldn't you like to know? Read this book and you be the judge about yoga in schools.

With Respect and Humility,

Rebecca Melton, PhD, MBA

Foreword
by Alicia Hall

"Would you like to go for coffee?" said one brave mother to the new face in the crowd. The new one was desperate for friendship and a sense of belonging in her new surroundings. That "Yes" was the beginning of something that neither woman would have been able to comprehend at the time. The brave one, Jennifer Sedlock, is THAT kind of friend. Her willingness to step out of her comfort zone and extend a welcoming smile to me was a moment of long-lasting impact on my heart. She's the one that you want in your corner, that you want to go to for advice, that you want praying for you, and that you want to continue to have coffee with.

Since that day, in 2008, we have faced a lot of things together.... tough things, real things. Jennifer never waivers in her faith, nor in her desire to follow God's truth. Simply put, whether it be for her own family, for her loved ones, or for the sake of Christ, she is a Warrior.

The sacrifices that Jennifer and her family have made to stand strong against the deceptive practices of yoga have been excruciating to watch. I don't know that I've ever seen a friend fight so tenaciously for truth and continue to operate under the umbrella of joy as much as my friend, Jennifer. The message in her book is riveting and worthy of your time. So armor up and grab a cup of coffee as you read through one woman's journey as she takes you through darkness and back into the light. I'm sure as you finish the final pages, you too, will see why I call her friend.

Alicia Hall

Dedication

This book is dedicated to those harmed, led astray, and lost, due to yoga.

And, for the parents who have lost children to suicide over yoga. May our country (and others) wake-up to the *Yoga Crisis* you already know so well!

These sites are dedicated to the education of yoga in America.

www.truthaboutyoga.com

https://www.facebook.com/factsaboutyoga/

https://twitter.com/truthaboutyoga

Contents

Illustrations, Diagrams and Textboxes

Introduction
by Jennifer Sedlock

Wake up and smell the coffee – Is Yoga the *New PE* in America?

Years ago when I first heard about yoga, I thought it was just a new fad of exercise entering the gyms, similar to step-aerobics or kickboxing. Yoga appeared to be designed for an older crowd as a low-impact activity. At the time, I was in my 20's and preferred high-impact, fast paced aerobics, so I wasn't interested at all in yoga.

I never dreamed that years later I would write a book about yoga. I never wanted to write this book, nor did I see a reason to be concerned when the Jois Yoga program entered our elementary school district in Encinitas. But that's exactly what transpired over the next years.

Photo credit: Brian Chernicky, ImagineDynamic.com

Our beachside California community is about twenty-five miles north of downtown San Diego. Encinitas includes nine elementary schools. As a mother of three children ranging in age from 7-14 at that time, I simply didn't see the problems with yoga at first. But, just like many other families, I wasn't aware of the backroom decisions and handshakes by our school district officials that would entangle our children and decrease the physical education program. When I did finally look, I couldn't believe what was happening in public schools right under *our* noses.

Many other parents began researching the new Encinitas Union School District yoga program long before I was invited to pay attention. The snowball began with an increasing number of parents each week who shared their concerns at school board meetings for four months the fall of 2012.

With little to no response from the school district, beyond dismissal of parent questions and concerns, frustrations grew as the months passed. The focus shifted to talk of litigation options toward the end of the year, and parent outcry ballooned. The *group of concerned parents* continued to gather research and began educating the public on the type of yoga program entering our elementary schools. In late 2012, there was a decision to file for removal of the Jois Yoga program. The lawsuit filed February 2013 instantly gained international attention.

The impact of this lawsuit reaches far beyond this one form of yoga, and the Encinitas Union School District. Yoga practitioners, former yoga instructors, scholars and law students are discussing and writing articles about the trial, and the issue of yoga in public schools. Several other countries are responding in their own legal systems whether to allow yoga in their schools.

Clearly, yoga is growing exponentially in our country. But, does yoga belong in elementary schools replacing cardiovascular PE and shaping the minds and future norms of children in America? In the pages ahead are many details and evidence that will help you discern and decide for yourself with many facts that were unable to be presented at trial, nor would the media expose due to the current public "pro yoga" bias in California. As the trial proceeded, so did the work of the parent group; we produced a website, social media, newsletters, and public education events. Exposing the truth was the goal, and what was unraveling was beyond disturbing. And now to sum up the events, as your eyeballs roll across the words, a book.

This is a story about a yoga program targeted and created for the American elementary school system. We are parents raising children in America today with many influences shifting into the school systems to reshape the way our children think and form their worldviews. News media portrayed a very different side of this story than you will see here. From pre-trial steps attempted by parents to "inside the courtroom" scenes from the trial, to the aftermath of unintended consequences that have already surfaced from children doing yoga in schools; *This is the side of the story that was never heard, until now.*

A website of the concerned parents is referenced throughout the book (www.truthaboutyoga.com) with links giving further information. You may want to get the *eBook version* offered there, so that you can click on the many links provided in this book. The coupon code to get $5 off the eBook price (of $9.99) is: bringbackPE.

I hope that this *behind the scenes* look into the Encinitas Elementary School Yoga Trial and plethora of research, gives you a better foundation of information about the impact of yoga in schools. As a mom from the Midwest, raising three kids in this dynamic day and age in California schools, along with others looking into this yoga program, noticed that *something wasn't quite right.*

Photo credit Adnan Abidi: http://tamildiplomat.com/ narendra-modi-leads-thousands-in-international-day-of-yoga-celebration/

Try to picture some elementary children before you begin. Maybe drive by a local school and watch the playground, or take a tour. At a minimum, imagine through the next few statements.

Observe some children to:

Remember the innocence.

Remember the sponge-like quality young children have naturally.

Remember the fact that if you are nice to a child, they are instantly drawn to you.

Remember how easy it is to get them to do almost anything. They trust quickly.

Remember how important it is to protect them, and why laws and fences are in place.

Then, read this book.

For the children

Section One: Stepping Stones Leading to a Trial over Yoga in Schools

CHAPTER ONE

Something wasn't quite right ...

I couldn't believe what I was hearing. As I sat on a warm, soft couch in an unfamiliar home a few blocks from my own, I was in shock. I was listening and soaking up everything the parents said about their children's experiences with the new yoga program placed in our elementary schools. I knew a few of the parents, but there was a crowd of others I didn't know. So many that they were filling the living and dining rooms, and a few were standing as there simply weren't enough seats. I could hardly believe my ears. Although the October chill was outside, I began to feel it inside that night. There was even an attorney and a pastor in the room. Why were they here? How long had these people been meeting? My mind was racing with questions and thoughts as parent after parent told what was happening to their children in yoga. All were parents concerned for their children. I had *no* idea the deception we would soon find. I had no idea the miles we would walk in this journey. All I knew right then and there was that "something wasn't quite right." I knew I needed to find out more. I could hardly wait to get off the couch and start investigating. I had no idea the depth and breadth of what I would find, and it would be more chilling than the drive home that night in October.

Fall 2012 - *"Back to School Night"*

Backing up a couple months to August 2012; the school year started much like the eight years prior. We headed back to the familiarity of the same elementary school. I was busy transitioning back from summer into my own work along with three kids settling into classes. Our boys were entering eighth and sixth grade while our daughter was starting second grade. We were meeting new teachers and filling out a lot of forms, as usual. Nothing seemed different. The awareness could have started at *back-to-school-night*, but it didn't for me. The principal announced we had a new program by a grant from a generous foundation for weekly yoga in every grade. Little detail was presented about the new yoga program, but my husband said the hairs on his neck went up and he wondered, "Why yoga?" He joked: "What happened to dodge ball?" I didn't think much about it that night and told him not to worry. We didn't ask anything and neither did anyone else. It was merely a short announcement sandwiched in between others. Perhaps that is why most of us didn't know what was coming.

What wasn't said ...

The principals didn't announce that yoga would replace sixty of the one hundred minutes of physical education (PE) each week. They didn't mention that the grant was from a highly religious organization that only taught and promoted "Ashtanga" yoga. They skipped the part about weighing and measuring our children for a three year "study" to later promote yoga to other schools. Parental permission and signatures weren't even acquired the first year that these biometrics were taken. They didn't mention that the Jois Foundation would be paying the grant through a third party in order to have their own yoga instructors paid more than other specialized teachers in our district. It was never mentioned that curriculum would be created by these yoga teachers. Nor did they tell us the Jois Foundation was going to spread Ashtanga curriculum to more schools in the US. They didn't mention the three-year contract with Jois Foundation, or the fact that the half-million dollar grant would cause the district to be unable to offer an option of regular PE. No, we were only told that it was a very wonderful gift that we should appreciate.

Shortly after back-to-school night, I began hearing other parents share their concerns about the organization that was contracted and funding the *Ashtanga* yoga. I'd never heard of Ashtanga, but, at that point I thought yoga would be fine and healthy for the kids. Other moms kept asking me to look into the Jois Foundation and the teachers' backgrounds and their ties to India for their training. I didn't. That year, I was the leader of a group called "moms in prayer" for our school, which is an international program (https://momsinprayer.org/) [1] that is a group of moms praying weekly together for the school staff, teachers and children. Therefore, after multiple members requested, I felt like I needed to check into it, given their concerns. It didn't take longer than that first parent meeting and a couple hours on the internet to see we had a potential landmine entering the district. How had this slipped through? How had something this all-encompassing taken over so much PE time? Did the board members have any time to look into this foundation and grant that the Superintendent brought to them in one board meeting (according to board meeting notes) the summer of 2012?

October 4, 2012 - Concerned Parents Meeting

The first time I heard the designation "concerned parents" was when I was invited to the October 4, 2012 "concerned parents meeting" about yoga in the Encinitas Union School District (EUSD). A group was forming that not only named themselves, but had a private Facebook page to share information. Their first meeting was in August or September of 2012. Three separate calls from concerned moms from other schools in Encinitas in August had invited the same attorney to the first meeting. He was known locally for handling cases to protect religious rights and freedom. Years later I was told that the attorney was reluctant to meet with the parents, but after the third call, he agreed. He became concerned at the first meeting. I wasn't sure why he was there in October, and I wasn't sure what to expect out of the meeting. I was just seeking information.

The meeting was well-organized with an agenda and there was a sign-in form requesting that we include our names, email addresses and phone numbers. There were *two* attorneys, a pastor, and twenty five to thirty parents present. The parents there represented not only themselves, but their spouses at home taking care of their kids. Five schools in the district had started yoga and the other four were due to start in January. My school was slotted for January, so my kids had not said anything about yoga. The parents of children already doing yoga expressed their concerns over what was happening to their own children in the yoga classrooms at their schools. With very little information about the program, I was all ears, listening.

Statements about yoga by Concerned Parents

Some of the concerns included the following statements:

> *"My son was reprimanded in yoga class and told to sit staring at the corner for thirty minutes. Do these teachers have any experience with children and discipline?"*

> *"Capri Elementary is my school and we piloted the program. The Ashtanga Eight-limbed poster was on the walls and I asked the teacher about it. She said they are only teaching the first few limbs for now (Samadhi is "limb 8" meaning—"union with the divine"). I do not want religion taught to my children in the form of movements. This is pagan worship."*

> *"My child is ADHD and needs to release some energy like any little boy in elementary school. Why is stretching for thirty minutes seen as good for this age? Kids are limber at ages five and six and twelve! They need to get the energy out, not sit more."*

> *"I was invited here and my kids are not doing yoga yet, but now I am concerned and will be researching more about this. I did some research on our child's yoga teacher at El Camino Creek and she spent three years in India. I*

also know the "head teacher" is Jen Brown and she too "sojourns" to India practicing Hinduism, according to her website. She also now works for Jois yoga and EUSD and you can find her on the Jois website, as well as her own."

"My daughter was told to say Namaste to the teacher upon entering and leaving the room."

"My son told me they rang a bell to signify when to stop doing the last task they were told in order to clear their mind of thoughts. I think these are Hindu bells used in meditation."

"My kids said they have to take their shoes off before entering the room and place them facing north and that they face that direction for some poses."

"My daughter is worried about the cleanliness of the mats and it has only been two months—the August and September heat and coupled with multiple kids using one set of mats for the whole school. I asked the yoga teacher and they had no cleaning plan for the mats."

"My kids don't like yoga and neither do their friends—they want to run and play. This is an extension of quiet time they have for six hours already."

"My child's class was put into circle on the floor, in lotus position, with their hands palms together in prayer position and bowing heads to one another closing eyes and repeating Namaste over and over to different children in the circle. "(Park Dale Lane)

"My yoga teacher told me she is very upset because these classes of thirty to forty kids are way too big for her to make a difference with any one child. Yoga is ideally taught one-to-one she said, and yoga teachers are trained to teach

a small group of adults, not a room full of rowdy kids!"
(Mission Estancia)

*"There are many children pulled out of yoga in our school
already, I think we will pull out tomorrow after hearing
all this. I'm very concerned. "(Olivenhein Pioneer
Elementary—OPE)*

*"My son was told the Sanskrit names for his body and I am
not sure what that all means but I think it might be a part
of traditional yoga—does anyone know what Sanskrit is?"*
(Flora Vista)

*"My 1ˢᵗ grade daughter is pulled out of yoga and I have to
pick her up during yoga class because there is no supervision for her. She loves it because now Friday is "Daddy and
Panera" hour. We need an alternative PE or supervision
solution for these kids."*

*"This yoga IS pagan worship and Ashtanga is known for
"Sun Worship" which is what the "opening series" sequence
is teaching these children." (El Camino Creek)*

*"I'm concerned that these teachers aren't credentialed and
are alone with my kids saying who knows what? If I, as
a caring trustworthy parent, am not allowed by state law
to be alone with a class, then why is a young yogi alone
with them?"*

Utter Shock and Disbelief

To say I was in shock would be an understatement. What I was
hearing was nearly unbelievable. When the sharing came around to
my side of the room, I offered my initial thoughts that I had come
to the meeting *because I was invited, not because I was all that
concerned.* Two of my three kids attended El Camino Creek, so we
hadn't started yoga yet and I came to gain insight into *all the fuss*

8

about yoga. I shared that I was now troubled after listening to all of them and realizing that yoga might be *more than stretching* in these elementary school classes. My initial apprehension was also perhaps simpler than most of theirs.

My main *concern* was that I wouldn't want any form of exercise or sport to dominate a PE program. Kids need variety for fitness and to learn what they are good at, while burning some energy and building healthy bodies. Since our students have one hundred minutes of PE per week (our state mandates 200 minutes every ten instructional days https://www.cde.ca.gov/ls/fa/sf/peguideelement. asp)[2] and yoga had become sixty minutes of that week, then that means two-thirds of their PE time *had now been dedicated to …just yoga? For Seven years?* I wouldn't want volleyball for that much time! Nor, would any other single sport dominating their PE time be good. Just as volleyball isn't for everyone, neither is yoga. But if all US students play volleyball for sixty minutes weekly, for seven years, we would become a volleyball nation in just one decade. I tried at the time, to imagine the US as a yoga nation in just one decade. (And ha, I don't have to conjure that image up for long—it is happening rapidly!) I remember thinking there was more here than meets the eye. Over a half of a million dollars that fall of 2012 was paid to EUSD to implement *just Ashtanga yoga.* Why?

What Could Parents Do?

The attorney at the parent meeting was Dean Broyles from the National Center for Law & Policy (NCLP—http://www.nclplaw. org/).[3] He was also trained in "Alliance Defending Freedom" as an affiliate attorney at National Litigation Academies (NLA). This is an important distinction to note—ADF lawyers have additional training to defend our freedoms as Americans. He is part of ADF's honor guard, after being invited and receiving, advanced training at NLA.

Broyles let us know there was a school board meeting on October 9, 2012 and asked if anyone would like to share their thoughts in person with the district. He also explained to us that the meeting format for our school board meetings allowed for only five to seven speakers for two to three minutes each during public comments section of the meeting. This meant we only had fifteen minutes to present our case to the school board. Due to lack of response, it became clear that despite many were upset, most parents were too afraid to speak at a board meeting. At that moment, I knew one reason I might be involved.

Express concerns to the EUSD board?

Many people are terrified to speak in public. Toastmasters clubs are available in most cities to help with the paralyzing fear of speaking in public for so many. I realized I might be able to be an advocate to speak up for the adults who were in fear and the children, who had no voice or platform to share. A loud and clear message rang in my ears; call it conviction or resolution. I didn't have a clue what would unfold and be revealed in the days, weeks, months and years ahead, but I knew to trust and take this seriously that night. *Something was not right.*

A Little Research Goes a Long Way

Twenty minutes on the Internet showed enough to be even more concerned! Three hours later and I knew the Jois Yoga Foundation had a mission to put Ashtanga yoga into schools across the nation, and that our district was the target to create the curriculum for them. It was clear from the board meeting that our superintendent was boastfully proud of their new "partnership." The EUSD elected school board was led straight into a pen like sheep. But how much did they know? We would soon hear them claim they didn't know much. Had the $533,000 grant grabbed their attention? Had the board been led into a July contract with very little information? Did they make a quick decision to hire and train Ashtanga yoga teachers for a program to be up and running just weeks later by the start of school in mid-August?

Going to Board Meetings

Many of us went to the EUSD board meetings to express our physical, fiscal, religious and various other concerns. We had many. They were valid. The board did not respond much after the first meeting. They did not attempt to answer our questions nor respect our words or requests. In fact, the Superintendent did the opposite; he was disrespecting us to reporters multiple times, such as calling us "just a few" and misrepresenting what we said (media proof below). When one hundred people show up to a board meeting that usually drew only a few people, is that really *just a few*? And even if it was just five on an issue, wouldn't those concerns still be valid and important? Following are some details of those board and parent meetings in the fall of 2012.

October 9th, 2012— EUSD School Board Meeting

About sixty parents (representing spouses, too) attended the EUSD school board meeting in October of 2012 to share our concerns about the new yoga program. The board seemed very interested to find out why we were there and listened intently to what we had to say that evening. Perhaps the fact that media reporters and a large number of parents were there piqued their interest. Given this was the first meeting to draw media, no parents attended in support of yoga. Seven of us spoke during the *public comments* section of the board meeting.

I had three topics I chose to address:

1. Is any *one* form of PE good for kids at this age to dominate 2/3 of PE time?
2. Why no PE alternatives if we opt our kids out of yoga? How will they get graded?
3. Why are kids pulled from core subjects like math to be "measured" for the Jois Foundation study, rather than during

yoga time? (I observed this when volunteering in Mrs. Weber's second grade math class.) The answer given by the board was that they didn't want to embarrass the children. Hmmm. I watched those kids line up outside the math room to get weighed and measured right in front of each other, while the person weighing reported out loud the weight for someone else to write it down! Talk about embarrassing! And the bigger problem in my mind, *they lost math time*!

The other six parents spoke passionately and candidly about other concerns. One spoke about what was occurring in many of the classrooms, overviewing what parents had reported. Another presented concerns over the Sanskrit being taught to kids for names of their body parts. One talked about a yoga book being read to the children containing a lot of spiritual concepts, and the Ashtanga poster on the wall at Capri of the eight Limbs, including references to "*union with the divine*." Another parent discussed the problems of opting-out their kids and how the children were not supervised, left sitting in the back of another classroom using an iPad while missing out on state mandated physical education. Unintentionally, one parent stole the show.

Uproar in the EUSD Board Room

Since the local news media was covering everyone in the room, there was added pressure for those speaking, and unfortunately one dad's words would get pulled out of context and highlighted in the evening news. He said something to this effect— "Indoctrinating the children with yoga meditation like this twice a week, over years, is not unlike what Hitler did when he targeted the young children to teach them a new philosophy to follow." Well, that set off a bomb in the room for board member Marla Strich (who is a daughter of a WWII Holocaust survivor, she would tell everyone). She lashed out at him and spewed her frustration all over the room. The media loved it. This was the focus on the evening news instead of our multiple concerns. Unfortunately, many news reporters hounded this family at their home in the weeks to follow, causing them distress. His family also experienced harassment from adults at school. Many of us would soon endure similar treatment for simply sharing *any* of our concerns over yoga.

I wonder if he was onto something prophetic rather than a quick unintended comment. If yoga and meditation *can* change your worldview and thinking, as evidenced by a plethora of research covered in later chapters, then perhaps the indoctrination comment wasn't a stretch that night. Patience and strength have been incredibly hard in this journey, but for those of us who have walked this path, we have developed an incredible patience for the truth to come out over time. Having no idea what would transpire after that October 9th meeting, I was awake, alert, and now researching all about this yoga program.

Some of the media coverage of that meeting is located here:

Oct 23, 2012—Parents May Sue Over Yoga Lessons in Public Schools http://abcnewsradioonline.com/health-news/parents-may-sue-over-yoga-lessons-in-public-schools.html[4]

Oct 23, 2012—Suit Eyed Over Yoga in Public Schools https://www.yahoo.com/news/suit-eyed-over-yoga-public-schools-184622594-abc-news-topstories.html [5]

We parents *had a few questions*

Given the slick method of introducing the program into the district, and the reluctance to provide much information, we parents had a lot of questions. Over the next few months, we queried the board members, staffs, and principals at our schools. The answers given and the lack of responses became even more concerning than the original questions we asked! One question led to another. Answers revealed deeper issues which kept many of us continuing to look further into what this all meant for our children. Some of the initial questions are in the following box.

Some of the questions we began to ask:

Q—Should yoga replace the traditional variety of PE for 60 of the 100 minutes required weekly? (http://www.cde.ca.gov/ta/tg/pf/ [6] gives you what the California State Board of Education requires).

Q—Should a third party be able to buy their way into the school system like this? What precedent does this set?

Q—Why isn't yoga an optional PE or an after school program like all the other types of "extracurricular" activities?

Q—The kids were tested by a third party. Why were the parents not asked for consent prior for physical measuring of their children?

Q—Is stretching and breathing really what kids need after 6 hours of class time sitting? What about cardiovascular exercise and learning different sports, getting fresh air and sunshine?

Q—What if it was tennis, would anyone have a problem with that replacing 60 minutes per week for 7 years? We'd be a tennis nation in one decade! And there certainly isn't any holy tennis, so would that be okay? No. "Tennis isn't for everyone either," just like yoga isn't for everyone. So why pick *ANY* one form of PE to dominate so much time?

Q—Is yoga really in the best interest of the kids? Or was the money the district received too hard to pass up?

Q—California law states un-credentialed adults (such as parents) should not be alone in a room with children at school. Why then, are there non-credential yoga teachers allowed in the EUSD yoga classes?

Q—What about the warnings of physical injuries by doctors for youth doing yoga? https://truthaboutyoga.com/concerns-about-yoga/ [7]

Q—What "norm" are we conditioning in our children when they leave elementary school by setting up more hours in their youth practicing yoga than we do most other activities such as piano, art, sports, etc.? Doesn't this "normalize" yoga for kids?

Q—How many families actually had their children in yoga classes outside of school, prior to this entering the schools in 2011/2012?

Q—What about the cleanliness of the mats given that class after class uses them daily in these large elementary schools? There appears to be no plan and no cleaning.

Q—What are the sexual implications when sixth grade boys and girls in a class of 40 are bending down and all around in tight dark settings with regular school clothes on (have you seen what kids wear today?— with short shorts and blousy tops—not best for the yoga rooms)

Q—How did a program this spiritual get into the school system with current laws?

The Encinitas Union School District (EUSD)

Photo credit: Ch 10 ABC, Four members of the 2012 EUSD Board

It's important to note the reactions and responses of the EUSD board to the parents. Gregg Sonken, one of the five EUSD board members, was present at the October 9th school board meeting. He stood up in response to our comments and said "I am very concerned about what these parents are saying—did we not research this group enough [Jois Foundation]? We need to look into this and perhaps cut off the contract with Jois Foundation." *This was the only encouraging thing any board member displayed that evening and for the next several years.* The other board members did not respond much beyond the frustration from one woman I mentioned earlier. There was chatter from another elected board member, Emily Andrade, who said she does yoga and likes it and people like Julia Roberts and other stars do it so why would it be a problem? We can get into the fact that Julia Roberts evolved into Buddhism, but most of the comments were about whether the board members personally liked yoga. These comments were made to and facing one another - not addressing the public in the room. They were beginning to grapple with the question though—is yoga religious?

With sixty of us showing up to tell the board and staff that this yoga program crossed our boundaries of exercise with religion, we were clear that we didn't want our children subjected to yoga. The Superintendent's response to the news media (not to us) was *"this is not religious and these parents are wrong."* However, as evidenced by us all saying that yoga crosses our boundary line of physical and religious teaching, *it obviously does!*

So, we started pulling our children out of yoga classes, family by family, school by school. Many parents were still too afraid of the consequences though … (understandably!)

November 12, 2012—Concerned Parents Meeting

Number of Concerned Parents Increased

From the media that followed the October board meeting, more parents were becoming concerned, so numbers increased at the next parent and board meetings in November. Two attorneys battled over yoga on CNN and multiple national talk shows like "The Doctors" were beginning to cover the story in Encinitas. The superintendent admitted that the classes needed to be "cleaned up of cultural and religious references" because the curriculum was posted and parents pointed out the spiritual words and poses. Many were Sanskrit words which, converted to English, are highly spiritual words.

The parent meeting ran about the same as before with signing in, parents sharing what was happening with their own children and others in their schools. The newest twist was in responses from the staff as parents attempted to remove their children from yoga. It became increasingly more difficult. The school rules kept changing and it became obvious it was all sourcing from district directives. The staff tried to talk parents into watching another yoga class, made new requirements to meet with the principal, (which could take weeks to get an appointment) and asked parents to re-think their decision. Divisiveness was erupting in conversations and blew up into conflict among parents on school grounds.

PTA meetings were tense for the concerned parents because others tried to influence the perceptions about the yoga program and promote it to the PTA groups. In one school, La Costa Heights, the pressure from the principal in PTA was so strong that anyone against yoga kept silent for the first school year. Most of the parents and teachers across the district against yoga were simply silent. They could not afford to share their concerns at that point, given the ridicule and anger *over yoga*. I'll point out now that those of us against yoga in school were not angry. It was those that wanted yoga free-in-schools who became adamant and displayed loss of control, such as name-calling and harsh words or actions. Proof of this was captured in the media.

November 13, 2012 - EUSD School Board Meeting

More people and media sources attended the November, 2012 board meeting than prior. Many professional yoga community members (studio owners) also attended. Prior to the meeting, an offsite retreat occurred in San Francisco for the EUSD board with Superintendent Baird and Assistant Superintendent David Miyashiro. Other parents were questioning the legality (Brown Act requirement for open meetings) of the privacy of the offsite retreat, since it was not then a public meeting. They also questioned the financial costs of this retreat. Our group was primarily concerned with the fact that the board seemed to be synchronizing their actions in opposition to our concerns about the yoga program as a result of this retreat. Gregg Sonken (who showed concern prior) now sat with a glazed-over expression matching the rest of the board this month. We tried to appeal to many aspects of the yoga program problems, but the board did not respond at all this time. Our concerns grew, just as the numbers in our group multiplied.

The room was full of tension, media and angry-looking people who professed to love yoga and the program. The board smiled, nodded and gave feedback in verbal form to anyone saying anything positive about the yoga program, minutes after stating that they could not respond to anyone (against yoga) because it wasn't an agenda item. Note that two years later a parent would point out that there is no such rule in their bylaws for not responding to public about public comments off the agenda! They made it up. Or maybe they misinterpreted a bylaw. No one refuted it at the time though in 2012. Some of the board and staff even looked away as any of us spoke. We were now being called the *"anti-yoga group." We would not hear one verbal response to our concerns for the remaining board meetings that Fall or next year.*

One of the articles after the November meeting:

Group of Parents in Encinitas view yoga in elementary school as religious indoctrination http://articles.latimes.com/2012/nov/07/ local/la-me-yoga-20121107 [8] (Note: when you read an article, don't stop at the end of the article, read the comments from the public to see the vast scrutiny and ridicule. Separation of Church and State is merely *one* issue in a vast amount of issues surrounding the trial! The comments got downright vicious and hurtful. Ask: *Why?*

December 2012—Concerned Parent Meeting

The December, 2012 *concerned parent meeting* began with many more concerns and ended with this resolve: *this board meeting would be our last attempt to talk to the board.* The attorney was clear with us that if they would not listen after this, there was nothing he could do further to help us unless some of us were willing to take legal action. Of course none of us thought that would ever happen. We thought the board would listen since we had a petition and more evidence of problems with yoga. As you are reading this book, you will see that was not the case.

December 4, 2012—EUSD School Board Meeting

December. 2012 was by far the largest and most divisive of all the board meetings. According to several different news outlets, the audience was counted at 100—120 depending on which article you read. We in the group opposed to yoga noticed many of the "pro-yoga" people speaking and in the audience didn't appear to be parents in the district. We would find out afterwards while talking in the parking lot (where media was doing interviews) that many were local yoga studio owners, yoga enthusiasts from the community, and even yoga teachers from Jois Yoga. In fact, a pro-yoga website for Encinitas parents was created by a young studio owner who disclosed that fact to us directly (in the parking lot) and we had a lovely discussion with him. He understandably wanted to support yoga in the community. Another Facebook page and petition was started by an attorney. So those with a vested local interest came out to support yoga, not just parents but those who stood to gain a lot more business from yoga in schools.

A Heated Battle

Given that we had been to the board meetings prior, we knew that we would only be allowed fifteen minutes and seven speakers maximum. However, the rules kept shifting each meeting and this one would change the most to benefit the board's clear leaning to the pro-yoga folks. One of the rules was about filling out a speaking card, which you turn into the staff prior to commencement of the meeting. The board allowed just those who fill out a card and divide the time between all. But this day *nineteen* of the pro-yoga people ended up being allowed to speak! And most hadn't filled out cards! This rule by the board had not been "broken" until that night. Sadly, we were getting used to their changing the rules. In addition, the board again made verbal comments to pro-yoga people after claiming they were not allowed to respond to us. The board didn't speak to any of us. The changes to the rules simply displayed their obvious bias—to respond when they heard what they wanted to hear. To the media, and public watching the news that night, it looked like there were a lot more people in support of yoga than against, but that wasn't the reality in the room that night. It was simply the amount of speakers that were allowed to speak. Those of us against yoga in schools had easily double the amount of people there, yet those that were supporting yoga were granted triple the air time. Reports of the meeting were skewed when televised. Are these the actions of a school board showing the integrity and honesty we want our children to emulate? Whose agenda is being protected?

A couple of other trends began to appear: many of the "pro yoga" speakers that night started off by stating their own religion such as "I'm a Catholic and ...", "I'm an Atheist and ...", "I'm Jewish and ..." I wondered if they kept claiming yoga wasn't religious, then why did they feel the need to state what religious beliefs they hold? Watch and read the media. It's quite interesting. Second, the "heated" tone of most of the pro-yoga speakers, name-calling and labeled our group as yoga-haters or anti-yoga. We were called fanatics, fundamentalists, intolerant and much more and angry tones were evident. Ironically, we kept getting called judgmental by people who were actually displaying their own judgements. But you wouldn't see that anger lashing out from our side of parents at other parents. We didn't retaliate and we didn't call names back. Other parents were not our focus. Our objectives were to speak with the board members who were the people able to make changes. You can watch most any of the media to see this behavior contrasting the two sides. And *they* claim yoga is calming! *Hmmm ... something was not quite right!*

Dec 16, 2012—New York Times: Yoga class draws a religious protest: http://www.nytimes.com/2012/12/16/us/school-yoga-class-draws-religious-protest-from-christians.html?_r=1[9]

Medical, Religious and Divisiveness Concerns over Yoga

At that wild December EUSD board meeting, many parents expressed that yoga crossed their religious boundaries, among many other concerns. Of specific alarm was idol worship that had now been found as the root of Ashtanga yoga (by worshipping and bowing to the sun). Parents were educating themselves on the Jois Foundation, Jois Yoga, and what the EUSD had jumped into by contracting with Jois. [Details and links will be given in the Jois yoga chapter.]

One of the parents offered various credible medical findings opposed (physically) to children doing yoga, including the highly respected Mayo Clinic. Documents and information will be covered in the injuries chapter of this book and on our website, but the board was clearly warned about injuries to young women's hips in particular. Another parent discussed the religious nature of many things happening in the schools, summarizing many other parents' input. since we thought only a few could speak. She also shared the divisiveness erupting in the schools over yoga and even referenced the current room as evidence of the angry behaviors of the *pro-yoga* supporters.

Another parent covered the yoga curriculum created by the Ashtanga yoga teachers for EUSD, pointing to the many religious references and components shown in the November copy available from the District. She showed the hypocrisy of how this is a gateway to Hinduism and apparently fine with the board, but if it were a path to Christianity, it would be ousted already. In addition, it was shared that the spiritual nature of yoga is within the physical movements, not cerebral like Westerners tend to think of "religion." That is why learning about a religion in schools and performing it with their bodies, is different. Performing yoga is inherently a spiritual ritual to Jois Yoga, according to the yogis and the creators.

Another parent covered what the Ashtanga yoga gurus and Hindus themselves say about the religious nature of Ashtanga yoga. They are clear on their websites, in all their writings and promotion of their yoga. Yet somehow, the EUSD board was still denying the spiritual components after two months of our concerns being shared. Links to websites were given to them and they had the Jois Foundation and Jois Yoga at their fingertips, if or when they chose to look. The attorney spoke and did a summary of the legal issues involved. Broyles received a lot of ridicule and sneers both in and outside the meetings. The board was never receptive to him. He withstood a lot of scrutiny in the media, but stood his ground to protect the children's rights.

Armed with a Petition of 250 Signatures

We gathered a petition over Thanksgiving weekend with 250 signatures of community members, asking for removal of yoga out of the Encinitas elementary schools. We thought that, if the board was willing to look at this, it might make a difference. I didn't set up the petition, but happened to be the one presenting that part and gave each of the five board members a copy and one to Timothy Baird, the Superintendent. They didn't even look at me or the copies that were directly in front of them as I spoke. What does avoiding someone's gaze mean to you? Do you expect this from effective leaders you are to trust with your children's education and safety? [You can view this petition and all the comments online on our "how you can help" page: https://truthaboutyoga.com/how-can-you-help/.][10]

Given we had three minutes to speak that meeting, I gave a description of what was in the petition explaining that it contained the signatures of parents and community in the district and some very informative comments including those of MD's, teachers, atheists, and even a Hindu. The Hindu mom that signed the petition as petitioner #201 stated that yoga is not appropriate for schools. I read this point to the board, noting for the whole crowd that *a practicing Hindu parent* doesn't think yoga is appropriate in her child's elementary school! As a parent, I respectfully understand that our kids are not allowed to pray in school because that is not for everyone. This mom also understood that one religion should not be imposed on all other children.

Of the 250 signatures obtained, fifty-four people signed anonymously. The person who set up the petition and I saw who those people were. There were patterns to who didn't sign their names (PTA members, teachers and many Mormons for some reason). We obviously did not share those names, but it was fascinating that anyone would even feel the need to sign a petition anonymously, which speaks volumes to the controversial nature and fears building at EUSD over yoga. But the EUSD board ignored us and Baird continued stating to the media throughout the next year that the "majority" want yoga. And how did they know that? By people remaining silent to them? They certainly wouldn't survey any parents and saying *nothing* was support.

Divisiveness in the Schools

This became a constitutional legal issue by the Establishment Clause of the First Amendment, which is not up for public opinion or vote. The district wasn't responding to the parents and we would later find that was a pattern on various topics for Superintendent Baird. He has had multiple conflicts on topics such as the sale of a school property, to common core issues, to retinal screening of our children on iPads, to a "fake" farm lab and garden controversies, and many more. Each concern had many parents' support and some of these other issues are documented on other websites. It appears from these websites and from long-term parents in the district Baird was known for stirring up conflict, and dealing with a lot of upset parents by basically ignoring them. EUSD proceeded to add the Ashtanga yoga program in January to the last four elementary schools in the district. The divisiveness escalated at the school level. (See local television news footage on our website, www.truthaboutyoga.com).[11]

Three more articles are listed here for your convenience.

Parents Claim Grade School Yoga Classes Are First Amendment Violation

http://www.abajournal.com/news/article/parents_claim_grade_school_yoga_classes_are_first_amendment_violation.[12]

Union Tribune, Yoga Packs Board Meeting Dec, 4, 2012 http://www.sandiegouniontribune.com/sdut-classroom-yoga-topic-packs-board-meeting-2012dec04-story.html.[13]

Yoga BlogSpot discussing how to cover up spiritual language in Ashtanga yoga

http://grimmly2007.blogspot.com/2012/10/the-joisyoga-grant-and-yoga-in-schools.html.[14]

Religious Discussions, Hostility, and Emotions

Chatter at the schools was becoming very divisive, as mentioned, and there was great hostility toward those of us who spoke out against yoga. All of a sudden, people were talking about religion when there was no reason to do so for years before the yoga program. In fact, before yoga entered the schools, I didn't know the religious beliefs of fellow parents. But it became common discussion who was Methodist, Mormon, Jehovah's Witness, Christian, Catholic, Scientologist, atheist and more. I sat on bleachers and volunteered with parents in years prior and had no idea of their religion. Even the teachers came out of the woodwork in support or disgust when other staff wasn't looking. I had a teacher pull me aside in a copy room and tell me that there were many teachers in support of what we were doing and to please keep fighting yoga out because parents are the only way to get it out at the grassroots level.

Faith became clear. *Why all this discussion of religions all of a sudden if yoga is just exercise?* These new discussions, all centering on yoga, made it even clearer that yoga was not without a tie into something spiritual or religious.

Yoga was evoking all kinds of emotions and hostilities in people, not just spiritual discussions, which made us think, question, and research even further. Many of the emotions were hostile from those in favor of yoga at school, regardless of their religion. That made us ponder —*where is all this hostility coming from in otherwise nice people we'd known for years?*

Fear, Ridicule, and "Opting-Out" of Yoga

So many people were afraid to speak up, which made perfect sense. The ridicule was intense. Many families had already taken their children out of yoga. Many had written letters to the board asking them to remove yoga and had been seen in local media on TV and radio. The backlash to those in the media was inexcusable. As a result, months later, the attorney would recommend we (the filing family) not speak to any media.

Check video footage of the controversy to see that the *concerned parents* respectfully spoke the truth of their concerns about their children and specifics about what was being taught to their children. However, watch the pro-yoga supporters, and you'll see the verbal ridicule. They would refer to us as *"you conservative bigots"* and *"you fanatical Christians."* Even with television cameras pointed at them, they made all kinds of derogatory comments.

Their behavior is far from the *peacefulness* that yoga is purported to promote. And if this isn't about religion, why did they need to state theirs, or make fun of others'? There was nothing peaceful or healing or tranquil about their behavior. I would soon learn that the most venomous words would come from those who were actively doing yoga, and who I once knew as nice and friendly people. If it hadn't happened over and over, and with the same context of "over yoga," I may not have seen the patterns. Many of us experienced this, and collectively, we saw the repetition of lashing out.

Opting-Out

To be clear, there was no replacement PE if you chose to tell the school you didn't want your child in yoga. The only alternatives were non-physical options, because the point of the yoga program in Encinitas was to test our children (for the study), so physical activity at school needed to be controlled. Two groups were formed in August: five schools doing yoga all year, and four doing PE in fall and yoga in spring. EUSD was in fact forced to allow an "opt-out" *after* dozens of families across schools asked to pull their kids out of yoga, but *only because* so many of us were asking out. Principals scrambled to cover supervision of kids in various ways, none of which were PE. Some of the children sat in the back of another classroom on iPads to do individual assignments. Some did typing or repeated an elective class with another classroom such as music or computer time. Some were told to sit at the back of the yoga room! Parents didn't allow that for long. Some kids were found in classrooms alone and a couple of parents reported picking up their younger (5, 6) children because there was no supervision during yoga classes. Many situations arose from kids opting-out, and the rules and consequences changed constantly. For example, a "packet" to complete at three of the schools, for just the "opt-outs," became a huge frustration for the kids, claiming it wasn't fair for them to do all this extra work. "The packet" was busy work, about health and wellness, and was said to go along with what the kids

26

were learning in yoga class. The packets went away after parent intervention.

Principals were frustrated over kids opting-out because they had to find individual options for the children involved, and they had limitations of staff. Opting-out was not an easy choice for *any* parent because embedded in that decision is that you *cannot trust your school officials any more to decide what is best in school for your children,* a barrier most parents could not hurdle even if they saw a problem. "I don't want my child to *feel different"* were the words parents voiced. "I don't want to *cause waves."* In reality, these parents weren't the responsible parties for causing the waves; it was those deciding to implement yoga into the school curriculum who started the problems. Yet many opposed to yoga stayed silent. Many were watching and waiting and supporting (in the safety of anonymity) those of us speaking up about the issue.

Advised to Pursue Legal Action

After the December board meeting we heard a recommendation from the attorney who had attended four concerned parents meetings and four EUSD board meetings. He spoke at some of the meetings, he had appealed to clergy in the area, he listened to many parents, and he fielded calls from various community members all during the fall. He concluded after the December board meeting that legal action was the only thing that might get the board to respond. We all sat dumbfounded.

No one wanted to sue the district.

That was never the intent.

But what are we to do?

Do we just lie down and let them trample all over us, (like the filthy yoga mats in the yoga classrooms) ignoring our concerns and leading our children down a path they themselves as a staff and board don't even comprehend?

They had not responded to the many calls, or the sharing at meetings, or the letters, but they had become rude to us and belittled us in the local media!

Was it really time to take this to the next level?

A Big Decision

After receiving this feedback, there was silence. It was early December ... which is Christmas time for most of us. No one was responding to the attorney from all of the families involved. After a few days of silence, I responded with an invitation for just the parents to our home to discuss the situation. In that meeting, one by one, each family had really good reasons why they couldn't be part of a lawsuit, even though they wanted to be involved. Some examples include: One man had a heart condition, one couple was beginning a divorce, and one woman said, "My husband isn't the same religion as me, and he doesn't want to do this."

Another father was too concerned about how it would look for him professionally and resulting potential lost income. Others were too concerned for what it would put their family through. No doubt ... some just were afraid. It would impact all aspects of life — financial, mental, and spiritual. Our children's academics could be adversely affected. Fear was a huge barrier, for every parent, including us.

After listening to all their concerns about why they wouldn't or couldn't get involved in a lawsuit, I was asked if we could. I told them that I had been thinking that if ten couples would join in a lawsuit, we would do it. At that moment I would have even considered just three couples! But none? Silence. You could hear a pin drop. (Note that I hadn't even asked my husband yet, and he wasn't at the meeting — in our own home because he was off being a parent to our kids at a sports event, while the rest of us were choosing to miss activities and discuss this district's decisions). We all left that meeting knowing *not one* other family *was willing or able* at the moment to step into a legal battle. We questioned if it was the right thing for us to do. But we all knew that night it was either us as a couple or no one at this point. That realization immediately weighed heavily on our shoulders. It wouldn't be the last time I would feel that heavy feeling on my shoulders in this journey.

Later that evening, I asked my husband and his reply was "Yes we should continue to fight this, of course—how many other families are there?" I must have dropped my head and spoken softly when I responded: *none*.

A lot of questions to consider

For three days I struggled with the question: *why us?* I pondered a lot. Given my faith, I cried out to God, "How can you expect me to put my children in the limelight of a battle like this? How can we handle the pressure of this, given people are already so divisive over yoga? What about my role as chair of the Jogathon at school (oh, I will need to step down for sure) and what about my career as a professional speaker? Will companies stop hiring me if they see us as fanatics like we'd been called by others in media—a permanent record of comments? There might be a huge presence on the internet—how will that affect my kids for college applications and their future? How would this impact my husband, our privacy, our family, our home and our future? Would we be safe in our neighborhood? Should we park down on the next cul-de-sac to jump the fence to get to our car, if news people hound us, like they did with those other families already? How could you ask us this? Can't this be solved another way? Why us?"

The Trial *of My Life*

After three days of internal struggle, this was the peace I heard in the following phrases from above: *"I've called you. I've prepared you. Now it is up to you to decide. You are free to decide; freedom to choose yes or no. Do you trust me enough?"* Ugh, I thought, what??? *Trust enough? "No, I really don't" was what I wanted to scream, but a calm came over me as I realized the REAL need ... the children of EUSD.* My focus shifted off us and onto the kids.

It wasn't an audible sound. It may have seemed more like my own thoughts, but I've grown accustomed to asking whether my thoughts are from one of three sources—from me, from God, or from the enemy? Remember the angel and devil on your shoulder depiction? If we are in our heads ... it's one of these three. I knew it wasn't me, and clearly not the enemy on these thoughts, so it had to be from above.

I realized it was about my faith, or my lack thereof. I realized this was a calling, and the calling was to us, not to others, for this part. It was time to step into this or not, and time to walk alone to the next step of this journey that we didn't ask for, or want. A *yes* meant a lot of changes. A *no* would be so easy! A *no* would mean going back to our comfortable daily lives prior to the yoga in elementary schools controversy. Oh, but wait, we would still have to deal with yoga—for five more years for our youngest child. Maybe a *no* wasn't so easy after all.

After much prayer, I realized it's not about me ... it's not about us. *It's about the children.* Someone needs to take the stand. So I changed my question from *why us* to *why not us?* Why wouldn't we be a good couple to stand for this and slowly saw many ways we had been prepared, my husband and I for years, *for such a time as this.* "*No*" was an option that quickly did not seem like an option any longer.

I emerged from three days of prayer and struggle to tell my husband "*Ok, let's do this.*" My husband was as ready as he had been a few days prior, so we called the attorney who had been part of the journey to that point, and we let him know *we were in.* Dean Broyles was extremely surprised, as we would find out later. He would soon share, in meeting after meeting, that many injustices happen, but it is hard to find people to *take a stand.*

I know why.

You know why.

And the rest of this book shows why.

But we survived, and I am here to write and tell you—it's the best choice for freedom and liberty I've ever experienced. I wouldn't change my decision even after all the losses. We lost friends. We lost volunteer positions. I lost work. We lost respect of others we'd known for years. We lost the ability to walk through the school without being stared down. We lost staying at the same school for our youngest when the ridicule began to impact her. We lost many things over the course of the trial. Others questioned us and didn't believe the warnings. No one wanted to believe it, and truthfully, we all just wanted yoga to go away. We lost *Christian* friends who had known us and our character for over ten years. People just "moved further away" down the bleachers as if we had a plague or something. They didn't sit near us or talk unless they had to address us. You can see easily when others start to "avoid" you when you walk in their direction. Their eyes gaze downward, or their path shifts right or left; they pretend to be texting someone. It became the norm, sadly, especially in our public schools, because people didn't understand. They didn't have time or energy to try to understand, and for that we understood their actions.

However, the flip side is we've made many amazing friends with depth we never expected and new friends from almost all nine of the elementary schools. We would have never met these families any other way. I have more new and deeper friendships than most of the acquaintances I lost. I can't find enough time to even spend with the amount of wonderful new people I have met. And we've met people all across the country too. We get calls from supportive people who are cheering us on and understand the battle we are enduring. We get letters from folks who have walked other similar battles and know what we are up against. For those new friendships and especially deep sisterhoods, I will never regret the choices we made.

20 Seconds of Courage

There's a great quote in the movie *We Bought a Zoo* that is reminiscent of what happened next. In the movie, Matt Damon's character (the dad, who bought the zoo, based on a true story) says it only takes twenty seconds of courage. See trailer for that part right here: https://www.bing.com/videos/search?q=we+bought+a+zoo+20+seconds+

of+courage&view=detail&mid=BF4EA8C498890F
7265B3BF4EA8C498890F7265B3&FORM=VIRE.[15]

Our *twenty seconds of courage* would set off a series of events that would lead to a whole lot of countries discussing yoga in schools. I give that badge of courage to my husband. His positive response led me to examine and pray over seriously considering being the only couple. Later, I learned why. I would never have wished some of what we would experience next on any other family—whether friend or foe. Ironically, a few of the new friends would actually share that they were jealous and wished they could have filed! Seriously?

Humor became important along the path. The pressure could break some marriages, and it would bury some friendships. Our faith was tested. Our commitment was tested. Our friendships, patience, security, schools, and more would be tested. India and Pakistan news outlets would be calling our home within twenty-four hours after filing the lawsuit.[16]

Would we be ready?

Ready for the Challenge

On December 19, 2012, I wrote what I felt like was my *last appeal to educate parents* [17] in the district about what was going on in an email that would hopefully get read and passed to others. A copy of it is on the website. It was chock-full of links and information and warnings about yoga: injuries; statistics from the American Yoga Association against Yoga for sixteen-year-olds and under; facts from the Mayo Clinic against yoga; churches and ex-yogis against yoga; and so much more, including the petition. It was my last public effort before *"going silent"* for a lawsuit that would take the entire next year. I also wrote a letter to the board prior that month.[18] We were told by the lawyer not to speak to anyone, especially the board, about anything. Many others had written many emails and an FAQ[19] too, attempting to educate people on what was transpiring. I was just one of many. The only difference was that I knew this was my last chance for a long while.

You may or may not know by now, but my work is as a public speaker. Ask a speaker not to speak and there is a little bit of a challenge. Luckily, I was up for a challenge. I learned to bite my tongue (literally, at first). We had already learned that just the subject of yoga in elementary schools was divisive, and that we should not bring it up in social settings or school settings or really at all. We (the group of concerned parents) learned to wait for others to bring it up. One-to-one conversations seemed to be the best ones, and safest for both parties.

Our goal was to speak the truth in love, especially when dealing with sensitive topics. And we learned that this was *as sensitive* as bringing up abortion, gay marriage, ISIS, racial, or political issues (well Trump and Hillary have raised that to a new level for our country now). But yoga has become just as bad to bring up, given the spiteful, sudden, and violent reaction of others. It is almost taboo—that which claims to be peaceful and accepting! Yoga is complex and deceptively packaged, yet it seemed to magnetize people like your children's favorite cereal on the lower shelf in the grocery store. We found ourselves uncovering so much evidence. People didn't want to see any of it if they already enjoyed yoga. The defensiveness was incomprehensible without more research.

While the concerned parents of Encinitas were there for support, we would take this next step alone. We began to prepare privately for what would become public in the New Year.

CHAPTER TWO

Stepping into the Fire ... *and Surviving!*

Although we became two people at the center of this trial, there were many varied and wide opinions from people on both sides. I included what happened to people who initially stood up against yoga replacing PE in our schools. This book *will not contain all that each family* went through (for space and privacy), nor all the families that were impacted as a ripple effect of these decisions by our school board. But there are far-reaching implications for what we went through in our community. And in the force of the beach tide here, many got tossed around and pulled under water at times. We knew this issue could impact our entire nation, which is why the concerned parents of Encinitas were troubled. The Jois Foundation's stated mission was for every elementary child in the US to be doing yoga in school. Meanwhile, most parents didn't see any problem and wouldn't see some of the consequences for years. Thus, we knew we had to act.

Lawsuit Filed in Court of San Diego County

On February 20, 2013 my husband and I filed as petitioners a "Writ of Mandate"
https://truthaboutyoga.files.wordpress.com/2015/01/sedlock-complaint-final.pdf.[1] When you click on that link you will find a warning message, but it is the attorney's website and safe to open. Every document on his website will give that warning. I have also made it available on this page of our website due to that issue:

https://truthaboutyoga.com/about/lawsuit-in-encinitas-2/.[2] This was an expedited hearing given the nature of children involved, and requested that the EUSD Superintendent Timothy Baird and EUSD Board *remove the Ashtanga yoga program as curriculum from the nine elementary schools within the district immediately.* [The press release for the filing is located here online, and a copy is in the resources for Chapter Two: http://www.nclplaw.org/wp-content/uploads/2011/12/NCLP-Complaint-Press-Release-FINAL.pdf].[3]

When we asked for the removal of the program, the superintendent dug in harder to keep the contract. In the "Sedlock vs. Baird, et al." filing, two of our three children became the plaintiffs because they attended the district in question. My father, a respected retired professor, stood in as guardian, representing the children's best interest, as is required in most trials involving both the parents and their children. There was *supposed* to be no jury, one expert witness per side, and a speedy two-day trial. *That is not what happened.*

The judge quickly realized there was more to this case than he originally thought. Media cameras peppered the jury box each day. One recorded the full trial, start to finish.

We had no idea the amount of reaction this filing would cause around the globe. The small spark in Encinitas lit off a firestorm in many states and other countries.

Worldwide Media Attention

Within two to three hours of the filing and press release, we had calls at our home from the major US television networks including ABC, NBC, and CBS. We were contacted by the producer of the show *The Doctors* and many more news outlets. The press release regarding the lawsuit specified contacting our attorney's office for queries, and many in the news did respect that, but many did not. *We were bombarded with calls to our own home.* We did not reply to any of them, as per the advice of our new attorney. Instead we directed everything to the attorney's office so he and his staff could handle all media requests. We learned in the fall just how much controversy surrounded two of the moms who went on news interviews and weren't treated fairly. Their views weren't represented as expressed, and they were verbally attacked by readers. [Here is an NPR interview of the attorney Dean Broyles and a director of KP Jois Foundation on "Does yoga Have a Place in Public Schools?" from Dec 2012 http://www.scpr.org/programs/airtalk/2012/12/17/29724/ does-yoga-have-a-place-in-public-schools/].[4]

Pakistan and India News are calling!

Within twenty-four hours, we had news outlets from Pakistan and India calling our home phone number asking us to interview! Wow. There were *moments* in this whole journey where we would wake-up to the fact that this was *huge!* This was global. Yoga is extremely controversial, beyond San Diego, and people were solidly ready to fight both sides of the issue. Yikes, what had we unknowingly stepped into? Poke a bear and you know there is trouble. Poke around ancient pagan rituals, and yogis say that very angry spirits rise up and create chaos. We had no idea the depth of anger we would encounter. At home however, it was a bit amusing as we daily walked by the phone as it rang and yelled out to others in the house "*ABC* is calling" or "the *India Times* is calling" and continue on to the next thing we were doing. A new normal was happening, to say the least. My kids learned to never answer the phone, but it was important to keep our humor and shield the kids from as much of the negative publicity as possible.

Two Moms in the News

The two moms in the district, Mary Eady and Samantha Vigil, had gone on multiple news interviews, and most of the media had painted a very negative picture of the parents wanting yoga removed from schools. This told us early on that, culturally, this was a huge, uphill battle. America wasn't ready to deal with this topic because of their newfound love of yoga. But many countries have been battling this for years and were poised to help. Many people called in support, and many called in anger. Here are three news articles (and comments) interviewing Mary and/or Samantha:

Controversy won't stall Encinitas Yoga Plans:

http://www.kpbs.org/news/2013/jan/02/controversy-wont-stall-encinitas-yoga-plans/[5]

Yoga programs in Public Schools Face Backlash:

http://www.foxnews.com/us/2012/12/17/yoga-programs-in-public-schools-face-backlash.html [6]

Parents Object to Yoga classes in Schools: http://www.thepostgame.com/blog/training-table/201210/parents-object-yoga-classes-schools [7]

Hate Emails Spewing Wrath

Hateful emails began and then calls. Finding our contact information was all too easy. I am a public figure in my work as an inspirational speaker, and I have a business website. It didn't help to take it down for three months, because others have my number posted anywhere I spoke in the past. As they say, hindsight is twenty/twenty (20/20) and I had no forewarning thought of being in the center of such a firestorm. The wrath of many disenchanted, albeit angry people, poured in on the line. I was quite shocked how awful and hurtful people tried to be to us. *All we did was say that mandatory yoga crosses our religious boundaries as a choice for our family and we did not want it in the public schools' weekly curriculum*. We suggested yoga be optional or after school, and you'd have thought we committed a crime or something. But what most of these angry folks did not understand are the facts of the case surrounding the yoga placed in Encinitas. It became very personal for many, and they lost control for some reason. Fortunately, we quickly learned not to take any of it personally. Things said were more about the person saying them, than about us. I am pretty certain I'm not the worst mom in the universe, but I suppose that mom in Virginia had a reason for saying so, and perhaps *she* may need some help.

Yoga Haters?

I wasn't prepared for the onslaught of emails from folks who acted as if we did something that offended them personally and figuring out what to do at first was confusing. One term we were called was Yoga Haters (and that was one of the nicer names). In fact, I think it is ironic that people constantly call us "intolerant" when they obviously aren't respecting our wishes or opinions while demanding that we respect theirs. We were called judgmental, but we were not judging others doing yoga. We were simply asking that it not be mandatory for the 6,000 elementary age children of Encinitas enrolled in the public school system. We had to separate emotions from the facts. And part of the problem with this lawsuit since day one, was that most people didn't know the most important facts about what was going on in the Encinitas schools. They thought things, such as that yoga was optional for us, and that we were only people whining over a small program or wanted some money out of this. They didn't realize who KP Jois Foundation was, their plans to evangelize and spread yoga, how much money backed them, the politics involved, and famous people who were backing this *movement*. They simply didn't know. There was so much more.

We could not seem to get all the information into the courts, nor into the media effectively. And we knew there was so much more going on than we could prove or even knew at the time. Many facts were never reported accurately in the media or lawsuit, and even when they were sorted out and stated plainly by our attorney in court, the judge somehow missed or ignored some of the most important facts! Many people made all kinds of assumptions, filled in their own blanks, rather than seeking or seeing the facts.

A Barrage of Vicious Communications

The phone calls were ridiculously vicious. We were called all kinds of names, both in and out of the newspapers, usually in the comments section of articles. Emails and voice mails were the worst. One morning about five o'clock the office phone rang. I didn't want the kids to wake up, so I stumbled over to my office and answered, half in a fog. The man on the line called me a Pharisee, which actually made me laugh later. I was so tired that all I could think to say was "can we talk about that?" and he hung up. They always hung up. They only wanted to spew their wrath and never wanted to actually have a conversation. One lady contacted us three times during the middle of the night. People usually said whatever they had to say very quickly, and then slammed their phone down or click; silence after the yelling. At some point, we just turned off the ringers and quit answering phones altogether. If it was work or friends, they would leave a message. Life moves on, and you change your habits.

After I read the first ten or so toxic emails, I contacted our attorney who said to quit reading them, but to send them all to him. I filed them in my computer in case we needed them later at trial. I created two files: Supporters and Haters. The first sentence of an incoming email was very telling; I immediately knew to which folder it belonged. In my business, and in being a busy mom of three, teachers and coaches and parents send emails, so I couldn't turn off the exposure to them, but needed to comb through the incoming emails daily. Eventually, but not initially, we did get emails and calls in support of the case. As for the few letters via regular postal mail we received over the past few years, they were all in support. Thankfully, we did not receive any hate mail delivered to our home mailbox nor did any of the threats materialize. This demonstrates that many of the emails and voicemails were communicated "in the moment" of anger and hostility, usually without a filter. But why were they so angry... *over yoga*?

The well-thought-out appreciation and support came in all forms. Random hugs from strangers and the letters would help to sustain us during the onslaught of hate at any given moment. And since we are parents, you can imagine how we tried to protect our children from the negative communications of others. I shared *every supportive email, letter and call with all of my family.* However, to this day my husband has not even seen most of the hate emails I received. He need not ever see those. When we changed over our number to a digital line, I lost all my messages. On the mailbox were several hateful messages I don't know why I was still keeping. Evidence, I guess. Now, they are gone for good, and that's probably for the best.

I printed the emails for the trial and a year later I read all of them thoroughly and it saddened me that people can be so mean-spirited. Years ago, I might have taken them personally, but clearly they weren't about us. I see that as God's protection, provision, and wisdom over me and over my family. The same vicious communications that were meant to stop us only helped fuel our resolve. Something was very wrong with yoga, if it brought out this kind of venom in people. Something was very wrong.

Threats Against Our Family

Although none of this is about us, it still happened to us and I share these things for you to be aware that all is not copasetic over yoga. For five years, I've not responded to those email threats, verbal abuses and telephone messages that are downright vile. Friends (or I previously thought they were) whom I'd known for years quickly also turned on me and said hurtful things, which was worse! This was baffling to me because I wasn't saying anything about anyone else doing yoga, but calmly stating *my opinion that I think yoga should not be in schools.* I told these same people I felt it was okay to do it outside school hours if they wanted, but I firmly believe it should not be forced upon an entire district of kids with no choice. I became a voice for the many parents who were afraid to speak up, and those who had no idea anything was happening.

I really didn't choose this position. It happened, and I accepted it because it's not about me or any of these parents. It's a much more important issue. We as parents don't need to agree on everything, but we should give the courtesy of respecting free choice and freedom of speech. I find it very interesting how the most judgmental people often call others judgmental and don't see it in themselves. Face it, we all make judgements every day. Our brains sort through loads of information, and sometimes split decisions are necessary. Our ability to respect others is a different story. There was such a lack of respect coming out of the mouths of yoga supporters, and I would soon find out the connection between those doing yoga and their venom. I actually think some people don't even know what they are saying or why—it just spills out. When they walk away, I wonder how they view what they just said. But in anger, people will say a lot of stupid things—self included. We all fall short. We all need grace. Former Yogis would begin to teach us why people doing yoga act this way.

If I hadn't needed to be *silent* due to the lawsuit, I think my response now and in the future will always be exactly the same to every nasty email, call and comment people made to and about us. My response would be: *If yoga is so calming and centering, and creates peace for you, then why are you so angry, and why would you say what you just said to me?*

Testimonies from Ex-Yogis warning about yoga

The emails that surprised and intrigued me most were from ex-yogis, or we could call them former yogis, people who formerly practiced yoga. Out of the woodwork came people who encouraged both the attorney and us that this was more important than we understood. These former yogis were in favor of us fighting for these children with everything we had, to get yoga out of the schools. Some say they had been caught up in cults, and it took years to get free. They shared that they see clearly now how they fell into the attraction of yoga and how it took them places they never wanted or intended to go. I learned a great deal about these *unintended consequences* while researching yoga, and will report on them in later chapters. These former yogis were adamant that we protect the children from a path unintended. Thus, there is a chapter on the specific warnings from these former yoga instructors. As you can see, though, with a mountain of concerns surrounding yoga being brought to my attention, I knew I needed to keep researching for the truth. There was more to be discovered. I'll share with you next where some of that research led. And starting with the beginning, the origins of yoga, and following with the yoga being practiced in our district, seemed to make the most sense.

CHAPTER THREE

What's the Big Deal with Yoga?

O ur concern about children performing yoga in the United States public elementary school system grew as we studied the history of yoga, the objectives of the organization, and the promoting of this specific form of yoga called Ashtanga. The weekly yoga classes began in Encinitas, California at the Encinitas Union School District (EUSD) in August of 2012, and by January the entire district of nine schools was doing yoga at least twice weekly. We found in our research that yoga has religious origins. You may think the opposite as I did (*it's just stretching*), so a look at the following information will lead to understanding the current debate over yoga in America. Once you begin to see the web of roots, dig a little more, and it becomes as obvious as the idol statues you find in yoga studios.

Religious Roots

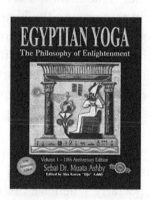

Photo credit to Sema Institute of Yoga, www.egyptianyoga.com

Found on amazon at: https://www.amazon.com/Egyptian-Yoga-Enlightenment-Muata-Ashby/dp/1884564011/ref=sr_1_1?keywords=egyptian+yoga&qid=1559062619&s=gateway&sr=8-1

To fully understand yoga, one needs to go back to how it started, by whom and why. There are numerous books on yoga dating back to Ancient Egypt. The bookstores are stocked full of titles, such as: *Egyptian Yoga: The Philosophy of Enlightenment* and you can look online to find the rich history of yoga recorded. India, with a predominant religion of Hinduism, is the powerhouse of yoga. Hinduism is based on the belief of reincarnation and controlling your mind to try to gain a "better life" and higher caste for "next time" you re-turn to life, in a new form. Hinduism has over 330,000 deities and gods, and they take the form of all kinds of common things around us, such as cows, tables and statues. This religious system is significantly different than the majority of American families' system of belief years ago. While we were allowed to exercise religious freedom, the majority of Americans' worldview was based on a monotheistic belief. One Creator equals One God. But that has shifted through yoga and many other influences, such as immigration of varying religions and belief systems, travel, and transforming of beliefs or non-beliefs.

As creators of yoga will tell you, yoga was not created for physical exercise. Yoga is mental control, worship and *centering* meditative time with your mind, your gods and for "sitting long hours in focus." The Western World has taken yoga and morphed it into body "movements" that stemmed also from contortionism, which you would see in researching the history. Contortionism is still viewed as a bit odd and more for entertainment, but for the people practicing it, they call it exercise as it takes great physical challenge. America has crafted yoga even further to the extent that many claim it is just exercise and can be separated from any spiritual roots. This is the start of why the spiritual root of yoga *is a big deal*.

"The spiritual cannot be separated from the physical" many Yoga Gurus and Yogis claim, (such as Rabi Maharaj in his book, *Death of a Guru),* especially when we are talking about young impressionable children. http://www.amazon.com/Death-Guru-Remarkable-Story-Search/dp/0890814341/ref=sr_1_1?ie=UTF8&qid=1462194141&sr=8-1&keywords=death+of+guru

In the Encinitas Union School District (and other districts across the country now) *the big deal* is that children ages five to thirteen (kindergarten through sixth grade) are participating in yoga weekly because the yoga curriculum has replaced their Physical Education time and in some cases, core subject time. If Encinitas district really did, as claimed in court, "Add sixty (60) minutes of yoga as PE, to the one hundred (100) required minutes," then what in the six-hour day did they take away to get those extra 60 minutes? It would have to be core classes! It is simple math, and the District staff didn't think that claim through! One hundred sixty minutes (160) of PE per week is far over the standard requirements and *certainly not happening* in Encinitas. Other chapters give you more detail and references to those facts.

Photo permission: Harvest House Publishing

Photo credit: Rabi Maharaj (former Hindu) speaking on yoga and how it cannot be separated from Hinduism

Not Just Exercise—**Say Hindus**

Many India-based organizations both in the United States and in India are not happy with this *"sac-religious"* attempt to *change* yoga. A few examples:

1. The *India Times* contacted us at home (http://economictimes. indiatimes.com/topic/Hindu-American-Foundation)[2] less than twenty four hours after our filing Feb. 20, 2013 for yoga classes to be moved out of the regular school day curriculum.
2. The *Hindu American Foundation* has published and been involved in many articles showing their concern for the "Americanization" of Yoga and began a campaign in 2008 to "Take Yoga Back." The article on this link lists fourteen other articles (by dates) of the progression of that campaign over the years. (http://www.hafsite.org/media/pr/ takeyogaback).[3]
3. The link to the Hindu American Foundation (http://www. hafsite.org/)[4] and their Facebook link, (https://www.facebook. com/Hindu-American-Foundation-105243818008/)[5] hold a lot of information as well.
4. In one of their articles to note, they quote PB Jois: "The essence of yoga is to reach oneness with God," Pattabhi Jois (http://www.hafsite.org/media/pr/yoga-hindu-origins).[6]

Many organizations are trying to educate America on what yoga is, but *is America listening?*

One of the parents at El Camino Creek (from India) thanked me for respecting their religion enough to ask that it be removed from the schools. Many are quietly disappointed with what the schools, and American culture here, is doing *to* yoga. The *World Faith Foundation* wrote an amicus brief on our behalf for the trial, dated Oct 17, 2014, asking the trial court to reverse their decision based on both religion clauses of the first amendment and conclusions that the school-sponsored yoga program violates the constitution. They pointed out thirty-seven prior cases that support our position. A copy of this is available through the offices of Dean Broyles and the National Center for Law and Policy (http://www. nclplaw.org/).[7] In addition, a Wheaton Undergraduate Law Review article recently discussed our yoga litigation, challenging the ruling on the 2013 Encinitas Yoga Case and explained how the judge got it wrong in (Sedlock v. Baird) (https://wculrcom.files.wordpress. com/2016/04/wculr-vol-1-no-1.pdf).[8] Law schools and Religious Studies departments across the country continue to study this case and question the line of governmental intervention of religion, as well as, how this impacts our rights and current laws.

Many other Indian, Buddhist and Sikh-based organizations are in support of our case, claiming American-based organizations have attempted to cover up the religious roots of yoga. They state "The movements and meditation *are* the worship". In the West, we think of religion as cerebral—learning, praying, reading, and worshipping through song, so our definition of religion is focused on learning and thinking vs. a *movement based* spiritual encounter. Hindu and some other religions are *worship based* through movement vs. using words out loud. Their texts promote their religion, as well. So when America starts tweaking yoga in the West, this may be annoying *to Hindus (and others we have found)*, but doesn't change *their (Eastern) knowledge or belief* in what they are doing. They are worshipping and know it, during yoga, whether Americans choose to believe that or ignore it, or attempt to change it for themselves. The Sikh Foundation here called to support our battle, sharing that Sikhs too are forced (in India) to do yoga along with the Christian and Buddhist children, and it is against their religious beliefs.

We are not alone by a long shot here. We are not just some fanatical Christian couple in California that has lost perspective. Yet we hear that and turn the other cheek knowing that "they do not know what they are saying." It is sad that others would put the focus on Christians or us, when that is not the issue at all. Like an addict who would try to put the blame and focus on others to distract from the truth or in denial. The problem is the root that some are trying to cover up. We cannot ignore that the main philosophy behind yoga is to yoke to a god within ourselves. Yoking by historical definition is a wooden crosspiece that is fastened over the necks of two animals and attached to the plow or cart that they are to pull together. Thus, yoking is to attach two or more entities. To ignore this fact of its being *yoking*, is similar to "ignoring the elephant in the room." And after a while, you just can't any longer. He gets in the way. He blocks you. He needs you to pay attention to him. He needs to be fed. Yoga feeds on itself and the person practicing craves more and more. If yoga is devoid of spiritual experience, then why the defensiveness and lashing out from yoga loving folks?

Why Ashtanga Yoga?

A great article titled: What Makes the Encinitas School Yoga Program Religious? https://www.huffpost.com/entry/encinitas-yoga-lawsuit_b_3570850[9] is available to help you begin to see that "The Encinitas Union School District (EUSD) did not implement just *any* yoga program; it selected one of the most highly religious ones. The terms of the $533,000 grant with the Jois Foundation *obligated* EUSD to promote Ashtanga yoga https://truthaboutyoga.files.wordpress.com/2014/01/jois-moufinal.pdf.[10] *Ashtanga* (eight-limbed) yoga was developed by Krishna Pattabhi Jois from the *Yoga Sutras*, a sacred text for Hindus. Ashtanga emphasizes postures and breathing on the premise that these practices will automatically lead practitioners to experience the other limbs—including union with the universal (Brahman) eventually—whether they want it or not. Jois Foundation promotes nothing else besides Ashtanga Yoga.

Whereas Protestant Christianity focuses on words and beliefs, Ashtanga yoga is action: practice and experience. Nevertheless, Ashtanga is "religious." It explains ultimate problems and connects individuals with *suprahuman* energies, beings or transcendent real-ities (such as worldview, or big-picture reality) and cultivates spir-itual awareness and virtues of ethical and moral character (such as ethos, the philosophy of how to live) … Brown's article mentions *"EUSD used funds from a religious organization with a missionary agenda to implement a religious yoga curriculum that furthers the goals of the funding foundation. US and California constitutions prohibit this kind of complicity of government and religion."*

48

It's Not Just "Going through the Motions"

Let's take Catholicism as an example. There are Catholic rituals of standing, sitting, kneeling and signing the cross over one's heart. Others can perform or make fun of the rituals all they want, but Catholics understand fully the meaning of the motions, which are a respect and reverence to God. I'm not Catholic, but I understand this and even a five year old can quickly comprehend that the motion is a universal sign of the cross. Similarly, some EUSD fourth grade boys popped up onto a bench in the lotus position outside the Self-Realization Worship Center in 2013 while on a field trip, putting their fingers into the jnana mudra. One of the chaperones was concerned on that field trip and snapped a photo. She became troubled because the only information on the permission form was "historical sites" for the parents who gave permission. Most would never find out where the kids went that day. And even if the boys didn't know the name juana mudra, they knew the finger formations went with the lotus position already and spontaneously performed it having less than six months of yoga "experience." Kids understand much more than the EUSD District and the judge claimed they would!

*Elementary kids on a field trip to Self-Realization Center
spontaneously jump on bench into lotus position*

Photo credit: parent in EUSD who prefers anonymity

Let's try to set religion aside for a moment. Let's call the motions of sitting on the floor in yoga lotus position something else, like *crisscross applesauce* (Incidentally, this is what our school district did to try to mask the Sanskrit term padmasana for lotus). Still, the lotus position with hands in *jnana mudra* is a universal sign that even a kindergarten five-year-old comprehends quickly. Kids linked chanting *Om* and closed eyes to this sitting position very quickly. "Are you Smarter than a Fifth Grader" is a TV show for a reason. By fifth grade, children are learning a lot about the world that they can recall faster than adults. Let's give the kids a little more credit for the sponge-like nature of this age. And this is likely the true reason Jois Foundation targeted this age group. Kids learn quickly and trust their teachers. We must vet their teachers better than this. Most of these yogis do not have teaching credentials for schools.

Other religions have split to change certain rituals. Christianity, for example, has hundreds of different denominations, varying in some aspect of theology, but perhaps generally closer in doctrine for some, and far opposing in others. Hinduism is no different, in that many Gurus (yogi leaders) have created their own forms of yoga and their own "followings"—especially in this latest century. There are many forms of yoga and offshoots for which each has a head Guru that others follow. Many have even made the news lately in the US and it hasn't been for good leadership, but for sexual predatory accusations. One subject we ran across in our research was the sexual oppression of women through yoga in India and other countries. Gurus have a power over their students moving beyond just being physical fitness leaders. We won't touch on that much in this book—but it is an important area to mention because it has a critical impact in other countries. Multiple links to sexual litigation cases, investigations, and photos of the accused in precarious positions, are linked to our website.

Does it really even matter if children don't cognitively understand it is religion (as the court questioned) if the ridicule toward other children has increased? EUSD claimed one goal of adding yoga was to decrease bullying. For those opted-out of yoga, bullying has increased. And not just bullied from children, but from other teachers, principals and staff. There are multiple examples of this from the parent stories found on the website testimonial page here: (https://truthaboutyoga.com/testimonials/),[11] and the bullying is not just *to* the children, but to the parents. Some would claim that it's the parents' action of pulling the children out that caused the bullying. But once again, that is like an addict trying to cover up the truth pointing fingers at everyone else. The truth is that those families wouldn't need to pull their children out if the district wouldn't continue to implement a program that they are well aware is a religious problem to many families. Again, we see a root cause rather than the resulting actions. Over a dozen entire families with multiple children have left the district over the implementation of weekly yoga. And if you don't think sixth grade boys bullied each other *over* yoga moves, you need to hang out at a school and watch current eleven and twelve year olds.

Entangled?

This book is not against any religion. This is an attempt to understand how these blatantly religious and spiritual rituals could make their way into the curriculum of public schools in the United States. The US laws to keep a separation of religion and government are fairly clear. So why did a judge (an elected governmental official) decide whether yoga in the public school system, taught to elementary-aged children, is *too religious* or *cleaned up enough*?

Isn't that entanglement right there?

A government official decided whether a yoga program is religious or not. Who would be less entangled to make that decision? Who should decide the extent of "religiousness" in yoga? Is *spiritual* a more palatable word used so that yoga can be allowed in public schools? Would a person who has studied religious studies and/or religion as a practice (a pastor, a priest, a religious scholar, a Hindu leader or a yogi who is not tied to the outcome of the benefits of the decision) decide differently whether yoga is religious or not? Absolutely, they would have. But that wasn't the plan, and clearly ... this would be a much larger discussion than just for the

Encinitas District. And did Judge Meyer, by practicing Bikram yoga, impact his own decisions? As you'll see, he declared "Yoga is religious" (which should then automatically lead to taking it out of schools) but his second statement didn't match the first when he said "but, it's cleaned up enough for the kids of EUSD." The yoga trial chapters will unfold surprising details and how Judge Meyer worked so hard to understand this very complex subject.

Yoga Uncoiled

Yoga Uncoiled—The Satanic Roots of Yoga (http://yogauncoiled. com/)[12] is a video that answers the question of whether yoga can separate the physical from the spiritual teachings by asking many of the experts who created yoga. This author has been researching the NewAge development for years and will help you understand the foundation of the problem in just a few minutes time. This video deals with the false belief that one can practice yoga postures, breathing, and focusing techniques devoid of yoga's spirituality, not realizing that yoga is an inherent part of Hindu philosophy which teaches that man and nature are one with divinity.

Another video by Caryl Mastrisciana is a 16 minute version of "Wide is the Gate" https://www.youtube.com/ watch?v=bDBoBhIqfwQ[13] rather than the six hour video that shows how yoga came into the US, and what is happening as it relates to much more than yoga. The video covers yoga entering the US through the drug culture and the Beatles (Rabi Maharaj also talks about this) and how yoga is part of *the new age religion* and the *emergent church*. If you watched just the two videos linked here, you would have a clear taste of how Christians then might find a contradiction between practicing yoga and practicing Christianity.

The Meaning of Namaste

The message has been loud and clear on not having *religion* in schools, until now. For the past several decades in America, prayer in schools and references to Christmas have been removed (or at least in our schools in California we are not to say "Merry Christmas" at school, and celebrations are called "holiday parties" and now it's "spring break" not "Easter break"). However, yoga is a religious practice by definition in our dictionaries,. Yoga is yoking. Yoking to what? Or rather, one might ask, to whom? Yoga is a ritual relatively new to the West and is not understood by our Western culture the same as in the East. For example, if you see a person motion in the shape of a cross, most Westerners know what that means. However, if you say Namaste, most Westerners *do not* know what that means. Most think Namaste is a benign greeting of hello such as: *Aloha*. But one doesn't put prayer hands together and bow when saying Aloha. Namaste does not mean hello and goodbye. Namaste is defined in Wikipedia (https://en.wikipedia. org/wiki/Namaste)[14] as "I bow to the divine in you" and the return Namaste from the other person means "I also bow to the divine in you." Divine what? What is the definition of divine? Look it up!

Whether one knows it is religious or not, the reasonable mind who thoughtfully considers the definition understands Namaste as more than a simple greeting. Teaching young, impressionable children this greeting—bowing to each other, closing their eyes, hands together in a prayer position to do with your yogi teacher—*is far from unimpressionable*. When 3rd grade kids were put in a circle at Park Dale Lane Elementary School in Encinitas and told to bow to each other and say Namaste, one mom observing (Mary Eady) knew the true meaning of Namaste. She knew to ask for this to stop when the children did not have a voice for themselves, nor know this was a *practice*. Most of these children knew nothing about what they were being taught to do. And yet, many children went home and told their parents of all the religious things going on in yoga. Some told parents that they didn't think they should do yoga due to lessons at church (see the "testimonials" page of the website and Chapter 1 in this book for detailed stories). In addition, you can find the Eady letter to the district on the Encinitas trial page and the news where she was discussing these incidents and more, included on the trial page of the website https://truthaboutyoga. com/lawsuit-in-encinitas-2/.[15]

Yoga stretches into the main classrooms

Today, in the Encinitas Union School District, for every student *practicing yoga,* this *is the standard:* Every child bows and greets each other every time they walk into and out of the yoga rooms. This *practice or greeting* has spilled into the classrooms where teachers implement Namaste greetings, forced breathing before a test, or the children stand up to do "yoga stretches."

Poster of Covey's 7 Habits with yoga lotus pose,
La Costa Heights Elementary, 2016

The yoga pose woman was posted[16] in every third, fourth, fifth and sixth grade room at La Costa Heights during the 2015-16 school year. We asked the teacher to remove it and she agreed. But the principal, Christie Kay, then said no. The pictured yoga posters remained all year long, Yoga is clearly being weaved into the main classrooms daily, not just taught in yoga room twice a week. Gardens are replacing large portions of campus grounds. "Teaching wellness," by using yoga methods *to relax,* and now eating based on the same philosophies (Meatless Mondays).

You will see in the chapters to come, that the Encinitas Union School District claimed in court "the children do not know there is any religion in yoga" therefore, it is fine. Do you think the children are smarter than that? Children know a lot more than these adults claim. The children's own actions are proof. The children spontaneously chanting "om" and jumping into lotus and finger/thumb together, is evidence of knowledge given their location at the temple. "Om" is Sanskrit for "I am god," did you know that? I didn't until I looked it up! The Om symbol is popping up on cars all over the roads here.

(https://en.wikipedia.org/wiki/Om, https://www.learnreligions.com/om-or-aum-hindu-symbol-1770511)[17] Children seem to know yoga isn't just exercise as evidenced by their questioning and behaviors. In Sanskrit Om is:

Sanskrit for Om

My daughter came home one day telling me she had learned some "new names" for her body parts. What I would later find out is that they were Sanskrit terms for some of her "limbs." The yoga teachers taught the kids Sanskrit, which is an ancient language written for spiritual ceremonies. The definition (https://en.wikipedia.org/wiki/Sanskrit)[18] of Sanskrit is *an ancient Indic language of India, in which the Hindu scriptures and classical Indian epic poems are written and from which many northern Indian languages are derived."* The language was written specifically for ceremonies, called "pujas." [For a fuller description, go to the above referenced link and also google "puja's" to find the spiritual Hindu definition].

The children of Encinitas were invited to a Puja in 2013 (chanting, worshipping, adoration) ceremony in downtown Encinitas.

Clearly, there was something different about yoga than other physical activities. One does not need a "new language" for most sports. Take gymnastics, for example. For kids to understand gymnastics, they don't need *a new language* (especially a highly religious one written for religious rituals). Children learn that a horse is not a live horse and bars in the gym are different than bars on a bike or a street corner. These are just new definitions that apply *in context*, yet not a whole new language is needed.

Sanskrit is different. And children know it, as evidenced by the elementary students popping into lotus on the benches in front of the Self Realization center, placing fingers in jnana mudra, closing their eyes and saying *"om" during a field trip*. Clearly they had already learned this at school since we couldn't find any gyms or studios offering yoga to kids in 2012. So since the kids visited undisclosed "historical sites" on the field trip signature page— what's up with that lack of disclosure ending up inside the Self Realization gardens? Kids may *understand* that yoga *is religious,* and they are using the new body part words knowing they are not usual words in our language. In fact, in many cases, the boys this age are blatantly making fun of yoga and, at that moment, they have no intention to *exercise* or *worship*. They are being 5th grade boys, making fun of something they are being subjected to do now. This is one way of expressing their feelings since they are stopped from expressing any dislike of yoga to the teachers or staff at school. Kids joke about a lot of things, and sometimes it is because it is uncomfortable. That's what makes it funny to others, the discomfort. Thankfully, some children knew Sanskrit was odd and told their parents right away, mine included. She was only in second grade (seven years old).

The Question Is ...

Researching the origins of yoga is important to answering the question—"What's the Big Deal?" It is tantamount to the lives of

5,600 children in Encinitas ... and for the countless others who will be affected by similar school district decisions. In the following chapters, you'll see this story unfold. You'll learn more about the type of yoga (Ashtanga) taught to our children. And you'll learn about the Jois Foundation, which provided all the funding for the program, which to date is over Four Million Dollars. You'll see the connections between Jois Foundation and the EUSD Superintendent. You'll see that the school board did not understand the origins of yoga and that they had trusted the Superintendent, Timothy Baird, and his Assistant Superintendent, David Miyashiro, regarding what they had researched and presented at the school board meetings. There wasn't a lot of time between when the EUSD board was presented with the new ideas and grant, (according to the meeting notes of 2012 EUSD board meeting notes—all available on their own website—http://www.eusd.org/board_agds.htm),[19] and when the board needed to vote on the grant in July 2012. School *happened* to be out of session.

The origins of the Ashtanga Yoga/Jois Foundation grant, program, and *study* on the children, are in direct conflict with many beliefs of most families in these schools. Most parents just didn't know what Ashtanga yoga was, nor could they view it before implementation. And even if they had, they would not even be able to see the opening sequence as what it is, a specifically crafted set of movements making up what is Ashtanga yoga by design. Parents just wouldn't know what they were looking at beyond cute little kids rolling around on a mat. They would be adorable doing almost anything.

If yoga is not *just exercise*, as so many people warn, then it is well worth the time for parents and administrators to search for the truth. Turning to look the other way is not an option when the stakes are this high for our future generation. History repeats itself and knowing history can teach us to make better choices next time.

The History of yoga is *a big deal;* particularly when you choose to put it into elementary school curriculum, on a weekly basis, and replace other traditional subjects important to parents.

Compliments of Coast News: The children at Paul Ecke doing yoga to the Ashtanga opening sequence still on the wall in 2016, after Superintendent Baird claims (in court, 2013) EUSD won't do Ashtanga yoga.
https://www.thecoastnews.com/eusd-to-pay-800k-for-yoga/

CHAPTER FOUR

What Is Ashtanga Yoga *and* Who is the Jois Foundation?

Ashtanga Yoga

Ashtanga Yoga is the granted yoga to the children of the Encinitas Union School District (EUSD). It is said to be one of the most highly religious forms of yoga, ideally taught by one guru to one student at a time, according to Sri K. Pattabhi Jois, the founder and top Guru of Ashtanga Yoga from India. You will learn about him in this chapter. His philosophies and beliefs are clear on the Jois Yoga website http://joisyoga.com/.[1] As one of many concerned parents in Encinitas, I did a lot of research on Jois Yoga and the Jois Foundation in 2012. So did many other families in our school district. What we found were clearly stated goals by Jois Foundation to spread Ashtanga yoga throughout US elementary schools. Why? This troubled me. So I continued my research.

Sri K. Pattabhi Jois, photo credit to: ashtangapictureproject.com

The Eight Limbs of Yoga

According to the official website for Ashtanga yoga (www.ashtanga.com)[2] this form of yoga is a *system* of yoga transmitted to the modern world by Sri K. Pattabhi Jois (1915–2009). This *system* of yoga involves synchronizing the breath with a progressive series of postures—a process producing intense internal heat and a profuse, purifying sweat that detoxifies muscles and organs. On this website you can see that Ashtanga yoga literally means *eight-limbed yoga*, as outlined by the sage Patanjali in the *Yoga Sutras*. To find out what those are, google "yoga sutras"—one site is here: http://www.yogajournal.com/article/yoga-101/beginning-journey/.[3]

According to Patanjali, the path of internal purification for revealing the Universal Self consists of the following eight *spiritual* practices:

The Eight Spiritual Practices of Ashtanga Yoga

Yama [moral codes]

Niyama [self-purification and study]

Asana [posture]

Pranayama [breath control]

Pratyahara [sense control]

Dharana [concentration]

Dhyana [meditation]

Samadhi [absorption into the Universal]

I would be fine with the physical benefits of posture and concentration. But "self-purification and absorption into the Universal" seemed way beyond the worldview my family believes, and what I teach my children. I asked myself, how can this be considered *just exercise*?

On another website http://yoga.about.com/od/yogabooks/ fr/yogamala.htm [4] you'll find this definition: Ashtanga means "eight limbs" in Sanskrit,(https://www.verywell.com/what-is-asana-3566793)[5] which refers to the eight limbs of yoga laid out in the *Yoga Sutras of Patanjali* (https://www.verywellfit.com/ yoga-beginner-4157112). [6]

The Ashtanga method of Asana (https://www.verywell. com/what-is-asana-3566793)[7] practice was interpreted by T. Krishnamacharya (https://www.verywell.com/krishnamacharya-father-of-modern-yoga-3566898) [8] and Sri K. Pattabhi Jois from an ancient text called the *Yoga Korunta*, which they claimed described a unique system of hatha yoga developed by Vamana

Rishi. Point being, the more you start to look, the world of yoga is very connected: connected in its practices, roots and its various versions. One cannot spend a couple of hours on the websites of these forms of yoga and not realize that yoga goes far beyond simple stretches. My concern grew deeper. The following is one clear example that yoga is not *simply exercise*.

The Significance of Moon Days

If yoga is *just exercise* why can't one *exercise* during a full moon? Read about Moon Days at http://ashtanga.com/html/moondays.html [9] "Ashtanga yoga practitioners should not practice on the days of the new or full moon" is stated on this website and many others (learn why here: http://ashtangayogacenter.com/moon-days/.[10] The day you rest is the day of your regular practice time nearest the new or full moon. Check with your local studio for its observed moon dates. Doesn't this make you also question whether yoga is really just exercise?

Ashtanga—Series of Poses

The first, or primary, series is described in *Yoga Mala*. The primary series is called Yoga Chikitsa, which means *yoga therapy*. It is intended to *realign* the spine, *detoxify* the body, and build strength, flexibility, and stamina. This series of about seventy-five poses takes an hour and a half to two hours to complete, *beginning with sun salutations*, and moving on to standing poses, inversions, and backbends before relaxation. The children in EUSD are doing the sun salutations and calling them "opening and closing" sequences rather than the original names (unless they've changed the names again by the time you read this book): Opening or Surya Namaskara A - https://www.verywell.com/surya-namaskara-a-3566700 ,[11] Closing or Surya Namaskara B - https://www.verywell.com/surya-namaskara-b-3566701).[12]

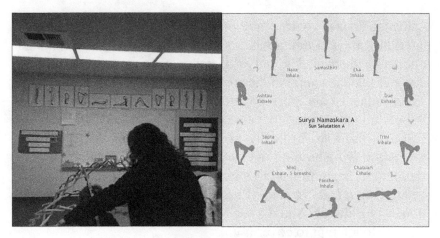

Ashtanga Yoga Opening Sequence Diagram

The wall at La Costa Heights elementary at open house 2016,

Ashtanga opening sequence still on the wall, despite EUSD claims in court in 2013 of not doing Ashtanga.

It's important to understand, as parents, what the poses truly mean. The above photo was taken at La Costa Heights Elementary School during open house night in 2016. (Find these and other photos on our website on the Encinitas page https://truthaboutyoga. com/about/).[13] The chart on the right is the opening sequence for Ashtanga yoga. The poses match identically.

This was troubling to me because the district claimed in the final days of the trial (June 24, 25, and 26th of 2013) that they *"never"* did Ashtanga yoga. And that they would *not do Ashtanga yoga* in the future. And yet, as you can see from the photos in the room three years later, the movements taught to the children on the photos posted in the room match identically to the Ashtanga yoga poster called Surya Namaskara A or Sun Salutation A (opening sequence). We pointed this out in the trial (in 2013) and the district (Baird and Miyashiro) blatantly led the judge to believe they were not doing Ashtanga yoga by claiming it was different. In May of the trial, they did not use any term for the yoga, but a month later in June, they had created a "new name" for *their* yoga: "EUSD yoga". Clearly, the statement they made that kids were not doing

Ashtanga yoga is not true, as evidenced by the fact that three years later they are still doing what is globally known as the Ashtanga opening sequence. The only difference between the two images above is that the *names* of the poses are changed. They are the same exact sequence and pose positions as you and any child can see. Why is this important? Because Ashtanga yoga Guru and creator PBK Jois had a strict rule that every class must begin with this Sun Salutation (worshipping the sun). If a parent does not know this standard of beginning a class by Jois, then this seems but a small detail. But, *it is a big deal*. It's a big deal to Ashtanga yoga practitioners worldwide. And it's such a big deal that the superintendent appears to attempt to cover it up.

A Typical Day for EUSD Kids Who Participate in Yoga, as of April 2016

Written by a parent in EUSD in 2016

The kids (K-6th) walk into the yoga room (after placing their shoes outside and north). They enter the room and proceed to get their mats and begin the sun salutations on their own. Each does the opening sequence with no direction because they have memorized it now. The sun salutation includes ***sun god worship*** (*whether they know it or not*) and many movements that ***are signs of worship*** (ex: palms pressed together in some, specific poses). *My addition:* Kids may not be aware of the significance of what they are doing, but you can bet the yogis know the significance!

Banned Stretching Pose in US - Still in Use at EUSD

Also notice that twice in the opening sequence there is a pose that has been banned from stretching in the United States as per doctors http://www.memetics.com/5-reasons-you-why-you-shouldnt-lock-your-knees/[14] and that is the stretch where you lock your knees straight and bend to touch the floor. We were told decades ago not to do this type of stretching and yet, our schools are now promoting it in yoga classes, by yogis. Injuries from tendons and ligaments being pulled from the bone come from this type of stretching http://www.regenexx.com/knee-locking-up/.[15] This is one of the common injuries in yoga: *muscle tearing from the bone and tendons*.

Other injuries come from the large number of children being taught at one time (there are up to forty to fifty students in a room with one yoga instructor). It is difficult for one yogi (yogi is the term for yoga instructor) to guide all the students to be careful enough in this stretch, or any movements for that matter. I was an aerobics instructor for years, and the larger the class, the less control you have over seeing if someone is performing a move incorrectly. Nor are the kids guided to bend their knees (not lock them) as they would in regular exercising, for any sport or traditional PE. *This is a clear and present physical danger for our children.* An entire chapter ahead is devoted to childrens' yoga injuries and physical concerns by doctors.

The spiritual issues are just as concerning as the physical. Former yogis claim the worship poses *invite in s*pirits of the gods, in worship, which are exactly what this yoga was created for, as per Jois' own website: http://joisyoga.com/.[16] Yikes, what? Read that again. There was a whole chapter needed on those warnings. Back to who is Jois first?

Who Is Sri K. Pattabhi Jois?

Sri K. Pattabhi Jois (1915-2009—also known as K.P. Jois) began his yoga studies with Krishnamacharaya in Mysore, India, at the age of twelve. He became the leading practitioner and teacher of Ashtanga yoga, which is a structured set of poses done in a flowing Vinyasa style. From biographies about him (http://yoga.about.com/od/yogabooks/fr/yogamala.htm) [17] to articles such as this one, you can learn his history and purpose: http://yoga.about.com/od/ashtangayoga/a/ashtangs.htm.[18]

In 1958, he published his treatise on Ashtanga yoga, *Yoga Mala* (https://www.verywell.com/yoga-classics-yoga-mala-by-sri-k-pattabhi-jois-3566934 and (http://yoga.about.com/od/yogabooks/fr/yogamala.htm[19]- giving both links, in case they take either down). His first Western students began to arrive in Mysore in the early 1970s. Through them, Ashtanga spread westward and profoundly influenced the way yoga is practiced today. After Pattabhi Jois died in 2009, his grandson Sharath took over the *leadership role*, including teaching the many students who continue to flock to Mysore in order to *deepen* their practices. Sharath also teaches at Jois Yoga in Encinitas. Some EUSD yogis sojourn to Mysore.

The Ashtanga method stresses daily vinyasa flow practice using *ujjayi breathing* (https://www.verywell.com/ocean-breath-ujjayi-pranayama-3566763),[20] mula bandha (https://www.verywell.com/how-to-use-mula-bandha-in-yoga-3566803),[21]uddiyana bandha, (https://www.verywell.com/uddiyana-bandha-3566811),[22] and drishti (https://www.verywell.com/how-understanding-drishti-can-help-your-yoga-practice-3566795). [23] There are six different Ashtanga series, through which a student progresses at his or her own pace. The leading yogi for EUSD, Jen Brown, shared in court she was not yet to level six after multiple trips to India and years of practice. "In fact," she said, "you will find very few make it to level six." *Why is that?*

On this website: http://ashtanga.com/html/background.html[24] "*Ashtanga yoga* is a system of yoga recorded by the sage Vamana Rishi in the *Yoga Korunta*, an ancient manuscript said to contain lists of many different groupings of *asanas*, as well as highly original teachings on *vinyasa, drishti, bandhas, mudras,* and philosophy (Jois 2002). The text of the *Yoga Korunta* "was imparted to Sri T. Krishnamacharya in the early 1900s by his Guru, Rama Mohan Brahmachari, and was later passed down to Pattabhi Jois during the duration of his studies with Krishnamacharya, beginning in 1927 (Ashtanga Yoga). Since 1948, Pattabhi Jois has been teaching *Ashtanga yoga* from his yoga *shala,* the Ashtanga Yoga Research Institute (Jois 2002 xvi), according to the sacred tradition of *Guru Parampara* [disciplic succession] (Jois 2003 12)." (These references are on their article linked above, not this book, so see end of article for those). Have I lost you yet? If so, imagine how difficult court was for the judge and others who don't know Sanskrit to sit through definition after definition. Press on, you'll be fine.

Sonia Tudor Jones: Good Intentions?

Photo of Sonya Tudor Jones in front of one of her multiple Jois Foundation locations - from Jois Foundation now defunct website, but still found on historical website engines.

We learned that this goal to spread across the US was funded and sourced by a devoted Ashtanga yoga student, Sonia Tudor Jones. Sonia had traveled to India multiple times over the years and was a direct student of K.P. Jois. She wanted to bring Ashtanga yoga to the United States. She formed a foundation to do just that. Her husband, Paul Tudor Jones, a hedge fund investor who is a billionaire, could easily finance her efforts. There were many others involved who will come into play. Two children of Sri K.P. Jois, Manju and Saraswathi, and two women, Salima Ruffin and Sonia Tudor Jones, were co-founders of Jois Foundation. See their kick off video for the Jois Yoga Shala in Encinitas (eight minutes: https://vimeo.com/21459292).25

Vanity Fair, March 7, 2012, Sonia Tudor Jones,
Jois siblings Saraswathi and Sherath, Salima Ruffin

http://www.itsallyogababy.com/
yoga-for-trophy-wives-vanity-fair-profiles-sonia-jones-jois-yoga/

Sonia Tudor Jones probably had good intentions. She probably had a really good experience in healing, or a strong spiritual connection in Ashtanga. She probably wanted to help others. Why not target easily teachable children? And why not give children, whose PE programs had experienced budget cutbacks, a good alternative? Good intentions aside, Ashtanga yoga is highly spiritual and ritualistic, as evidenced by The Eight Limbs definition at the core of Ashtanga. Sonia certainly knew this, having practiced and sojourned to India over and over. Our EUSD board could have easily figured that out. One very telling article that includes stars, such as Gwyneth Paltrow and Madonna as devoted *Ashtangis*, uncovers a lot about Sonia and why she is starting all these yoga shalas (yoga studios of compassion and "goddess of grain offerings"—look it up!) as there were at least four at the time of the article in 2012: http://www.vanityfair.com/news/business/2012/04/krishna-pattanbhi-trophy-wife-ashtanga-yoga.[26]

Paul and Sonya Tudor Jones at Jois Yoga event,
photo compliments of anonymous donor

Jois Yoga: More than Just Shalas

This is the story found on this webpage as of July, 2016: http://joisyoga.com/about/story/.[27]

At its simplest, Jois Yoga is an extension of the Ashtanga philosophy and practice developed by Sri K. Pattabhi Jois in Mysore, India in the early 20th century. At Jois Yoga shalas in Encinitas, CA, (where Ashtanga was first introduced in the US in 1975), Greenwich, CT, Islamorada, FL, and Sydney, Australia, hundreds of students receive instruction in Ashtanga yoga though the vehicle of parampara–uninterrupted succession–in a lineage that traces directly back to the Mysore teachings of Pattabhi Jois, R, Sharath Jois, and R, Saraswathi.

But Jois Yoga is more than just a collection of shalas. It is also an instrument of outreach, through the newly formed Jois Yoga Foundation, which was created to bring the Pattabhi Jois philosophy to youths in underserved communities. The Jois Yoga Foundation is currently partnered with two schools, one in Virginia and one and Kenya, and intends to bring Ashtanga instruction to upwards of 7,000 youths by midsummer 2012, with much more ambitious outreach goals on the horizon.

Additionally, Jois Yoga is a spiritually conscious line of clothing, created in keeping with the Jois philosophy of non-violence and sustainability. Jois Yoga apparel is designed to allow physical flexibility, with the intention of inspiring spiritual flexibility as well. Proceeds from the apparel boutiques will go to the Jois Yoga Foundation.

Through these three integrated efforts–instruction, outreach, and socially conscious apparel–Jois Yoga pursues its mission, to bring the philosophy, teachings, and values of Sri K. Pattabhi Jois to as many people as it is able to reach.

Wait! Did that say "partnered with two schools?" Yes, one is in Virginia and as you will see they also began the "study" on our children in Encinitas. However, studies must be conducted in an unbiased manner. The ambition to instruct "upward of 7000 children by midsummer 2012" refers to, and would be realized by, adding the Encinitas Union School District (just under 6000 children) by contract during that summer, which is exactly what transpired with EUSD approval in July. Yoga teachers with three years Ashtanga experience were hired in a rush, and trained prior to mid-August school openings. Did you catch the words—underserved communities? Encinitas? Ha! There is more money in Encinitas families to put kids into programs and probably would be described a little more as affluent and privileged (for the most part) - not "underserved." Notice also the statement "with much more ambitious goals on the horizon." Yes, there were. And some of us watched it all come to fruition—in Texas, in New York, in Cajon Valley (with our former EUSD Assistant Superintendent Miyashiro), and beyond by the time you read this book.

The photo of the four folks displays the original partnership for the Jois Foundation. See the Jois Shala kickoff video (linked above) and their Facebook page for postings which on Jois yoga in Encinitas: https://www.facebook.com/joisyogaencinitas.[28] Jois Foundation was linked to the two universities that were performing the "study" on the students. In fact, Jois Foundation's Paul Tudor Jones funded (twelve million dollars) for the start of the contemplative studies department at the University of Virginia (UVA). Thus, there is a conflict of interest where they were obviously in relationship for studying effects of yoga on school children. Later there would be connections revealed about Scott Himelstein who was running the study at the other university, the University of San Diego (USD). We parents didn't know at the time of the trial how very deep the ties and payoffs would become. Note that the Jois Yoga spiritually conscious line of clothing proceeds go to the Jois Yoga Foundation (see them in shala video above), their way of tapping into the vast million-dollar industry of fitness clothing in America. Perhaps Jois Foundation aimed for a wider target than *underserved*?

What is up with The Jois Foundation?

This article - *What is up with Jois Foundation* points out that something is fishy http://www.thinkbodyelectric.com/2013/06/ yoga-train-wreck-in-encinitas-or-whats.html.[30] or rather a "train wreck" in Encinitas. The author gets some of the facts right, but still makes many assumptions that were incorrect at the time. What they have accurate is that there are problems with the Encinitas ties in the District and the big promoters of Ashtanga yoga through the Jois Foundation. More has been revealed to the public since that article such as one that reveals some of the problems and links in the web of political, spiritual, celebrity and other relationships, with the district Superintendent desperately trying to hang onto this program four years later (after Jois Foundation pulled the funding). The Coast News started digging and found a plethora of what they titled: "The Ties between EUSD and yoga program foundation and schools, raises concerns: https://www.thecoastnews.com/ ties-between-eusd-yoga-program-foundation-and-school-raise-concerns/.[31] These are some of the same concerns the Judge in the initial case had (see ruling on Lawsuit page of truthaboutyoga.com website) and that we have had all along. However, let's walk you step by step and details on more recent activities will be revealed in final chapters. One peek at this article though, and you see the ties that concerned us all. The truth will surface over time. Even upon publication of this book, and the expert witnesses' book (back cover endorsement), so much more will be revealed.

New Name—Sonima Foundation

Note that after the lawsuit ended at the first level on July 1, 2013, Jois Foundation abruptly changed its name to Sonima Foundation. The new foundation name was a combination of two of the founding womens' names put together: Sonia (Tudor Jones) and Salima (Ruffin). Son + ima. The initial foundation appears to have been between not only these two women but two of the Jois

children, but now it's not clear if they are also part of this newer named foundation (see videos above in Jois Shala section and their own website for evidence). Eugene Ruffin, Salima's husband and Chairman of Jois Foundation, was also very involved and attended the trial. If what Baird said was true about there not being ties to Jois Foundation and that the kids were not doing Ashtanga yoga, why would Ruffin feel the need to be at the trial? Why did Ruffin speak to the media in June after judgement on the case if EUSD was doing their own yoga? Why did Jois Foundation change their name the day after trial? What reason did they give? None we could find …

There was a grand opening for Jois Foundation prior to trial on Coast Hwy 101 in Encinitas involving Encinitas folks. There was a big *ceremony* at which children of EUSD were invited to the ashram during the trial timeframe. There was a second year celebration that is also available on Vimeo. It is three minutes located here and includes a talk on *Karma* by Sanjeev Vermi. http://joisyoga.com/events/jois-yoga-encinitas-2nd-anniversary/.[32] Find all of those links on our concerned parent website as well.

Encinitas: The Entry of Yoga and Ashtanga Yoga

Encinitas is a small, Southern California beach community. It's known for its world-class surfing, quaint-yet-quirky downtown on Historic Highway 101, and for being home to a premier botanical garden. It is also the home to the Self-Realization Fellowship (SRF), a beachfront temple that has meditation gardens overlooking the water and located by Swamis beach. The SRF is important to note because it was founded by Paramahansa Yogananda. Thus, Encinitas was an "entry point" to yoga entering the United States.

This is found on their website:

"Today, Self-Realization Fellowship has grown to include more than 500 temples and centers around the world, and has members in over 175 countries. In India and surrounding countries, Paramahansa Yogananda's work is known as Yogoda Satsanga

Society of India (YSS), with more than 100 centers, retreats, and ashrams." https://yogananda.org/self-realization-fellowship.[33]

What type of yoga do you teach? "Paramahansa Yogananda taught the path of Raja Yoga, which includes the practice of definite, scientific methods of meditation — known as Kriya Yoga — that enable one to perceive from the very beginning of one's efforts, glimpses of the ultimate goal — union of soul with Spirit. The Kriya Yoga path also embodies a complete philosophy and way of life. Through the practice of Kriya Yoga, one is able to calm the mental and physical processes so that one's consciousness, freed from limitations, can realize the bliss and omnipresence of God." Found here: http://www.yogananda-srf.org/faqs/Frequently_Asked_Questions.aspx#1.[34]

Encinitas: The Perfect "Target Demographic"

Encinitas school district was the perfect target for the Jois Foundation's goals as it was home of the 1970's Encinitas Ashtanga Yoga Movement by K.P. Jois. EUSD is located in the heart of Encinitas, bordering Carlsbad, and is comprised of the nine elementary schools. There are no mid or high schools in Encinitas District. Kids move to the San Dieguito District after their elementary years. The grandson of the founder (K.P. Jois) happens to be married to a schoolteacher at Capri Elementary. Capri was the first school to Pilot Ashtanga yoga twice weekly in the spring of the 2011–2012 academic school year. Prior to that, you might find a volunteer mom teaching one or two yoga classes, but nothing this encompassing.

There are many other connections and reasons why Encinitas schools were targeted and the administration was ripe for the opportunity. The fact that the grant got "passed" with three professing Christians on the board is surprising until you understand some details behind the decisions. First, the board wasn't given much time to think about or research the background of the organization with whom they would jump into this three-year commitment. Second, funds are tight in Encinitas for schools, and PE had

already been cut for years leaving regular teachers in charge of PE. Third, personal connections to the grantors and others involved. Thus, the perfect storm was brewing with financial needs, wealthy contacts, and political aspirations.

Jois and EUSD moved quickly

Over the following summer after the pilot, EUSD and Jois Foundation together, recruited, hired, trained, and placed yoga instructors into all nine schools at the start of the fall in 2012. Four more schools started yoga in August 2012 with the other four due to begin yoga classes in January of 2013. The "yoga" teachers at the four schools without yoga in the fall taught other subjects such as art and foreign languages (such as Sanskrit).

Therefore, all nine schools had experienced Ashtanga *yoga teachers* in place in August 2012. Although some were teaching *other subject matter,* it is interesting to note that they were all brought on board (paid for by the grant) in August. In November of 2012, I had a conversation with Kristin McCloskey, who is a mom of one of my daughter's then classmates. She was also the new yoga teacher at Olivenhein Pioneer Elementary. She had over three years Ashtanga yoga experience like the other new yoga teachers, and she revealed to me that all the yoga teachers met on Fridays with the head yoga teacher named Jen Brown who led them in writing the curriculum. McCloskey never mentioned Leslie Wright from EUSD, who may or may not have been at the meetings.

In court, the Superintendent would claim that Leslie Wright (from the district) was writing the curriculum (not the teachers). Tax forms would later prove otherwise—that the yoga instructors were hired for the full time hours in order to write the curriculum and Leslie Wright's job description and tax filing changed from 2012 to fall 2013. In court, during the May 2013 sessions, Baird said Wright sat in on the writing some weeks, but by June he changed his story to her being *the* head curriculum writer. Given Jen Brown was proven in court to be working for both Jois on the payroll and EUSD (through Regur) there was clear proof of entanglement which they wanted to avoid by highlighting Wright as the lead and not Brown (Regur Development Group, as I explain further in Chapter 6, is the contracted entity between EUSD and Jois Foundation to employ all the yoga teachers). Wright's position and pay immediately changed according to tax records and District documents for 2013. We just wouldn't have those for trial, but are available on www.encinitasparents4truth.com[35] website if you want further details. We have embedded them into our website as well if needed one day. However, the yoga instructors met and wrote the program together as Kristin told me and if Leslie was even there, she was clearly not the expert in the room on yoga. According to records, she began helping the curriculum development part in the fall of 2013.

The Study

There was an explanation given for why some schools would begin yoga right away, and others would wait until January 2013. Two universities were conducting a study on our kids on the effects of yoga. So four schools would have half a year of PE, and the other five had yoga all year as a comparison study. Parents were not asked to sign anything for the study, which is extremely odd, and I'm pretty sure illegal, given children would be touched. In any study the subjects need to give signed consent, especially for minors. I'm not sure, to this day, how they got away without parental consent for the first year of the study. Just one more fact we were unable to get placed by the judge into the trial.

At El Camino Creek (ECC), the school two of my children attended in the fall of 2012, the new yoga instructor was assigned to teach *art* until January, 2013. (This will become pertinent later when you learn *art* became drawing mandalas and she taught the kids Sanskrit unbeknownst to our principal.) Or rather, that is what Carrie Brown, the ECC Principal, would testify to in court. In November of 2012, when I sat down and talked with Principal Brown in her office, she said she "wished this would all go away because it was a scheduling nightmare for the principals," and that she couldn't figure out a way to have the fourth through sixth graders do more than forty minutes of yoga because it would cut into their core curriculum time. ECC may have been the only school doing just forty minutes of yoga weekly for the upper grades. In her testimony, she made many mistakes, such as saying I talked to her about the mandalas, but that was not I, it was another mom, Samantha Vigil. She had many details wrong in her affidavit. Among her mistakes, the PE minutes for my kids was by far the most frustrating of the erroneous facts written, and in which she clearly knew the truth; but there would be no platform to share any of that at trial.

Further, after filing the lawsuit in February, 2013, Ms. Brown avoided me and never spoke to me again unless required to do so as her role as principal. Prior to yoga in the schools it was very different, I was the chair of our annual Jogathon (the largest fundraiser in the school year), and she had nothing but appreciation and thanks for me. Not any longer. I was clearly now on a blacklist, even after nine years of service and volunteering in that school. I'd been there longer than she had, and now teachers I'd known for years, began also avoiding me. Yet ironically, our young yoga teacher would have access to every child in the school—alone. That is something even caring and devoted volunteer parents were never allowed to do.

A whole lot of change was happening in this school district, and lack of parent knowledge and transparency from the leadership and district continued.

The Impact of Jois Foundation in EUSD

The Jois Foundation offered the Encinitas Union School District $533,000 initially to implement weekly yoga for sixty to eighty minutes and to have our 5,600 children available for *testing* of several indicators of fitness and bullying. The Jois Foundation provided most of the teachers for the school district to interview and hire. The only requirement for teaching yoga to the EUSD students, as per their advertisements, was three years of experience practicing Ashtanga yoga (photos of the captured screen shots available on Ashtanga yoga in Encinitas page of truthaboutyoga.com web-site), *but no experience working with children was necessary*! The initial grant information about Jois Foundation is recorded in many places, but here is one from Paul Ecke Central Elementary School. http://pauleckecentral.com/jois-foundation-grant/.[36]

Who is Tim Miller?

Let's take a shift from the Jois family and Encinitas to Tim Miller. Miller claims to be among the first to bring Ashtanga to the United States after David Williams. This is written by Tim Miller on his website, on this page: http://ashtangayogacenter. com/a-brief-history-of-ashtanga-yoga-in-encinitas/.[37]

By Tim Miller: "Encinitas holds the distinction of being the American birthplace of Ashtanga Yoga. David Williams began teaching here in the early seventies and sponsored Pattabhi Jois and his son Manju to come here for the first time in 1975. Brad Ramsey and Gary Lopedota, two of David's students, opened their own yoga shala, and called the Ashtanga Yoga Nilayam, after David moved to Maui. ... I became involved in 1968." (see more on link above) If you peruse his website more you will see such topics as the Alchemy of yoga, retreats, classes, and a picture of K.P. Jois on the homepage.

Did Superintendent Timothy Baird invite Tim Miller to EUSD schools? Miller was spotted at Park Dale Lane in late 2012. There was a "demonstration" of yoga going on and we (the concerned parents group) wondered "why is Tim Miller there?" The best answer we had at the time was that Jois Foundation's coming into Encinitas with such a big presence was either 1. competition to Tim or 2. would be a good flow of children to his studio as yoga would become second nature to all these kids after seven years. Miller's Ashtanga studio is in the Forum shopping center on El Camino Real and Calle Barcelona—planted right in the middle of the 9 Encinitas Elementary Schools now doing the very type of yoga that he teaches. Miller was never seen at the trial or the schools since, to my knowledge. He continues as the main teacher at the

Forum Ashtanga location as of April, 2019. Some news articles have noted that he was offered the opportunity to become a part of the incoming Jois yoga shala, but that he chose to keep separate from the whole new Jois Foundation plans. Smart man if that is the case.

Sharath Jois

Did the Superintendent invite Sharath to events at the school as well? Sharath is the grandson who performs most of the Jois Yoga classes even today in the Ashtanga shala in Encinitas. The last found location was a fairly hidden spot off Westlake after closing down the elaborate 851 South Coast Hwy location on 101. The Westlake location wasn't easy to find. It is merely a set of stairs on the side of a large fitness building with one sign posted showing "Sherath with his leg up to side." Upon going up the stairs, the door was locked. It was a day before full moon. Only a photo of Sharath was posted on the door. The location was a far cry from the celebration days just two years prior in the kick-off videos.

There are several more Ashtanga and Jois folks involved who will be mentioned in the Cast of Characters chapter. For now, this is plenty to get you started.

Many questions remain unanswered, but over time, many get answered and that is why asking questions is so important to the scientific process of discovery. And wow, has this been a journey of discovery!

Photo by author of Sherath Jois on door to Ashtanga yoga studio in Encinitas, June 2016

Photo by author of stairs leading up to Ashtanga Yoga Studio in Encinitas, June 2016

Photo by author June 2016, former "grand opening" location in downtown Encinitas on HW101

EUSD Superintendent Baird and California PE funding

I would like to believe that EUSD Superintendent Timothy Baird had no idea the harm he would bring to the district and that he intended to bring a good program that would help the children of his district. However, the fact remains that he was given multiple warnings of physical, mental, spiritual and religious problems with the program in 2012 by hundreds of parents coming to meetings, signing a petition, and writing letters, and he denied them all. He ignored the parents without responding in meetings while he chose to respond to pro-yoga parents in support. He kept yoga with a very strong arrogance in his demeanor. He would not open the door for any communication, and to this day we have never spoken. He never called me back from emails, letters and even a filing in court! Never once has he attempted to speak to me. His only response was an FAQ which didn't address all the issues and only made an attempt to cover up others as they appeared to scramble to change policies and procedures almost weekly. As we uncovered famous people involved (such as Deepak Chopra, Stedman Graham, Oprah's significant other, the Tudor Joneses, etc.) that he was rubbing elbows with, his pompous and confident attitude became understandable, and just made us dig even deeper into asking, why? He is a crafty man who chooses his words carefully — too carefully. There always seemed to be a reason. He is responsible for the consequences that will come for the EUSD District, and many others will bear some responsibility in those schools that the EUSD board chose to bring yoga in as curriculum, just as any leader who makes these decisions. The fact that so many staff, teachers and principals are afraid to speak up, is part of the "influencing" that became a huge problem. Was there more of this going on than that which was obvious to us?

PE funding cuts in California led to a long tradition of regular teachers (not trained in PE) being in charge of their own class PE in most California schools. Regular classroom teachers have been teaching PE for over a decade at least. Growing up in another state, PE was taught by a qualified teacher educated in physical education. In California not only is every teacher required to teach PE, but, there is a PE manual to follow to get ideas of how to run certain activities. Many of us parents filled in the gaps teaching PE when teachers needed help. I taught PE to a 4th grade class at El Camino Creek Elementary when one of my sons was in 4th grade. No one checked any credentials or asked if I had any experience. I was handed a binder and thanked for helping. That's just how it was in Encinitas.

Covering PE in CA — a ripe budget problem

Principals grappled with ideas on how to cover the required PE minutes by others when possible. Some purchased programs with funds parents donated (such as the karate at El Camino Creek in 2012) and some used parent volunteers. Some teachers just had the kids run laps. Lack of funding for PE teachers and PE state requirements of 200 hours per two weeks is a big part of why the District was so open to an outsider with funds. We needed better PE. We needed money or volunteers. What we didn't need is a program (of any type) to dominate two thirds of the time for PE when any one *activity* isn't the best for everyone. We needed an alternative to the yoga right away, and that was simply denied. The contract spelled out why. Baird readily denied optional PE—it was yoga or non-physical alternatives in 2012 - 2013. That's where the media and people *assumed* we had a choice for PE alternatives when we didn't.

So when Jois Foundation approached the District (or however it happened), Baird was ripe for a program to fill the Physical Education needs, and what he got was a whole lot more that he would become enamored with, and lose all perspective (in my opinion) on what is entanglement and conflicts of interest. He didn't care what the children thought and wouldn't dare ask them in a survey if they prefer PE or yoga because he knows the answer. But the end isn't written, and everyone pays the piper eventually. For that we will wait, and watch and record history as it unfolds. We have a monthly newsletter posting news articles and developments, if you are interested in watching this unfold along with us.

Defining many people and terms became important in this case. Ashtanga Yoga, Eight Limb yoga, Jois Foundation, Sonia Tudor Jones, Salima Ruffin, Sonima Foundation, and more. The foundational information researched made it understandable for the "perfect storm" to flow right into Encinitas, at this time in history, for purposes you will continue to see revealed in this book. The timing was no accident, nor were any of the players involved. In an upcoming chapter, a cast of characters will help you follow the scenes of the trial.

Follow the Money ... Bravo to Jois

Like so many investigations, follow the money and you'll find the motivations. Jois Foundation was crafty and strategic in creating devoted followers—their yoga teachers.

The initial contract at $533,000 would blossom to over four million dollars in four years for the Encinitas District. Multiple other districts across the country have now accepted $500K initial implementation grants from now named Sonima Foundation. Follow whose hands the money goes through, and to whom, and see who is on the Sonima Foundation Board of directors. Most of that money though, is going to "Jois Yoga" instructors and a small amount to supplies in the districts. Genius plan, Jois Yoga! You found a way to take part-time yoga instructors (how many classes per week did each teach prior?) and give them a full-time forty-hour-a-week job, creating devoted Ashtanga yoga followers in the meantime, undivided in their time and focus. EUSD/Jois yoga instructors became devoted to writing curriculum for Jois while spreading Jois Yoga unbeknownst to most kids and parents. Now, the curriculum sits on a website of Scott Himelstein, who did the CEPAL University study—further entanglement the court would somehow overlook. Bravo, Jois. It was a genius plan to spread your yoga and beliefs. Jois Foundation fooled the district and public along the way. Or did they? Haven't they been quite upfront about their spreading Ashtanga yoga mission right on their website from the beginning? Why did so many people miss that? Yes, the EUSD board missed that somehow too, or rather ignored it when we told them. They may not have "intended to" spread Ashtanga yoga, but intent isn't the issue, when the results are hurting others, such as children who have no choice and no voice in the matter. Most parents didn't have time to look fully into this. We didn't either. But we did anyway. We put aside time in our jobs, in our school volunteering and with our own families. Going to meetings, researching and spending valuable time of ours (many parents), having to ask for the removal of yoga—but it was well worth the effort, *for the children*. We spent the time because something greater than ourselves, led us to *take a deeper look* for the sake of the children and each step was fueled by the hidden facts and agendas we found.

SECTION TWO—

Behind the Scenes—*Inside the courtroom each day*

CHAPTER FIVE

Inside The Yoga Trial of 2013—San Diego, California

T he next few chapters were written to give you an "inside the courtroom look" of the trial. Many of the *behind-the-scenes* events of the trial are worth reporting because they impact so many people beyond the children of EUSD. Many statements and direct quotes will be highlighted from the Yoga Trial of 2013 and the Appellate trial of 2015. The legal documents of interest are attached to the *Truth About Yoga* website on the following page https://truthaboutyoga.com/about/lawsuit-in-encinitas-2/[1] and many are also linked on the website of the Attorney for the case, Dean Broyles at the National Center for Law and Policy http://www.nclplaw.org/resources/.[2] What we experienced as a family, with other supporters both internal and external to the school district, was sharing more than just seats on the left side of the courtroom, as the trial progressed.

Not about us, Nor just about yoga

This trial was not about us—no matter how much anyone tried to focus on us as a family. Nor was it just about yoga. The trial was about enforcing the laws of church and state and protecting children from programs that don't belong in elementary school curriculum. There were problems beyond the program, not only with who was offering it, but also with the ties of relationships and payments, how it was being implemented, and why. Yoga could have easily been an after-school extracurricular activity or an optional elective, to avoid the need for a trial. That was not an option for Superintendent Baird, nor the EUSD board, for forthcoming reasons.

For starters Baird and Encinitas Union School District would not consider other choices for PE than yoga because they had already hastily signed a three-year contract that included testing of the 5600 children in our school district. That testing needed to control the amount of PE. The two universities doing the testing were linked financially and relationally to the Jois Foundation. This was another big concern, and why we filed. We hoped to have EUSD remove yoga completely, move to an optional program after school, or at the very least, gain PE as an alternative to yoga within the school day. It was apparent the intent was for all the children to do yoga weekly for seven years through their elementary school years. That was very concerning.

Separation of Church and State

You may think this trial was about separation of Church and State Laws, and you would be right. You may think this trial was about protecting the children, and you would be right. What you may not have thought much about, though, are all the other various concerns many parents had, having nothing to do with whether laws were broken, but for the best interests of the children. You may also not have heard about the concerns of which the former yogis warned us and pointed to more dangers when children do yoga. Dangers none of us saw at first glance.

Never could have been prepared

Quietly preparing for what would happen when the case became public was our concern between the December decision and the February court filing. We prepared our children, our jobs, our home, and our extended family for what was coming in the next months. In hindsight, we could never have fully prepared for what was about to happen. The attorney could prepare the documents, but he could not anticipate, nor plan for, the calls and media requests he would receive. We could not be prepared for being called "Yoga Haters" or any of the worse labels that would come to pass. We could not even begin to understand the magnitude of people we would impact by our willingness to stand up and question yoga and the EUSD decisions. Thankfully, we couldn't imagine it; that may have held us back. The circus began the very day we filed.

You can see the press release and court filing (links below here) where we asked for a speedy trial in order to get yoga removed immediately from the schools and allow children to return to regular PE classes. The expedited trial was supposed to have one expert witness on each side, no jury, and last only two days. That is *not* what transpired.

The *Writ of Mandate* filed on February 20, 2013, is on these two websites: https://truthaboutyoga.files.wordpress.com/2015/01/sedlock-complaint-final.pdf [3] and https://www.nclplaw.org/wp-content/uploads/2011/12/Sedlock-Complaint-FINAL.pdf

The press release that same day: http://www.nclplaw.org/wp-content/uploads/2011/12/NCLP-Complaint-Press-Release-FINAL.pdf.[4]

Media Surrounding Trial

Here are some of the articles you would find if you did a search about the trial. Most of these were published on the actual days of the trial in 2013.

- Yoga Lawsuit, Encinitas Union Schools Feb 1, 2013, ABC News. https://abcnews.go.com/US/yoga-lawsuit-encinitas-union-school-district-california-sued/story?id=18561237[5] Encinitas School District Yoga Trial Starts, May 20, 2013, Fox News http://fox5sandiego.com/2013/05/20/encinitas-school-district-yoga-trial-starts/[6]
- Trail Begins in Lawsuit over Yoga in Schools, May 20, KPBS http://www.kpbs.org/news/2013/may/20/sd-yoga-lawsuit/[7]

- Doctor (Religious Studies Professor) Testifies at Yoga Trial http://fox5sandiego.com/2013/05/21/expert-witness-testifies-teaching-yoga-is-a-conspiracy/[8]
- Yoga Trial Underway, May 21, 2013. Coast News: https://www.thecoastnews.com/eusd-yoga-trial-underway/[9]
- Definition of Yoga as Religion on Trial May 21, 2013, Yoga Alliance https://www.yogaalliance.org/Learn/Articles/Questioning_the_definition_of_religion_as_the_trial_begins[10]
- Yoga Lawsuit, Schools Accused of Spreading Gospel, May 22, 2013, NBC News http://www.nbcsandiego.com/news/local/Yoga-Class-Encinitas-Lawsuit-San-Diego-Reglious-208538581.html[11]
- Encinitas Yoga Trial over Religion in School, May 23, 2013, Huffington Post http://www.huffingtonpost.com/2013/05/23/encinitas-yoga-trial-religion-in-school_n_3327247.html [12]
- Trial without Resolution adding days in June, May 23, Yoga Alliance https://www.yogaalliance.org/Learn/Articles/Yoga_trial_without_resolution [13]
- Trial on Yoga in Schools resumes, June 24, 2013, Fox News http://fox5sandiego.com/2013/06/24/trial-on-school-yoga-classes-resumes/[14]
- Parents Testify in Yoga Trial June 25, 2013, NBC News http://www.nbcsandiego.com/news/local/Parents-Testify-in-Encinitas-Yoga-Class-Trial-212831061.html [15]
- Yoga on Trial in San Diego, June 26, 2013, Charisma News http://www.charismanews.com/us/40019-yoga-on-trial-in-san-diego-religious-lawsuit [16]
- Attorneys Deliver Closing Arguments in School Yoga Trial, Coast News https://www.thecoastnews.com/attorneys-deliver-closing-arguments-in-school-yoga-trial/[17]
- Closing Arguments Underway, June 25, 2013, KPBS http://www.kpbs.org/news/2013/jun/25/closing-arguments-begin-encinitas-yoga-trial/ [18]
- School Sun Salutations Here to Stay (Encinitas Yoga Case), Encinitas Patch, July 1, 2013, https://patch.com/california/

encinitas/candy-gunther-brown-school-sun-salutations-here-to-stay-encinitas-yoga [19]
- Yoga Can Stay in School: Looking More Closely at the Encinitas Yoga Trial Decision, July 2, 2013, http://www.huffingtonpost.com/candy-gunther-brown-phd/what-made-the-encinitas-p_b_3522836.html [20]
- Huffington Post on yoga and the Church vs. State Battle in Encinitas https://www.huffpost.com/entry/encinitas-yoga-trial-religion-in-school_n_3327247 [21]
- What Makes the Encinitas Yoga Religious, Huffington Post July, 24, 2013, http://www.huffingtonpost.com/candy-gunther-brown-phd/encinitas-yoga-lawsuit_b_3570850.html [22]

Seven Days in Court

Quickly the judge realized we had valid concerns and this wasn't going to be a quick slam dunk trial as he'd perhaps imagined and others had articulated. "This claim has legs to stand on" one reporter at the Union Tribune would quote in the news. Members of the Media filled the jury box daily, rather than jurors, for the entire seven days of the trial. We were in court for three days in May. 2013. Then, due to lawyer and court schedules, we were back in court three more days in June of 2013. The verbal verdict was given July 1, 2013. Six long days of trial, and one day of verdict would result. What was to be a two day trial resulted in seven days.

My overall impression was this: Court was comical, frustrating and fascinating all at once. Perhaps unique to our case, there were so many *religious* and *non-English words* presented that needed to be defined for the entire courtroom. This made the day very tedious and then amusing after a while. People got tired and punchy, especially the judge. He was downright jovial at times. We enjoyed his humor; yet, he seemed to seriously contemplate the facts while peppering the room with funny comments. I will share many of his comments with you, but one of the first things the judge said on day one, after one of the lawyers offered that the judge stop him anytime to ask questions was "Well I'm not a potted plant, I do intend to ask you questions."

A while later that first day when the judge almost skipped the opening arguments of a third lawyer (for the district), that lawyer piped in with copying comments "I'm not a potted plant either, may I proceed?" That third (not district and not plaintiffs) attorney would attempt over and over to joke with the judge, and I counted at least three times over six days (in the trial court reporter notes) where he called himself a potted plant after the judge made that joke once the first day. It was apparent this lawyer was trying to be humorous to win points with the judge.

Honorable Judge John **MEYER:** *Photo Credit, Coast News*

One day in court I laughed more than watching a comedy show on TV. We laughed so hard we had tears, and my sides were hurting. It was hysterical. We understood that the judge was "lightening" the mood, but I also wonder, given the heavy content and hefty words: *was he using humor out of discomfort in his own knowledge on the topic?* Does he always hold his head in his hands the way he did in our trial? Does he hold his hand against one cheek when trying to figure something out, or is it just a habit? He appeared to be contemplating the information. Body language can be tricky to read, but it does speak volumes. He tried hard to "figure out" the different language used in the trial. I now wonder if he just kept trying to fit the pieces into how he wanted to rule. Why the four extra days of trial, if he knew? The truth is that he couldn't have known in two days; he needed more information. He stated at the opening of his verbal verdict that he had reviewed and re-reviewed everything on the case. Perhaps he adds humor most days in court, not just in our case; this is his daily job, and, no doubt, some levity is needed at times.

Sanskrit Language

Many words used in court were in Sanskrit, which is defined as the ritual language written for group worship ceremonies. The definition here is what you would find on the link given.

> *Sanskrit is the primary sacred language of Hinduism, a philosophical language in Buddhism, Hinduism, Sikhism and Jainism, and a literary language that was in use as a lingua franca in Greater India.*
>
> https://www.bing.com/search?q=sanskrit&form=EDGHPC3&qs=LS&cvid=864ea0fdac7b481e8583196209fa5fdd&pq=sanskri

The reference to the different languages used in yoga went beyond just definitions and spelling for the court reporter. Demonstrations were used for clarity at times, before we could proceed. Constant interruptions occurred like this, and then we returned to the point being made. This became somewhat exasperating for not only the attorneys and judge, but for the whole room.

It was common in court for the judge to scratch his head or hold his head in both hands and ask: "Now what does that mean?" He'd say, "Tell the court the definition of that so we can understand what you are saying." One of my personal favorites from the Judge: "That looks like a pretzel to me—can any of the kids even sit like that? What kind of exercise is that, and how is it helping a child?" All of these queries, and the many more he asked, caused the courtroom laughter to erupt, then we wondered and concentrated together to figure out the responses from yogis and experts. We even defined and discussed the words yoga and religion. The basic definition of yoga is "to yoke." *And to yoke to what? To become one with what?*

To Yoke ... Not a Joke

The very definition "to yoke" is the basis of the foundational concerns with yoga in public schools. There was constant starting and stopping to define terms such as Jnana mudra, Samadhi, lotus position, Corpse pose, Namaste, Vedas, Bhagavad Gita, Jois family names, and Ashtanga yoga. So, you can imagine the confusion for the judge and the media and the court. You are starting to get the picture of why we had to stop and have each word defined. After the distraction, someone had to work their way back to the statement they were trying to make that included the word, and then move forward. At one point the judge said, "This is a trial by Wikipedia," and we all laughed with him at many jokes like this. The media would pick up on little quips and the evening news would, unfortunately, focus on that rather than the more important content. The truth was, the definitions of all these words for and in yoga were at the core of the problems in this case. The words define the substance of the problem. The fact that most Americans don't know what the yoga lingo actually means in a foreign language adds to the complication of understanding that there even is a problem.

"The Yoga Lawyer"

At some point along the trial our attorney became known in the news as "the Yoga Lawyer." A title we would all laugh about, but eventually he would grow to accept when, call after call, people would ask him "Hey are you the yoga lawyer?" Once, when I met someone and told her my name was Jennifer and she responded "Jennifer yoga?" I just had to laugh … well, yes, that would be me I guess, but I never thought of that as a word defining who I am prior to her question. Some things just stick, whether we want them to or not. Those of us battling this all had lives before this, and none of them had to do with yoga.

The *Yes* Lawyer

The "extra lawyer," added to the district's side, attempted to portray our lawsuit as frivolous in the media and in his social media circles. This attorney "pushed into" the case and called us names (such as fanatical Christians) in his opening statement. This became his mode of operation to attempt to "pigeon-hole" us in the minds of others as something negative. He became referred to as "the yes lawyer" because he started a "yes" campaign with parents to try to gain support of the yoga program for what appeared to not only benefit him personally for his kids, but also professionally to gain a lot of exposure.

He was also a parent in the District. He asked to be part of the trial even though EUSD already had attorneys on the case. Our attorney, Dean Broyles, and my husband and I, as petitioners, allowed him to be part of the trial because we value that others have the opposite opinion on yoga even though the trial wasn't about popular opinions. Our goal was to educate more people in the process about the conflicts of interest over yoga in EUSD. By allowing him into the trial proceedings, we would hopefully show that we were not concerned with his attempts to injure our character, nor were we concerned about the fact that some people love yoga. Liking or disliking yoga was not the issue. He did not appear to sway the judge in the opening statements with his name-calling anyway. However, he made negative statements and used derogatory terms about us throughout the trial, displaying negative bullying of his own. He was entirely inaccurate on many facts and made erroneous assumptions. Some of them would never be clear to the judge, but, I'm sure the judge didn't miss the fact of the bullying comments in the courtroom that were also court recorded "for the record."

Once, at the court of appeals, I stepped into an elevator to correct "the yes lawyer" directly about his inaccurate statements about my beliefs and specific strategic untruths he had just stated about me during trial. He called me Catholic and I am not, but my husband is, so perhaps he "assumed" and when we assume – well, you know the saying. We all deserve respect and to have our opinions, but interestingly the "pro-yoga" side (parents and this lawyer) tended to degrade and call names with hostility, rather than treat others with peace and respect. There was no sense of their *Namaste* (he considers it a respectful greeting) during this trial ... But one parent in the district noticed that after trial, his offices (next to the self-realization center in Encinitas) went through a pricey upgrade. Not sure if that was related, but the timing is awfully questionable...

Who attended the trial?

The entire courtroom was visibly mentally and physically exhausted at the end of each day. I now know more than I ever cared to know about every one of these words and dozens more in Sanskrit[23] and about yoga. (And I love learning!) I'd imagine most people in that courtroom loved learning (after all, most were in education, supporting a school district, so I hope so!) I'm referring to the approximately twenty to thirty people from EUSD that were sitting on the other side of the court each day. Some were teachers, some principals, some yoga teachers, some Jois Foundation people, and several district staff there daily. Not sure what that cost ... but educators sitting to be educated on these terms was entertaining when the yawns began. I sat wondering why so many of them came each day and why they were so adamant to throw so much effort at this yoga program. Ironically, the same educators to our right were not open at all to information that the very program they put into the schools was not appropriate for children to be led to do weekly. They clearly hadn't even educated themselves on the religious nature of the foundation that provided funding. Or worse - they knew and were covering it up to move forward on their plans and contracts.

Somewhere around ten to fifteen people were sitting on our side, and I'm pretty sure no one was paid for their days sitting in court or their gas to get downtown, nor the parking lot fees outside. No expense reports were available on our side. I didn't even know some of the people sitting on our side who came to support our case. Most of the parents with kids in school and jobs couldn't come to court. Some were probably scared to show up, given the divisiveness in the schools already. Many questions I received, and still receive, about court helped me realize that many were interested in what happened.

The following chapters will show answers to most of those questions people asked, in detail with quotes from court reporter notes. From reviewing more than 1400 pages of court reporter notes for the seven days of trial, I pulled the most interesting and important factual information from each day for you. I assume less than five percent of you reading this book would ever want to read through all of the trial. If you did, you would find it humorous and educational, but, my assumption is that only a few attorneys will comb through those pages. Therefore, you will find the highlight points that each witness gave, testifying in court, providing you many facets and interesting details of this trial. Page numbers are referenced (to trial notes) in those chapters in case you wanted to check further into details. Knowing who is involved, their backgrounds, and their role in the trial will help make sense of chapters seven through thirteen. To begin, I will introduce the roles and importance of each person involved.

CHAPTER SIX

Cast of Characters

B efore getting started on the trial quotes, it would be really helpful for you to know the characters involved. After much thought about how to untangle the web of confusion that could easily snare anyone reading or researching about this trial, the following idea emerged. Lay out bullet-pointed details of why each person is important to the trial, and display their relationships or involvement in the yoga program. This solution will hopefully "keep it simple," giving you background before you start reading the in-depth trial chapters. You'll find some links to the evidence noted here, but most items will be cited in the next chapters, as revealed in the trial. This list of people can be a reference for you when a name is used in the following chapters. Read this chapter first though, because it will give you a vast amount of background and foundation. These points contain the very concerns of many parents in Encinitas, in addition to exposure from the media and lawsuit. There was so much more than ever got reported ...

Jois Yoga

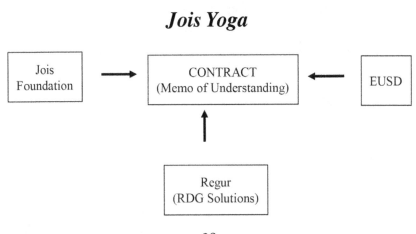

Cast of Characters for the Yoga Program and Trial

Compliments of http://www.indiawest.com/news/global_indian/yoga-poses-new-questions-for-st-century-practitioners/article_3d4cd8c0-72ce-11e5-895f-17a2ef13b575.html

Timothy Baird
Photo credit Coast News: https://www.thecoastnews.com/school-yoga-program-continues-to-anger-parents/

Superintendent, Timothy Baird
- Superintendent of Encinitas Union School District.
- Former Sonima Foundation Advisory Board Member.
- Implemented Jois Foundation Yoga into all nine EUSD elementary schools in the fall of 2012, after a pilot program done at Capri Elementary in 2011/2012.
- Implemented IPads into all schools, a $2.7M program involving Scott Himelstein, prior to their partnership over jois yoga http://encinitasparents4truth.com/baird-himelstein/. [1] Also found: https://www.thecoastnews.com/encinitas-school-district-rolling-out-ipads-for-k-2/
- Baird sued Encinitas over Pacific View Property, 2011. http://encinitasundercover.blogspot.com/2011/10/eusd-superintendent-tim-baird-sues.html. [2]
- Baird's travel expenses exploded from 2012-2015, during Jois Yoga implementation http://encinitasparents4truth.com/timothy-baird-eusd-board-travel-costs-exploding-higher/. [3]
- Seen on large cruise ship photos with Scott Himelstein, although he claimed to not be entangled in any way with Jois Foundation and the researchers doing the "yoga study." (Himelstein directed Jois/EUSD yoga study at USD).
- Testified not to be "partnering" with Jois Foundation, (while documents used that very word, partnership), while Baird carried the title Board of Directors for Sonima, appeared on Jois promotional videos, and spoke at events with Sonima partners.
- Baird's daughter, Kelsey, first volunteered, then a paid worker for Jois Foundation.
- Baird traveled to seminars to speak with Deepak Chopra and the other Board Members, seen in photos at prominent Jois Foundation events, etc.
- Former Superintendent in Ojai Schools before coming to Encinitas (see news section for details of "web of lies" from news in Ojai with his entangelements there.)
- During the peak of the partnership between Encinitas, the Jois Foundation and USD's research, Baird attended numerous conferences alongside Himelstein and Sonima

representatives where he touted the district's yoga program. One such event was a three-day symposium April 2014 in Lenox, Mass.

- Baird told Coast News in 2016 that Sonima paid for some of his travel expenses. His travel expenses for the district (taxpayer's money) also rose a great deal in the same time frame (2012-2015). Details given in closing chapters.

Assistant Superintendent, David Miyashiro

- Assistant Superintendent at EUSD implementing Ashtanga yoga in the fall of 2012.
- Testified in court in June of 2013 and left EUSD right afterwards that month.
- Became the Superintendent of Cajon Valley schools in August of 2013.
- Implemented Ashtanga yoga into Cajon Valley schools by January, 2014, with an identical grant from Sonima of $500,000 to start yoga in his new schools.
- Called the pastor at Skyline Church attempting to stop an event in June, 2014, to educate the public about yoga in the schools. Miyashiro attended the event since he couldn't stop it. He asked to be a speaker. Broyles declined. He stayed to watch.
- He appears to be in good standing with Sonima Foundation as evidenced by him speaking at same events as Baird.
- You won't want to miss what Miyashiro claimed when he testified in court! In June, 2013, he conflicted with and opposed many facts Baird testified to, just one month earlier in court, in May. A coincidence or a hatched plan? Read and decide for yourself the court reporter notes in next chapters.

K.P. Jois Foundation (name changed to Sonima Foundation)

- Co-founders are Sonia Tudor Jones and Salima Ruffin plus two of the Jois family children, Sharath and Saraswati Jois (video proof referenced in chapter).

- Also called "Jois Foundation" for short, (formed in 2011 during EUSD yoga pilot).
- Renamed Sonima Foundation, right after the EUSD yoga trial in 2013.
- Contracted a "partnership" (exact contract wording) with EUSD for Ashtanga Yoga to be taught by Ashtanga teachers full time for a 3 year study.
- Grants given of over $4 million to Encinitas Union School District, as of 2016.
- Jois Foundation (funded only by Paul Tudor Jones) donated $12 Million to start the University of Virginia's Contemplative Sciences Center https://csc.virginia.edu/class/ashtanga-yoga-monday-saturday-mornings.[4] UVA was one of the two Universities selected to do the yoga study by these same people funding it.
- Awarded USD Center for Education Policy and Law, known as CEPAL about $500,000 in grant funds to research the foundation's yoga programs between 2012 and 2014, including the Encinitas program. ($90,000 in 2012, $377,000 in 2014). Funds grew as the programs expanded across the country.
- Paul Tudor Jones, Billionaire, Hedge Fund Manager (Sonia's husband).
- Executive Director, Eugene Ruffin (Salima's husband).
- Current Executive Director Terry Grier, who formerly served as Superintendent of the San Diego Unified School District.
- The Foundation's fundraising exploded in 2013, rising from $1.3 million to nearly $3.2 million, with most of the donations coming from two sources: Sonia Jones and the Dalio Family Foundation, (founded by Ray Dalio, the billionaire businessman who founded the Bridgewater Associates Investment Firm).
- In 2014, the Sonima/Jois foundation and school district's partnership reached its height. The district again received $1.4 million in grant funding, and the Sonima Foundation received more than $4.4 million in donations.

Regur Development Group, Inc. (aka RDG Solutions)
- The Regur Development Group was founded in 2011 in Downey, California, by Steven Regur—which happens to be the same year the initial (pilot) yoga started in EUSD at Capri Elementary School.
- Regur Development was contracted to payroll the yoga teachers between the Jois Foundation and EUSD in July, 2012. Jois Foundation funded and EUSD received, the yoga teachers. The three-way contract was for Ashtanga Yoga to be taught by qualified and experienced yoga teachers during a three year "study."
- Regur Development website at http://www.rdgsolutions. com/ [5] displays "Innovative Solutions for Learning Organizations" as a header on their website, and with only one principal in California, and no other employees listed in company online records.
- John H Regur is listed as the Treasurer for Regur Development Group in Nevada. The company is incorporated in both California and Nevada. In Nevada, two principals are listed, both Steven and John Regur.
- Steven Regur is also listed as an "Education consultant from Newport Beach" and owner of Educators Cooperative: https://educators.coop/ [6] (IPad palooza, digital badging, and global common core). Partners listed include: Cajon Valley (Miyashira's district) and EUSD (surprise?).
- Grants given of over $4 million flowed through Regur Development Group, as of 2016. This way the yoga teachers could be claimed by EUSD as "not employees of the district" but rather "employees of Regur."

Scott Himelstein
- Director of Research, University of San Diego (USD).
- Director of the San Diego Center for Education Policy and Law (CEPAL) at USD.
- Contracted to do the CEPAL yoga study (at USD) for Jois Foundation for $104,167.

- Awarded nearly $500,000 in grant funds to research the foundation's yoga programs between 2012 and 2014, including the Encinitas program. This included $90,000 in 2012 and a $377,000 grant in 2014, as the program expanded to other districts across the country. (All proof in documents provided in later chapters!).
- Owns both the Chandler Hill Group and Portico Educational services, LLC, two separate organizations that Sonima Foundation contracted with in 2012. According to business records both are owned by Scott Himelstein.
- The Chandler Hill Group first received a $104,167 contract in 2012: this increased to $318,000 and $481,000 in 2013 and 2014, respectively. According to the tax returns, the company was to, among other things, "develop a partnership with the University of San Diego ... to research and report on the results of the Sonima programs," as well as to "support required public relation/public policy changes on the state and local levels to make health and wellness best practices an integrated component of the public education system." (read that again... *to change policy*!) https://www.thecoastnews.com/ties-between-eusd-yoga-program-foundation-and-school-raise-concerns/.[7]
- Portico Educational Services received payments of $35,000 in 2013 and $80,000 in 2014 to perform data collection at the various sites, including Encinitas.
- Business records show that both the Chandler Hill Group and Portico Education are companies owned by Scott Himelstein, who currently serves as the director of CEPAL — the center that performed the Encinitas yoga research study.
- Himelstein formerly listed as an Advisory Board Member for Sonima Foundation.
- Seen on Cruise ship photo on the large staircase with Timothy Baird.
- Hosted parties for principals and school officials on the "High Spirits" yacht in San Diego, owned by Multi-millionaire William D. Lynch. CEPAL was founded by the

William D. Lynch Foundation in 2007, and Himelstein was also President of the William D. Lynch Foundation.

- Himelstein received nearly $1M in payments in 2012–2014 (to his Chandler Hill entity) from Sonima, for the "unbiased research of Jois/Sonima yoga in schools" according to Sonima Tax records those years (see others parent website for links http://encinitasparents4truth.com[8] to documentation).

- Himelstein is the owner of the new website that holds the Sonima curriculum for Schools named *Pure Edge -*: http://pureedgeinc.org/).[9] Sonima website sends you to this website. Sonima Foundation is spreading this curriculum to any Districts they can get into, which is in several states so far and clearly Himelstein (who did the *"unbiased"* research) is very involved. http://pureedgeinc.org/partnerships/.[10]

- So through various entities Himilstein has received funding/payments: William D Lynch Foundation, CEPAL at USD, Capitol Hill, Portico Educational Services, and perhaps others now such as Pure Edge. https://www.corporationwiki.com/California/San-Diego/scott-b-himelstein/42111831.aspx.[11]

- Does Himelstein's research lack independence needed due to potential financial conflicts of interest?

- "Appointed Deputy Secretary of Education in 2005 under Governor Arnold Schwarzenegger." One of the contracted https://www.linkedin.com/in/shimelstein[12] items between Jois Foundation/Sonima Foundation and Himelstein was for him to:

"Support public relation/public policy changes on the state and local levels to make health and wellness "best practices" (yoga, **meditation**, and nutrition) an integrated component of the education system, including education of the members of the legislative and local school boards, also the benefits of the health and wellness programs in public schools, working with the Curriculum Commission to gain support for the JOIS Self Mastery programs as part of school curriculum."

Photo of Scott Himelstein at an EUSD Public Event

http://encinitasparents4truth.com/
sonima-foundation-tax-returns-and-usds-scott-himelstein/

Note: "EUSD "in collaboration" with Jois, USD and UVA— proof of collaboration, denied in court

Paul Tudor Jones
- Billionaire, Hedge Fund Manager.
- Husband to Sonia Tudor Jones.
- Funded $12 Million to start the University of Virginia "Contemplative Sciences Center" (one of two universities to do the yoga study on the children of EUSD).
- Ties to Jois Yoga in India with K.P. Jois and family, through wife Sonia. Photo of Eugene Ruffin, Paul and Sonia Tudor Jones, Salima Ruffin and Eddie Stern available.

Eugene Ruffin
- Director of KP Jois Foundation.
- Husband to co-founder of Jois Foundation, Salima Ruffin.
- President of Ed Futures, Inc. found on Highway 101 in 2016 in Encinitas. sharing a business space with 1. Jois Yoga and 2. Salima's travel company: Creations World Concierge and 3. Ed Futures.

- Attended yoga trial court proceedings (while Superintendent Baird claimed EUSD had no ongoing ties to Ashtanga yoga or the Jois Foundation).
- Has started and incorporated multiple organizations. President of each of the following: Nubia Leadership Academy in 1997; School Futures Research Inc., 2000; Good Schools for all, 2000; New Life Leadership Foundation, 2005; ESR Leadership Institute Inc., 2010; and Kpj Couture, 2010. All of these are now inactive except Ed Futures, which is showing a Florida location with Ruffin as President in Carlsbad HQ address, his home presumably since the HW 101 office shutdown.
- Co-founded American Education Reform (as CEO) with John Walton (The Walton Family) as Chairman, According to Ed Futures site and in 2001 after developing over 60 schools nationally (charter) supporting the development of successful fiscal and academic models, Ed Futures was founded. http://www.edfutures.org/ [13] (note, in 2019 as I revise this, Ruffin moved location: http://edfschools.com/about/history/ to the .org one I just noted (so anytime you can't find something – google and they've simply moved it, just as Jois/Sonima keeps moving items, so do Himelstein and Ruffin.).
- Ed Futures appears active and current with six people on the website and once again we find Scott Himelstein involved, on the board of directors. So Scott is tied to Sonima, Eugene is tied to Sonima (his wife) and they are tied together in the Ed Futures organization as well,
- Eugene Ruffin listed as Executive Director of Pure Edge, Inc., now https://www.guidestar.org/profile/45-3182571 [14] (Himilstein owned).
- Eugene Ruffin speaks to the media http://www.nbcsandiego.com/news/local/Yoga-Lawsuit-Encinitas-Judgment-Ruling-School-Class-Controversy-213853341.html#ixzz2XrSK81Zt [15] in June after watching trial in court.

- So why was Eugene Ruffin in court watching the trial if he truly had no vested interest in the yoga program (as per Baird) in the Encinitas schools?
- Greg Ruffin, his son, is on the Ed futures website with this as some of his role: Tour Director for Live Sonima Tour, with the Sonima Foundation organizing and participating in motivational tours that uses the performing arts and character development to inspire over 100,000 students in grades 6th thru 12th.
- "Greg has brought dynamic programs to his charter schools and works closely with Stedman Graham working with teens to build a sense of self and place a step by step process to become lifelong learners". (Stedman Graham was in Cajon Valley schools with the Tudor Jones' daughter teaching these seminars, June of 2014 ...).

Sonia Tudor Jones
- Married to Paul Tudor Jones, billionaire.
- Co-Founder of Jois Foundation with Salima Ruffin, Manju Jois and Saraswathi Jois.
- Devoted Ashtanga follower, practicing under KP Jois himself, in India

Sonia + Salima = Sonima

Salima Ruffin
- Married to Eugene Ruffin.
- Original Co-founder of Jois Foundation also with Manju Jois and Saraswathi Jois.
- Renamed Sonima, using "Sonia + Salima = Sonima.
- Owner of Creations World Concierge, Travel Agency (Jois Foundation travel appears to have been booked through Salima's company. Conferences for speaking on yoga programs include Baird, Himelstein, Miyashira, and Graham).
- There appeared to be a "falling out" in 2016 when these offices on 101 closed, Salima's name and photo taken off

of the Sonima website. She is no longer a presence as the co-founder. You don't find the Jois children mentioned either on Sonima as co-founders any longer.

Sonima Foundation

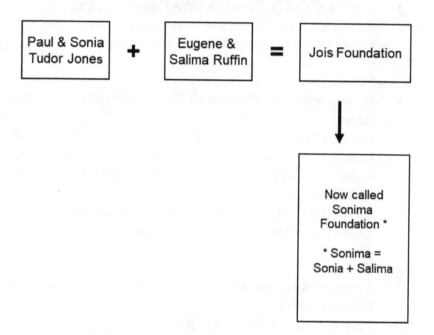

Nancy Jois
- Teacher at Capri Elementary School in Encinitas.
- Married to Manju Jois, son of Sri K. Pattabhi Jois, founder of Ashtanga yoga in India.
- Capri was the first school in Encinitas (pilot program) for Ashtanga yoga in 2011.
- Sharath Jois, Manju Jois' brother, was the yoga teacher to our lead yoga teacher for the district, Jen Brown. This reveals the connections among Manju, Jen, Nancy and Sharath.
- Thus, with Nancy Jois in teaching position at Capri Elementary School, Capri was an easy starting spot and connection for Jois Foundation.

Stedman Graham
- Most popularly known for his romantic partnership with Oprah Winfrey.
- Teaching Leadership programs alongside Tudor Jones' daughter, seen in Cajon Valley schools in June of 2014.
- Sonima Board of Directors https://www.sonima.com/.[16]
- Working with Ed Futures as evidenced by claims on the Ed Futures website: http://www.edfutures.org/.[17]

Michael Corke
- Interim research director at CEPAL. Author of first CEPAL Report on EUSD yoga.
- Corke is now the Sonima Foundation's "Director of Research. (Article: Former USD researcher Michael Corke, author of "Yoga in San Diego Schools" gets research job with Sonima).
- Baird, Greer and Corke often travel together, reportedly to support their agenda to wealthy billionaires.

Terry Grier
- Former Superintendent for San Diego Unified School District.
- Former Houston Superintendent.
- Grier helped 52 schools in Houston implement Sonima's Ashtanga yoga.
- Currently the "Executive Director" for Sonima Foundation.
- Listed with Pure Edge company records.

Russell Case
- Yoga Advisor for Sonima Foundation (overseeing CA and Texas programs). Title at Sonima: Western Region Program Director.
- Screened every candidate for Encinitas yoga teachers in a week-long program July of 2013, advising Miyashiro and Regur on whittling down from 22 to the top 10 qualified candidates to teach in the schools.

- Visited curriculum planning meetings with the 10 Encinitas yoga teachers and Leslie Wright, bringing his Ashtanga expertise to the room.
- Case named one of the most influential Ashtanga yoga teachers in the US http://downtownyogashala.com/apps/mindbody/staff/100000232.[18]
- Case called a "Level 2 Ashtanga-yoga instructor" for Stanford in 2014 http://events.stanford.edu/events/418/41803/.[19]
- His classes in San Francisco, 2010 https://www.yogagardensf.com/ashtanga-yoga-at-the-garden/.[20]
- Introduced Jen Brown (knew her from India) to this "new yoga in schools" project and invited her to get involved. (As per Jen Brown's testimony Day 3, p. 96). (*Posted under court reporter notes each day of trial on the truthaboutyoga. com Lawsuit page under Encinitas tab.*)

Eddie Stern
- Director of Ashtanga Yoga New York, studio http://a..yny.org/.[21]
- President of the Broome Street Ganesha Temple.
- Trained by Pattabhi Jois in 1990 in India.
- Head of curriculum development for Jois Foundation.
- Program manager for Encinitas Union School District (EUSD) yoga program.
- Leader of lobbying group for New York to avoid taxation due to being "meditative and spiritual, not exercise." New York exempted yoga from taxation in 2012.
- Noted as the downtown New York guru for serious yoga students http://tmagazine.blogs.nytimes.com/2012/02/27/pose-posse/.[22]
- Gwyneth Paltrow on you tube with Eddie Stern and he says "I teach Ashtanga yoga and I run a Hindu temple" https://www.youtube.com/watch?v=Xw_6ore09UU.[23]
- See him in EUSD Curriculum videos discussing how these classes will change the way kids think and that is the goal of the program! (EUSD/Jois video referenced over and over in trial).

- News reported he was asked to help with CA schools, but he declined and stayed in New York.

Andrea Silvia, OM yoga studio
- EUSD's "yoga expert" from Canada.
- Limited to testify her personal experiences and beliefs about yoga.
- On stand confirmed she knew little about Ashtanga yoga or EUSD curriculum.
- Although her company name is "Namaste Om" she claimed not to know what Om meant (Day 3 p. 127 of testimony).
- Silvia testified that yoga had no religious meaning to her at all.
- Her testimony fell apart after she admitted she was not an expert in Ashtanga yoga.

Brown, Brown and Brown *(we can't make this stuff up)*

Professor and Expert **WITNESS:** *Candy Gunther Brown*

Candy Gunther Brown, PhD.—Professor Brown
- Expert Witness in Encinitas Yoga Trial.
- Three Degrees from Harvard:

- o B.A. summa cum laude in History and Literature, Harvard, 1992
- o M.A. in history department, Harvard, 1995, Honors thesis – religion and women
- o Ph.D. in History of American Civilization and American Studies dept, 2000.

- On sabbatical in Oxford UK when first heard about the yoga trial.
- Tenured Professor Position of Religious Studies at Indiana University.
- Taught also at Harvard three years, Lesley University, Vanderbilt, and St. Louis.

  Brown taught classes about Hinduism, Buddhism, Western metaphysics, and yoga.

  The courses ranged from Religion, Illness, Healing; Religion Health and Healthcare Management; to Sickness and Health; Religion and American Culture; and, to Women and Religion.

- Her research contributes to several areas in religious studies. These areas include: religion and science, ethics, globalization, spiritual healing practices, complementary and alternative medicine including yoga and meditation, comparative religions, Evangelical/Pentecostal Christianity, Hinduism, Buddhism, Taoism, and additionally, Western Metaphysics.
- The list goes on and on of her credentials. To find more go online or read more on the court notes ... pages 202–210.

Carrie Brown, PhD — Principal Brown
- Principal at El Camino Creek.
- Testified at trial (erroneously) that Sedlock children got all 200 minutes of PE every 10 days.
- "Teacher planner calendars" were the proof given that our kids PE actually occurred.

- Email proof that the January, 2013, plan from the Principal was that one Sedlock child went to math lab and the other went to typing lab during yoga classes.
- Claimed she "supervised" the yoga room daily at her school.
- When Samantha Vigil complained about Mandalas being colored by children in the yoga teachers classroom, principal Brown looked into them and all the artwork "disappeared" never to be seen by any parents at ECC. Only the testimony of children drawing them remains, along with Christina Reich (ECC yoga teacher) admitting to having the kids draw them and knowing that mandalas are Hindu religious drawings tied to yoga (seen in Vigils parent declaration). Carrie (erroneously) testified that I reported the mandalas.

Jennifer Brown—Jen Brown—Lead Yoga Teacher at EUSD
- Yoga instructor on payroll at Jois Yoga Shala in Encinitas.
- EUSD yoga instructor on Regur Development payroll for EUSD.
- Curriculum Writing and Staff Development (Baird's words, Trial Day 1, p. 42,43)
- Lead Curriculum Developer in 2012/2013 school year.
- Lead Yoga Instructor and Trainer (I "gave feedback on every yoga teacher to their Principals" was in her testimony).
- Testified in Court on Day 3 and performed yoga positions in court.
- Testified that although she had "sojourned" (her website wording) to India multiple times to learn yoga from Sharath Jois (PK and his family members), that she "never saw yoga as religious."

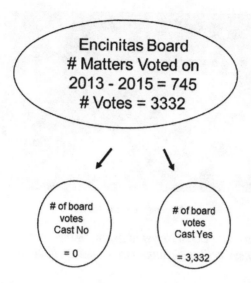

Encinitas Board votes

EUSD Board Members in 2012/2013:
- Emily Andrade, Maureen Muir, Marla Strich, Gregg Sonkin and Carol Skiljan.
- Encinitas Union School District board members, who have supported the yoga program, may have been unaware of many of the details of the district's partnership with Sonima and USD.
- These five were given ample information and warnings about the dangers of yoga in elementary schools the fall of 2012 and beyond.
- As diagram shows, in 745 matters with over 3332 votes cast, the five board members cast 3332 yes votes and zero no votes over a two year period.

Attorney Dean Broyles

*Photo credit Coast News: https://www.thecoastnews.com/
attorneys-deliver-closing-arguments-in-school-yoga-trial/*

Attorney Dean Broyles, Esq.
- National Center for Law and Policy, President.
- Lead Attorney for parent group against yoga curriculum in schools.
- Contacted by three separate EUSD families in Aug/Sept 2012 over yoga in schools.
- Attended and spoke at multiple school, parent and EUSD board meetings fall of 2012
- "The Yoga Lawyer" (a new title he would not be able to shake).
- Juris Doctor degree from Regent University School of Law, in Virginia Beach, VA
- Affiliate attorney of the Alliance Defense Fund (ADF).
- ADF affiliate attorney and member of ADF's honor guard.
- Mentored in law school in constitutional litigation by Jay Sekulow of the American Center for Law and Justice (ACLJ),
- Clerked for several years at the National Legal Foundation, a religious liberty non-profit organization.
- When asked why he took on this case he replied, "I reluctantly went to the first meeting of parents after receiving a third call from third set of parents in this district. Once I heard their complaints, I became compelled to help, and one thing led to another."

Rob Reynolds, Attorney Assisting Broyles.
Brad Abramson, Attorney Assisting Broyles, Alliance Defending Freedom (ADF Attorney).
Jack Sleeth, EUSD. Lead District Attorney.
Paul Carelli, EUSD, Assisting Attorney Sleeth.

David Peck, Coast Law Group, Assisting Attorney Sleeth
- Attorney requesting to be added to trial; agreed to by Broyles and Sedlocks.
- Also a parent in EUSD.
- Representing "pro yoga in schools" families.
- Coast Law Group is located next to the Self Realization Center off 101 in Encinitas.
- Peck targeted religion of Sedlocks multiple times during trial: "Wear their religion on their sleeve" (Day 1, p. 33) "Devout Christians" and "skewed fanatical religious prism" (Day 1, p. 34) and much more saved for trial chapters.
- Expensive upgrades to his offices after trial. Offices are also across the street from the 101 offices of Jois yoga, Ed Futures and Salima's travel agency.

John Campbell
- Religious Studies Professor at University of Virginia (UVA).
- Paul Tudor Jones donated 12M to start Contemplative Sciences Center at UVA.
- Campbell was scheduled to do an EUSD yoga study for Jois Foundation at UVA.
- Ashtanga certified yoga instructor.
- Worked for Paul and Sonia Tudor Jones teaching Ashtanga to Jones' employees.

The Contemplative Science Center at the University of Virginia (CSCUVA)
- Scheduled and announced to EUSD as one of two universities conducting studies on our children, but this one never produced any results and may not have started.

117

- John Campbell headed up the CSCUVA.

University of San Diego
- CEPAL (*Center for Education Policy and Law*) study run by Scott Himelstein.
- CEPAL Study produced two reports for EUSD:
- Jan 30, 2014—https://truthaboutyoga.files.wordpress. com/2015/01/eusd-yoga-student-effects-2012-13-formattedforwebsite.pdf [24] (you can trust our website when you get warning box)
- Nov 8, 2013—https://truthaboutyoga.files. wordpress.com/2015/01/cepal-report_implementing-yoga_2013-2014.pdf [24]
- Analysis of the CEPAL reports—https://truthaboutyoga. files.wordpress.com/2015/01/cepal-bulletpoints.pdf [25]

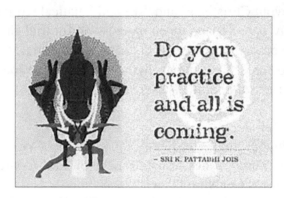

Do your practice and all is coming.

– SRI K. PATTABHI JOIS

Photo Credit: Sri K. Pattabhi Jois Yoga Website Photos purchased online

Ashtanga Yoga
- Ashtanga yoga, which is based in Hinduism.
- Certified Ashtanga Yoga Instructors, "trained by Jois Foundation teachers." (MOU).
- 8-Limbed yoga—8th limb is Samadhi– "Absorption into the Universal" or also called "Union with the Divine" (a merged identity with "gods").
- Contains Breath control, Meditation, Sun Worship (opening sequence).

- Based in polytheism (multiple gods) and reincarnation.
- Purpose of Jnana mudra—to open the channel of energy.
- Purpose of forced breathing—open "channels of chakras up" to elicit euphoria and eventually "bliss" (known as third eye chakra healing).
- Chakras according to the Chopra Center: http://www.chopra.com/articles/what-is-a-chakra#sm.01pahbe910lcfc 611rw22umdt0y36. [26]
- Chakras open "prana" (invisible energy) providing "vital life force" (wording used in EUSD curriculum, Nov 2013).

*Photo credit: WND http://www.wnd.com/2015/06/
parents-opposing-yoga-for-kidstake-campaign-public/*

Complaints from parents in EUSD about yoga in the schools
- "Namaste" circles—kids bowing with hands together in prayer poses saying Namaste to one another (meaning—I see the god/ in you).
- Mandalas being drawn and taught as a form of Hindu art, connecting to inner self.
- Sun Salutations (worshipping the Sun).
- Inability to get standard amount of PE if opted-out.
- Sanskrit taught to children for body parts. Sanskrit is a religious language written for rituals, not a cultural or language issue.
- If the yoga program needed "scrubbing" (district used this word), wasn't it religious in the first place?
- Children are taught to channel energy through certain poses.

- Children are taught "Ommm" to channel energy through vibrations and meditations.
- Ashtanga 8-limbed poster on wall at Capri.
- 8-limbed Ashtanga trees made and placed up on walls at many schools, fall, 2012.
- Book being read by yoga teacher to students about kid yoga, religious looking cover and inside ... banned from the school by district once a parent complained.
- Sample curriculum in Nov, 2012, district said it was all scrubbed of Sanskrit language and yet, there was still plenty of spiritual guidance and use of Sanskrit words in the curriculum. More revisions were made.
- Meditation and guided visualizations still being used while district said the yoga teachers would not meditate during yoga anymore.
- Lotus practice still taught in 2017. Told it would stop and be *crisscross applesauce* in 2013 not the case ...
- Even if fully stripped of *Sanskrit*, is this "grey area" of spirituality of yoga and thus not appropriate for schools/gov't institutions to promote and practice?
- Kids entered into a study with biometrics taken but no parental consent in fall of 2012 (proof in parent letters from Vigil and Hevrin).
- Need a PE option for opt-outs. All 9 schools.
- Oct 12, 2012, Broyles sent an email to the EUSD board and Baird showing relationships in conflicts of interest between Jois Foundation and the UVA study.
- CEPAL research was not independent (Himelstein tied to Jois Foundation and to Baird) so could produce misleading, biased research conclusions.
- The Relationship Baird had with Jois Foundation was of large concern. His reactions to parents made the concerns grow. Additional research found more concerns of his involvement with Jois Foundation in multiple layers of curriculum writing production, promotional videos produced with both Jois and EUSD people in them, and follow

the money to find more concerns. More in "What's current with EUSD now" chapter.

Jois Foundation

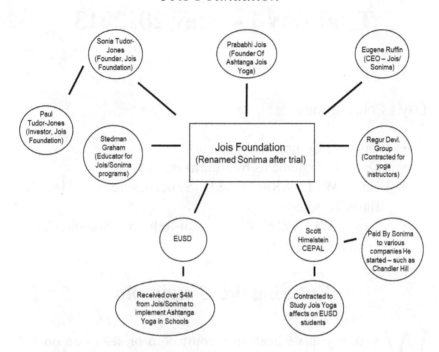

Hopefully, this cast of characters will be a useful resource for you as you read through the chapters of the trial, given the various people involved.

Let's step into the courtroom now.

CHAPTER SEVEN

Trial Day 1 – May 20, 2013

Day 1 Court Agenda

- Opening Comments by Judge
- Opening Statements by Attorneys
- First **WITNESS:** EUSD Superintendent, Timothy Baird Testifies
- Expert **WITNESS:** Professor of Religious Studies, Candy Gunther Brown Testifies

Entering the Courtroom

Whether you've been in a courtroom or seen one on TV, you can imagine the setting: two sides of benches with an aisle down the middle that ends with a swinging door on a short wall between the public seating and the floor where the desks of Attorneys and clients sit. To the left of those tables was the jury box on the same level of flooring. A large "desk" at the back center of the room for the judge is the highest level in the room. Two box seating areas to either side of the judge are a level lower than the judge and a higher level than the rest of the room and are for the witnesses being questioned. The judge sits the highest in the room, by design. The court reporter is seated on the main floor with the rest of us, positioned sideways and looking usually at the machine she or he is tapping upon, so little to no eye contact with others. After a while she became invisible, while perfectly visible. She isn't the focus of the show, so you might overlook her while you put your attention on the main act.

This could be a great metaphor for how a magician can "trick" us to look at what he is showing you and do something "hidden" while you are distracted. This fits what happened in EUSD yoga. We were told to look at certain aspects and to "trust them" while other elements occurring simultaneously were "hidden" in plain sight. We were in this courtroom to expose hidden relationships and multiple problems with the yoga Baird and EUSD selected.

Walking into Court – Day 1

The moment we stepped into the courtroom, we weren't sure where to sit, so we paused. Do we go to the benches at front or up to the attorney tables? Right or Left? There were TV cameramen in the jury box on the left. A bailiff moved around busily doing something. Our attorney entered the front area of the room through the low swinging door, set his briefcase and belongings on the table to the left, signaling to us it must be left. Then he must have noticed our hesitation, and pointed toward the front row of benches, left side. Whew. We would not need to sit up at the front table with him which was a bit of a relief, media wise.

The air was crisp and no water bottles were allowed in court where the judge could see them. I guess it was a pet peeve of his and a "judge's rule" so the bailiff delivered the news: "No water bottles on the table please" he quipped to the attorneys; "only glasses of water from the pitchers provided." It was the bailiff's job to fill up the water when it ran low. Another rule we all seemed to lose sight of daily was "no gum in court." More than a few times the bailiff had to ask people to spit out their gum. He quit asking, and just walked around with a trash can, and if it paused in front of you, no words were necessary for you to remember why. Mints available in the downstairs store became more popular as the days wore on, and lunches sat on stomachs. Lunch time was not a time of relaxation, but power meetings to cover what happened, what was next. Food was "thrown down" quickly and ninety minutes seemed to fly by without a minute wasted. Three attorneys, three of us and, for two days, our expert witness. I'm pretty sure the rest of the folks from our side of the room in support were eating a more pleasant lunch than we were, but no doubt they were also chattering about the trial. Most people in lunch spots near the courthouse were focused on a trial of their own, whispering or discussing details except for a few attorneys copiously writing notes and cramming down their own bites of sandwich alone. I've read just about every John Grisham novel, so noticing details about the trial in and out of court, were like devouring his words. I enjoyed parts of the process and learning.

The box on the right for the district was full daily. There were principals, two to three school board members each day, district staff, teachers, yoga teachers, Eugene Ruffin and probably others from Jois, whom I didn't know, all filling up the seating on the right hand side. I'm pretty sure at least one day that some of *their side* had to reluctantly sit on *our side*. Our side contained many parents from the district and others unfamiliar to me at the time. Gestures of support such as a smile, a wave or a thank you in the halls outside, made it clear they were on our side of the debate. I heard there were people outside on sidewalks praying for the trial as well. They must have been standing next to the media that would miss us on the way out because they had no idea what we looked like. We even asked what the reporters were following and they would say they were waiting for the yoga trial to get out. We would laugh about it on the walk to our cars, knowing that they had no idea who we were.

Judge's Opening Comments

Judge John Meyer opened with asking for appearances (introductions of all attorneys present) and then mentioned reading a lot over the weekend to prepare and noted that this is a very interesting case and that the documents were well presented. He denied a motion right away that the District Attorney Sleeth had attempted to exclude our expert from testifying (Day 1, p. 2). Meyer thought she would be worth hearing. And wow, was she worth hearing!

Meyer went on to set the scene, asserting that the case would hinge on whether yoga taught in the Encinitas Union School District (EUSD) was religious, so he asked the attorneys to answer a simple, yet important, question: "What is religion?" Meyer explained his question and asked the attorneys to address the difference between western religion and Judeo-Christian beliefs versus Eastern religion, such as Hinduism or Buddhism. He addressed PE minutes and his thoughts that the fact is the district must follow the state mandated Education Code. He preferred not to get involved in anything further than necessary since government cannot make any recommendations on curriculum. His final question was whether Jois Foundation is religious or not and to make sure that is covered (Day 1, pp. 4, 5). Then he called on Broyles to proceed with opening statements. (Note: Broyles opening lasts until p. 25, Sleeth pp. 25-31, Peck pp. 31-35).

Photo of Trial: Attorney Broyles speaking, EUSD Attorneys Sleeth and Carelli, Superintendent Baird

http://www.kpbs.org/news/2013/jun/25/
closing-arguments-begin-encinitas-yoga-trial/

Dean Broyles' Opening Statements

Broyles began: "Your Honor, Counsel, parties, this case is fundamentally about religious freedom, a liberty that is protected against the tyranny of corrosive government power. As George Washington said, "I beg you will be persuaded that no one would be more zealous than myself, to establish effectual barriers against the horrors of spiritual tyranny. And every species of religious persecution, for you doubtless remember that I've often expressed my sentiment that every man conducting himself as a good citizen and being accountable to God alone for his religious opinions ought to be protected in worshipping the deity according to the dictates of his own conscience" (Day 1, p. 5).

"The consciences the petitioners are working so hard to protect in this case from the spiritual tyranny of the state, Your Honor, are the tender consciences of our youngest citizens, some of whom are as young as five years old. What will the evidence in this case show? Simply put, the evidence will clearly demonstrate that the Encinitas Union School District is teaching religion to young impressionable children in its care, in the form specifically of Ashtanga yoga. And that as a result, the district has not been providing the mandatory minimum PE minutes required by California law to its students who, for very good reasons, for religious reasons, Your Honor, decide to opt-out of the district's unconstitutional program" (Day 1, p. 5, 6).

The *Story* of Jois Foundation

Broyles began to explain how Jois Foundation became involved with EUSD, their motivations and mission, their pathway into Encinitas, and the connections that were conflicts of interest for the District related to the religious foundation and the two universities, "studying" the children. He spoke in "story form" of their mastery to attain 5600 children for their "scientific" study, with goals to promote their yoga nationally to schools afterward when the newly written curriculum would become available, created by Ashtanga teachers for yoga in Encinitas.

Broyles stated: "And being quite clever, the organization camouflaged its religious designs by wrapping the whole religious program in the cloak of respectability, the cloak of science, by claiming the program had measurable physical and mental benefits and by acquiring the aura of academia by asserting that the study was being done by respected universities" (Day1, p. 8). Broyles continues, pointing out that Jois Foundation was already in an Encinitas school the year prior with a "pilot program" and that more would be revealed about the connections to that during testimony.

A New Partnership

He discussed the "partnership" between Jois Foundation and EUSD in documents (the language from the contracts - p. 9). The requirements in advertisements for the "Ashtanga yoga" positions of "certified yoga instructors" with three years Ashtanga experience, and trained by "Jois Foundation teachers (p. 10). He submitted that: Ashtanga yoga is a particularly religious form of yoga, and read descriptions of the eight limbs from an Ashtanga yoga brochure. "Ashtanga yoga means eight limbed; it is an ancient system that can lead to liberation and greater awareness of our spiritual potential," Broyles said, quoting the brochure (pp. 11-13) and submitted that Candy Gunther Brown would testify to the religious nature of this yoga (to be yoked) and 8th limb being "union with the divine" and other religious language from the documents. Broyles goes into answering the judge's questions about Ashtanga yoga (p. 15, 16) and described how Jois influenced much of the district's yoga program. He pointed out some of the parent complaints occurring in the children's classes (up to p. 19) and then moved on to the PE minutes that all the opted-out-of-yoga children were missing. He described opting-out and how that was never given as an option from the district until multiple families across the district forced the issue by asking for their children to not be placed into yoga classes.

THE COURT: So the objective of Ashtanga yoga is to achieve unity of self with a divine god?

MR. BROYLES: Yes, Your Honor, that's basically it. And again, I'm going to allow my expert to elucidate more on that concept.

THE COURT: And that's what's being taught?

MR. BROYLES: Yes, Your Honor. Until concerned parents complained, the Ashtanga tree with all eight branches was on the wall of many of the classrooms early in the school year. Until parents complained – and the Sanskrit names were on the tree. Until parents complained, the Jois trained Ashtanga yoga teachers were teaching the students to say "namaste" to each other, which is a religiously laden Hindu greeting that, in essence, means the divine in me bows to the divine in you. Often, namaste is accompanied by praying hands and a bow. If you bow to someone even without saying "namaste," it's my understanding that it means the divine in me bows to the divine in you even if you don't say the word "namaste."

THE COURT: Namaste? And so on…

Spreading Ashtanga Yoga is the heart of the case

Broyles finishes opening comments – "Yet this case is not about whether we like or dislike yoga, whether yoga has health benefits, nor whether other forms of yoga that are taught and practiced in the United States are religious or not religious, as delineated in the intervenor's brief. This case is only about whether Ashtanga yoga, which involves religious beliefs and practices, may be taught to young and impressionable children in the public schools. Once you've heard all the evidence, Your Honor, the petitioners will be asking this Honorable Court to order the district to suspend its religious Ashtanga yoga program and order EUSD to comply with the law regarding mandatory PE minutes" (p. 22).

What is Religion?

Then Broyles answered the judges original questions "But let me just say from my perspective, from kind of a common sense layman attorney perspective, religion is about ultimate beliefs about who God is and who man is and about our position in the universe. It often deals with comprehensive worldviews. Often Hinduism is misunderstood and has been called in some places in America a philosophy or a worldview. But Hinduism, as you'll hear from Ms. Brown, is actually a world religion with specific religious beliefs and practices that specifically make up Ashtanga yoga. Now, as you were asking also questions about the concept of, you know, how we define religion, oftentimes people who are following Eastern religious beliefs and practices like Hinduism, like Buddhism, like Jainism, especially Westerners here in the United States, they don't like to call their beliefs or practices that they're engaging in religious. And why?... because they would rather call their beliefs and practices spiritual or philosophical" (pp. 22, 23).

"And the reason that is, Your Honor – and you'll hear from our expert witness – is because many Westerners now object to the Judeo-Christian biblical worldview that says that we have a God who shows us how to live and has prescriptions for how we live. So many people who rejected Judeo-Christian worldview would rather not be seen as religious because our culture brings in all the baggage of what people see negative about those Judeo-Christian world views. And so it's convenient to call it spiritual, but don't let the euphemism "spiritual" fool the Court. When we say – use the word "spiritual" in the context of Ashtanga yoga and Hinduism and Buddhism and Eastern religions, what we're really saying is religious, and the evidence will show that" (pp. 21, 22, 23)

Broyles said he was sure of one thing: Yoga falls under the umbrella of religion. Consequently, he maintained, EUSD violated the separation of church and state by incorporating the practice into its curriculum.

You can see the full webpage dedicated to yoga Gurus, pastors, the Vatican and more answering the question of whether yoga is religious but here is an example of just one.

Is yoga religious…?

Consider what Yogis themselves say… Quoted in Hinduism Today: Professor Subhas Tiwari of Hindu University of America. "The simple, immutable fact is that yoga originated from the Vedic or Hindu culture. Its techniques were not adopted by Hinduism, but originated from it… The effort to separate yoga from Hinduism must be challenged because it runs counter to the fundamental principles upon which yoga itself is premised… "Efforts to separate yoga from its spiritual center reveal ignorance of the goal of yoga. " (HinduismToday.com – 9/13/09).

BROYLES: The evidence will show that in making inaccurate and self-serving claims, the district desperately does not want the public or this Court to peek behind the curtain and see what's really going on. But, we must look behind the curtain and understand exactly what is going on" (p. 21).

Jack Sleeth Opening Statements

Sleeth purported in his opening statement that what we will find is just a "health and wellness" program with physical and mental benefits for students. He presents that it doesn't matter if Jois Foundation is religious and whether they are doing Ashtanga yoga or not. He states that isn't the issue, either. He asserts that the issue is whether the yoga that they are currently doing violates the constitution or the amount of PE minutes (p. 26).

Sleeth continues on to state that there is no Sanskrit and each of the poses are now in English, that the kids are learning healthy breathing and that the district believes the science (study) will show the benefits psychologically. He dives into a definition of religion for the court and Meyer interrupts him (p. 27) to ask "But isn't the test an objective test as a five- or six-year-old child? It's not looking at it from the perspective of someone who's been educated and –" to which they go back and forth about entangling, advancing or inhibiting religion and whether this program might or might not do that, but the law is that it cannot. Sleeth claims that the District has "removed" any of the religious beliefs in the program and words that might lead one to believe it is religious (p. 29).

THE COURT: So we're not going to just peek behind the curtain, you're going to throw the curtain open?

MR. SLEETH: You can have the curtain.

THE COURT: All right.

MR. SLEETH: Come on down. We'd be happy to have the Court come on down and see everything we're doing.

THE COURT: That's absolutely going to happen (Day1, p. 30).

What? Did the judge actually say he would visit a school? I doubt he did, and there was no further mention of this during the trial so I'm fairly certain he did not. Sleeths' entire opening statement covers just 6 pages (25-31) and the judge seems a surprised and responds "That's it?"

DAVID **PECK:** Opening Statements

This is where the judge calls for the first witness from Broyles and Mr. Peck pipes in "I'm not a potted plant either ... (Day 1, p.

32). The judge apologizes and Peck is allowed to intervene with his opening statements. He makes it clear that he is representing 150 students in the district (is he counting his "Yes" yoga Facebook page followers I wonder?). He states that yoga is not a religion. "We submit that the evidence during this trial will show that the yoga taught in the school district is not religious. It is not religion. The United States Constitution and the California Constitution are not violated in any regard, by the maintenance of that program." (p. 32). To which the judge asks:

THE COURT: Is it called Ashtanga yoga?

MR. PECK: It's not, Your Honor.

THE COURT: It's not.

MR. PECK: "It's not called Ashtanga yoga. It's interesting Mr. Broyles brings up the fact that in the MOU (memo of understanding), an initial document, before there was any yoga practiced in the school district whatsoever, there was a memorandum of understanding between the school district and Jois Foundation, which referenced once to Ashtanga yoga."

In reality, as Peck was well aware of, there was a grant written by Baird prior to the MOU which states Ashtanga yoga in it, as well as contains wording of Jois-certified yoga teachers. He also knew that Jois Foundation only does Ashtanga yoga and nothing else. In addition, The MOU and several other documents including an FAQ by Baird in December months later, all contain the word Ashtanga, which was well *after* the start of yoga in the district. And finally, the pilot program at Capri which was also funded by Jois, was the year prior and included the word Ashtanga (along with posters on the wall saying Ashtanga, etc.).

MR. PECK: "The families that I represent stand steadfastly against the promotion for the inhibition of any religion whatsoever in the schools. What they see, though, is a program that's designed to eliminate bullying, to eliminate stress, to help with the hyper competitiveness, to help with obesity. And, in fact, Your Honor the yoga program is working. Parents, students, teachers alike have raved about it. The plaintiffs *wear their religion on their sleeve* in the case. All the declarations submitted by the plaintiffs and their witnesses make it very clear they throw the curtain open, so to speak, on their own *religious beliefs, and they are devout Christians.* And that's fine. My clients include devout Christians and atheists, folks who have no religious beliefs whatsoever. There's no way plaintiffs can meet their burden of proof in showing objectively, not through a subjective skewed *fanatical religious prism*, but objectively, that the program that's being performed in the school district today…" (P. 33).

THE COURT: From the objective perspective of a student.

MR. PECK: "Correct, Your Honor, from the objective perspective of a student."

Foreshadowing the challenge ahead; the burden of proof will lie in what a child perceives. And you'll see that the judge didn't even want to hear from children, he didn't believe them over adults. Hmmm. But whether a child perceives something is wrong is a standard that doesn't protect them from what they don't know. You'll see how this unfolds.

And in 5 pages, Peck was done.

Note: First Witness Timothy Baird testifies until well after lunch (from p. 35 - p. 173). Sleeth direct examines up to p.184, then Peck to p.190, Re-cross by Broyles to p.202. Second Witness called by Broyles, Candy Gunther Brown, who testifies until the end of day, pp. 202-240.

First Witness – EUSD Superintendent Timothy Baird

Tim Baird in Court, 2013

Photo credit NBC San Diego: https://www.nbcsandiego.com/news/local/Yoga-Class-Encinitas-Lawsuit-San-Diego-Reglious-208538581.html

As Broyles said in court "Baird does not want you to 'peek behind the curtain'…where all the master controls are…" and it doesn't take long to unravel the curtain when you know where to look. EUSD demonstrated in court (Baird's testimony) that he did not even understand the very program they had contracted to do: Ashtanga yoga. In fact, he claims to still not know what Ashtanga yoga is, even after plenty of parents gave him the information in the fall of 2012, and he is in the middle of a lawsuit over it in 2013. Incredibly, he still claimed in court to not know what it was, even though he used the word himself over and over in documents and emails.

It's not Religious…*Trust Us*!

EUSD Superintendent Timothy Baird claimed that the district - not the Jois Foundation - crafted the yoga program. He claimed it was created purely to promote health and fitness. He denied he hired Ashtanga yoga teachers for the district (but see grant pro-posal, grant MOU and MOU for the truth). His claims are because EUSD hired through Regur, so *technically* the yoga instructors are not "district" employees, nor are they "Jois Foundation" employees but "Regur" employees. Thus, they were contracted by EUSD as full time "external consultants" to the district. The statement of not hiring Ashtanga yoga teachers is a clear attempt to hide the fact from the judge. The fact remains that experienced Ashtanga yoga teachers were hired for teaching the EUSD kids and they created the curriculum for Jois Foundation to use nationwide. Just because Baird claimed the yoga "wasn't religious" and to "trust them," doesn't change the fact that Ashtanga yoga is foundation-ally religious.

"It's just us"

Jen Brown led the other yoga instructors in developing the cur-riculum every Friday. The majority of the instructors' yoga teaching experience was in Ashtanga. Thus, Jois Yoga instructors' input was the foundation to build the curriculum. "It's just us developing the curriculum," Baird claimed. What he didn't say is that the "us" is ten *Regur employees* that are yoga instructors, *certified by Jois*, for EUSD. He slides in statements that are not factually false, but mis-leading (as you see, they are not technically district employees due to his ingenuity). The clever wording escapes most people, until you start listening closely and watch the facts.

Later, Baird claimed Leslie Wright (a District employee) wrote the curriculum, but she began without any yoga experience offered in testimony, and her pay, according to w-2's and 2013 tax records, is for a different job. The yoga teachers in the room had the yoga experience, so if or when Wright did help with curriculum writing, she was still not the expert developing each pose and creating the curriculum. The experienced yogis were there for a reason.

Baird testified that all of the opted-out students were getting the required minutes of PE. However, consider this - if all the opt-ed-out children across the nine schools were getting the required

PE minutes, why would we make that part of the lawsuit? Reality was, opted-out kids didn't get PE alternatives in 2012 or 2013. We testified that our daughter got thirty minutes of Karate and ten minutes of running per week. That was all because they assigned her to sit with an iPad during one yoga class and to attend an extra computer option during the other. Many kids had similar stories of little to no supervision in another classroom or worse - they were seated at the back of the yoga room! The district didn't seem to understand that we didn't want our kids exposed to yoga by being in the room. Some incidents happened in schools where students walked around unattended or hung out at other recesses. These parent discussions are all noted on a Facebook page still in existence and some documented in letters, and to the district, and in affidavits for court.

For simplicity of facts, this list will notate the testimony of Timothy Baird that needs consideration of whether it is truth or hiding the truth (intended or not). Some items are facts he stated, and then later denied.

Did Baird mislead facts on purpose?

1. Baird claimed all kids opted-out received the required 200 PE minutes per two weeks (for 2 weeks prior to trial and summer, PE increased briefly – P.175). Evidence to the contrary was given to the court from many parent letters and emails.
2. Testified he "usually tried to meet with parents that complained" (p. 44). But this did not happen. Out of all the parents who addressed him all fall of 2012 in meetings, letters and calls, he never attempted to contact most of us. He never once responded to any of my multiple inquiries. Out of all the people in our group communicating (over 100) he responded to one mom's emails to my knowledge. (Cindy Gray who he knew prior. Those emails are in evidence - p. 44).

3. Baird admits yoga teachers are certified (p. 47), and trained by Jois instructors (p. 49), but don't have teaching credentials in district (p. 47). Later he denied this.

4. Claims he doesn't know what Ashtanga yoga is and that he didn't research it before contracting with Jois. He didn't think they were doing Ashtanga. Yet, he wrote the grant for Ashtanga yoga, agreed to creating curriculum for Jois Foundation to take to other districts *and later claims not knowing it was Ashtanga?* (pp. 49-55).

5. Baird responded that only district employee David Miyashiro was in the meetings with the yoga instructors every Friday (p. 43) and the next month would claim that Leslie Wright was the writer of the curriculum, although NO mention of her here prior when asked the question. On p. 64, Baird states "our teachers are doing the work," writing the curriculum, when he would later switch to saying that it was Leslie writing the curriculum (who had no yoga background). Page 129 again, Baird states it was David and the yoga teachers writing the curriculum.

6. Baird said he communicated with Eugene Ruffin, but didn't mention John Campbell of UVA or Scott Himelstein of USD until pushed by Broyles directly (pp. 57-63).

7. Baird and Broyles spend many more pages discussing whether Baird researched Ashtanga yoga or Jois Foundation to which Baird said he did not.

8. However, he says multiple times "and that is why we formed a partnership" (p.97) moments after stating that Jois just gave them money and they have no say in the yoga at EUSD, nor any ties. Then goes back and forth calling it a partnership – which is also the exact wording in the contract MOU between Jois and EUSD. In June at court, he would claim there was no partnership.

9. Baird claimed he received *thousands* of emails from parents over yoga in the district (p. 109). Yet in media, he would say "a few."

10. They go on and on over the contract documents and it appears by the dialogue that Baird is very argumentative,

trying to deny the very items in the specific contract, while appearing vague and careful in his answers, not taking ownership of the contracts he wrote and signed for the district (up to p.127).

11. "Regur agrees to pilot this curriculum in EUSD schools, gathering feedback from district representatives and representatives from the Jois Foundation to improve the curriculum." And Baird responds that Jois Foundation wasn't involved, yet Regur contract clearly states they are all three giving feedback (P. 128-129).

12. Jois Foundation was involved in hiring (ads, recommendations, and requirements), training (via Russell Case and Jen Brown) and writing curriculum (Jois yoga teachers) p. 130. Steve Regur was in those meetings sometimes, as well (p. 136).

13. He testifies that El Camino Creek School (and all in district) had 200 minutes of PE every two weeks on top of yoga (for 120 minutes every two weeks) which is one of the biggest fabrications in the trial. If that were even possibly true (320 minutes of PE in two weeks) – then what core subject lost those 120 extra minutes for every two weeks if it were not now PE? He clearly *stretched* any truth here. My daughter didn't get 100 min of PE per week after yoga began, nor over the subsequent four years. Actually, in 2013 she got forty minutes at best, any given week, made up of thirty minutes of karate and ten min of running time one morning per week with her normal class teacher. Our situation was similar to other parent stories that children simply lost the sixty minutes of PE each week, not just in the beginning like they claimed at court. He may not have known the truth, or the principals who had to cover themselves, but the teachers knew for sure and had to cover up that fact as well. I never blamed the kid's teachers for that, because they were just doing what was directed to them to do to keep their jobs. For two weeks prior to trial, it appeared they upped the PE minutes, but it couldn't be sustained without taking 120 minutes from somewhere and the district never

defined where (because it didn't happen beyond those two weeks!). The judge never asked, and the Attorneys missed that fact too! The superintendent is the responsible party for creating an environment where everyone else had to choose to *fudge* the truth in fear of losing their jobs (p.141-156, plus declarations of Carrie Brown as Principal and the two teachers of the Sedlock children). Is fear of retaliation to speak up unlawful or unethical when children's rights are involved? The law is clear on PE minutes.

14. When asked about "meditating" as a word used on a document put out by a district principal describing the yoga program, Broyles asked Baird if meditating is a word he is comfortable with the children doing. Baird claimed it wasn't a word they were using in their discussion about yoga (P. 166).

15. Another issue discussed was the non-district-certified teachers being alone in a room with a student when parents are not even allowed alone in a room with children. (P.187) This comes up again (on page 198) where Baird again confirms that sometimes kids are alone with a yoga teacher, then turns around and denies it and says that a yoga teacher leads and another sits in the yoga room. Opposing testimony shows the reverse that the wheel is "by design" time for teachers to do their own staff meetings with others of the same grade (Carrie Brown testimony).

16. I find this question from Peck particularly amusing:

PECK: Dr. Baird, on your frequent visits to these elementary classrooms, would it be correct to say that you're looking for inappropriate as well as appropriate teaching methods?"

BAIRD: "Exactly" (P. 189).

First, the use of the word "*frequent* visits to see yoga classrooms" is problematic and leading right away, but then for Baird to say he is looking for appropriate teaching methods after he already testified to not even knowing much about yoga or Ashtanga yoga makes this all the more laughable. Again, court was comical on a daily basis. But this misleading is no laughing matter.

17. Another conflict of testimony:

BROYLES: Now, programs that might be offered to adults in a yoga studio include Ashtanga yoga taught by Jois; correct?

BAIRD: Yes.

BROYLES: So that's one of the yoga programs that you might be referring to. Now, what you said here, though, sir, contradicts what you actually told Mr. Peck earlier. It says, quote, "Although the poses themselves are the same physically demanding poses used in adult yoga, students have an easier time remembering our terminology." Do you see that?

BAIRD: I see that, yes.

BROYLES: So what you meant by that is the poses themselves aren't changed; isn't that true, sir?

BAIRD: Yes.

BROYLES: Okay. And you meant that the poses are still strenuous or physically demanding; correct?

BAIRD: Yes.

BROYLES: And that's why you have it as a part of the PE program; isn't that true?

BAIRD: Yes.

BROYLES: Okay. So since you don't really understand or know what's involved in Ashtanga yoga, you wouldn't really know whether the poses themselves were modified; isn't that true? (p. 193).

18. One last point important to the case and the strategy of the district is to try to separate what happened in the pilot program from what happened in the rest of the District. The testimony on this either confuses or convinces the judge because the attorneys on the district side keep trying to separate (p. 199) and say there was no Sanskrit, Namaste or other things throughout the district schools in yoga, only the pilot school. But these words were used in all the schools with examples such as the testimony of Sanskrit at ECC, Namaste at Park Dale Lane, and more. Sanskrit language was used and taugh, even after the pilot in the other schools, as evidenced by the fact that most of the parents concerned weren't from Capri, the pilot school. Various testimonies and declarations demonstrate the truth.

Liar, Liar, Pants on Fire?

Day 1, page 67 – Broyles used the term "inculcating" and the judge said – "that's a big word", and Broyles apologized. Then Baird said:

BAIRD: We don't do a lot of inculcating.

BROYLES: Well, "inculcating" is a fancy word for teaching. So hopefully, you do a lot of inculcating.

THE COURT: If he had said yes, I think we'd all get to go home.

"Jen Brown was contracted to work with both the District and Jois yoga. The crossover is clear. Baird's own daughter worked for Jois Foundation and he claims no relationships. Hmmm…where is truth? Truth was in the facts, but the facts were hidden, camouflaged and so obviously covered up by confusing statements made to impact the judge." Written by a parent in the district, Sian Welch,

141

who sat in court each day then blogged each night. Blog available at https://sedlockvseusd.blogspot.com/?spref=fb[1] *called "3 days of testimony" and "Sedlock vs EUSD."*

Expert Witness, Candy Gunther Brown, PhD

There were three Ms. Browns in the trial court (we can't make this stuff up!) and therefore, I will refer to our witness as Professor Brown, as her credentials deserve (p. 202) from the three Harvard degrees she holds and her professorship at Indiana University. Professor Brown has many articles, books, case studies and websites full of information on what she has researched so she speaks with authority on the topic of this trial. She gives talks at professional, collegiate and association events; and as a professor, teaches regularly in the Religious Studies Department at Indiana University. I'm not sure I will ever meet a brighter, more articulate person than she revealed herself to be in court. She is brilliant, articulate, factual, connecting, scholarly, and *she found us!*

She was informed about the lawsuit by others while on sabbatical in England. Two different law professors, aware of her research, e-mailed Brown links to news stories about the controversy. Brown, in turn, e-mailed Dean Broyles promotional material about her forthcoming book, *The Healing Gods: Complementary and Alternative Medicine in Christian America.* This book discusses many of the issues of yoga and meditation in schools, along with other alternative medicines and practices entering into American culture. Broyles, in his turn, asked Brown to serve as an expert witness. She was ready and prepared for this trial. She knew more about this topic than most will ever attempt to grasp. You can find the professor's books, lectures and information on her website at Indiana University: http://indiana.edu/~relstud/people/profiles/brown_candy.[2] In addition, she just published a book containing details of this trial and is titled: *Debating Yoga and Mindfulness in Public Schools: Reforming Secular Education or Reestablishing Religion?* available on Amazon.

Declaration and Expertise

The declaration of the expert witness is attached to our website on this page: http://www.nclplaw.org/wp-content/uploads/2011/12/DECLARATION-OF-CANDY-BROWN-FINAL.pdf. [3] Candy Gunther Brown had studied this field for over twenty years. Most of the rest of the room had studied it for about twenty minutes. And it was obvious the EUSD attorney could not keep her from running circles around anything he asked. She was brilliant. Everyone in the courtroom was in awe of the content and delivery of information and facts articulated by Professor Brown each time she spoke as evidenced by their reactions.

Even Attorney Sleeth for the district stood up at one point during Dr. Brown's questioning and stated "There are not any more questions I can even ask to this woman because she is so much smarter than anyone in the room. I can't even formulate any more questions for her, I'm not smart enough." We laughed at the truth he stated. Yes, this very intelligent attorney said he wasn't smart enough to ask her questions. She had read every book or scientific study he asked her about, and would correct him on the lines he mentioned and would tell him the entire premise of the book. She would then offer additional literature connected to the same subject, and what the author had said or written elsewhere. She was a force to be reckoned with!

Judge: *One of the brightest witness' I've ever seen*

Judge Meyer was visibly in awe of Candy Gunther Brown during her amazing testimony, as demonstrated by him keeping her forty five minutes after the attorneys were done with their questioning. He was talking directly to her asking questions and the two just looking at one another having a *private* conversation *publicly*. Additionally, in the privacy of the chambers with the two sides of attorneys, the judge stated she was the brightest expert witness he had ever seen.

The judge lightened the room with humor a few times in response to Professor Brown speaking too quickly. He said:

"Professor Brown, we've got a court reporter who is going to need some alternative medicine or something (if she doesn't slow down)." Brown said, "Apologies" and attempted to speak a little slower (p. 220). Brown goes on to Sleeth – "You are making an ontological or metaphysical statement, and I'm making a descriptive or an empirical statement."

Background to Expertise in Religious Studies

In response to the question "What have you been researching and publishing?" Brown answers: "I've been conducting this general program of research on complementary alternative medicine. I'll just say CAM for short. So including yoga, meditation, and these other practices we've mentioned and the relationship specifically to religious traditions, including Christianity, Hinduism, Buddhism, Western metaphysics. And I've been doing this for the past ten years. The research includes historical and literary analysis of both written texts and audiovisual materials. It includes ethnographic research, surveys, interviews, observation. It includes sociological study, including qualitative and quantitative analysis, including statistics. My work includes biomedical and clinical studies of the empirical effects of health practices or healing practices on health, and it includes the analysis of scientific publications and systematic reviews of medical literature in clinical studies. And this research builds upon training and experience that I've had since 1989 in historical, literary, religious, and cultural analysis, including close readings of texts, historical and cultural contextualization of practices and documents, assessments of what people mean when they use terminology such as 'religion' and 'science,' and comparisons of scientific research with popular use of scientific language. And so this has resulted in a number of books (p. 212)."

Establishing documents and
information reviewed

Broyles asks what she will base her opinion of EUSD on and she responds:

PROFESSOR BROWN: "So that includes the MOU between EUSD and the Jois Foundation; the EUSD grant proposal to the Jois Foundation; the MOU between EUSD and the RDG; the EUSD yoga program FAQ; the GLPD Gazette dated 9/12; both the original and revised EUSD, On the Mat curriculum; the Capri quiz study guide; the Ashtanga Yoga Institute asana poster; the ABCs of Yoga for Kids poster; the Timothy Baird e-mail to the parents; the Sedlock letter to the EUSD board; the Gray-Baird correspondence dated 10/12; C-Ville article on UVA CSC; the Southern California NPR interview; trial briefs by plaintiffs, defendants, and YES; respondents' answer to verified petition; declarations by Eady, Hevrin, Gray, True, Nordal, Vigil, Sedlock, Baird, Miyashiro, Carrie Brown, Reich, O'Keefe, Weber, McCloskey, Cooney, Bergeron, Campbell, Paul, Ruzic, Gerbarg, Enjedi, J. Brown, Wood, Chapple, Singleton, Hartsell, Borak, designations of expert witnesses and motion to exclude expert testimony and motion in limine, and also publications that are listed in my bibliography related to my long-term research on yoga, meditation, and CAM, a true and correct copy of which is appended as Exhibit B to my declaration originally (p. 22).

She continues: I've also spoken with parents from EUSD who – families who have observed EUSD yoga classes, and I've also read written statements by those parents beyond the declarations that were submitted today. And I've done Internet searches on organizations and individuals who are referenced in the trial materials, including websites and linked videos from the Jois Foundation, JoisYoga.com, K. Pattabhi Jois Ashtanga Yoga Institute, Mysore, India, Ashtanga Yoga Center, Ashtanga.com, Core Power, Radiantly

Alive, Integral Yoga Institute, as well as news articles and blogs reporting or commenting on this case (p. 220).

Hinduism

They talk about Hinduism a while (p. 234):

MR. BROYLES: Q - Does Hinduism involve religious beliefs and practices?

PROFESSOR BROWN: Yes. I mean, Hinduism is a multifaceted religious tradition. It's actually the most complicated of the world religions. It embraces wide varieties of beliefs and actually is intentionally very embracing and welcoming of differences in belief. That's kind of one of the differences between, say, Christianity and Hinduism where for Christianity, it's very important to have correct doctrine or your heretical, right? You don't belong within the fold.

For Hinduism, you can believe a lot of different things and still be Hindu. That's – it's this practice-oriented kind of religion, not this belief-oriented religion. Nonetheless, there's – there are a lot of shared beliefs among many Hindus. So, for instance, those would include belief in, say, reincarnation; that there's this cycle of life and births and deaths. And actually a goal of Hinduism is to escape that cycle of births and deaths, and that's seen as liberation, is to not have to continue being reincarnated, but to become enlightened and to enter into kind of this union with the divine so that you don't have to keep on going in this endless cycle of births and deaths. There's a shared belief in this kind of Brahman, this greater reality, this divine, this kind of universal everything. That's also very important. And there's a sense of kind of multiple manifestations of that divine. So this can be a point of confusion (Day 1, p. 240).

We had to close for the day but the plan was to start the following day with continuing testimony from Brown.

Media covering the day

- Encinitas School District Yoga Trial Starts, May 20, 2013, Fox News: http://fox5sandiego.com/2013/05/20/encinitas-school-district-yoga-trial-starts/[4]
- Coast news reported from the courtroom: https://www.thecoastnews.com/eusd-yoga-trial-underway/[5]
- Trail Begins in Lawsuit over Yoga in Schools, May 20, KPBS: http://www.kpbs.org/news/2013/may/20/sd-yoga-lawsuit/[6]

CHAPTER EIGHT

Trial Day 2 – May 21, 2013

Day 2 Agenda

- Daughter of Petitioners, Plaintiff FS (7 years old) Testifies
- Continuation of Expert **WITNESS:** Professor Candy Gunther Brown Testifies

Trial needs another Day

The second day of trial opens with the Judge and Attorneys batting around the issue of whether they will finish today or if they now need a third day. Broyles asks to interview the Sedlock children briefly about the amount of PE minutes they receive. After some discussion, both Meyer and Sleeth agree. Sleeth contests that "discovery" is needed for these new witnesses and the Judge says "no", to any postponing of the trial. He also states that they will likely move into tomorrow for a third day.

Testimony of a 7 year old

Originally our children weren't called to testify. The reason we brought two of our children to the trial, was in response to the testimony of the Superintendent. Baird told the court (the erroneous statement) that all children in EUSD were getting the state required 200 minutes of PE every ten instructional days including those opted-out of yoga. During Baird's testifying we (my husband

and I) looked at each other and said "let's bring in the kids." We knew the truth needed to be revealed, whether Baird believed his own words or not. Additionally, our Principal had written the same version of cover-up for PE minutes in her affidavit. So when Baird claimed this, only furthering our frustration, it became a tipping point of deciding to bring in the children. We knew that for fifty to one hundred opted-out-of-yoga children across the district, that getting the full and mandated 200 minutes wasn't happening. The best way we knew to display the reality going on in the District was for the children to tell the court the truth as proof. Our discussion that night confirmed to us that no matter what, being in court would be a learning experience for our children. Our oldest son would have enjoyed court the most, but he was in another school district due to his age. Ironically, he is the most likely in the family to become a law student, and it wouldn't surprise me if he became interested in cases of religious freedom just like this. One day, he can read this book to learn about the case we went through before he began high school.

FS testifies (Day 2, p. 4-8). She answered a few questions about how many minutes of PE she had the past week, and the week before. She answered that she only got 10 minutes last week in PE and she wasn't sure about the week prior, but that is probably about the same since that's what they do pretty much (running) every week. Judge Meyer pipes in and asks her if she can answer for weeks prior without guessing. She responded "no." Suddenly, he decides he doesn't want to hear her testimony or from her older brother sitting in the courtroom. Meyers abruptly replied "I'm not going to…let's move on" then interrupts Broyles after the next question and says, "I want you to rethink this…call your expert witness and maybe we will deal with this (kids) later, but I want you to rethink this." And with that, he ends her testimony and excuses her, not realizing how he also startled her. For your clarity: *Given she wasn't including the 30 min of weekly karate she gets at school in her PE minutes, her testimony was just as inaccurate as Baird's claim she got 100!, although, that was Broyles' next questions (about karate) which would have made it clearer to the judge. She actually got 40 minutes per week according to the teacher and the schedule that I saw weekly at school for her class while volunteering. The 60 minutes per week she lost was due to not being in yoga. During yoga she was in computer class doing a typing (type-to-learn) program by herself and the other session she sat with an iPad in back of another teacher's class.*

FS retreated quickly on her little legs to the benches where her father, brother, grandfather and I were sitting. She was very worried and confused about what just happened. "Did I do okay? Why is he mad?" FS asked me. I assured her that she did a great job and everything was just fine. I recall the judge say he would not believe a 7 year old over a principal, as she left her seat from testifying... However, the court reporter notes don't contain his comment, which is odd. Our son JS was a little sad he couldn't testify, yet perhaps secretly relieved. The reward for bringing the kids to court that day would come about 20 minutes later.

JS was 12 at the time and didn't fully grasp why he was not doing yoga with his buddies beyond that it was against what we thought was best for him. However, after listening to 20 minutes of Candy Gunther Brown's testimony, that little boy leaned over and said, "now I understand more about why you pulled me out of yoga; thank you so much" and then he went on drawing since he is a little artist and although might appear "bored" and "busy" to some (by drawing), in reality he was soaking up every word Brown said from the witness stand. Therefore, as you can see from this example, even a 6th grader could quickly decipher the religious nature of yoga when hearing about it for 20 minutes. And no matter the source (court, school, radio, TV, studio advertisements around town, or wherever), these kids see how yoga is spiritual and not just exercise. Whatever their first exposure, the Districts' argument that just because the kids are not taught it as religious in school, doesn't mean they won't connect the dots without explanations. And that's another aspect of concern. In a short few years, these kids will be "conditioned" to do yoga and with full endorsement by teachers, schools, and parents. The standard is then embedded as *the norm* for them.

Continuation of Expert Witness Candy Gunther Brown Testifying

BROWN: "Yoga is a Sanskrit word (Day 2, p. 9) - the word "yoga" comes from what we think of as Hindu texts. So the Upanishad, Bhagavad Gita, both describe yoga as meditative disciplines. So really it's mostly about meditation. And the purpose of meditating is that you withdraw your senses from the world and you focus on the divine. And so the goal is to yoke with the divine and to have devotion through this benevolent, this omnipotent being."

Brown goes on to define "Brahman, Krishna and Om (p. 9), Prana (vital energy) and Atman (universal spirit) on p.10, Nadis, Kundalini and asanas (p. 11), Shiva, bliss Maksha and Samadhi (p. 12) then gets into American Academy of Religion and what Ashtanga means (pp. 13-18) going into the 8 limbs and what they mean to the Ashtanga Hindu worldview (p. 21). She discussed forced breathing: But you do that purification, you do that asanas, and then breathing or pranayama is very important for hatha yoga. And the purpose of pranayama in hatha yoga was not just kind of union with God, but actually it was to get supernatural powers so that you could like telepathically take over other people's bodies. So there are kind of other powers involved as well."

Asanas, Prana and Worship

BROYLES: What is the religious significance to the asanas in Ashtanga yoga?

PROFESSOR BROWN: Asanas are not just physical movements or postures, but they're performed in a very ritually significant way. They're taught to be performed in a very precise manner, in a precise order repeatedly in the same way every time, going deeper into the posture every time. This is because Jois said so, and he's the charismatic authority figure through parampara, but it's also because asanas embody symbolic meanings. And they, therefore, instill moods and motivations. And they're believed to ultimately lead towards union with God (p. 26, 27).

Professor Brown quotes from book "There's a book called the Myths of the Asanas. In fact, it's a textbook that Jen Brown taught from at Capri Elementary School in 2011 to 2012." And what Myths of the Asanas says is that, "Asanas can be viewed as a kind of prayer." I'm quoting from the book, "and they have a significant and wholesome effect on our physical body, our psyche, and our emotional health" (Day 2, p. 27).

BROYLES: Who is Surya? (p. 29)

PROFESSOR BROWN: The Sanskrit means supreme light and refers to the chief solar deity of Hinduism. Surya is worshipped at dawn by most Hindus, and there are many temples dedicated to Surya across India.

BROYLES: Is there any religious significance to the Surya Namaskara?

PROFESSOR BROWN: Yes. It's a highly symbolic religious ritual of devotion to the solar deity Surya. In fact PB Jois says there is no Ashtanga without Surya Namaskara which is the ultimate salutation to the Sun god. [Note: This is why kids *must* to do this opening sequence in EUSD yoga to remain compliant with the Jois/EUSD contract.]

BROYLES: What is virabhadrasa? (p. 34)

PROFESSOR BROWN: It's a warrior pose, and it's one of the asanas in the Opening Sequence B or the Surya Namaskara B. It's also explained in the book the Myths of the Asanas and specifically was taught by Jen Brown at Capri. Like many asanas, the pose is taught because it embodies symbolic meaning. Parallel to how taking communion commemorates the Last Supper of Jesus, the warrior pose commemorates and it honors a Hindu warrior god.

BROYLES: What is the Lotus Position? (p. 36)

PROFESSOR BROWN: Well, the lotus flower is a sacred symbol of purity and enlightenment. The Hindu god – or a Hindu god sat on a lotus and the posture is believed to help the flow of prana or vital energy to get you grounded spiritually, and it facilitates meditation. So even though it's hard to do, once you can do it, it makes it easier to meditate. That's the idea.

Then they move into discussing breathing techniques promoted in Ashtanga and why (for prana flow), mandalas, mudras, anjali mudra, yama mudra, (up to p. 48) when they circle back to Sun Salutations. She tells why Jen Brown was teaching from Ashtanga sources of posters, Sanskrit and books with Sanskrit terms as all the above.

Onto p. 53, 54 with Drishti and vinyasa,

BROYLES: Just to be clear, it's the one that talks about the gazing points or drishti; right?

PROFESSOR BROWN: That is correct. And all nine of the drishti are also listed on the first version of the curriculum used the following year.

BROYLES: Okay. Focusing just for a moment on this document, it defines asana there; right?

PROFESSOR BROWN: It does.

BROYLES: And it defines other vocabulary like samadhi?

PROFESSOR BROWN: Yes, it does.

153

Proving over and over that the curriculum contains very religious levels of Sanskrit words that have deeply religious meanings whether the children (or district) know or not.

Self-Mastery?

A great point Professor Brown makes on page 57 and 58 is that the word "self-mastery" was used 11 times in the first version of the EUSD contract that was signed by Regur and EUSD. In a later version, every time "self-mastery" was used, it became replaced by "health and wellness."

Judge commends her expertise

THE COURT: "Let me just say, with all due respect to your obvious overwhelming expertise…" (Day 2, p. 61) The judge asks her to point out what was religious in the fall curriculum (Day 2, p. 63).

PROFESSOR BROWN: Okay. So I find it religious, that the children are learning Sanskrit. I find it religious that they're still saying "namaste" and that they're still sitting in the lotus and that they're still doing this. Those are religious to me. And that they're coloring mandalas in their classes and talking about reaching the center of themselves. So that's all I'll say, then. Those are the religious elements I see in the fall. Then they go into the spiritual language of each of the yoga teacher testimonies because they use many spiritual references (p. 71) like mindfulness, centering, and balance.

Kids making religious connections

PROFESSOR BROWN: So another thing that was very interesting to me in the teacher declaration was that children are making religious connections from what's going on in the classrooms, which suggests to me that the context of the EUSD classes isn't really all that different from another context (p.72). Let me give some examples from teacher testimonies:

- Reich – asks children to sit in lotus and touch fingers to thumbs in circle (jnana mudra).
- Enyedi said on occasion she hears a few kids chanting. She tells them to stop praying because we cannot do that anymore (note, she called chanting praying, interchangeably) and they do it while in lotus connecting the two (Day 2, P. 72).
- Jen Brown – "kids say Namaste to me when they leave class but I don't reciprocate." She also said kids chant "om" but not because she taught them, she said their parents must have shown them (p. 73). Similarly, I have students who use the Sanskrit names like shavasana," the corpse pose, "and I don't correct them because I don't want to draw attention or encourage it."
- McCloskey – "The kids can reflect back to yoga class and use the tools we've taught them in life." (Life skills – by un-credentialed teachers…more in next section below.)

One of the defenses of the district was that kids were learning the religious parts to yoga outside the classroom and not inside.

Seriously – did the parents teach their kids all these religious parts? This is what became so hysterical in court. The fabrications seemed so steep that even the judge couldn't miss them. But did he? I don't think he was "concerned" for no reason. He had "reasonable doubt" as to whether these classes taught spiritual things. These kids are doing non - physical, very spiritual looking things in yoga (praying hands, palms together) and even the yoga teachers point them out in their own declarations, yet plead the 5th on being the ones who taught them (even though that is exactly what Ashtanga is and does and all instructors know that). Truth? Was stretching the truth part of their day while talking about stretching their bodies and minds?

WITNESS: So to me this is interesting because the students are chanting "om" when they're in this position, and "om" again is the sacred sound of the universe. And Brown (Jen) finds it inappropriate, so she shouldn't encourage it. But instead of telling them not to do it, she just ignores it. So this is from January 2013 to the present. This is Jen Brown's current declaration that the kids are chanting "om" in the lotus position and they're saying "namaste," they're using Sanskrit terms like shavasana, and she's not correcting them.

BROYLES: Is what you just described that's happening in the classroom, the connections that children are making, is that religious, Ms. Brown?

PROFESSOR BROWN: They're making religious connections, right? I mean, what they're doing in the classroom is the children, to me it sounds like they're interpreting it as religious; that they should pray, that they chant "om"; they should put their hands in this special position that symbolizes this kind of connection to the universe. Those are religious connections, in my opinion (Day 2, p. 74).

There is something "more" to this

David Miyashiro (in the video, Exhibit 14 to court, 4 videos of the curriculum) uses "our yoga instructors…" and I, "Dr. Miyashiro," was sitting in the back of an assembly where a kid walked up to do some yoga to calm the room down. He said he began thinking, "There's something more to this" (Refering to "more than stretching and breathing"). And note, this assembly would also contain all the opted-out children, now once again being subjected to yoga philosophy and poses while outside of yoga classrooms.

These teachers don't have teaching credentials and yet, McCloskey talks about teaching life skills and Professor Brown points out that these "life skills" and tools are philosophy or ethos and therefore aspects or features of religion (p. 81).

Professor Brown goes on to share all the religious movements the kids do in the video such as the yoga teacher saying "go into lotus" (not crisscross applesauce) and hands in praying mantis, coordinating of breaths, use of triangle "bell" with every change of movement (used in all Hindu yoga). There's an emphasis in the video on coordinating breath with movements, the vinyasa, and the movement of prana. There's the guided meditation and visualization. So the first version of the yoga curriculum actually gives guided meditation scripts. The second version of the curriculum doesn't give the scripts, but there's more going on in the video than what's in the curriculum. And so they have the guided meditation.

Eddie Stern

Professor Brown quotes Eddie Stern (from EUSD yoga curriculum video) *Reminder from cast of characters chapter, Eddie Stern is the guy who was trained by K.P. Jois and began the New York Ashtanga studio and is called the "Downtown NY Guru."*

Here's a fascinating quotation from Stern in the Jois/EUSD video. "The position that we hold our body in affects our mind. We have taken this idea and we have modeled our health and wellness program on this fact." And so he's saying that, "What we do with our body, it affects our mind," right? "It doesn't just express what we already believe with our mind, but it changes our mind. And that's the basis of why we're doing this entire curriculum" (p. 84).

She goes on to explain how he talks about balance (pp. 84, 85) and "Stern uses really interesting language that – you've got to unpack this, a little bit. He says, "If we deal with the breathing and make the nervous system balanced, if we relax the mind and understand that we can consciously relax ourselves, what this does is it creates the condition for attention. At that point when our body, our breath, our mind are all in good shape, then we're attentive." So let's unpack this just briefly. The program is shaped around the idea the body affects the mind. The postures are transformative.

The breathing he mentions, remember it's prana. It's vital breath. It's Atman. The triad body breath and mind, often its body, spirit, and mind. This makes a lot of sense given that breath is vital breath. It's prana. It's spirit. Energetic balancing (p.86)."

Yikes!

Religious words still in Curriculum

Another 20 pages goes on about the curriculum, then focus on the Jois family and their beliefs, definitions, *internal* changes come about as we practice...etc. (p. 91, 92). And she says "there also are systematic studies that have been done by sociologists other than myself who say for whatever reason people begin practicing yoga, we can see that at the end they make this spiritual transformation" (p. 96).

Brown addresses the very concern we have over kids coming out with their worldview changed after seven years of yoga in elementary years: "And what's interesting, actually, is if you look at yoga promoters, for instance, those publishing in the Yoga Journal, author after author says the same thing; that most people when they start doing yoga, they start doing it for health benefits. But if you look at a dedicated yoga practitioner who's been doing it for a year or two, most of them will have embraced the entire yoga life philosophy and the entire life worldview. And they'll use the words 'life philosophy' and 'worldview.' I could cite example after example of this from people promoting yoga who say, 'Well, of course people start doing it for physical reasons, but then that changes over time.' And that gets back to the point I made earlier where we tend to think that what you intend by doing an action is what determines whether it's religiously meaningful (p. 96)."

Then they cover the camouflaging the district is doing over yoga, hiding behind science when there is no scientific evidence to support yoga over PE even with their own study... (pp. 101,102) camouflaging in the FAQ, the curriculum, etc. (p.107).

Cross Examination of Professor Brown by Sleeth (pp. 110-139)

Another humorous time in court for many of us, is when Sleeth tried over and over to catch Professor Brown in a question (say about a book) but she would answer circles around him. Not only would she have read the book, listened to interviews of the author and commentary about the book, but she would be able to name other sources that clearly Sleeth had not heard of yet. She is after-all, the researcher and expert! She clearly displayed her intelligence to us all (pp. 116, 117), and he exclaims here in the next section that a smarter lawyer is needed to ask her questions, as mentioned earlier. Starting on p. 117 and lasting many pages, Sleeth asks questions about how yoga might be stripped fully of any religion and they go on tangents of what is religion and spirituality.

SLEETH: I heard in your direct examination – I thought I heard you say that yoga is intrinsically and essentially spiritual.

PROFESSOR BROWN: No.

SLEETH: What did you say?

PROFESSOR BROWN: The way that yoga is theorized and practiced is pervaded by spiritual and religious ideologies. That is a different statement from what you're saying.

SLEETH: How is that different?

PROFESSOR BROWN: You are making an ontological or metaphysical statement, and I'm making a descriptive or an empirical statement.

SLEETH: We need a smarter lawyer up here.

[And if an attorney can't sort it out, how can the children?]

(Laughter) (Day 2, p. 120)

Sleeth then attempts to separate spiritual from religious… and the Judge is not sure we need to spend time on spiritual questions, and we may be wasting our time.

THE COURT: Okay. Fine. Anyway, we'll be here the rest of time in an interesting dialog, but I'm not sure how productive it really is.

SLEETH: Well, I'm not sure either. But some of the things that she's said have led to the possible conclusion that yoga is religious, and it starts with a subset of religion being spiritual. So we have to talk about spirituality.

THE COURT: Okay (Day 2, p. 126).

Then a little later – (p. 136)

THE COURT: That changes the question. What do you mean by a layperson?

MR. SLEETH: I mean a person who's not got three degrees from Harvard.

THE COURT: That what?

MR. SLEETH: Who's not got three degrees from Harvard?

PROFESSOR BROWN: Yes. And I think that the parents in the EUSD school district who have opted their children out of the program perceived that there was something religious. And the children of those parents who came home and said, "I'm not going to do that posture. It feels religious to me," they perceived it as religious. They – I don't think they had three Harvard degrees.

[Again – Professor Brown ran circles around Sleeth and would not be caught. Her answers stunned us all at times. She eloquently articulated the problems with language that made sense, yet was hard to grasp without a clear explanation. Many times there would be a pause after she stopped answering, as if every other brain in the room had to catch up to her words.]

What is religious in the yoga positions?

Judge Meyer asked what is religious about the movements:

PROFESSOR BROWN: What Westerners can get is the movements of the body. And specifically the sense of Jois is these are sacred movements. These are sacred sequences. They're not just like any kind of set of callisthenic routines. So the Ashtanga philosophy is that these very particular sequences are what are going to produce the spiritual transformation even if you never say anything about it. They will automatically, they will spontaneously lead to the last four limbs of Ashtanga, including Samadhi, whether you want it or not (p. 130).

More importantly, she then talks about the progression of yoga, that even if right now, in the district, there were no talk of spiritual words, that yoga is a progressive pull that the kids will normalize to yoga, come out of elementary school so used to it that they will at some point move to more advanced levels and enter studios and those are overt (not camouflaging) the religious aspects of yoga (idols in the room, bells, many spiritual words, smells, signals and more)...

It's "Scientific"

BROWN: on p. 133 "And, so that's the demand side of this. And then there's the supply side of this with the camouflage. And you say, "Well, it's not religious. It's scientific. It's physical. It will give you health benefits. It will give you something spiritual that's universal," and this very intentional marketing and saying, "Well, here, we're going to lead with the physical benefits, and then we'll introduce the spiritual later." And, I mean, I could give you quotations where people admit to this who are yoga marketers and marketers of meditation. They'll say, "I go in gradually. I don't say anything about the spiritual things at first. But then I let them see some benefits, and then I will introduce the spiritual components later." So it's sometimes actually very deceptive and intentional the way that teaching about the philosophy comes later.

Camouflaging

Here is an example of admitted camouflaging in a recent similar case where yoga was put into schools promoted by the yoga teacher making it appear that yoga isn't religious, but later admits publicly to not telling the truth about the religious nature of yoga so that she could get it into the schools (p. 133):

PROFESSOR BROWN: Hartsel refers to Yoga Ed and the program there, which is in The Accelerated School in L.A. And I think this is a very relevant example. Because there was a big school board dispute, and what the promoter of Yoga Ed said, Tara Guber, was that, "We'll change the terminology. We won't change the word 'yoga,' because yoga means yoking, and we've got to have that word 'yoga.' But we'll change all the words. We won't say, 'pranayama.' We'll say 'bunny breathing.' We won't say, 'samadhi.' We'll say, 'oneness.'" And they substituted language. And as they were having these school board disputes, what one of the promoters said was, "It's just semantics. We'll just change the words and we'll get it in." Well, they got it in, and then – here's the camouflage at play – Tara Guber admitted in an interview with Hinduism Today – and the article is subtitled, "A Vedic Victory" or "A Hindu Victory." What she said was, "I was disingenuous when I said yoga was not religious and I got it into the public schools. I just changed the language, but the yoga practices will go within."

Cross Examination of Professor Brown by Peck (Day 2 p. 139 -186)

Within minutes of cross examination Peck seems as flustered as Sleeth with Brown's responses to his questions.

PECK – (to Brown) Well, if you can't answer with a "Yes" or "No," be so kind to let me know why you can't, and I'll try to rephrase it. But I can't match brain power with you up here, so I'm trying to make it as simple as possible (p. 146).

The Mission to Spread Ashtanga

The judge seems to understand something here by his question that Peck doesn't, so he jumps in and asks Brown. On page 145, 146, the Judge asks Brown if she thinks that EUSD is promoting the path to Ashtanga for later in these kids' lives. She responded that it's Jois Foundation and the Jois yoga teachers now in the district that are the "foot soldiers (the judge's term) to spreading their yoga with a planned mission. She refers to the evidence on the Jois Website of their mission to spread to every US School and to the language in the contracts and video promotion such as "we want to export this program." I'll add here that *Timothy Baird is even on the video stating that he doesn't just want this for our country, but for all the world!* What? Okay that goes way beyond EUSD and yoga…and displays his invested vision.

Another example: BROWN – (p. 153) And if an empirical effect of practicing Ashtanga yoga at EUSD is that there's this religious change that Jois Foundation thinks is going to happen and that happens, then that's an empirical effect just like prayer practices can have an empirical effect.

MR. PECK: Your Honor, again, I have a few questions here. And if I get a reversion to the whole theme of the case here in every response to every question, we're going to be here all day. Peck touches on the very important topic of mindfulness meditation which is another push into the schools and contained within yoga (p. 155).

PECK: Okay. You've talked a lot about this concept of mindfulness. Is mindfulness necessarily religious?

PROFESSOR BROWN: - According to John Cabot Zinn, the foremost promoter of mindfulness meditation in America – (interrupted by judge)

THE COURT: What is that? What is mindfulness?

MR. PECK: Why don't we start –

PROFESSOR BROWN: I won't – I mean, so his definition is it is the heart of Buddhist meditation, yes. Mindfulness is religion.

MR. PECK: But *mindfulness* isn't that something that sports psychology is all about; in other words, living in the moment?

PROFESSOR BROWN: No.

MR. PECK: That's not what sports psychology is all about?

PROFESSOR BROWN: That is not what mindfulness is about. It's a very specific term. It's the seventh limb in the eighth whole path of Buddhism. It leads towards enlightenment.

MR. PECK: So when we tell our kids to be mindful of their conduct, aren't we telling them to be aware and focused in their conduct?

PROFESSOR BROWN: This is an example of where words that can be used in multiple directions are used expecting and hoping that people will interpret it like what you said, but what they mean is actually Buddhism in this case.

MR. PECK: Well, in what case?

PROFESSOR BROWN: The case of mindfulness meditation.

And so on… Like I said, court was entertaining! And tedious! And a little exasperating for the district and especially for this attorney, as it pertains to questioning Candy Gunther Brown. No one could touch her intellect or corner her into their definitions of words. She was simply not going to be pressured into anything they tried.

And it goes on: p. 156…

THE COURT: I'm not sure where we're going. I'm a little lost, frankly.

MR. PECK: My question is mindfulness, this concept of mindfulness, or living in the moment.

THE COURT: What's the question?

MR. PECK: Well, isn't living in the moment, being aware of oneself in the moment, another definition for the term "mindfulness"?

PROFESSOR BROWN: No, not in the context of how it's being used in EUSD curriculum. It's referring to Buddhist mindfulness meditation. According to if you look at any of the websites from the Jois Foundation, from the institutes that train the yoga teachers, if you look at how it's being used in the literature.

Peck and Brown address Christian confusion over yoga

PECK: Well, Christians the world over practice yoga; right?

PROFESSOR BROWN: Yes. And Christians the world over, dispute yoga. And this is – this is fascinating. I can – I can explain to you why that is, I think (p. 166)

PECK: Because they're being fooled?

PROFESSOR BROWN: (ignoring his comment) - If you look at – if you look at the Roman Catholic Church's statement on yoga, it describes it as New Age and warns Christians to avoid it. If you look at Muslim authorities, they – for multiple countries, they say that yoga can destroy the faith of a Muslim and they shouldn't practice it. Protestant Christians don't have an overall governing body, and they've got this word-oriented definition of religion. And so it's the Protestants who are actually the least likely to recognize the religious rituals as religious. And then there's this demand-and-supply dimension. So Christians, like other people, may not be getting their needs met from their churches or their medical doctors or their jogging around the track, and they want the something more, the something spiritual or religious from yoga. So they want the yoga. They want to rationalize it as something that fits with their faith. And then there's the camouflage dimension or the marketing that we've already discussed (p. 167).

PECK: Are you personally aware of any parents from the EUSD district who don't identify themselves as devout Christians who are objecting to this program (p. 169)?

PROFESSOR BROWN: I'm not personally aware of them, no.

Unfortunately, Brown did not know that the petition contained multiple different religions, and atheists, but that wasn't public knowledge nor did any of us ever tell her that. It just so happened that of the parents who emailed and wrote letters to the district, all were Christians. What that shows is that these were the parents willing to take the risk of objecting in written formal letters to the district and declarations for trial. For example, the Jehovah's witnesses were opted-out before others at various schools, yet never spoke aloud to anyone that I have knowledge of to date. Many Mormons (Latter Day Saints), atheists and a few Hindu parents were also not happy with yoga in schools. They just were not the ones to write letters or stand in the front lines of this battle. Why? Perhaps Biblical verses pertaining to this whole subject gave some Christians the courage to stand up publicly. Nothing personally about any individual made us any more courageous than anyone else, but for the trust of the truth of the Bible, versus our own knowledge or courage. No one wanted to go against a district and live through what we went through. But there comes a line crossed that must be defended, by someone, and Christian parents were willing to stand publicly.

They go on to discuss the significance of Sun Worship (170) Hindu Bells again (p. 173, 4), life skills (174), transformative effects of yoga (175), what is religion (176), Hindu prayer postures (177). More humor is shared between Judge Meyer and Peck (p. 179): He refers to the "Gods must be Crazy" a movie in the 80's he claims where a coke bottle is worshipped and the judge responds "That wasn't in the 80's…" yet in fact, with a little research, it was a 1980 released movie. Perhaps consider watching it to add a little levity one day.

PECK states he is done (p. 186) and BROYLES says "No Questions" to which the Judge says "Huh?" as if surprised, then goes on to question Candy Gunther Brown himself until page 193. The judge allows re-examination questions from both Sleeth (189) and Peck, only to have her put them right back where they were to start with, referring to all the spiritual parts of the curriculum, district actions and Jois contracts for Ashtanga yoga, and their signature opening and closing sequences which are, by definition, Ashtanga.

Ashtanga certified yoga teacher, JEN BROWN, Testifies

Broyles begins (p. 193) with establishing Jen Brown's Ashtanga yoga training in India (3 trips for a total of 9 months) from Sharath and Saraswati, the grandson and daughter of founder, PBK Jois. Three trips were one month, 6 months and 2 months later in testimony. She received her certificate in 2011 to teach Ashtanga through Sharath Jois in India, from the Mysore (p. 197, 198) and now listed on the Pattabhi Jois Ashtanga Yoga Institute website as one of the teachers, Shala – Indian word for school (according to Jen Brown p. 199), three shalas worldwide. "Three worldwide that I'm aware of: One in Sydney, one in Encinitas, and one in Greenwich, Connecticut, I believe."

Then the court goes specifically into the certifications, qualifications of Jen Brown and then into the actual Sequences that are in Question: Surya Namaska A (or opening sequence 1 – renamed at EUSD) and Surya Namaskara B (opening sequence 2 at EUSD) and primary series (all of which Jen Brown is certified to teach, but not the next level up, considered intermediary).

As the judge tries to understand – he adds humor for all to enjoy: (p. 209, 210)

THE COURT: It looks like – some of these poses look like pretzels.

(Laughter.)

That's kind of – that looks kind of hard.
MR. BROYLES: So stipulated, your Honor.

THE COURT: No. I mean, it's –

MR. BROYLES: Okay.

THE COURT: I mean, it almost looks like – well, like pretzels. I mean, not everybody can do that. Maybe Cirque du Soleil or something.

(Laughter.)

Where – I'm just curious, where does the district's program stop?

MR. BROYLES: Well –

JEN BROWN: Is that question to me?

THE COURT: No. I'm just curious. I just -

MR. BROYLES: Your Honor, there's been a lot of testimony, and it's been shown -

THE COURT: Just in general.

MR. BROYLES: They do Surya namaskara A, Opening Sequence A, they do Surya namaskara B, Opening Sequence B, and they do other poses, and then end with the lotus typically.

BY **MR. BROYLES:** Q Is that true, Ms. Brown?

THE COURT: It's essentially the primary series, the first – the top, second, and third down, and then that's –

MR. SLEETH: The district respectfully requests we ask the witness.

THE COURT: Okay. All right.

JEN BROWN: May I answer that question?

THE COURT: Sure, if that – Is that okay?

MR. BROYLES: Yeah.

JEN BROWN: Okay. In our curriculum, there are a number – (interrupted by judge)

THE COURT: We're not jumping ahead. I just – there are a whole bunch of poses here, and some of them look –

JEN BROWN: We don't use all of the poses in the primary series. There's a handful of them used, but we also have a handful that are not seen anywhere in Ashtanga yoga.

MR. BROYLES: Okay. But you do use Surya namaskara A and Surya namaskara B; correct?

JEN BROWN: Yes, we do.

MR. BROYLES: And that's how you start your classes; right?

JEN BROWN: Yes.

This is the proof needed to meet the burden of proof that the district is doing Ashtanga yoga and her responses show that they are doing the Ashtanga sequences. Thus, the burden of proof (on us) is established right there from Jen Brown. Yet later the court would not use this important admitted evidence.

Did Jen Brown collude with the District?

Jen Brown not only stated the kids are doing the Ashtanga Surya namaskara A and B, but those contain the Sun Worship poses *and* a pose that is banned in the US for health reasons (pulling muscle off the bone – covered in injuries chapter). Brown submits and has shown that EUSD is doing Ashtanga yoga, from an Ashtanga yoga trained teacher, who is paid by both Jois Yoga and EUSD (through Regur) that year. Additionally, she appears on the Jois website as a teacher, and she is thus entangled between the district and Jois as well as the leader who oversees and, in speculation, probably reports back information to Jois, or could be asked "her feedback" in her words. But did the judge see all that?

Next, Broyles goes on to ask about her studying Sanskrit and she claims to have done it "for fun"… (p. 216/17)

MR. BROYLES: Why did you study Sanskrit?

JEN BROWN: I think its fun.

MR. BROYLES: Okay. Why is it fun?

MR. PECK: Objection, your Honor; relevance.

THE COURT: Huh?

PECK: Relevance as to why she thinks it's fun.

THE COURT: Well, I don't know. I'd like to hear the answer.

(Laughter.)

PECK: I'll withdraw the objection.

JEN BROWN: I've also studied Spanish because I think it's fun. I like the way that other languages sound.

THE COURT: Which is more fun?

JEN BROWN: Honestly, I think Spanish is a little bit more fun because I have the opportunity to use it more frequently. I work at a dual language school, so I can use that on a daily basis there.

THE COURT: Cinco de Mayo.

MR. BROYLES: Have you ever chanted in Sanskrit?

JEN BROWN: Yes, I have, sir.

MR. BROYLES: You have chanted in Sanskrit?

JEN BROWN: Yes, I have.

MR. BROYLES: Did you learn to chant in Sanskrit from Laksmish Bhat in Mysore, India?

JEN BROWN: Yes, I did.

Does the Court Reporter need a break?

THE COURT: Did you get that? (He says to the court reporter)

(Laughter.)

JEN BROWN: Laksmish Bhat. The last name is B-h-a-t-t (sic).

THE COURT: That's why I want it.

MR. BROYLES: I agree, your Honor.

MR. SLEETH: And, your Honor, I have no idea how to do that. I'll try to help, but –

THE COURT: What's the poor court reporter going to do? Come on. She's going to have to go to India and take Sanskrit?

(Laughter.)

MR. BROYLES: What –

MR. SLEETH: The problem is we're not doing that. They're bringing in the Sanskrit. (the kids?)

THE COURT: I don't care. Just -

MR. BROYLES: What did Dr. Laksmish Bhat teach you about chanting?

MR. PECK: Objection, your Honor. There's no relevance to what's going on.

THE COURT: Who is that? Is that a name?

(Laughter.)

MR. BROYLES: That's a name, your Honor, yes.

These bits of humor may not seem funny to you, but sitting in a courtroom, with all the tension that goes along with that for everyone but the Judge and Bailiff, the concern for the court reporter was humorous because it was also hard for all of us, with one exception of perhaps Candy Gunther Brown, who had studied and likely knew every word used. Even Jen Brown might have needed a dictionary, and if not, point of Sanskrit use well made... Remember Sanskrit is a religious language for rituals, not akin to other languages that are "cultural."

The Judge asked for a glossary of terms for the court reporter... (Day 2, p. 213).

JUDGE - I would like counsel to give the court reporter a glossary because there very well could be a transcript of this, and it's going to be difficult, if not impossible, for her to try to retrieve these names and things. So if I could ask you to prepare a glossary of these words so that she won't have to spend the next six months tracking down these elusive names.

MR. BROYLES: Yes, your Honor.

THE COURT: Okay. I mean a joint glossary to give to the court reporter.

MR. REYNOLDS: Just a suggestion, we could probably sort the briefs and declarations and get most of the words.

THE COURT: No, but I want counsel to do it. I don't want her to have to –

MR. REYNOLDS: Yeah, we'll do that.

THE COURT: She's had a hard enough time.

And yet, they were not elusive, they were all another language! Sanskrit names were all over this case and made it very challenging to move at a clip pace; stopping and defining was imperative to the understanding of the questions.

Next, Jen Brown admits to teaching Ashtanga yoga to students at Capri through the Jois Foundation and a grant, 2011/12 school year (p. 225-229), and to teaching at the yoga shala in Encinitas that year as well; and that she has no background in teaching children. EUSD trained her during the summer of 2012 in what to expect in a school setting, but she also admitted to holding no teaching credentials. She then testifies (p. 230) to the curriculum being written on Fridays from 1pm - 3 pm each week as a "collaborative project" and a "group effort" where everyone's input is equal – that she is not any more influential than the other yoga teachers. There was no mention of anyone else involved from the district.

Therein was the proof we needed. Would the judge use it?

One last revealing moment

THE COURT: How old is he? (In reference to Tim Miller – one of the most experienced Ashtanga instructors in US), (Day 2, p. 225).

JEN BROWN: Gosh, in his fifties. So...

MR. PECK: That old?

THE COURT: He's off the chart. (the judge being well past 50 himself).

(Laughter.)

Day 2 ends with unfinished testimony from Jen Brown, so she will return the next day and then the witness from the district side, Andrea Silver, is scheduled to testify.

- Sedlock v. EUSD Trial Transcript Day 2 -May 21, 2013: https://truthaboutyoga.files.wordpress.com/2015/01/day-2-annotated-court-notes.pdf [1]

Media covering the day

- From NBC news of trial: http://www.nbcsandiego.com/news/local/Yoga-Class-Encinitas-Lawsuit-San-Diego-Reglious-208538581.html[2]
- Yoga Trial Underway, May 21, 2013 Coast News: http://www.thecoastnews.com/2013/05/21/eusd-yoga-trial-underway/[3]
- Definition of Yoga as Religion on Trial May 21, 2013 Yoga Alliance: https://www.yogaalliance.org/Learn/Articles/Questioning_the_definition_of_religion_as_the_trial_begins[4]

CHAPTER NINE

Trial Day 3 – May 22, 2013

Day 3 Agenda

- EUSD Lead Yoga Instructor, Jen Brown, Testifies
- EXPERT WITNESS: Yoga Studio Owner and Teacher, Andrea Silver, Testifies

Dean Broyles questions Jen Brown

To start off the third day of testimony, Broyles questions Jen Brown. (Sedlock v. EUSD Trial Transcript Day 3—May 22, 2013: https://truthaboutyoga.files.wordpress.com/2015/01/13-05-22-part-03-court-reporter-notes-day-3.pdf).[1] He establishes from her that the kids in EUSD were indeed doing Ashtanga exactly as the first five lines of an Ashtanga poster depicts, and that she was taught by Sharath Jois in India and Encinitas. Saraswati was also there, but didn't directly teach Jen. Locally, Jen Brown said she practices daily yoga and teaches at the Encinitas Jois Shala. She testified that she sees Manju Jois at the shala, but he is not her teacher. She also said she knows Nancy Jois, a kindergarten teacher at Capri, Manju's wife (Day 3, pp. 1-14).

The questioning moved into the realm of character building and the "extra life skills" taught along with yoga classes.

JEN BROWN: "When I met with the principal prior to beginning my program, one of the things that she said she really wanted to incorporate into the yoga class were things like character traits that the school worked on. So I talked to her about how yamas and niyamas are things like, you know, practicing kindness towards others and not stealing. And so she really liked the idea of bringing that type of lesson in, so that was why I included them."

Broyles goes on to draw out that Jen Brown learned Sanskrit in order to be able to teach Ashtanga yoga with the proper words and pronunciations to adults (Day 3, p. 16). They also discussed how there was an Ashtanga poster up with all 8 limbs (including Samadhi, meaning union with the divine) for the entire school year at Capri (Exhibit 9), a tree of 8 limbs up for a day and a ½ or so, and some other papers that were the poses of Ashtanga, all attached to the wall. By page 24 they get into other teachings for the kids like "shaucha" which is about bathing and cleanliness (which is a big deal when you research Deepak Chopra's website), and they go over the fact that yama, niyama and shaucha are all Sanskrit words and from India (she admits) so that the origin of these lessons she was teaching the kids was from India.

"If I'm being Honest" she says

They begin to discuss Jen Brown's use of the book "Myths of the Asanas" at Capri Elementary with the children. We have to pause and note that she says over and over and over in her testimony comments of "if I'm being honest"…"I have to be honest here", "if I'm being honest"…"honestly"…. And here it is again on p. 30. There are over a dozen "if I'm honest" statements from her. If someone says that phrase repetitively (especially during testimony!) then at some points, isn't it quite possible they are *not* being honest? Just asking the question…you read the notes and decipher for yourself. Also, if you could visually see her testimony (the entire case was recorded) you would see an entirely different demeanor from Jen Brown when Broyles was asking the questions, than when Sleeth was asking. Sleeth's were probably pre-planned questions and answers for her, and she was calmer. Jen Brown appeared a lot more nervous with Broyles, as displayed by her face and neck being red, quieter answers, stumbling over words at times, and the many "to be honest" statements used. She didn't use as many of those statements when answering Sleeth's questions and was a bit more methodical and scripted. Body language can show a lot, and she was noticeably different based on who was questioning her. Normal? Well partially, yes, but sitting in that courtroom some of the differences appeared dramatic with her, while not with other witnesses. I would imagine, hypothetically, that it would be harder to answer if you are trying to cover up something, or stick to a story someone encouraged you to tell, than if every answer is the simple truth that comes into your mind. Thus the saying, "the truth will set you free." Unfortunately, in our justice system many can be set free on the lack of truth, as well. It would have been fascinating to see what a jury would have added to the flavor of the whole trial!

Sun, Elephant and Monkey Deity and Worship

Next, they dive into other Sanskrit like Surya, which Jen Brown shares is the Deity of the sun (solar deity), the pujas (Hindu ceremonies) that she has attended in Encinitas and India where there were statues of gods such as Ganesh (Elephant Deity) and Hanuman (a Monkey Deity on a bell). At the pujas, she describes, there were flowers, incense, chanting in Sanskrit, dancing, and more. There was a video of the *puja* (called Ashtanga NY – a documentary on Ashtanga yoga), and she showed the kids in Encinitas the video, with the idols of the gods Ganesh and Hanuman and the puja going on with a large group of people in New York in a Sun Salutation [Note: Sun salutation is the Surya namaskara A and B which is called Opening Sequence 1 and 2 in EUSD yoga, which most clearly is described as "Worshipping the Sun") (Day 3, pp. 36-42).] The video was filmed in 2001 after the twin towers went down (p. 36), so some of the meaning behind where and why they filmed is important to note. Brown testifies that she thinks discussions of Greek gods and goddesses are not religious in nature at all (p. 49).

No more Pujas, Namaste or Om

Then they start to cover what Brown, as a yoga teacher now of public school children, stopped doing this year (pp. 50-58) – no more reading "Myths of Asanas," No more showing the video that contained pujas and Ashtanga poses, no more use of "Namaste" and other Sanskrit, Ashtanga poster off the wall, 8 limb tree poster off the wall, chanting "om" in class, postcards of kids in Ashtanga poses off the wall at Capri, and her postcards from India on wall at Capri. Now, on the walls of yoga rooms, you find big colorful posters titled "The ABCs of Yoga" (Exhibit 12 in trial). By page 61, Jen Brown offers to show the court the lotus position, and the judge tells her he won't censor anything and that she will end up on the news, but she is okay with that so she goes ahead and provides visual "because she is wearing pants" she says… (pp. 58-61).

Jen Brown demonstrates yoga for court (and TV)

Jen Brown admits that lotus is dangerous to hips and knees so she doesn't "generally" teach it to the kids, but she allows it if the children *decide to follow her example* (p. 64). http://www.nbcsandiego.com/news/local/Yoga-Class-Encinitas-Lawsuit-San-Diego-Reglious-208538581.html.[2]

Jen Brown in Court

Photo credit to NBC San Diego News: https://www.nbcsandiego.com/news/ local/Yoga-Class-Encinitas-Lawsuit-San-Diego-Reglious-208538581.html

BROWN: So crisscross applesauce is here. If they want to, they can do a half-lotus, which means lifting one leg up. Or if they're very flexible and they've already done it – like if they've come into class knowing how to do this, then they can do lotus. I don't generally teach it because it can be dangerous on your hips and knees if you don't have the correct flexibility." [Note she uses the world "generally" as in I generally don't teach it, but ask yourself – isn't demonstrating it the same as teaching when the kids all watch for how to do a pose? And does "generally" mean sometimes she does but mostly she doesn't?]

BROWN: "And then only for the bigger kids, I might do like pick your lotus up off the ground. So, then they just bring their palms to the floor, they press down, and then they try to lift something up off the ground."

[Notice she uses the term "pick your lotus up," not "your crisscross applesauce." Over and over, these slips of Sanskrit happen by yoga teachers in the schools, even in demonstrations to the parents when the yoga teachers were clearly told not to use Sanskrit any longer. The yoga teachers simply cannot help Sanskrit slipping out of their mouths, as it is the foundation of Ashtanga yoga. To separate the words from the actions is hard, even for the informed instructors during those "on stage" moments. Contrary to what the principal said, we observed this at the schools, and over 90% of the time, the yoga teachers are not being watched, but by children.]

Jen Brown confirms in the following dialogue that she and the other instructors developed the curriculum. Later, the District claims it was Leslie Wright developing curriculum, so notice how Baird hadn't even mentioned Leslie as being in the meetings, but that it was Miyashiro with the yoga instructors developing the yoga curriculum. Baird claimed Miyashiro was involved with all of the meetings and that he himself, only sometimes (Day 3, pp 65, 66).

BROYLES: Now, we've been focusing a lot so far on the poses that you teach in the classroom, but poses aren't the full extent of what you teach in the classroom; right?

BROWN: Primarily, yes. There's also some character education that we teach as part of our curriculum.

BROYLES: Yeah. And the prior year, you – in the pilot program, those were explicitly called yamas and niyamas; right?

BROWN: Yes.

BROYLES: You worked on the curriculum that was developed this year; is that correct?

BROWN: Yes, our entire team does.

BROYLES: Those were the Friday meetings that you mentioned yesterday?

BROWN: Yes.

BROYLES: And at those Friday meetings, the yoga teachers had input into the curriculum; right?

BROWN: Yes.

BROYLES: And the district had input into the curriculum; right?

BROWN: Yes.

BROYLES: Did you work specifically – or did you personally work on the curriculum that was being developed in the fall of 2012?

BROWN: Yes.

Broyles then asks why Jen Brown chants "om" and she says she never learned it from anyone but that *maybe it comes from the vedas*, which she isn't sure. But she does chant, in conjunction with mountain pose and lotus (p. 73). (Vedas are a spiritual Hindu text – Om is called the "Shanti mantras" from the Veda texts). She said she chants the sahanavavatu mantra, as well, which is Sanskrit for teacher/student relationships (p. 75). She goes on to claim that none of this has any spiritual significance to her. "Honestly?" Another chant she does is called "asatoma" which she describes as "bring me out of darkness." (We can't make this stuff up – I mean how can that not be spiritual?). She goes on to say she knows what it means, but not why she chants it. Seriously, check the court document; that is what her testimony says, *for the record* (p. 76).

Quite a few pages and minutes are then spent on discussing breathing and the different types of breathing and breath control taught to the students of EUSD: "Belly breathing, ball breathing, floating arms breathing, and dragon breath, etc." More importantly, she says, is the breathing taught with the movements that make Ashtanga (p. 93).

Cross Examination by District Attorney Carelli of Jen Brown

Carelli starts by asking Jen Brown about Russell Case. Jen Brown testifies she ran into him in Encinitas and knew him from India. Case told her he was working on this new "yoga in schools" project and asked if she would like to get involved. She interviewed with him, and the rest is becoming history (p. 97). Russell Case, as a reminder, is the level 2 Ashtanga yoga instructor for Stanford http://events.stanford.edu/events/418/41803/.[3] He was also named one of the most influential Ashtanga yoga teachers in the U.S. http://downtownyogashala.com/apps/mindbody/staff/100000232[4] and does classes such as https://www.yogagardensf.com/ashtanga-yoga-at-the-garden/[5] in 2010 before becoming the Western Regional Program Director and Advisor for the Sonima Foundation. He now covers both CA and Texas schools for Sonima.

Preparations for Pilot program

Carelli goes on to establish that Jen Brown was talking with another teacher piloting the Ashtanga yoga in a Florida school, at the same time she was piloting at Capri in the 2011/12 school year. That school was also "sponsored" by Jois, which likely means another grant. Then they spend quite a big deal of time on what she actually taught and how she taught the opening sequences the first year and how it was all progressive (build on more and more as you go). She said the girls who had done gymnastics were the most limber and able to do the poses easiest, whereas others grew in flexibility over the year. She claims (on p. 117) that she was the only person developing the curriculum and that when she was gone for 6 weeks, another teacher subbed for her while she went to India, but they were "in contact on email weekly" so she could tell the sub what to teach (p 114).

Brown became the leader of the EUSD yoga teachers and displays that (p. 118) by stating she observed all the other yoga teachers at each school once they started the district-wide yoga program and gave feedback to the principals. She also mentioned that they received a curriculum writer (Leslie Wright) who had no yoga background, but who started taking yoga soon after. So, clearly from her testimony, the expertise Wright brought to the table was curriculum writing, but the experienced yogis supplied the content.

At that point, it was time for lunch break, Day 3. Jen Brown's testimony had gone a lot longer than anyone expected. The attorneys for the district asked if their expert witness could go next, given she was from Canada and needed to return after testifying today. All agreed and we proceeded to lunch.

So Silver would testify, then we would go back to Jen Brown later today.

Testimony of Andrea Silver, Witness for EUSD

The *expert* witness for EUSD was flown in from Canada for the trial. Her testimony appeared to be the biggest disaster for the district during this third day of court. Remember, each side could only choose one expert witness. Why not a yogi from the United States? With months to search for a qualified expert, how was she their top choice? Or was it they just couldn't find one whose website would be white-washed enough to not show too much "religion?" Silver's website must have passed the test of no references to spiritual practices of yoga http://www.namasteomwinnipeg.com/.[6]

Silver responded to questions about her background including a BA from University of Manitoba, but she couldn't remember what year in the 70's so she guessed 1978 (starting Day 3, p.121). Silver lives in Winnipeg, Manitoba (Canada) and appeared to be a very nice woman. She said she taught yoga over 20 years in Canada, US and India. She learned both Iyengar yoga and Ashtanga. She taught yoga at the Winnipeg Yoga Center for around 10 years, but now teaches out of her home, about 8 years then according to her testimony (p. 124-126).

"Om," *ummm*

A ridiculous twist came when Silver, whose company name was "Om practice," claimed to not know what the word *Om* means. Additionally, she said the word *Om* was not religious to her, even though she would admit to using the word *Om* to chant daily. But it meant nothing to her, and she didn't know it's meaning when chanting it daily? These types of oddities occurred daily in court and it was humorous, if it weren't so blatantly an attempt to cover something at the same time. She was so unimpressive that the judge dismissed her fairly quickly within the hour. Our expert witness testified for multiple hours over two days and the judge even kept her well past when the lawyers were done asking questions. The judge asked Professor Brown many of his own questions as if they were the only two in the room having a coffee chat and swiveled looking just at each other while conversing. With Silver, it was the polar opposite: in and out. Included are a few details here to illustrate.

While Silver lacked credibility in anything Ashtanga, as you'll see here, she did express warning and concern for flexibility and that a person should *build up to the lotus position with all the poses prior.*

SLEETH– Focusing on the positions, is there any particular reason for using the lotus position toward the end?

SILVER–Well, lotus position requires a certain rotation of the femurs into the hip socket that actually causes the spine to be in a very aligned and erect position. If you can manage to get your legs into that position and sit like that, it's very light. It's very easy. You can sit for a very long period of time if you choose. A lot of the poses, you know, *could be looked at getting prepared* to sit in this complicated posture (p. 133).

Cross examination starts on p. 127 so you see how short the District attorney's own use of her is in entirety (6 pages). I was glad to see she had taught around 20 years, so at least she had some yoga experience. The name of her website, "NOW," stood for "Namaste, Om, Winnipeg." She said she formerly called the business "Om practice" (as if practicing Om she said). However, she claims she has never said Om in meditation, but that she has chanted Om. (Yes, we were just as confused – if you are chanting aren't you meditating perhaps too?). She agreed to understanding that Om is a Hindu chant, but then she goes on and on saying that although she *does* Om she *doesn't teach it* because it's uncomfortable for her to sing, and she doesn't want to make anyone else uncomfortable. Yet, she named her company "Om" – "because it was like home" she states (how she came up with that part who knows? – court notes, p. 150).

BROYLES: Do you know what "Samadhi" means? (p 157)

SILVER: I know what it means – I know what it means when you read it, but I don't know what it means experientially.

BROYLES: Okay.

SILVER: You know, I read it and I say, "Oh, union with the divine" or whatever it says, but personally I don't know what it means, like I don't – haven't experienced it. I've read it, I've seen it, *and I know its common knowledge*. However, in my experience, I don't know what that means.

BROYLES: Okay. So you've never experienced personally union with the divine. Is that what you're saying?

SILVER: Yes.

BROYLES: Have you talked to other practitioners of Ashtanga yoga who have experienced union with the divine?

SILVER: I don't think I've talked to any yoga practitioners who would say they had union with the divine.

BROYLES: Okay. Would they say anything similar to that to you?

SILVER: No.

BROYLES: Isn't it true that you're not really an expert on Ashtanga yoga, ma'am?

SILVER: I'm not an expert on Ashtanga yoga. I was called as an expert on yoga.

BROYLES: Okay. Just yoga generally?

SILVER: Yoga generally.

BROYLES: And there are literally hundreds, if not thousands, of different types of yoga; right?

SILVER: Absolutely.

BROYLES: There's Broga; right? Have you ever heard of Broga?

SILVER: No, but I'm a little afraid of what that might be.

(Laughter.)

Basically, Broyles draws out that she is not an expert in Ashtanga, nor yoga in general as she does a "mix" of things, that are not qualified by schooling in any of the things that would impact the witness for the children such as; physiology, anatomy, biology, kinesiology nor physical education (pp. 127-165 for Cross examination from Broyles).

Peck cross examines Silver in less than 2 pages! Sleeth grabs the floor again to "redirect examine" her (just 2 pages), then back to Broyles to "re-cross-examine," starting p. 169 to 174. Not much else to report from any of that.

Done with Silver, back to Jen Brown

More Camouflaging – "Brain Highways"

And now we move into another very clever camouflage that appears to be directed from the district on how to answer or avoid answering questions. Jen Brown responds that she really doesn't know what a jnana mudra is (second finger to thumb on each hand palms up while in lotus position) which she does daily. She pleads the fifth and plays like she has no idea what that is until they introduced it in "Special-Ed class" as a "brain highways" activity so the kids don't have to just sit there with palms up, *bored*. Okay, no one bothers to ask her why she's in a Special-Ed class, but I can guess she's teaching them yoga and one of them mentioned *just like brain highways* when asked to go into lotus (I mean criss-cross applesauce), and then palms up on knees with second finger and thumb in a circle. I'm sure they didn't tell the kids that this is to channel energy, but if it really does - then we need to ask - does it matter if they are told or not? Can they channel without knowing? I don't know, but I also don't want 5600 kids to find out.

Brain Highways has a purpose for tapping each finger to the thumb, and it is a whole different purpose than in yoga. But it was close enough to try to use as a distraction technique in court. Well, ahhhem. That's a nice distraction for a magician, and the district has another win in court of *camouflaging the real issue* and what the yoga teachers are really doing with that finger and thumb together. And we all know it except the judge, apparently. I speculate here that the kids said Brain Highways and that it became handy for court. Slick Baird, but the fact is that there is a purpose behind Jnana mudra to channel energy, and EUSD is allowing that in schools. We see it in the videos, the curriculum and even in the children's actions outside yoga class. Who is responsible?

Leadership

We find out more about Jen Brown's leadership role on p. 185 when Broyles draws out that Jen Brown interviewed with Miyashiro, and then sat in to help interview the other yoga instructor candidates with the district. She was the Ashtanga expert sitting in observation of each interview. She claimed at least 6 teachers had Ashtanga experience (3 had gone to India and 3 had learned though Jois Shala in Encinitas) and seconds later she states only 5 when judge and attorneys move to strike and add back information. So somehow her answer changed in seconds when 6 were Ashtanga trained (not including herself), but note that she also said two others were from the district and one was a PE teacher in the district and the other taught art in the district. But all 10 had yoga experience of some kind and only 3 were "fairly new to yoga" (p.187). And if that seems confusing to you, perhaps you see what the judge had to do in sorting out facts!

More proof EUSD is doing Ashtanga yoga, 2012-2013

JEN BROWN - So, for example, like if you were going to do, you know, the Ashtanga primary series during the standing poses, you would do the pose on the right, do the pose to the left, come back to mountain pose, which means come back to stand at the front of your yoga mat with your feet together and your arms by your side, and then you would start the next pose by stepping out to the right and doing the right and the left. And so in between each pose, you always come back to mountain pose, which is the correct Vinyasa or flow in Ashtanga yoga primary series. We don't teach it that way. We teach, "Okay, we're going to – today we're going to do these three or four standing poses, but we're going to step out and we're going to do them all, going back to mountain pose each time" (p. 194).

She testified to using bell sounds (p. 198), and then it just went on and on about parents visiting her classes and what her typical day with the kids looks like. She described teaching 8-12:30 with the children, then coming back after lunch to teach parent offered yoga classes, and teachers were offered classes right after school. She also discussed her conversations with other yoga teachers in the district (usually Fridays) of how their plans worked or didn't for the week.

189

Peck cross examining Jen Brown

Brown responds to Peck's question pointing out that her Ashtanga classes with adults are different, in duration, names of poses, intensity, etc. (p. 214). Pecks questions become a little badgering and making fun of our expert witness, which causes the judge to get a little frustrated with Peck. Meyer stated to PECK: "Did you really think she would say yes?" (p. 217). The Judge also asked "if she says anything different, I'll fall over" (Meyer is being funny again). Then Peck calls Jen Brown an "expert" and Broyles jumps in with "that hasn't been established, and their yoga expert just left the stand for Winnipeg" (Remember we were only allowed to bring in One expert, and theirs was not Brown, although clearly she is a yoga expert, as we would all learn).

Judge Meyer then starts clarifying and interrupting Peck. It appears more and more confusing about what defines Ashtanga yoga. Meyer confuses Ashtanga (opening sequence being in a specific order), with thinking the whole 30 minute yoga session has to be in order (which can be hundreds of poses). Meyer then leads everyone down a rabbit hole in his confusion of these differences, and Jen Brown could hardly answer (many pages up to page 226), nor did she want him to see clearly that Ashtanga designation is only the first few "sun worship" poses to identify it as Ashtanga. Meyer even asks her to perform a tree pose which, by then, I think he was literally just distracting and humorous for the audience at her expense. But, she was young and open to doing more yoga in the room. As she performed a pose he asked: "And is it hard to balance on one leg for most kids at first" (Judge Meyer, p. 222)?

Re-Cross Examination of Jen Brown

Re-cross begins again by Broyles on p. 227. More humor from the bench:

THE COURT: There are only so many contortions the human body can go into.

(Laughter.)

I'm just saying that it – I don't want to get this silly because –

MR. BROYLES: No, I understand, your Honor.

And again, p. 233

THE COURT: Which Jois is that?

MR. BROYLES: The Guruji, your Honor, the dead guy.

THE COURT: The dead guy.

(Laughter.)

THE COURT: When was he asked that?

MR. PECK: He's in corpse pose.

(Laughter.)

MR. BROYLES: Before he died, hopefully.

The day regressed and got more punchy in tone, for the last 20 pages or so of court notes. The judge asked the opposing attorney if he'd already packed for his trip (since we couldn't continue the trial due to the one attorney had a trip previously scheduled – work I presume, but no one asked) and a lot of other nonsense. In the midst of the chaos and side conversations, the attorneys (7 of them I think) tried to find the next court date in June that everyone would be available to meet for *two more days tops* the judge said.

And that of course isn't what happened.

It would become three more long days of trial, plus another day for verbal verdict.

That's it for May 2013.

More Media of Trial Day 3:

- Encinitas Yoga Trial over Religion in School, May 23, 2013 Huffington Post: http://www.huffingtonpost. com/2013/05/23/encinitas-yoga-trial-religion-in-school_n_3327247.html[7]
- Trial without Resolution adding days in June, May 23, Yoga Alliance: https://www.yogaalliance.org/Learn/Articles/ Yoga_trial_without_resolution[8]

CHAPTER TEN

Trial Day 4 – June 24, 2013

Day 4 Agenda

- Judge Meyer begins with opening statements (a month has passed since last court day)
- Petitioner, Stephen Sedlock, Testifies
- Petitioner, Jennifer Sedlock, Testifies
- Principal of El Camino Creek Elementary School, Carrie Brown, Testifies
- Assistant Superintendent of EUSD, David Miyashiro, Testifies

Sedlock v. EUSD Trial Transcript Day 4—June 24, 2013: https://truthaboutyoga.files.wordpress.com/2015/01/2013-06-24-sedlock-baird-trial.pdf[1]

Judge Meyer's opening statements

THE COURT: Let me just suggest an issue, and I think this is where we – This is getting down to the nitty-gritty, as they say. The primary legal test that the court has to apply here, I think is the Lemon Test. And you might recall in Lemon, Parochial schools were given money to teach secular subjects. And the court, in essence, said we can't trust the nuns, the Catholic teachers, to teach secular subjects and for the state to monitor that; make sure they teach the way they're supposed to teach would involve excessive entanglement in religion. So the court said no can do. Now, that is the law. If you assume in this case that Jois is establishing Ashtanga yoga in the public schools and if you further assume—I'm not making a finding but I'm saying assuming, for the sake of this discussion that Ashtanga yoga is Religious, and we have had significant evidence of the district trying to cleanse the yoga program of religion, which some would argue the district knows its religious or feels it very well might be religious my question is how to you square that scenario with Lemon?

In other words, if the Ashtanga Yoga is religious and Jois is establishing it in the public schools, and the District is trying to make it nonreligious, which seems to certainly arguably not square with Lemon, what can the district do, if anything?

MR. SLEETH: The first –

THE COURT: I don't want to have closing argument. I'm suggesting that that is this case, perhaps. You understand?

MR. SLEETH: I do understand. I see the case as being exactly the opposite.

THE COURT: Okay. It's going to be one way or the other. This is not a case where everybody is going to be happy.

MR. SLEETH: Factually, we will address the issue of how they're trained and who does the oversight with some testimony today.

THE COURT: I'm just saying this seems to be arguably Lemon in Reverse.

MR. SLEETH: Yes.

THE COURT: And if you make the assumptions that it's religious, we have Lemon in reverse. It's the same scenario, only instead of the state giving religious school money for secular purposes; we have got an arguably religious organization giving a secular public school, money for religious purposes. But that assumes that

Ashtanga yoga is religious. And again, if it wasn't religious, why is the District going to great pains to change the curriculum as we speak, almost?

MR. SLEETH: Any statement I make in response, your Honor, would be argument.

THE COURT: I'm just saying that is, I think, the case. And when you – again, I don't want to invite argument, but here we have got – this is not a high school elective. This is an elementary school and it's a required subject, which I'm sure you'll at some point remind the court.

I'm not making any findings. I'm suggesting that it seems to be –I mean, there has been – over the last session there was a lot of kind of interesting and almost entertaining dialogue with Dr. Brown about all sorts of things, which is interesting, and as I say, perhaps somewhat entertaining, but not where we are or where we should be. I'm just trying to refocus on the issue and that is the law which the court has to follow. So saying that, where are we?

MR. BROYLES: Your Honor, we would like to call Stephen Sedlock, The Petitioner and Plaintiff in this case.

Mr. Sedlock, Father and Petitioner, Testifies

After covering some background about his schooling, work and family, Mr. Sedlock is asked about his involvement in the community and schools. Basketball coach for National Junior Basketball, AWANA leader for youth at church, and volunteer at Brother Benno's soup kitchen are among the responses for the community. He responds that his involvement at school mostly centers on events his own children are participating in at the time. It was during one of these events where he found out about yoga in the schools for the first time (pp. 8-11).

Sedlock testifies that yoga was introduced by Principal Carrie Brown at back-to-school night at El Camino Creek in August 2012. He became concerned right away due to the lack of details and simply that it was yoga. During further examination by Broyles, Sedlock explained that the yoga teacher at El Camino Creek was teaching art in the fall of 2012 and taught Sanskrit to our daughter (we were a test school so no yoga yet, but we had a yoga teacher). Mandalas were drawn at ECC in this yoga teacher's classroom, although at some point in the back and forth the judge and attorney and Steve all start saying it was at some other school, and I'm not sure why none of them remembers it was at El Camino Creek. Confusions like this added to challenges in clarity of information for the judge. Another example of confusion is Carrie Brown's declaration where she says we complained about Mandalas at ECC, when in reality it was Samantha Vigil at ECC that complained to Carrie Brown about these. I don't think she remembered correctly, but other points in her declaration are not accurate either, such as the kids PE minutes. But the truth here is that the yoga/art teacher Christina Reich at ECC taught Sanskrit and Mandalas in her art class fall of 2012, prior to starting the yoga classes there in January.

As a father, he also shares his concern for physical safety for children, lack of credentialed teachers, and that as he learned more about Ashtanga yoga, he realized it was in opposition to his faith as a Catholic. Specifically, the bowing down to "other gods" as this yoga program promotes, in the sun worship poses and more (pp. 12, 13), and against biblical teachings. In summary, Sedlock testifies to his concerns, his community involvements and why he doesn't want yoga to be a curriculum class in elementary schools (pp. 8-30).

Mrs. Sedlock, Mother and Petitioner Testifies

I'm asked some of the same questions as my husband about my education and work background and living in this community for 11 years. This was our 9th year, as a family of 3 kids, in the school being discussed. I respond to community questions that our boys are both competitive basketball players, and our daughter is involved in various sports. Further, we are involved in our community with events, volunteering and helping run programs. I'm asked about volunteering as the Chair of the Jogathon Committee for the last three years (largest fundraiser for the largest district school), Vice President of the board at Oak Crest, (our oldest child's school at that time), and classroom volunteer in math and language arts for the past 9 years. One of the most pertinent experiences Broyles draws out for me to testify regarding, is that I taught the elementary Physical education curriculum called "Sparks PE" at El Camino Creek elementary one semester when a pregnant teacher needed help. So I learned the PE guidelines and standards in the "California Education Code Guidelines for Physical Education" in 2011. Additionally, in my past, I was a certified aerobics instructor for many years giving me a base knowledge about the process of fitness teaching certifications. As an assistant coach at Torrey Pines High school, for track and cross country (pp. 30-34), I had worked with children and fitness as a hobby and voluntary position as well. These experiences and this knowledge would impact my view of this yoga program.

Fitness and Kids

Therefore, fitness and kids are near and dear, to my heart. You won't find those words of how much I care about kids in testimony – but it may help you understand that my biggest concern here has, and always has been - the physical, mental and spiritual growth and freedoms for our children and all children in our nation.

I love working with kids and understand their fragile nature, allowing us to so easily steer them in directions such as Ashtanga yoga, that are not in the best interest of all the children. The physical issue is not something you can easily bring before the court of law, but the religious is an area we could. So, although many people think we are "Bible thumping fanatics" because of our "name calling opposers," it was some of the only criteria which we had available with which to file to try to eradicate the yoga before it grew further. I am just as concerned for the physical problems brought on by having one sport dominate all 7 years of elementary school (EUSD is K-6ᵗʰ grade so = 7 years). The only sport I see that kids should do almost every week of their lives is jogging to keep up some endurance - for all the other sports they used to get to do. And if you watch elementary kids at recess – you never need to tell most of them to run around and play. You rarely have to instruct them to do it; they just do it! Run, jump, climb, shoot a ball, throw, jump rope, it all comes naturally if you give the environment of some blacktop, some grass and some items to play with or monkey bars to hang on. Now, in less affluent schools or areas where that is not the case, make 'em jog! Put down the yoga mats and run around! Yoga just isn't the best fitness option for elementary school age children, in my opinion.

Five Concerns of a Mom

I testified that I had 5 primary concerns.

1. Yoga replaced 60 minutes out of 100 minutes required for PE every week and that I would not want *any one sport* to dominate 2/3 of PE for the entire elementary school years where multiple units of sports were learned prior. I was even fine that yoga was one unit years prior, but not that it took over the whole district for 2/3 of PE (p. 35).

2. All the opted-out children did not get a PE alternative given the nature of the Jois/EUSD contract, so kids were losing up to 60 minutes of PE across all the schools. Principals were well aware that they were giving us "non-physical" alternatives (as evidenced by emails to me from my own principal, Carrie Brown, for typing and computer work instead).

3   I was concerned that yoga was planned for three years in our district, and that the Jois Foundation's stated mission was to reach the entire nation to replace PE for elementary

schools. I was and am very concerned about their mission (p. 35).

4   I was very concerned about the spiritual nature of the yoga program and that this is a *physical practice* they are doing in schools. I don't mind my kids learning about various religions, but practicing one in school is what I'm not okay with and opposed. Knowing that this is a *participation* religion, not one of sitting to learn about cerebrally as we westerners think of religion, but one of action and "practice," this is similar to the active verb used of a doctor who "practices," one practices yoga, and the spiritual part grows over time, we learned.

5   I was concerned our children were being tested and studied without our written consent and that they were taking pulses, weight, etc. during math time. I was a volunteer in math in the second grade, Mrs. Weber's class. Kids were pulled out of that class to be tested, and parents were not informed nor had consented to this for their children. I am certain most parents to this day never knew that their kids were being pulled out of math, science, and English to do these measurements. Why wouldn't these "yoga study" metrics have been taken during the yoga class time? Why weren't the institutions required to gain parental permission through signatures?

Religious Concerns about Yoga

When asked by the defending attorney why I was concerned about yoga at EUSD for religious reasons, I responded that practicing Ashtanga yoga is a violation of the first and second commandments in the Bible. When asked specifics, I stated that in Hinduism there are over 300,000 gods and that in Christianity there is one God. I explained that to "bow down" to other gods is in direct conflict with the first commandment to not have other gods. And, the second commandment is to not create or bow down to idols (p.38). Then I was asked if I ever voiced my concerns to anyone. I gave five examples of the board meetings where I spoke, the emails and letters sent to the entire board and Baird. All these communications were between the months of October 2012 to December 2012. I testified that I never received a response from any of my communications. In addition, I shared that we presented a petition including over 250 people in December that was gathered a few days over Thanksgiving from people who want yoga out of the EUSD schools. At that point, the Judge stops my testifying and doesn't want to hear more, stating that it doesn't pertain to the law and the choices he needs to make.

Visiting Yoga Classes at EUSD

Note that I did testify to seeing a yoga class, but the attorney for the district and the judge later state that I never saw a yoga class, which wasn't accurate (p. 44). Carreli spends a lot of time trying to draw out of me that Carrie Brown reassured me that the children would get 200 minutes of PE, but over and over, I responded "no" to his questions, as it was the opposite. She could not offer my kids PE alternatives for yoga when we opted-out. Clearly, in emails she stated that the kids would go to typing and math lab. Finally, Carelli gives up, realizing he will not get what he is looking for me to say, because the reassurances simply didn't happen. Not once did Baird or the principal reassure us that we would get our required PE minutes, and the judge even asks Baird why he didn't trumpet that once, if at some point he did ensure 200 minutes *above yoga* in 2013)? But Baird doesn't respond because he never communicated that to the district. Neither did Brown. And I'm still not sure it ever happened more than the two weeks prior to court in May. One day, a week before the court proceedings, my daughter came home saying "Wow, we actually played a game of baseball today for a long time."

Note – five years later, we moved to a new school district for 6th grade that not only provided the full PE required, but our daughter was able to play volleyball, softball and basketball in after school sports – for last year of elementary. She may not have learned those in early elementary if yoga replaced 2/3 of PE. Stop for a moment and think of the incoming Kindergarten class of 2012 at EUSD. Those kids were in 6th grade as of summer 2018, and have completed six years of yoga. By 2019 when this book will be published the kids of Encinitas graduating elementary school will have 7 years of yoga under their belt. What will the impact of that be on their future? Will those children know how to play volleyball, softball, kickball or basketball when they get to junior high? Yoga is now offered at Jr. High and High schools in our area as well (but optional). Will kids keep this new tradition going? It still concerns me... On becoming a Yoga Nation... Jennifer Sedlock (p. 30 – 61).

Carrie Brown, Principal, Testifies

MR. CARELLI: "Your Honor, if we may, the defense calls Carrie Brown. Another Brown" p 62

THE COURT: Another Brown.

Principal Carrie Brown testifies about the hiring process of the yoga teacher for her school, PE minutes for the Sedlock children, Mandala art, and whether or not yoga teachers have other (credentialed) teachers in the room or not.

Brown testified that she interviewed candidates that had been selected by David Miyashiro, Steve Regur and the Jois representative, Russell Case (from the hiring process that occurred in June and July of 2012). She also made the point that she had never received any "other type of consultants (than yoga)" from Regur, but that she thinks maybe they provide the district with other consultants. It was established that the yoga teachers do not all have teaching credentials, but she chose Christina Reich because she had an art background, and they got along right away. Reich's philosophies seemed to match what Carrie Brown was looking for, for her school, she states (p. 62-70). Note that Reich's only experience with children was being a "nanny" which to Brown was a big plus.

Brown testifies that she told Reich to have the children draw mandalas in class because Reich would be busy helping take measurements of the children, and it would give them something to do. However, the measurements I saw taken during Ms. Weber's second grade class (my daughter's) were during math, not even during yoga or *mandala drawing*. I find it interesting that Brown would tell Reich a specific assignment to do, given that she hired Reich to handle lesson planning and teaching. Carrie Brown stated in an email to Samantha Vigil that she (Brown) didn't even know they were drawing mandalas. Furthermore, the mandala art all got thrown away after Carrie Brown told Vigil she would investigate what was going on with Mandalas. Art not coming home is rare. We get every small thing our children make, and I've never heard of any art ever getting thrown in the garbage at school, let alone an entire school's worth. In fact, in 9 years at El Camino Creek, I've never heard any other instance of art being tossed (p. 73).

19 children at ECC "Opt-out" Fall 2013

Carrie Brown mentions that 19 families opted-out at her school (p. 77) and a couple lines later she says 19 children. So, not sure which one is accurate, but she goes back and forth interchanging 19 students and 19 families. Either way, she states that at some point she had to "make PE time" above and beyond yoga, due to the growing number of opted-out children.

Ironically, the question that never got asked by any of the attorneys or the judge is this: if you still start and end school at the same time and take the same lunch and recess breaks, then what in the schedule is this extra 60 minutes "elective" of yoga replacing if not PE time? Is it Math? Science? English? What? 60 minutes has to come from somewhere, so in their new story of yoga not replacing P.E, yoga has to be replacing something else. This also means they get 160 minutes of PE per week in a school district that struggled to give 100 per week! That's just quite surprising, isn't it? Do the Math, and it becomes absurd!

This *new* claim doesn't even make sense from Baird or Brown. It was simply a scramble to cover themselves temporarily for the state mandated laws of 200 minutes every 10 days. Opted-out children simply did not get 200 minutes every 10 days. And certainly not 320 minutes with yoga! Not even close! 40 minutes per week is what my daughter got, so every two weeks she got 80 of the 200 required minutes! Our son got 60 minutes each week because his 6th grade class only had 40 minutes of yoga per week, so for 10 days he would get 120 of the required 200 minutes. For him, this only lasted one semester before he graduated to a new district. For her, missing PE minutes would last another projected four years (p. 80-84). If you got lost in the numbers, you see why the court could have easily gotten lost just as well.

Physical Education Minutes

Brown continues saying that kiderate (30 min of karate for K-3) is also *now* an elective – so that would be 60+30 or 90 "extra" minutes of PE each week, she claims on top of the 100 required, (or for 10 days that would be 190+190 for 380 minutes of PE for K-3rd graders!!! p. 84). Seriously? That was laugh out loud material in court! Not possible. Didn't and couldn't happen. Her testimony is not credible, nor provable. The only proof she offered was that if you open teacher's planners, the PE time was scheduled. I can't imagine the scrambling that went on to back date all that log of time. She goes on to testify that I never asked to watch a yoga class at ECC on record. The district moved forward, constantly stating I'd never seen a yoga class at EUSD. But I had. I am on campus frequently and there was not a "rule" that you had to check in through the principal's office until months after yoga started in the school. Checking school ledgers to *sign in and out* you can see I was there frequently, volunteering in the classrooms, and walking by the yoga classroom. However, I don't need to peek into the

Mormon temple on freeway 5 to know it's religious. It's a given. After I knew how religious Ashtanga yoga and the Jois Foundation were, I didn't need to look long to see the worship poses. Weekly, I could see into yoga rooms until one day someone decided to put blockers up in the windows of the yoga rooms at more than one of the schools, and they started closing the doors and turning down the lights. Then, you had to make an appointment with a principal and go in with a staff member to watch. That gave them ample time to do whatever was needed such as place a certified teacher from the school in the room during a visit. The rules were a "moving target." If nothing was happening, then why were these blockers needed, one has to ask? What was being held private?

Shifting Rules

Another example of shifting rules in the district is when all of a sudden one day you could only view a yoga class if you were a parent of that particular school. That change was in response to two of us setting up appointments to view a class in every school (in 2014). After viewing yoga classes at OPE, Mission Estancia and ECC (where Principal Brown is), we still had more appointments. Carrie Brown didn't waste a minute before calling Baird after we left her school. We started getting calls from all the other schools cancelling the appointments with messages stating a new "rule" from the superintendent. And to top it off, Brown knew there was no yoga class scheduled at the time she booked us, and she did not cancel the appointment. So she took us in the room to ask the yoga teacher questions, but there was no yoga class to watch. She could have avoided this with one phone call to cancel, but she chose not to do that and then quickly alerted Baird after our visit. So it was a sliding scale of hoops to jump through... They didn't make it easy to see a class, but I and others saw many over the last few years since the trial and the concerns remain with lights out and a growing set of issues. In 2016, you could see crystals placed in the front of the room. How do crystals help your exercise?

Principal Brown uses the word "honestly," just like Jen Brown, and the judge catches it and makes a joke at her expense:

PRINCIPAL **BROWN:** Well honestly, the first thing I do –

THE COURT: Of course, Honestly. That's a good start (p. 69).

Cross Examination by Broyles of Carrie Brown

Cross Examination starts by Broyles (p. 91), and they go over the hiring process of yoga teachers, the teaching of character traits in yoga, schedule of classes, and more (p. 102). Redirect starts by Carelli for EUSD (p. 109) and he establishes (for us!) that regular teachers are not always in the classroom with the yoga teachers. This is a very important point that the judge lost sight of later. This is another law that was broken. Not even a caring parent can volunteer and be alone in a room for 5 minutes with a class (p. 109).

Overall, Carrie Brown's testimony supports the efforts and changes that the Superintendent has made, even specific detail changes not pertaining to her school. She explains the hiring process the same way Miyashiro will next, which doesn't match Baird's. This means that they are "all on the same page" now in June with their new descriptions of old information including Ashtanga yoga, PE minutes and more.

Lack of Consistency in Testimonies from District

The ever shifting terms and rules added to a serious lack of consistency coming from the district witnesses. There was a continual effort to cover up their own stories to keep the fabrications going. It was a moving target. For example, at the beginning of trial, Superintendent Timothy Baird said they were doing Ashtanga yoga in the schools and that the district had "cleaned it up" of any religious rituals. (Don't miss the fact that if it *started religious* it shouldn't be in public school anyway). Yet by Day 4 of the trial here, Miyashiro starts claiming the opposite of Baird, that EUSD really didn't ever do Ashtanga yoga, and that Baird had that wrong. The new name "EUSD Yoga" emerged as the name for their yoga program.

A New Strategy by EUSD

So, on this fourth day of the trial, a month after the first three court days, a new strategy came from the district. Enter the EUSD Assistant Superintendent, David Miyashiro. As a last ditch effort from the district, and seemingly in response to the judge's comments that they better provide something, Miyashiro claimed that they were never doing Ashtanga yoga. Yes, he made this claim even though the contracts with Jois Foundation and Regur Development both stated they were doing Ashtanga yoga. Yes, he made this claim knowing that Jois Foundation *only* promotes one thing – Ashtanga yoga. Yes, he made this claim knowing that his boss, Superintendent Timothy Baird published a Q&A document about "Ashtanga yoga" in the district in December of 2012. Clearly, this new name "EUSD yoga" was a strategy they came up with for court. Would the judge fall for it? The switch up was so blatant and obvious, that there is no way the judge wouldn't catch it. Or did he? Would the judge fall for it? Or did this just give Judge Meyer the "out" he needed to side with the district?

Brilliant Strategy

Ask yourself a logical question: "if the district never taught Ashtanga yoga, why then did the Jois Foundation, that only promotes Ashtanga yoga and has no other mission, give the EUSD District over four million dollars over four years to *do a study of our 5,600 children* and for EUSD to write curriculum to give to

Jois? And if it was really "EUSD" yoga, why would Jois want that? The contract was for yoga curriculum created by EUSD that Jois Foundation could use across the nation. The curriculum is being used now across the country.

I think Jois Foundation was brilliant here in its strategy. Let's take a look at what they did and what they gained. Jois Foundation took over a dozen yoga teachers that taught a *few* hours of Ashtanga yoga classes a week each for them and gave them *full time jobs* via the school district to *write curriculum* to spread to other schools through Jois. If you do the math adding up all the classes (K-6th grade), there is no need for yoga teachers for 40 hours. But because they were meeting and collaborating and writing curriculum, they must have somehow fulfilled 40 hours. Bear in mind, there was never a 40-hour PE teacher prior to the Yoga program in any of these schools, which was why it was hard to keep good PE teachers with part time hours of 15-20 at most. By the second year, each school *had two "yoga" teachers for a total of 18!* This curriculum being developed would be used to spread Ashtanga yoga across the country as a model via Jois Foundation. As per the Jois (now Sonima) Foundation website, http://www.sonima.com/[2] their mission was clearly stated and we pointed that out to the district back in 2012. It is and was: To spread Ashtanga yoga to the children of the United States.

A Win-Win for Jois Foundation

In the meantime, Jois gains full devotion to Ashtanga yoga by fully immersing these teachers into their mission. These yoga teachers went from teaching a few classes of – let's conservatively say – three to six hours of classes per week to a 40 hour position. This is a win for Jois. Jois gave EUSD the money who then paid the teachers via the Regur Development Group – another genius move – adding in a third party so that the contracted teachers could be called *district employees*, a point that confused the judge into thinking they were really district employees. So sometimes Baird would call them district employees and sometimes he would point out they were not, depending which way it benefitted his points. Someone came up with the brilliant idea to farm these hires through Regur. This helped the district to solve some other hiring issues since all these teachers were not going to be qualified and/certified like most credentialed *teachers who are alone* with our children.

No loving and devoted parent volunteer is ever allowed to be alone with the students at school, but with this hiring process, these *teachers* would be! And there was a problem with Regur Development Group, which, at the time, we could not prove. But we knew that the man who is the sole person in the "development group" was linked to Timothy Baird and had just started the "Regur development group" that year. We needed more proof, but knew it would come. That proof is in the chapter at the end of the book on what's happening in EUSD now.

Miyashiro left the district after testimony

Another interesting fact is that *Miyashiro left the district right after his testimony*! He disappeared to another district, and within six months, he would then attain another $500,000 contract from Jois Foundation to start Ashtanga yoga in the Cajon Valley schools where he was the new superintendent, August of 2013. Now, knowing some of the above, let's take a look at David Miyashiro's testimony.

David Miyashiro, Assistant EUSD Superintendent, Testifies

Questions began with Miyashiro's responsibilities in the district and in overseeing the yoga program and principals. Miyashiro begins by telling about his role when yoga first entered the District because he was filling in as a principal for Paul Ecke. Since the principal was on maternity leave, and the school needed an "enrichment teacher," Miyashiro hired a yoga group called *Next Generation Yoga* to provide instruction in 2010 (p. 110). He expanded it to a second school, Park Dale Lane, based on positive parent comments about the yoga program (Day 4, p. 114). The Jois Foundation grant offering yoga in 2011 to Capri Elementary enabled Principal Beth Cameron to hire Jen Brown. Miyashiro states this was not a pilot program, but the responsibility would fall on Beth Cameron and not himself (p. 116). However, Jois Foundation did fund this yoga program in the fall of 2011 at Capri. [So one place it's called a pilot and here Miyashiro claims it is not.]

MIYASHIRO: In the summer of 2012, almost a year ago, Dr. Baird and I met with Gene Ruffin, who is the CEO of the Jois Foundation, as well as, Scott Himelstein, who's our former Secretary of Education under Governor Schwarzenegger and currently the Dean of the University of San Diego Center Policy on Law.

CARELLI: (Attorney for EUSD). Who set up that meeting?

MIYASHIRO: Tim did (p. 116)

CARELLI: And you met, I take it, over at the District office?

MIYASHIRO: I think we met at the pancake house across the street. (That would be one called "The Pancake House" on Encinitas Blvd. and Rancho Santa Fe Road).

CARELLI: All Right. And what was discussed at that meeting in terms of yoga curriculum?

MIYASHIRO: Tim and Gene had spoken about possibly expanding to a few schools, that there might be funds to support that. And then we talked about overall goals of what a program might look like. We discussed the possibility, "well, maybe online schools are possible." And so we brainstormed a little bit and we started with the goals of the program, which would be –
 Gene Ruffin (Jois Foundation) gets called "The fabulous guy" by Miyashiro and that sticks, then the judge and attorneys call him

the fabulous guy. So now we have the dead guy (PBK Jois) and the fabulous guy. Lots of laughter (P. 117).

CARELLI: So you asked for yoga, but you asked for other things beyond yoga?

MIYASHIRO: Right. Because the Health and Wellness Program, is more than just physical exercise. It's healthy eating, teaching kids about organic foods, how to prepare it. And it's about behaviors, how to deal with stress and anxiety as part of the comprehensive health and wellness program supported by our school board.

CARELLI: So you drew this up yourself?

MIYASHIRO: with help. Tim and I pretty much in his office had a very short amount of time to put a grant proposal together. We asked for everything, and they came back to us and said, "we'll support this." And "this" was the organic farming, the culinary arts, the physical education which in this case was yoga, and character development.

THE COURT: This is the Jois Foundation?

MIYASHIRO: Yes. (p. 120).

We were under the impression that they would have a yoga curriculum in place for our teachers to use and that they would be funding the development of the farming and culinary arts and character Ed so that I could employ a team to develop this curriculum for implementation in 2013-2014 (p.120).

Recruitment Fair, Hiring, Training or All of these?

Miyashiro talks about a *recruitment fair* put on by Jois that he attended every day, and the judge interrupts to re-iterate that the district needs to understand that rather than link themselves to Jois and their recruitment, that they need to distance themselves and make sure to provide evidence that they had control over the curriculum and not Jois (pp 122-124).

This is significant because it was the Judge's second attempt today to focus the district on what they needed to do to win this case. It was confusing why Meyer would *lead* them this way, unless you speculate that he wanted to rule in favor of popular opinion (yoga stays in district), but Meyer needed some evidence, as most of the facts were stacking up on our side.

MEYER: So is the District going to, at some point, indicate a way to avoid that issue with Jois (referring to Lemon case)? Do you understand what I'm saying? You're nodding (looking at Broyles) but you're the one that should be nodding (looking at Miyashiro). That would help the court perhaps a great deal.

MIYASHIRO: Yeah, so I can address that.

JUDGE MEYER: No, No. I'm just—I've got to make a difficult call here. And, you know, I think there are issues that are relevant and issues that are not. This one I think is relevant. (p. 123).

"Judge Meyer will rule with popular opinion"

Near the end of the day, Judge Meyer looked straight at the district lawyers and Superintendent Timothy Baird sitting with them and stated *"it's pretty obvious how I have to rule unless you pull something out of your hat tomorrow."* We saw this incredulous statement being made, and understood many facts to be on our side, but we also knew something else about the judge. Historically, he chooses popular opinion, according to a source that came two months prior, so we were only cautiously optimistic at that point.

I say cautiously optimistic because of this insight into the judge's potential decision from a lawyer in the community, who knew the judge. I met this attorney while I was standing at a table offering information on the yoga trial on a Sunday at our church. He approached the table and asked who our judge was for the trial. When I responded "Judge John Meyer," he shot back that our judge would rule against us due to popular opinion. That was in April, one month before trial began. At the time, I tucked that into my head as *interesting information…*

Back to the training *(or workshop…)*

Steve Regur (Regur Development Group), Miyashiro (EUSD), Russell Case (Jois Foundation) ran a *workshop*. During the second part of the trial, Baird and Miyashiro renamed it *"a workshop" to downplay that it was a training and recruitment program. EUSD was essentially trying to get distance from the word "certification" because to "certify" yoga instructors would presumably be different than giving them a "workshop."* So, Regur, Miyashiro and Case took 20-22 experienced yoga instructors "to train them in what it would be like to teach to kids" (in July 2012 – p. 129). The purpose was to recruit and interview candidates. Regur was there for the employee payroll aspects (fingerprinting, screening and paying), and Case was there as "the yoga expert" (p. 132). The judge asked if this was "the fabulous guy" but Miyashiro responded no that Gene Ruffin was the fabulous guy, but that this guy (Case) was fabulous too. Then the judge catches himself and says "I'm sorry, this is pretty critical testimony and I want to make sure I get it right."

During the *training (and decision which 10 yoga teachers to hire)* the three men whittled the 20-22 yoga teachers down to 12, then Baird, Miyashiro, and 8 of the 9 principals together interviewed all 12 and chose 9 for the schools. All nine began work a month later in the EUSD district teaching yoga (plus Jen Brown makes 10). All were paid through Regur from the Jois Foundation grant, as consultants for 40 hour work weeks, and began their Friday meetings (1pm – 3pm) for developing yoga curriculum (pp. 135-138).

Miyashiro's testimony does not match Jen Brown's in that he claims three of the yoga teachers formerly taught PE in the district and one was a science teacher, while Brown said two were teachers and one was PE. They go back and forth about how the teachers were trained and Miyashiro begins claiming they didn't really follow the grant in their "workshop," but the judge stops him and says:

JUDGE - The Grant Proposal says, "This program will be taught by certified yoga instructors selected and hired by the District and trained by Jois Foundation teachers" (p. 140). And the judge pointed this out because Carelli was asking questions leading Miyashiro into testifying that the program wasn't taught by certified yoga instructors, weren't hired by the district, and weren't trained by Jois Foundation teachers –- which is ALL in the grant! Remember, Jois Foundation does nothing but Ashtanga yoga!

Changing stories, conflicting with other testimony

The judge further catches Miyashiro when he is stating that they "ended up" not following the grant, but wait, says the judge "the grant is dated July 24th" which is AFTER you did the *workshop*, so how can it be incorrect?" (Day 4, p. 124) To which Miyashiro stands firm that they had no tie to Jois nor to Ashtanga yoga, even though that wording is in the grant proposal, and the grant, and even though most of the teachers were Jois trained and certified (even some from the district had the 3 years of Ashtanga requirements on Jois advertising these EUSD positions – screenshots on our website available). Miyashiro was knowingly leading the judge to think that these teachers had less Jois experience. For example, one of the "PE teachers," as he refers to her in the district, also had 3 years' experience teaching at the Jois shala. I know that for a fact because I knew her before this trial. Miyashiro led the judge to hear that Jois Foundation had a lot less to do with the hiring, training and influence from Russell Case, from Gene Ruffin, from Jen Brown, and from all the other Ashtanga-experienced teachers giving input

213

into the curriculum weekly as the experts. While Leslie Wright "wrote the curriculum" – wasn't it really based on the expert advice from the yoga teachers who, for the majority, had Ashtanga experiences (up to p. 152)?

Then the judge asked more about the curriculum and the qualifications of teachers if they needed to hire again? The judge moves into asking about other components Miyashiro referred to, and one is gardening. Meyer draws out that now the district has a garden at each of the 9 schools (p. 160-162). Some of the gardens take up quite a large chunk of what used to be space used for PE such as Flora Vista where the baseball fields were taken out and gardens now grow.

To point out a little clearer how Miyashiro's comments misled the judge – as evidenced by yet another example on page 162:

MIYASHIRO – So it was at a public school board meeting, and *a couple parents* came and said some of the things I just said, untrue statements, regarding the health and wellness program that we had, specifically the yoga class.

(So, although over 60 parents attended the meeting, Miyashiro called it a "couple parents." Seven parents spoke which is all that is allowed in the timeframe of 15 minutes per subject at a District meeting (while others clapped and made noises to show their opinions matched those speaking), and he claims here that only *a couple* parents came. A couple in Webster's definition is 2. This is a clear example of Miyashiro attempting to mislead the judge).

Miyashiro no doubt recalls there were more than two parents, so the question becomes, why is there a need to mislead the judge? Why not state that there were several or many people? Why a need to mislead if there is no problem with the yoga in the district?

The next topic the Judge picks up on though. Miyashiro goes into having pastors come to check out the program, and the judge starts wondering why they would do that if they think it's not religious? (p. 167, 168) The humor begins again:

THE COURT: You understand why. It's an interesting – of all the people to say it's not religious, why have a pastor?

THE WITNESS: He's just one of the various people that -

THE COURT: You have a pastor, a priest and a Rabbi –

(Laughter.)

THE WITNESS: and a professional Baseball Player.

Then Miyashiro takes it to a new level and even says that they didn't take things out of the program like Namaste or anything beyond Sanskit (p. 173, 174). The judge doesn't buy it and points out to him that testimony has been established that there were many things happening in the schools and that testimony from district (meaning Baird) was that they cleaned up parts and took out all Sanskrit and Namaste and lotus and chanting. On page 176, Miyashiro refers to "some of the yoga he has taken," showing that he himself is a yogi practitioner, and he calls three of the teachers *"experts on Ashtanga"* (Christina Reich, Jen Brown and Erin Kuntz (p. 177).

Cross-Examination of Miyashiro by Broyles starts p. 182 and takes an excruciating amount of time to ask questions due to the redirections and questions of the judge and other attorneys and the argumentative style of Miyashiro's answers. See for yourself the notes if you'd like, but it was a long, drawn-out experience to get just a few simple questions answered. Bravo to Dean for hanging in there in a tough, tough group of people and case! Basically, Broyles was establishing that Miyashiro was in charge of the yoga teachers and curriculum and that he didn't have prior knowledge of any religiousness about Ashtanga or any other yoga, and after his research on the Internet and other places, Miyashiro has concluded all yoga is not religious and that the yoga at EUSD never had anything even slightly ("not even a sliver" he quotes) of religious in it.

MR. BROYLES: You're one of the stars in the core video clips, right? *(The video for Jois and EUSD containing many district employees and Jois Foundation employees promoting Ashtanga yoga).* You testify quite a bit in there, right?

MIYASHIRO: I talk about the program.

MR. BROYLES: Okay. And have you actually watched the videos that were produced?

MIYASHIRO: Yes (p. 204).

BROYLES: Are you aware that the videos actually show children in the full lotus position with their fingers like this in the Juana Mudra, not doing brain highways, as you said?

MIYASHIRO: I don't recall that, no.

BROYLES: Would that surprise you, sir?

MIYASHIRO: Yes.

BROYLES: Why?

MIYASHIRO: Because in the curriculum that we wrote, we developed, one of the teacher's input was, "I have done some training with Brain Highways and then to connect the fingers through this posture would be a good way to activate certain areas of the brain."

BROYLES: Are you aware that being in the Lotus with your fingers done in Jnana Mudra circle is a way to channel spiritual energy, according to Ashtanga Yoga?

MR. CARELLI: Objection. Lacks Foundation.

Now you, after reading this far, know as well as I do that second finger and thumb together done in the lotus position means something to yogis (whether they think of it as channeling the energy or not), that they all do this pose, and that this pose was not only role-modeled for the children of EUSD, but children are doing it in the EUSD yoga video and now Miyashiro is claiming that it's all due to one teacher who helped special needs kids with brain highways. This is yet another example of covering up the truth. He knows what it is; we can safely assume that, given his research and that he is an apparently bright man who has studied what yoga is by this point in time. He has certainly run across this pose. If not, my mistake, he is just telling the truth and does not know. I don't believe it for a second though, and I can give you about 20 more examples, but for space and time I'll leave it at the few I've given you to show how amusing court can be, particularly when a witness appears to be skating around the truth – there becomes a lot of slippery ice once you start, and some of the ice gets very thin.

Next, Broyles establishes Miyashiro's relationship with John Campbell of UVA [who was supposed to be doing one of the two studies at University of Virginia – but that study never happened due to some unknown reasons never announced to district parents (pp. 207, 208)]. Right after Miyashiro states that John Campbell wasn't involved, he mentions meeting Campbell once and talking a couple times. [Of course, we cannot be sure what Miyashiro means by a "couple" now. It could be 60, as in the instance of how many parents came to the board meeting…]. I doubt they talked 60 times, but just pointing out the slippery slope of comments that can come back to bite you.

BROYLES: Are you aware that Russell Case indicated in a radio interview several months ago that John Campbell was a curriculum consultant regarding the EUSD on-the-mat curriculum? (p. 206)

BROYLES: It also says you led and were in direct supervision of research study conducted by the University of San Diego and the University of Virginia; is that correct?

MIYASHIRO: The Researchers did the research study. I was the point person for communications (p. 207).

BROYLES: Let me be specific. As of Early March of 2013, this year, were you aware that EUSD students participated in the seminar here in San Diego called "Teaching Ashtanga Yoga to children, with special guest Manju Jois." Are you aware of that?

MR. CARELLI: Objection. Assumes facts not in evidence (p. 211).

THE COURT: Overruled.

THE WITNESS: I'm not aware of that.

MR. BROYLES: Okay. You don't deny that Jen Brown is one of your teachers, do you?

MIYASHIRO: No. She is great.

MR. BROYLES: She actually teaches yoga in the District, correct?

MIYASHIRO: Yes.

MR. BROYLES: So do you consider Jen Brown an employee of the district or an employee of the Jois Foundation?

MIYASHIRO: She is an employee of Regur Development Group.

MR. BROYLES: Do you have any idea why she was represented on a seminar calendar as a Jois Foundation teacher?

MR. CARELLI: Objection. Hearsay. Assumes facts not in evidence.

THE COURT: Do you know what he is referring to?

MIYASHIRO: I don't know what he is referring to.

MR. BROYLES: Is Jen Brown a Jois Foundation teacher, to your knowledge?

MR. CARELLI: Objection. Asked and Answered.

THE COURT: Do you know?

MIYASHIRO: I know she has a role. I am not sure what she does beyond the scope of what she does with our school district.

Again, Miyashiro knows that she is a Jois yoga shala teacher as she even said so herself in testimony that he claims to have been present for the entire time, and yet, he continues to act like he doesn't know what she does. And it doesn't even matter if he knew or not; she did work for both, but the District was trying everything they could to distance themselves from the very Jois people sitting (Gene Ruffin) in the courtroom. But they could not, due to the overwhelming number of facts showing the relationships, involvements and influence. That is why the judge stated that the EUSD and Jois Foundation relationship was "troubling" even though he may not be willing to judge it Entanglement. *Entanglement on steroids* was the term Dean Broyles mentioned in the halls of the courtroom.

Another example of the use of the word Ashtanga in a document: Broyles shows that in the FAQ that Baird wrote in November/December timeframe (which was well after August where Miyashiro now claims they weren't doing Ashtanga yoga).

BROYLES: Does this appear to be the FAQ written by Dr. Baird?

MIYASHIRO: Yes.

BROYLES: Okay. The first question – The question is "how is the District funding the program?" There is an A, B, C Answer. Answer B says, "All yoga instructors will be certified by Jois to ensure that they meet a high level of instructional quality." Do you see that, sir?

MIYASHIRO: Yes.

BROYLES: These FAQS were written and published sometime in October or November of 2012; Is that not correct? Do you see that, sir?

MIYASHIRO: Yes.

BROYLES: These FAQS were written and published sometime in October or November of 2012; is that not correct?

MIYASHIRO: I don't remember exactly when.

BROYLES: But they were after the yoga program had actually started in the District, correct?

MIYASHIRO: YES. (p. 214)

And in fact, the FAQ was in response (Baird's testimony) to parent concerns about the yoga program, so here we have in the fall of 2012 where Baird still claims Jois had a part of the oversight, and it isn't until a lawsuit is filed that he begins to separate EUSD from Jois "in his language" and clearly briefed all district witnesses to do this (or they somehow started to do that – Jen Brown, Carrie Brown, and David Miyashiro). The only problem is that the entanglement went too deep. Jen Brown working for both is enough, but the relationships between Baird and Himelstein and Ruffin and Miyashiro and Case and the videos, just prove that the cover-up wasn't possible forever. It may have fooled this judge at the time, but probably everyone in the room knew what was going on, and if they really didn't suspect foul play before, they might have an idea now.

So, the covering up of facts by the district witnesses, was not some theory, it was a conspiring of people all right. The judge acted like he was seeing through it. His comments led us to believe he was well aware of the reality that Jois was involved, and the district was doing a form of Ashtanga in the opening sequences and primary series and closing lotus and rest poses. For example on page 216 one of Meyer's comments was:

THE COURT: So I don't – I am wondering what you (Miyashiro) mean by your word "feedback." That makes it sound like Jois has their hand on this whole program to make sure that it operates the way they want it to (P. 216).

Miyashiro throws Baird's testimony under the bus, in order to attempt, again, to camouflage the issue with the court. Here he directly opposes Baird's testimony:

BROYLES: Did you hear Superintendent Baird testify that the teachers were in fact trained and certified by Jois?

MIYASHIRO: No. (But he was in the room).

BROYLES: Okay. So you didn't hear him say that?

MIYASHIRO: No.

THE COURT: If he did say it, it's wrong?

MIYASHIRO: It's wrong. There was no training or certification by Jois Foundation or Jois People.

> *Don't miss that this is why he called it "a little workshop" in the summer weeklong process of interviewing and selecting candidates. They were actually training the women to teach in a school environment, but he becomes careful not to use the word "teaching" or "training" or "certifying."*

THE COURT: Jois teachers?

MIYASHIRO: Jois teachers.

THE COURT: Anybody?

MIYASHIRO: No.

THE COURT: Yes, What I said was correct?

MIYASHIRO: That's correct. (p. 223)

Later on p. 226 Miyashiro concedes to knowing that Jen Brown does indeed work for Jois yoga for some percentage of time, and that he even has to fill in her teaching spot on that day at her school.

So, that concludes the testimony of Miyashiro. He then leaves the district taking Ashtanga yoga with him, and begins a contract with Jois for $500K in his new district in Cajon Valley schools just months later. Off and running into another set of schools with "EUSD curriculum," as he testified?

After testimony for the day, the judge claimed he had a "difficult call to make."

Media Trial Day 4:

- Parents testify, NBC News: http://www.nbclosangeles.com/news/california/Parents-Testify-in-Encinitas-Yoga-Class-Trial-213042641.html. [3]
- Blog site – Sian Welch: http://truthaboutyoga.blogspot.com/. [4]

CHAPTER ELEVEN

Trial Day 5 – June 25, 2013

Day 5 Agenda: Closing Arguments

Sedlock v. EUSD Trial Transcript Day 5 — June 25, 2013:
https://truthaboutyoga.files.wordpress.com/2015/01/13-06-25-part-01final.pdf[1]

One thing we didn't know when we decided to file to remove yoga out of the schools is that the filing family needed to have a young plaintiff because of how long cases can take in court. Many of the families had older children in 5th or 6th grade that might not still be in the district if this case dragged on to the appellate and supreme court levels. Once the children graduate 6th grade, they leave the Encinitas district, and the case would have to be dropped. Ironically, our daughter turned 8 on this 5th day of trial. She was only in 2nd grade, so we had plenty of time that other families would not. Rather than spend this summer day with her for her birthday, though, we were in court listening to closing arguments.

Broyles - Closing Arguments

Yesterday closed with Broyles stating he had about 2 hours of closing, Sleeth one hour, Judge Meyer wanted 30 minutes and Peck (who referred to himself as the potted plant again) needed about 20-30 min. That is of course, once again, *not what happened…*

Here is a summary of points of concern from Broyles in his Closing Arguments:

- **BROYLES:** "We are concerned with the precedent set when a religious organization, such as the Jois Foundation, gains access to an elementary school district to influence curriculum based on grants given to the district" (Day 5, p. 3).
- **BROYLES:** "The slant to try to make the yoga program look 'scientific' by the wording of the study was concerning because the basis was simply answers and opinions of children. So five and six-years-olds answers to probably biased questions, become the basis to allow a wealthy and religious foundation like Jois Foundation to take the yoga program nationwide with curriculum created – does that seem like a wise basis of information?"
- **BROYLES:** "This case was *not* about whether one liked yoga, or not. It was not even about whether it was beneficial in any way, or not, or whether it was popular."
- **BROYLES:** "Jois Foundation and EUSD partnership violates the Law of Lemon Test (p. 4) by entangling EUSD with religion."
- **BROYLES:** "We had asked the court for a writ mandate to stop the program right away based on the 1st and 14th Amendments. The establishment clause has come to mean that the government may not promote or affiliate itself with any religious doctrine or organization, may not discriminate among persons on the basis of their religious beliefs and practices, and may not delegate the governmental power to a religious institution, and may not involve itself too deeply in such an institution's affairs."
- Broyles touched on practice based religions vs. knowledge based (p. 8, 9).
- The Meyers case lays foundation in Supreme Court that the Judge (who also happens to be a Meyer) here need not delve into whether he believes in any of the actual beliefs (in Ashtanga), but the question whether the beliefs involved are objectively religious. Broyles goes on in-depth referring to this case and defining Ashtanga yoga.
- **BROYLES:** "In the *Malnak versus Yogi* case, there was a teaching of transcendental meditation based in Hinduism

in the public schools, which violated the establishment clause" (p. 11).

Specifics of Ashtanga

- Broyles covers the 8 limbs that define Ashtanga yoga and how they are about *relating in the world* and the belief attached to each.
- Many factors that make up a religion are covered, referring to the Meyers case and various aspects to religion such as who are the leaders, what the texts or beliefs are and where they come from, the holidays, rituals, and organization of structuring them. Then he leads into why Ashtanga fits into the definition of religion and rituals.
- Broyles covers specifically how Ashtanga yoga is religious (p. 21) from the founder (Guru K.P. Jois) to the text (Upanishads and Bhagavad Gita) to the special gathering place (Mysore, India) ceremonies, rituals (pujas), specific liturgical sequences of Sun Worship, (Sequence A and B), and again, there is no Ashtanga without the opening sequence so that is why it is more than a physical pose, and why the District is unable to cut that part out of the program, since Jois is granting them money to do specifically Ashtanga and the documents reflect that commitment.
- **BROYLES:** "So this is more than a physical pose, your Honor (p. 24). This is religious worship, prayer and religious liturgy. Sharath Jois, the grandson of P.K. Jois, teaches," quote: "Our Surya Namaskara A and B were created by Pattabhi Jois for two reasons: To pray to the sun god each morning would ensure good health and because most of us cannot correctly understand the svara, the up-and-down proper pronunciation of vedic chants. We should not recite them. The Surya Namaskara A and B is an easier prayer or salute to the sun god."
- Broyles describes the mudras in detail (p. 25 and 26) and how they are channeling to union with the divine.

- Regarding ceremonies and rituals, the whole philosophy of Jois yoga and Ashtanga yoga is that you just teach the practices or the asanas, the postures, and that will lead people to all eight limbs of Ashtanga. Pattabhi Jois said, "The reason we do yoga is to become one with God and to realize him in our hearts. You can lecture, you can talk about God, but when you practice correctly, you come to experience God inside. Some people start yoga and don't even know him, don't even want to know him. But for anyone who practices yoga correctly, the love of God will develop. And after some time, a greater love for God will be theirs whether they want it or not." That is a quote from P.K. Jois himself (p. 26).

Why Children and "Scientific" Approach

- Broyles continues into how (Professor) Brown explained why Jois selected children, because the process of transformation of thought takes time. You start with the asanas (poses) and over time, years later, move into higher levels of practice, but along the way, change eating habits (as they are teaching along with yoga and building gardens, taking meat out of school days, etc. pp. 29, 30).
- Broyles touches on the evidence of propaganda of appearing "scientific" in order to push into the schools and "camouflage" the religious components. He points out that, as in the Meyers case, we are not asking this Judge Meyer to deem yoga religious or not because prior cases have established this. This case revolves around whether elementary-aged students should be led to participate in weekly yoga curriculum during the regular school days, as opposed to an optional elective, or after school hours program (pp. 32, 33).
- **BROYLES:** "There is a direct and inextricable connection between yoga and the religion of Hinduism. That link has even been affirmed in several other cases. In the case of

Powell versus Berry, the Court found, quote, "Yoga is a method of practicing Hinduism through which the follower seeks to achieve the ultimate state of oneness with the universe." If that's not Ashtanga yoga, I don't know what is, your Honor. The *Cotton versus Cate* case affirmed it again (p. 34)."

- **BROYLES:** "The final case I'll mention, your Honor, is *Garvins versus Burnett*. And the Court said there: "Defendant Vilgos explained further that Buddhism and yoga have many common practices, such as postures, meditations, and beliefs in reincarnation and karma, but they are separate religions." If you notice there, the Court is not saying that Hinduism is a separate religion from yoga. It's saying yoga is a separate religion from Buddhism (p. 34)."

- **BROYLES:** "Okay. So the third point is that the core foundation of the program, according to the grant that was incorporated into the MOU as Exhibit A, as testified to by Dr. Miyashiro yesterday, the core foundation of the program was, quote, 'Ashtanga yoga.'"

Judge Meyer Asks Questions

THE COURT: But that was clearly addressed yesterday, and that's – that was denied, denied, denied.

BROYLES: For the first time yesterday.

THE COURT: Okay. All right.

BROYLES: I just wanted to point out. He tried to throw all the documents under the bus, and I'll talk about that more later.

THE COURT: He didn't try. He did.

BROYLES: Yeah, he effectively said that, "Don't look at what was actually in writing, what we signed off on, what we agreed to as a contract." They said, "Throw it all aside and believe me" on the last day of trial.

THE COURT: That's what he said.

BROYLES: Yeah.

THE COURT: He said that, "That is wrong, and don't believe what it says. It should have been changed in writing, but it wasn't because we were too busy." But he said it's not Ashtanga yoga. He said that the teachers were not certified by Jois. The teachers were not trained by Jois. That's what he said.

BROYLES: And I just want to point out that that contradicts many other witnesses who testified about those issues that you just mentioned, including Dr. Baird. He flatly contradicted Dr. Baird on several points yesterday. But I just want to point out that if there's a dispute between who's telling the truth, I think we need to look at the documents, your Honor. We need to look at the actual evidence, what they signed (p. 37).

If it isn't Ashtanga, is just yoga okay?

- They spend up to p. 51 going over documents that prove EUSD was teaching Ashtanga yoga, as well as testimony from Jen Brown, and Miyashiro confirming it. Then the judge asks whether yoga would be acceptable in the schools if it wasn't Ashtanga yoga. Broyles points to the fact that several courts have decided yoga is religious and so yes, it would still be unacceptable (p. 58).
- Broyles points to Jen Brown's testimony frequently for the proof they are teaching the elements of Ashtanga (Sun Salutations, opening sequences, jnana mudra with lotus, etc. - 60's pages) and took direct quotes from the EUSD yoga curriculum such as the following (p. 69): The

228

EUSD curriculum includes not just physical, but explicitly religious goals. For example, "The yoga students will connect more deeply with their inner selves, and yoga will bring the inner spirit of each child to the surface." Those are direct quotes, your Honor, out of the November 2012 curriculum, Grades K through 1, Session No. 1. That's our plaintiffs' trial exhibit.

- **BROYLES:** "So a lot – there's some confusion between what they said in court, and what the videos actually show as far as the renaming of poses, okay? And it always finishes with the four lotuses, as we discussed in court, and the resting corpse or shavasana pose. There's still the jnana mudra being performed with the praying hands position, the anjali mudra, which is putting the thumb and forefinger together in the lotus position. That's shown explicitly in the videos presented to this Court. The children are still chanting "om," and they're praying while meditating in the lotus position. There are still Sanskrit terms being used" (p 72).

- **BROYLES:** "More about curriculum, Jen Brown's testimony and the elements of Ashtanga that are religious and should not be in public schools (pp -80's) showing it is still in the curriculum, on the latest videos, and happening in the classrooms regardless what the district staff is saying "is not taught" – kids are learning it and doing it. What no one mentioned is role-modeling which I find interesting because as Jen Brown states she didn't teach jnana mudra, but she did do it herself in classes. Doing something, especially physically where children are to do the moves as you do the moves, then whether you say something out loud is not as important as if you role model it. So if a child sees you chant om, even once, they learn that it goes along with the lotus, the finger/thumb and the chant. And add closing the eyes, which is clear in the video as well."

- **BROYLES:** "Dr. Miyashiro's last minute desperate attempt yesterday to salvage the sinking yoga program by trying to claim that the terms of the Jois MOU, the grant proposal, Exhibit A to the MOU, and the RDG MOU were not actually followed, and were virtual toilet paper and they didn't matter, and they should have been changed. Really, his claims yesterday should strain the credulity of this Court because he was the first one to throw all those agreements under the bus on the last day of trial. Why? Because they showed the inextricable link between the Jois Foundation and EUSD and the massive entanglement that exists between the parties, that I'll talk about in a moment. I also wanted to point out again just to remind the Court that Miyashiro's testimony yesterday contradicted the documents in this case and the testimony of most of the other witnesses, including his boss, the superintendent" (p. 97).

When is *Enough* Religion "Stripped Out?"

- **BROYLES:** "And the question I asked rhetorically and I really have been asking myself from the first board meeting that I attended in this case is; who decides when enough religion has been stripped from the program? Certainly not Dr. Baird, not Dr. Miyashiro, Jen Brown, none of them are qualified, your Honor, to decide when enough Hindu religion or Ashtanga has been stripped from the program. No one was qualified to make that determination in this case except perhaps Dr. Brown the expert witness. None of those in charge of the program are religious studies experts, and all of them are, in fact, in complete denial that Ashtanga yoga or any yoga, for that matter, is religious at all. So why are we trusting them as the gatekeepers – why do we trust them to be able to "take religion out of" a program they deny is religious in the first place? It's absurd" (p. 98).
- **BROYLES:** "Now, I want to get into specifically the law, your Honor. And here I want to refer to a case that you referenced yesterday. And that's Lee versus Weisman. And it says here under the establishment clause, quote, and "The Constitution guarantees that the government may not coerce

anyone to support or participate in religion or its exercise or otherwise act in a way which establishes a state religion or religious faith or tends to do so. Lee versus Weisman, as your Honor probably knows, was a graduation prayer case where the superintendent had selected – asked a rabbi to come and pray and had given them guidelines for prayer and asked them to pray in a graduation case – in a graduation ceremony. And that practice by itself, simple once-a-year deal at graduation practice – at graduation, was struck down as a violation of the establishment clause. And the Court said here, "Even if students are not actively coerced to participate, they face subtle core or subtle pressure, as well as, peer pressure to participate passively." And then, quote, "This pressure, though subtle and indirect, can be as real as any overt compulsion." If that's true at the high school and middle school level, it's certainly true that peer pressure applies to younger children, your Honor" (p. 99).

More Case Law after Lunch

- Broyles then moves into the divisiveness in the district and the coercion to conform (p. 102). "Dr. Miyashiro praised that, and yet what he's, in effect, praising is subtle peer pressure on the kids who are opting-out of the program. It's inappropriate. There are just a slew of misrepresentations in this case that have come out from the superintendent, from principals, and from yoga teachers. They've said over and over and over again that the program is not religious. So the implication there, if the program is not religious, is that it's silly to object to it, it's silly to opt-out of it, and it's actually alright to participate, okay? That's the implication there. So they're implying that the parents and students who object are just being ridiculous. 'I mean, if it's not religious, why would you opt-out? I mean, are you crazy? I mean, are you a nut job?' I mean, that was implied by the opening statement by David Peck, that these parents were crazy nut jobs, you know, extremists because they wanted to opt their kids out of the program" (pp. 106, 107).

- **MR. BROYLES:** Entanglement between the State and the religious speaker. Because in Lee, the facts were simply they invited a rabbi to come and pray at the end of a graduation ceremony, and they simply handed him a non-denominational prayer guideline. That's all they did. And yet the Court in that case said this was entanglement. *If that was entanglement, your Honor – this case is entanglement on steroids* (p. 110).

- **MR. BROYLES:** Actually, you don't, your Honor. If you look at – if you look at the Lee versus Weisman case or if you even look at Lemon, the case you mentioned yesterday, Lemon only found that they were excessively entangled with religion. They didn't address whether they had –

THE COURT: I understand that. I'm just saying Prong No. 1 –

MR. BROYLES: I'm not disputing it.

THE COURT: Right, and I don't – I'm not – I'm not inclined to find otherwise.

MR. BROYLES: Yeah. Okay. Yeah. And so I'll – we'll put that aside for now.

THE COURT: Okay.

MR. BROYLES: So just again, I want to be clear, if a challenged government action fails any of the three requirements –

THE COURT: Right.

MR. BROYLES: – so we don't need to win on 1, 2, and 3 or even 2 and 3. We only need to win on one of these prongs, your Honor, to prevail. That's the point I'm making here. So what are the Lemon violations in EUSD's program? Well, first of all, it advances and inhibits religion, Prong 2 of Lemon. It also excessively entangles EUSD with religion, Prong 3 and is, therefore, unconstitutional in violation of the establishment clause. I'm going to go through Prong 2 and Prong 3 one by one now, your Honor (p 116).

- They go on and on for pages about reasonable knowledge of a child, or a hypothetical child, and which are the standard, etc., to page 140!
- We finally get to the 3rd prong of the case for entanglement: Broyles – "We can throw away even Prong 2 and still prevail on this case. And that is the issue of excessive government entanglement with religion. The EUSD program, according to *Lemon versus Kurtzman*, the third prong, must not foster an excessive government entanglement with religion (p. 140).
- **BROYLES:** "In the *Sands versus Morongo case*, the Court, interpreting these provisions in California constitutional provisions, as your Honor pointed out earlier, stated that, 'State supervision of religious beliefs and practices is fundamentally inconsistent with the concept of the separation of religion and civil authority. Specific practices which pose an intolerable risk of excessive government entanglement with religion include State inspection and evaluation of the religious content of speech.'
  That's exactly what we have in our case, your Honor.
  EUSD's Ashtanga yoga program excessively entangles the district with religion in precisely the very same two ways forbidden by the California Supreme Court in Sands and the U.S. Supreme Court in *Lee versus Weisman*. EUSD's program involves improper governmental selection and approval of, number one, religious speakers, Jois Foundation trained and certified Ashtanga yoga teachers; and two, the content of religious speech they communicate, the Ashtanga yoga curriculum. The yoga program involved EUSD in an ongoing extremely entangled partnership with a religious organization, Jois, regarding a religious program with religious goals. This is where I said earlier we'd get

to religious entanglement on steroids, as I call it" (p. 140). He goes on to further explain the many relationships that entangle EUSD to Jois Foundation. (Ruffin, Himelstein, Regur, Case, Brown, etc.).

- **BROYLES:** "Number two, EUSD violated Sands-Weisman entanglement principles by controlling and changing the content of the religious speech, the religious yoga curriculum. Here's a quote from the FAQ: 'The district is writing the curriculum being developed.' Miyashiro and Baird – Baird attended approximately four to five of these Friday weekly yoga training meetings. They actively developed the religious curriculum and directed religious curriculum changes on an ongoing basis, even to within a few weeks before this court occurred. And they may have ongoing changes to the curriculum we don't even know about yet. They also were working again with Jois-trained and certified Ashtanga yoga teachers." (p. 146) The judge just keeps arguing moot points, already in evidence over and over, as if to badger Broyles, but perhaps he really didn't understand, or remember. Still, he has all the documentation to go back to; he doesn't need to keep on arguing with Dean Broyles over and over. It's quite a hoot to read the circles over and over of the judge asking the same questions. One could speculate many reasons he did it and in hindsight the question becomes: *was he trying to find ways to refute the evidence? And if so, why?*

Jois Foundation Involved with Hiring and Training or Not?

- The judge continues to question and one question was about Jois stepping out after initial hiring, and yet, Jois representatives were there in the courtroom, so why? Doesn't the judge see that they are there (still entangled) for a reason, other than just selling them their yoga, or rather, giving them a grant to do something else – to make up

234

their own yoga? A far-fetched idea that the judge will hang his hat onto later? Would anyone give over $4 million to promote something other than what they care about? And couldn't EUSD yoga become a competitor curriculum if they weren't contracted to give it to them? (p. 151).

- **BROYLES:** "And as said earlier by Dr. Baird in testimony, the purpose of Jois was to take that curriculum and run with it nationally. And Dr. Baird has actually appeared in some videos on behalf of the Jois Foundation. So therefore, the curriculum is being developed primarily, not just for the students at EUSD, but for Jois' future sales and marketing purposes, another example of entanglement. So they have an interest in how that curriculum is developed, and how that curriculum turns out. EUSD's superintendent Baird admitted to appearing in promotional videos, as I said earlier, for the Jois Foundation *and* public schools" (p. 152).

- **BROYLES:** "Instructors at EUSD must be certified and trained by Jois. The curriculum at EUSD is based on Guruji's or Ashtanga yoga based beliefs and practices and is being actively developed by Jois-trained teachers. The beliefs and practices promoted by the curriculum are based in well-established Hindu religious beliefs and practices such as concentration, breathing, Eastern meditation, mantras, asana, samadhi – which means bliss or union with the divine. EUSD's aid in the promotion of yoga and Ashtanga yoga in particular, excessively entangles the district with religion. Also, the Court in Malnak determined that *SCI TM* (a Hindu monk founded SCI TM – Science Translational Medicine) was, in fact, a religious teaching based mainly on its analysis of the textbook which, while it did not mention God or any deity, spoke in spiritual terms of the creation of the universe, the ultimate goals of human existence, and asserted SCI TM to be an exclusive moral teaching dedicated to creating a society of fellow believers" (p. 155, 156).

235

Broyles Wrapping Up / Closing

"Here in our case, your Honor, Dr. Brown's un-contradicted expert testimony that EUSD's yoga program is religious, including spiritual terms and meanings that are pervasively religious like "namaste," the moral teachings of yamas and niyamas, the ultimate goal of human existence being Samadhi, union with the divine, et cetera. I won't rehash everything. In Malnak, the requirement that each student attend a traditional Hindu ceremony at which the student and the teacher recited prayers in Sanskrit praising various Hindu deities to whom they bowed down and offered presents, Candy Gunther Brown's – similarly in our case, Candy Gunther Brown's un-contradicted expert testimony about the curriculum and the program requiring students to engage in specific liturgical rituals which represent worship – this is according to Guruji himself – which represent worship, prayer, and bowing down to Hindu deities, and Sanskrit was also used before it was removed from the classroom. Here's another important comparison. That's – the disingenuousness of these SCI TM defendants and their efforts to deny the religious nature of their practice. In our case, your Honor, Dr. Brown's un-contradicted expert testimony about the disingenuousness of Jois' and EUSD's efforts to deny the religious nature of their practice. There's extensive evidence in this case of trying to hide or attempting to hide by cosmetic changes a pervasively religious program by re-naming poses and removing purportedly "cultural" references. For example, in this case Jen Brown said she never learned or taught anything that was religious, yet she chanted Hindu texts, sacred text like the Bhagavad Gita, the vedas, and Sanskrit. She tried to deny, for example, that the lotus was really the lotus calling it "criss-cross applesauce" over and over again, and yet we know that the lotus is the lotus and it's not criss-cross applesauce like I learned back in kindergarten. The circumstances of our case involving EUSD are even more constitutionally problematic than Malnak, however, because Malnak involved older students at the high school level and the TM course there was an elective; okay, it was a true elective as opposed to part of the regular curriculum as Ashtanga yoga here at EUSD schools" (pp. 157,158).

Broyles asks for consideration of parents who are opted-out of EUSD yoga who are universally reporting they are missing PE minutes (in declarations and testimony) to issue the writ to make sure the district gives them all 200 minutes every 10 days.

He concludes with: "We, as the petitioners, request a writ of mandate or injunction ordering EUSD to stop teaching yoga, prohibit the EUSD yoga-based health and wellness program, which is in violation of California and Federal Constitutions' religious freedom provisions. Going forward, permanently enjoin or order EUSD from implementing a yoga-based PE or health and wellness program, or any other religious-based PE program in the future. And then finally, order that all EUSD children are offered the mandatory minimum PE minutes of 200 PE minutes every ten days. In conclusion, your Honor, EUSD's Ashtanga yoga program violates the law because it violates the establishment clause in the California Constitution in that it both advances and endorses religion and inhibits and opposes other religions. It excessively entangles

EUSD with religion, and it fails to provide sufficient PE minutes to the kids who opt-out. Therefore, we ask the Court to respectfully issue a writ of mandate to order EUSD to stop teaching yoga to its students, and order the district to comply with the California minimum PE minutes requirements" (p. 171).

Jack Sleeth Closing Arguments

These will be summarized as well into bullet points of Sleeths' closing points:

- Sleeth begins with claiming the yoga program that is practiced at the Encinitas School District is not religious. It's not religious because it doesn't meet the test that's established in the State of California. It's similar to the test that counsel identified, but there's a little bit of difference in it. And I'm going to read the components and give the background here on the correct test, and then we'll talk about the facts. (p. 172). –So the California law that is effective on this decision whether or not this practice or belief is religious needs to use the test that is on Page 69 of *Freedman versus Southern California Permanente*. "First, religion addresses fundamental and ultimate questions having to do with deep and imponderable matters." (P. 175). Sleeth goes on to make the point that EUSD yoga is nothing but stretching and breathing and nothing more.

- **SLEETH:** "Now, I want to talk for a minute about un-contradicted evidence. Professor Brown testified to a lot of hearsay, which she's permitted to do as an expert. But the Court can accept or reject all of that hearsay information that she brought forward and accept or reject her opinion as the Court feels appropriate. The Court is somewhat more bound to listen to the testimony of the witnesses in this case and the other documents that were put before the Court, but an expert witness can be ignored by the Court if it thinks it's appropriate. I'm going to suggest that it's appropriate in this particular case because Dr. Brown – Professor Brown's position on these issues is inconsistent with State law and so extreme as to be preposterous" (p. 175).

Judge Meyer questions Sleeth

THE COURT: What about Malnak?

MR. SLEETH: What about Malnak? Transcendental meditation case where they said transcendental meditation that incorporated basic concepts of Hinduism, including deep and imponderable matters, of course it was a religion.

THE COURT: Okay.

MR. SLEETH: And Malnak is one of the cases that brought forward this particular set of tests here to determine if these new religious ideas, these nontheistic religious ideas, could have the protection of the 1st Amendment in the California Constitution in religion. So as we look through this, we have to ask this ultimate question thing: What does yoga do to answer ultimate questions? And the only way you get to that is if you listen to six hours of testimony from Professor Brown which incorporates the Jois website, which was never put in, which incorporates statements from Mr. Jois, and he was never subpoenaed to come here and testify (he's dead!). So, all of that hearsay is necessary in order to inform the yoga program, to get it to the point that you even think about it being religious. If you walk into the room, and you look at what people are doing in yoga, it looks like exercise. And if there are no words spoken about Hindu theological ideas, then there's no way to transmit meanings on issues of fundamental and ultimate questions. Now, I heard Professor Brown say that simply by doing the practice, doing this exercise in this ritualized way, in this sequence of events, you somehow start turning Hindu, I guess. You make a transferance, to a different philosophical belief.

THE COURT: Not right away.

MR. SLEETH: After a long, long time (pp. 176, 177).

THE COURT: Or are you saying that Dr. Brown made that up? Because I think that's a basis for her opinion. And the quoting teachings of Pattabhi Jois, who could be considered a holy man, where he said you go through this ritual of physical poses and you control your breathing and everything else that goes along with it and you will be beyond this continuum that ends up in becoming one with the divine, spiritual transformation.

MR. SLEETH: It seems to me that we have to teach that in the class or we're not matching the requirements of California law. It may be that Pattabhi Jois believed that. I don't believe it.

THE COURT: Apparently, he does. I think he does – or he did.

MR. SLEETH: I think he's dead now.

THE COURT: I think he believed it.

MR. SLEETH: He probably did believe it. I don't know if his grandson believes it. I don't know what the current Ashtanga- – whatever, the studio. You'll remember there is a studio – Jois studio and the Jois Foundation. The two things are separate. And while we're there, let me just get that. Jen Brown testified that she teaches at the shala, at the school, not that she works for the foundation. She testified to that. Jen Brown testified that five of the teachers that they hired had no Ashtanga background at all, and five did. So all of those ideas that somehow Jois is strapped into this thing is, first of all, wrong; but second of all, doesn't meet this test because those things weren't communicated to the students.

THE COURT: Let me ask you – I mentioned this before, and this is something that's somewhat troublesome. I don't think the evidence shows that the district is teaching religion; in other words, they're not proselytizing Hinduism or any other religion. And if you – if you assume for the sake of this argument that Ashtanga is religious, if the hypothetical reasonable student in the district doesn't have the wherewithal to know it's religious, in other words, as a hypothetical reasonable objective kid taking this class, he is of a mind that this is PE, this is stretching and doing something physical, but then because of the controversy over this or because of other kids whose parents practice yoga and who maybe have gone with them or understand what yoga is then start doing things that are religious or are told, you know, "This is Hinduism. You're going to become a Hindu. Do you know what a Hindu is?" and then start om'ing and doing this stuff, so then you have students who are learning – or who are connecting this with religion even though the district isn't preaching it or teaching it, what do you do with that? Do you understand my concern? (pp. 181, 182)

MR. SLEETH: I do understand. And I've been –

THE COURT: And then the district says, "Oh, we don't teach it. I don't know where they learned it." It's still an entanglement, isn't it? If the district is – if the district is opening the door to this dialog with these students, that's all they need to do. Once you open the door and you get these kids thinking, "Hey, Charlie told me this is religious" or to say to one of these kids, "Why don't you do this. This is cool," and they say, "Because it's religious. Because you'll become a Hindu" –

MR. SLEETH: I –

THE COURT: – "and that's not what I believe. I go to a different – I've got a different religion, and this is what I understand," and then you've got these kids – you know, it's like – it's like the kids that don't do a prayer in the '50s in school and they go to the principal's office because they're not of the faith and they get ostracized. And I mean that's what the district – by doing this PE class, the district has created exactly what they're saying – "We didn't do it." You understand? That's –

MR. SLEETH: I do understand.

THE COURT: That's of some concern (p. 183).

Jois Foundation Mission

THE COURT: Okay. But let me – you had said something – you said you don't care about Ashtanga yoga because this isn't Ashtanga yoga. Okay. But what we – at least what the petitioners would say the evidence shows is that the mission of Jois is to promote Ashtanga yoga and that if Ashtanga yoga is religious but if the district is not practicing or teaching Ashtanga yoga, you have the Lemon case almost to a T. The City – the State is paying public – or is paying parochial Catholic schools to teach secular subjects. So the schools that are getting the money say, "Oh, we don't teach religion. We're not teaching Catholicism. We're teaching secular subjects." And then the question is, "Well, who's teaching?" "Well, the nuns are. The Catholic nuns are teaching." (p. 186). That's all the Court needed. Now, what we know is there are ten instructors teaching district yoga, not Ashtanga yoga. But they're all certified by Jois. They've all been trained by Jois. They've gone – at least one of them has gone to India and taken Sanskrit. Not that there's anything wrong with that, but there's a real connection with Ashtanga yoga. And Jen Brown is kind of a – there's a connection between Jois Ashtanga yoga and the district. So she kind of keeps going back and forth. Now, how do you square that with Lemon that says, "We can't monitor the Catholic nuns. We don't trust them. They're Catholic believers. This is their faith. This is their job. This is their mission. Teaching secular subjects is fine, but there's a risk that they will be having some Catholic teaching inculcated with their secular teaching, and we don't trust the State" or in this case "the district to monitor it. And once they do, they're entangled"? p. 186

SLEETH responds by saying that the district employees are monitoring the teachers (and yet they are in rooms alone with the children, with no teaching credentials in most cases). He goes on to say that the distinction to the Malnak case is how the teachers are paid and how they are supervised.

EUSD brings in Pastor to decide if Yoga at EUSD looks Religious

THE COURT: If the object of yoga is to become yoked so that you become one with the divine, it probably is religious (p. 191).

SLEETH: I don't think we did that (p. 192).

THE COURT: You realize there's a certain irony in bringing in a pastor–

MR. SLEETH: I don't see that, your Honor (p. 194). The parents came to a board meeting and said, "You're teaching religion." So we went to the pastors of those parishioners (not true – see note) and said, "Come look at the program."

242

The irony is that the pastor they chose to ask was not "the pastors of those parishioners." They asked a pastor who was speaking up FOR yoga and authored a book stating that he sits in the gardens at the Self Realization Center to pray and read. In addition, he has a pastor in his church that does yoga in the SRC gardens. Does that sound like a pastor pro-yoga already?

The pastor of the parents filing holds the opposite view. Pastor Bob Botsford has been speaking out against yoga and idol worship for over a decade. Many pastors are just as confused about yoga as the rest of the world, so you can easily find pastors that agree or disagree with yoga. Why? Because yoga has effectively slid into our culture quietly without much fanfare by shifting the focus onto scientific ideas and targeting exercise to 'package and hide' some of the spiritual awakening that is the whole goal of it, at the core. That is why people from India and those that know what yoga unleashes are warning us, and why a book like this would even come into existence at this time. There are good reasons yoga is so divisive in the schools and churches.

The judge actually encourages a settlement on p. 199 stating "it's not too late" to Sleeth but Sleeth continues barely noticing and on p 205 Sleeth says that they are not advancing Christianity or Hinduism, but perhaps *advancing yoga*. Interestingly, note this for when the judge claims yoga is religious, which then would be EUSD advancing religion as per Sleeth right here.

The day ends with agreement that Sleeth had 30 more minutes, Peck 30 and Broyles 20-30. Judge Meyer said he probably wouldn't decide the case tomorrow. Maybe Thursday. And of course, that is not what happened either!

- EUSD's grant proposal to Jois Foundation: https://truthaboutyoga.files.wordpress.com/2015/01/jois-grant-2.pdf[2]

Media of Day 5

- Parents Testify in Yoga Trial June 25, 2013 NBC News: http://www.nbcsandiego.com/news/

local/Parents-Testify-in-Encinitas-Yoga-Class-Trial-212831061.html[3]
- Closing Arguments Underway, June 25, 2013 KPBS: http://www.kpbs.org/news/2013/jun/25/closing-arguments-begin-encinitas-yoga-trial/[4]

CHAPTER TWELVE

Trial Day 6 – June 26, 2013

Day 6 Agenda

- Closing Arguments – Sleeth
- Closing Arguments – Peck
- Final Closing – Broyles

Sedlock v. EUSD Trial Transcript Day 6—June 26, 2013: https://truthaboutyoga.files.wordpress.com/2015/01/13-06-26-part-02final.pdf[1]

Closing Arguments from Sleeth Continue

Sleeth points to three declarations brought in by **PECK:**

1. Dr. Mark Singleton claiming he is opposed to what Dr. Brown said and sees Ashtanga yoga as stemming from military calisthenics (p. 3) and not PBK Jois. This is interesting, given the vast amount of information about Ashtanga yoga roots from PBK Jois on the Internet. And in fact, with an Internet search of the name, he gave "Krishna Morzaria" as an alternative person who might have created Ashtanga yoga; only one person with this name appears all over the Internet as a young woman who is from India on *Linked-in* and is an interior designer. If he/she were the founder of Ashtanga yoga, it would be published all over (as is Pattabhi Jois as the founder). This was yet another "stab in the dark"

by the district to sway the judge that there was "testimony" to refute Dr. Brown.

2. Brandon Hartsell, the CEO of Sunstone yoga, who runs the Yoga Alliance registry claims yoga can be done without religion. Sleeth tries to downplay that Jois and his own thoughts about Ashtanga don't make it religious. The Judge argues with Sleeth about that and the stated testimonies say it has been established as religious.

3. Sleeth offers a 3rd declaration from Dr. Chapple. Dr. Chapple is the doshi professor of Indic and comparative theology at Loyola Marymount University. "I heard a lot of statements that nobody is qualified to refute Dr. Brown's testimony because she's the only religious professor here. That's not true. He received his Ph.D. at Fordham University. He's published books." Sleeth continues quoting one of Chapples' articles, "In my experience, yoga may be taught and practiced without promoting or advancing religion." That's as good an opinion as Dr. ---Professor Brown's opinion (p. 10). Sleeth goes on to say, "The use of term 'namaste' in the EUSD curriculum would be the equivalent of greeting students in a French class by saying, "bonjour." It's how you greet people in Sanskrit. It's not religious. (So, obviously he has not looked up this word!).

This is exactly the problem with the use of Sanskrit because we Westerners simply do not understand the meaning of the words. Sleeth may very well think this is a greeting, and most of us might, until you seek the definition of what the word means. Even the word "yoga," comes from the word yoke. Most people simply don't look that far into the word, and what it actually means. That's how something so blatant, can appear hidden while right out in the open! The elephant in the room… Big as anything, and yet, people ignore it like it doesn't matter. The definitions do matter. And the definitions matter whether children are or are not taught them, or go home and find them. If it was presented at school, it matters.

Conspiracy?

Next Sleeth begins a whole argument that appears he is concerned that Judge Meyer is going to be swayed by concerns of honesty given Miyashiro's testimony refuting Baird's. Sleeth actually appears to be grasping at getting the court to see that the court should throw out Candy Gunther Browns testimony (because she sees religion in other things, such as chiropractic, acupuncture and other practices that impact the flow of energy-chi, etc.) But Sleeth continues to call it a *conspiracy theory*, when in reality, it is the very words of Jois' mission and the district's hiding and sliding that concerned us. A trouble that continues to this day to plague us (even though dozens of us with over 50 kids have left the district)! We remain concerned for the other children.

Sleeth, ironically, launches an argument that Jois Foundation knows EUSD isn't teaching Ashtanga yoga, and Jois is fine with that (so spending $4 million just to be nice to EUSD?). The humorous part is that there are Jois staff members in the courtroom when he articulates this. So, if they have no vested interest, why are they there? Why did Gene Ruffin speak to the news after court, if he doesn't have a vested interest? Sleeth knows EUSD is still doing Ashtanga yoga, as well as the rest of us in the room, (as defined by opening sequence including sun salutations, lotus and closing – all Ashtanga trademarks), minus maybe the judge (p. 20). Yes, Gene Ruffin is clearly there for many reasons.

Unchanged Contracts

SLEETH - Now, the argument is – as I heard that argument, somehow because we failed to go back and change the agreement with Jois, we've done something wrong. Jois has not complained. There's no evidence that Jois is unhappy that we're not teaching Ashtanga yoga. And if they wanted to come back and file a donative lawsuit that they want their gift back because we violated the grant, they could do that. They have not done that. They know exactly what's going on. *(That's an interesting statement if Jois* *isn't "involved" anymore)*. They haven't sued us because we're not teaching Ashtanga yoga, because we told them. And they went along with it, and they're perfectly happy with it. They're interested in yoga. It's more probable that they're interested in yoga in order to create more people who like yoga who will pay them at their school than it is, that they're trying to advance Hinduism. It's more likely that Jois is interested in the money that will come from these students when they're adults and they want to continue taking yoga then it is that they're actually trying to advance Hinduism. But if you look at it through conspiratorial lenses, you see a conspiracy there, and it's not supported (pp. 20, 21).

For some reason Judge Meyer goes into saying that he thinks we (the Sedlocks) are sincere and have grounds for bringing this before the court, but goes off on some tangent saying we hadn't looked at the classes (as if that mattered – even though I did, it really doesn't matter – do you need to go into a restaurant to know there is the advertised food inside?). From the research about Jois, I was concerned enough about Jois and the program, not what happened on a one time visit to a yoga class. Over 40 parents observing problems was enough for me, but the judge *throws all that out* in these pages and only refers back to the pilot program for some reason, forgetting about all the parents' declarations, letters to the district, and separate testimony that had nothing to do with us or the pilot (p. 30, 31).

Certified or are the teachers just "Proficient?"

Sleeth tries to change the words "Jois certified" (which is on their court documents and in Baird's testimony) to "proficient" (p. 32). Convenient, but the whole word "certified," came from the advertising and requirements to interview for the yoga jobs. They go on further to mock the certified issue (including the judge), forgetting that the very person (Case) there to "certify" the teachers was from the yoga alliance *that is a certifying organization* amongst other things and that yoga teachers do and can get "certified"… (p. 33). If yoga is anything like aerobics, the certification process is important, and many gyms or studios will not let you teach if you are not certified, so the judge's and Sleeth's making a mockery of the certification word over the yoga instructors might be down-right insulting to the profession of yoga instructors, such as the ones through yoga alliance, given the hours needed and testing, etc., in order to get certified (p. 34). So Sleeth slips further into the mockery by playing with the Judge on the word conspiracy over and over and he refutes the entanglement argument based on his assumption it isn't religious so there is nothing to entangle about, and stating that Jois has no say over the program or the teachers. He, of course, doesn't mention that one yoga teacher, Jen Brown, works for both, and that Jois Foundation will be the recipient of the curriculum written by the yoga teachers. All that gets lost "on the mat" somewhere by Judge Meyer who appears now to be trying to grasp at how to fit all the evidence into his verdict.

Belittling Brown

Sleeth continues to belittle Brown's testimony, saying "Isn't that nonsense though?" (p. 42) referring to the places she points out there are "religious" items on the EUSD current yoga video. Not to mention that it is a promo piece for Jois and the EUSD staff, including that a board member and the superintendent are on the video promoting it for Jois (not for just EUSD use, but for Jois to use to spread the yoga to other districts. That is clearly the intent of the video). Sleeth uses words like "preposterous" for Brown's testimony (p. 43), and continues to attempt to undermine her testimony. This divisive language is on display in the courtroom, much like the divisiveness in the schools after yoga began!

Peck Continues the Bullying...

Peck stoops to much name calling on the heels of Sleeth, such as "absurdity on steroids" (p. 59) and "look through conspiracy glasses" and "your honor that's a ghost in the closet" (Peck p. 67) about Jen Brown being eyes and ears and overseer for Jois. But the reality is, she was the leader, the head teacher over the other 9 teachers to whom she "gave feedback" and met with every principal and traveled to each school to watch these teachers. To think she did not report back to Jois ever, when she works at the Jois yoga studio weekly and is clearly active in the Jois yoga community extending to India, is a long stretch. A stretch to absurdity perhaps, as he stated.

Peck continues: Plaintiffs have advanced *this voodoo* (more bullying) that they get the kids in with *the gateway drug*, (p. 67) – This "*fanatical parent's viewpoint*" should be ignored as *irrelevant*.

Does the Judge buy it all?

Peck's Pattabhi Juice

Peck decides to bring in a metaphor of Pattabhi Juice and gives a scenario of making a healthy fruit and vegetable juice and give a grant to the schools to drink this juice for health and wellness and that kids can *opt to drink it or not*. The judge gets punchy and plays along:

THE COURT: Do they call it school district juice?

(Laughter.)

MR. PECK: We'll call it Encinitas juice.

THE COURT: That's what they call it?

MR. PECK: Yeah.

THE COURT: Okay.

MR. PECK: I mean, it's not my Pattabhi juice, but they call it juice.

THE COURT: Why don't they call it Pattabhi juice?

MR. PECK: Because it's not Pattabhi juice. My Pattabhi juice is a special blend, just like you can't call cola – plain wrapped cola, Coca-Cola. It's not the same. You can't call fried chicken Kentucky Fried Chicken. It's not the same (Seriously, this continues pp. 50, 51, 52 etc.). In this juice example one thing was clear – Peck was drinking the district Kool-Aid.

Peck tries to distance Jois again from the hiring process, but on that part the judge will not slide away with him (pp. 64, 65), and they go over and over that Miyashiro, Steve Regur and Russell Case all narrow the 22 candidates to 10, which is clearly Jois putting it's hand in the hiring process of these candidates. Clearly, even Peck concedes "yes, this is a collaborative process" forgetting what he just stated that it wasn't. A "slippery slope" that even he referred to – and it's one slippery cliff when you stretch the facts…but they would skate only up to the edge (p. 66).

A Clue the Judge might see through the Curtain

PECK: Jen Brown spent months in Mysore studying. When is she getting hit with that stuff? She professed and testified credibly that she doesn't know the first thing about Hindu philosophy.

THE COURT: I don't know about that.

MR. PECK: That's what the record says. We've heard this "om" being this holy sound and that she says "om." She says, "Yeah, it's something I do as respect to my predecessors."

THE COURT: How many times has she been to India?

MR. PECK: She said multiple times.

THE COURT: I suspect she knows something about Hindu philosophies.

MR. PECK: As much as I might know from –

THE COURT: I'm thinking she knows more. Have you been to India?

MR. PECK: No, I haven't, your Honor.

THE COURT: I think she knows more.

MR. PECK: I've sat through six days of trial now and I've learned a few things. You may think she knows more. She was cross-examined on the subject. She credibly testified she knows very little. She knows a few words in Sanskrit.

THE COURT: Oh, I think she knows more than that.

MR. PECK: I don't know why the Court would say that.

THE COURT: Because she's studied Sanskrit, and she's been to India on numerous occasions. She's got a profound interest in India. I mean, for whatever it's worth, I mean, I think she knows a lot about India.

MR. PECK: Whether she –

THE COURT: – and Hinduism.

MR. PECK: Whether she knows a lot about India, there's absolutely no evidence before the Court that she's a Hindu, that she maintains Hindu beliefs, or that any of the yoga teachers –

THE COURT: She's disclaimed that.

MR. PECK: She's disclaimed it.

THE COURT: So if she's truthful and credible, then –

MR. PECK: I'll let the Court make that determination, but I submit that she was, that she wasn't impeached there (pp. 68, 69).

Dean Broyles Rebuttal

Broyles starts with no matter what anyone's opinions are, the facts need to stand in this case. Just because someone thinks something is or isn't religious, doesn't make it so or not (p. 81). He summarizes Brown's testimony. He covers her qualifications and then states:

1. Professor Brown said that yoga is pervasively religious and that that was the consensus of religious studies scholars.
2. She said Ashtanga yoga is the most religious form of yoga practiced in the United States.
3. After looking at the entire yoga program, including the curriculum, the declarations of Jen Brown, and the other teachers, everything in this case except some of the later testimony in the trial, she concluded that EUSD's yoga program is, in fact, religious.
4. Her testimony, your Honor, was not rebutted by any competent witness called by EUSD, including Pecks 3 expert declarations (p. 88).

Judge Meyer - flattering about the expert witness

THE COURT: No, no. I – I think – I think Dr. Brown is eminently qualified, is very articulate, is astoundingly well-read, and is impassioned with comparative religion. I mean, that's her life, and she's just bubbling over with information. And it's – I mean, she's a very well-qualified expert. I – I think that the hearsay that she relied on is probably pretty – has a firm basis with regard to Pattabhi Jois and Ashtanga yoga and Hinduism and the yamas and niyamas and the asanas. And, I mean, she could teach that anywhere. And so those opinions, I think, certainly are – have a firm basis and is very helpful – (p. 89).

Everyone in District testifying has a stake in the Yoga Program Success

Broyles goes through the three experts Peck offered and refutes each testimony since they did not review the yoga program, did not testify and did not have any cross examination. (pp. 89-92). Broyles points out how all the people testifying for the district have a stake and vested interest in the yoga programs success.

EUSD generally in this case, then, your Honor, attempted to contradict Dr. Brown's testimony primarily by unqualified lay witnesses who gave their personal opinion testimony. These were people like Dr. Baird, Dr. Miyashiro, Jen Brown, and others. And I just want to point out for the Court as far as their credibility, not only was there a lot of contradictory evidence and testimony between them about what the documents meant and what the program was really about, but all – each of these people have a personal vested interest in defending the EUSD yoga program (p. 93).

Broyles spoke more about yoga being a practice religion vs. cerebrally learned and spoken (p. 98) and that we need to avoid the cultural bias that just because we don't understand the Hindu religion, we don't ignore that it is one (p. 100).

Broyles proceeds and he and the judge go around and around the topic of what the standard will be for judgement of an "informed child" of a government program, i.e., yoga, or "imputed knowledge" of Ashtanga yoga, to the child and which the standard will be (p. 107). Broyles points to the *Wicca case* where the child is informed and Judge Meyer can't get past the idea that the average child wouldn't know what Ashtanga yoga is in America, which they wouldn't; and that is why the standard in that case is "imputed knowledge" (and why to not inform is to take advantage of children performing something they know nothing about or where it leads in the future) and neither do their parents for that matter (p. 116).

Broyles proceeds to the *Alvarado case* where again knowledge was imputed to child for judgment. Well, this is a case where actually the knowledge of ancient history was imputed – a bizarre Mayan Aztec deity was imputed to people whom the Court didn't find actually knew it, okay? So the people in the Alvarado case did not actually know that Quetzalcoatl was an ancient Aztec deity, and yet the Court imputed that knowledge to them (p. 118). Even a 5 year old would know when you put palms together in "praying hands" mode (p. 120). He goes on to remind the court of the things the children are doing spontaneously now (lotus position, finger and thumb together in jnana mudra on knees while sitting in lotus, closing eyes and chanting om).

Broyles points out the direct testimony of EUSD district conflicting with itself on the issue of Jois certification of instructors:

THE COURT: The certification?

MR. BROYLES: Certification of the teachers.

THE COURT: The yoga teachers?

MR. BROYLES: Yes. I think if your Honor would look at the first three or four days of trial testimony before David Miyashiro got on the stand, the consistent testimony from every witness was that the teachers were trained and certified by Jois. It was only when David Miyashiro got on the stand on the last day of trial that he started undercutting not only the founding documents themselves like the grant and MOU, but also, this whole issue of certification, trying to downplay it and water it down. (Day 6, p. 129)

"Let me just point out to the Court where it is because I – and there was a definite conflict in testimony between the testimony of Dr. Baird, who said during his examination that they – he confirmed that they were certified by Jois and trained by Jois. And if you look at Exhibit 5, your Honor, which is the *frequently asked questions* (FAQ), that came out in November or December of 2012 right – several months after the program started – and I asked David Miyashiro about this. It says, quote, "All yoga instructors" – I'm reading from Exhibit 5, the FAQ under Subparagraph B. It says, quote, "All yoga instructors will be certified by Jois to ensure that they meet the high level of instructional quality." Baird – Mr. Baird confirmed that orally; that this was, in fact, the case. That is, in fact, spelled out in the MOU and the grant document that is Exhibit A to the MOU. And it wasn't until the last day of verbal witness testimony that that certification was even questioned."

BROYLES: - So I submit that the certification actually meant something. The documents said it. Baird confirmed it. It was confirmed in the FAQ. And it's important, your Honor, not only that they were certified by Jois because Jois gave them the grant and wanted some say as to who the teachers were, but it's also important because there's an ongoing entanglement that the defense is almost completely ignoring, and that is they're still developing this curriculum that Jois will use. (p. 131).

So in closing, your Honor, not all speaking is religious, but speaking a prayer is religious. Not all kneeling is religious, for example kneeling to work in one's garden, but kneeling to pray is religious. Not all bell-ringing is religious, but ringing a bell in a religious ceremony or liturgy is religious as you saw in the EUSD videos. Not all breathing is religious, but breath control in yoga is religious. Not all pressing of your palms together in worship or prayer is worship or prayer, but pressing your palms together in the Surya Namaskara A and B in worship and prayer to the Hindu sun god Surya is religious. Even a five-year-old knows that.

Thank you, your Honor.

THE COURT: Thank you. P. 139

I (Jennifer Sedlock) walked away from court very concerned that the judge had many details wrong by the misleading comments

256

given by the district and the lack of those details being clarified when the judge guessed wrong at times. Here are the few I observed:

Seven Facts the Judge seemed to have wrong after last day

1. He said there was unrefuted evidence that the district was giving 200 minutes of PE which ignores the very declarations that we petitioners filed, and all the other parents' declarations in evidence. This statement also ignores the letters and emails to and from the district in evidence, and the testimony of FS (petitioner child on stand telling the court how many minutes per week running and doing karate she got). So there is evidence, he just chooses to ignore it all or not believe it, but there was plenty of evidence to contradict the district claiming they were giving these opted-out children 200 PE minutes every two weeks. As testified, my daughter got 40 min per week, 30 from karate and 10 from running, one morning per week, with the teacher. That's all for the entire 2012/2013 school year. Her teacher's affidavit contradicts that, and I don't blame the teacher for what she wrote, trying to keep her job, but even she knows that isn't the truth. She herself did not give that second-grade class 70 minutes of PE per week above yoga, it just didn't happen, period (p. 36 -38). The judge calls the declarations of all the parents on this: hearsay (p. 46).

2. Meyer showed confusion on what a yoga certification is in the fitness world. Certifications are important and he and Sleeth downplayed that word like it was used inaccurately as a *proficiency* rather than an achieved certification. Baird and signed contracts used the word *certified* because yoga certifications mattered. Russell Case works for a *certifying* organization (Yoga Alliance), as well as for Jois. (p. 32) Even Sleeth admits over and over (p. 34) that the teachers were certified. And why Sleeth and the others keep using

that language is because it was a qualification for teachers before they could be interviewed. Certification is on the recruitment documents, and thus, the "selection" of them wasn't based on certifying them afterwards, they were already certified yoga instructors. If any weren't, then we have an even bigger problem on our hands and in the classrooms with our children!

3. Meyer was confused about teachers being hired through Regur, as if other teachers currently in the district were hired through Regur, which they were not. Only yoga teachers were hired through Regur. Miyashiro knew this, and allowed the judge to think the wrong thing by not clarifying after the judge summarized that point (Day 4).

4. Meyer claims our declarations contain opinions and irrelevant facts to the case (Day 6, p. 16, 17). He says that some declarations don't contain competent evidence. Basically, he is setting up to throw them all aside (from the parent declarations) and ignore the facts parents wrote, calling them "not truthful," basically by saying he has to find the truth in them. There is not one lie in any of those declarations, and yet he chooses to ignore all these parents and believe the district whose testimonies refuted each other (Baird vs. Miyashiro).

5. *How the Judge Got it Wrong* was written by The Wheaton Law Review covering details of the law that Meyer got wrong in this case: https://wculrcom.files.wordpress.com/2016/04/wculr-vol-1-no-1.pdf[2] (available on the lawsuit page of our parent website as well).

6. Meyer asks if there is any evidence Ashtanga yoga has been taught in schools, completely ignoring all the days of evidence that, yes, the elements of Ashtanga are in the curriculum, in the testimony of Jen Brown, in the videos, specifically the opening sequences, the sun salutations, the lotus and the jnana mudra, the chanting om, and so on. Meyer ignores all this! (p. 24).

7. Once again Meyer erroneously focuses on that we (Sedlock's) didn't watch a class, when I testified that I did

(p. 28). He states there was no testimony about mandalas, which is inaccurate as well. Candy Gunther Brown defined what a mandala was, at least two of the parents wrote about them in their declarations, and a definition was given to the court. Even Carrie Brown testified about Mandalas, saying they are taught in 6th grade within a religious teaching, but this was the "practice of drawing them and being used in the context of yoga teachings with Sanskrit and yamas." How did the judge dismiss all that? Does he "ignore" these, or "forget." The evidence is there, in black and white.

A few comments from Sian Welch blogging on the day included a summary: "Much of the closing argument case presented by the district EUSD was about discrediting Dr. Brown's 6-plus hours of expert testimony. It took the court over 30 minutes to get through her resume of degrees, international honors and awards for her studies and published work in the area of World Religion study. The District recommended throwing it all out."

Media of Day 6:

- Attorneys Deliver Closing Arguments in School Yoga Trial, June 26, 2013, Coast News: https://www.nbclosangeles.com/news/california/Parents-Testify-in-Encinitas-Yoga-Class-Trial-213042641.html.[3]

- Yoga on Trial in San Diego, June 26, 2013
  Charisma News: http://www.charismanews.com/us/40019-yoga-on-trial-in-san-diego-religious-lawsuit[4]
  Broyles quoted in the article—This "represents the clearest case I have observed of the government advancing, endorsing, or promoting religion," said Dean Broyles, president of the National Center for Law and Policy, a nonprofit based in Escondido, Calif., dedicated to defending religious freedom, traditional marriage and the sanctity of life.

"In America we do not allow the government to pick religious winners and losers, especially when you have a captive audience of very young and impressionable children as we do in our public schools," he said.

Note: The Three prongs:

1. *The government's action **must have a secular legislative purpose;***

2. *The government's action **must not have the primary effect of either advancing or inhibiting religion;***

3. *The government's action **must not result in an "excessive government entanglement" with religion***

Key word "Entanglement"—no matter how you see this case, "entanglement in religion" is impossible to avoid when you are teaching children yoga. The proof of this is the constant revisions of the "religious" parts of the curriculum. If yoga didn't have religious tenets, there would be no reason to continually monitor, revise, and remove basic concepts of the yoga practice.

CHAPTER THIRTEEN

Verbal Verdict – July 1, 2013

Day 7 Agenda

- Verdict *behind the scenes*
- Facts the Judge got right and wrong
- Verbal Verdict
- Reactions to Verdict

Verbal Verdict

The morning of the verbal verdict, we expected a short decision, so I parked on a downtown San Diego street and filled a meter with quarters for a couple hours, rather than park in the *all day* lot where I'd been parking. Given nothing seemed quick in this trial, perhaps we should have known better. My father was with me, but my husband missed several days of work for this trial already, so he went into work that day. This day was different in more ways than one. My father and I sat up at the table with our attorney for the first time. With cameras to our left and all the district attorneys to our right, it felt a bit more "on the spot," and my mind drifted to the fact that the cameras were going to try to get our reactions no matter what the verdict. Keeping a cool head regardless and not looking around much seemed the best at the moment. Judge Meyer dove into a summary of facts and then his verdict.

Approaching two hours for my meter outside, I realized Meyer wasn't going to be done soon, so at a crucial part of his *speech*,

I leaned over to ask my dad if he would go feed the meter more money. The timing of my dad walking out of court ended up being a very interesting part of Meyer's personal speculations, about *me*. It may have been good that my father didn't have to listen to the judge's comments because he probably would have been very angry. At one point, I literally leaned over to attorney Broyles and said "how can the judge say these untrue assertions and make things up about me in his own speculations – isn't this defamation of character?" To which Dean Broyles responded "I've never seen anything like it." But protocol is that Broyles couldn't speak at that point, and neither could I. It's one of those times in your life when you want to stand up and defend yourself and explain that the person speaking about you is completely inaccurate, and to point out the obvious facts he has heard in the case. But you can't. You sit and wonder – why is this happening? It was surreal, and yet, why would Meyer even entertain this line of thinking? I'll get to my theory on why, but first let's dive into the facts of what he said for the verdict.

Sian Welch wrote about the verdict and this is an excerpt:

Read details of what informed observer is or is not, because that is what the whole case seemed to end up hinging upon for Meyer's decisions. However Meyer also threw out and didn't take into account most of the cases that Broyles discussed. In fact, Judge Meyer could not have included those cases and come up with the verdict that he did, so he simply left them out. (Cases found on - Day 5, pp 116-140).

Judge Summarizes Facts

The verdict court reporter notes are posted here: https://truthaboutyoga.files.wordpress.com/2015/01/statement-of-intended-decision-meyer.pdf [1]

The judge summarizes and gets the following facts correct.

- He gives background of yoga, Ashtanga yoga, and Pattabhi Jois (pp. 2, 3).
- He gives 8 limbs of yoga in Sanskrit (pp. 3, 4).
- He goes into Jois Foundation (pp. 4, 5), The UVA and USD studies.
- He states for the record, the district must give 200 minutes of PE every 10 days (p. 6).
- Timothy Baird, Superintendent EUSD, meets with Jois Foundation over yoga in a pilot program at Capri, 2011 (p. 7).
- Jois Foundation funded pilot program at Capri and Jen Brown taught yoga for Jois at EUSD (p. 7).
- Jen Brown has been to India 3 times, studied Sanskrit, is trained by Sharath Jois and teaches at the Jois Shala in Encinitas (p. 7).
- Jen Brown put on the wall an 8-limbed poster and posted postcards in the yoga classroom that she sent the EUSD children from her trip to India. She used Sanskrit words and "Namaste" in yoga classes. She testified none of this was religious to her (p. 7).
- Baird and Miyashiro expand the program in 2012 with all 9 schools, a study to be *monitored* by USD (p. 8).
- The grant proposal dated July 24, 2012, MOU (signed Aug 31, 2012) specifically stating Ashtanga yoga and a "partnership" between EUSD and Jois Foundation (p. 8). The contract with Regur to hire the yoga teachers for EUSD.
- He states that the three men evaluating the pool of candidates and whittling it down to 22 were Miyashiro from EUSD, Regur from Regur Development, and Russell Case from Jois Foundation. The goal was to make sure these instructors could teach yoga to children. (p. 10). What he gets wrong (below) is that he says Jois Foundation has no influence over hiring, when he forgets Russell Case was right there doing all the qualifying of candidates.
- The Judge refers to an FAQ by Baird created to address parent concerns (P. 14).

Where the Judge summarizes some of the facts wrong, and not matching testimonies:

- Meyer thinks other consultants and teachers are hired through Regur, such as for karate, music and technology. In reality, these teachers are outsourced or hired by the district and each school, *not Regur*. Meyer erroneously thinks this because Miyashiro didn't correct him when Meyer concluded they used Regur for hiring other *consultant* teachers. Regur was only for hiring yoga teachers in 2012 (p. 6). The testimonies of Carrie Brown and Miyashiro match the truth in that Regur was only for yoga instructors, but that in the past they had done "teacher trainings" through Regur. Yet Meyer gets it wrong, and Miyashiro knows it, but stays quiet instead of clarifying for the judge.
- Meyer states that Baird and Miyashiro testify that they never did Ashtanga yoga at EUSD (which is true; they did testify to that) but all the other evidence clearly shows that EUSD did and does do Ashtanga yoga, even down to the most basic definition of Ashtanga (ie- opening sequences containing sun salutations and lotus with jnana mudra - pp. 8, 9).
- Baird and Miyashiro denied that Jois Foundation helped hire or train or certify the teachers, even though they signed documents that Jois did all of these phases. And even though the facts show that Russell Case was involved with the recruiting, screening of the 22 before the MOU was signed, thus involved with hiring and certifying because if he says they are passing, then that certifies them, given his credentials: (Case works for Jois Foundation, Stanford and is a yoga teacher at shalas and works for Yoga Alliance, a certifying organization, p. 9).
- The judge states that 9 of these yoga teachers (of 22) were hired, but he doesn't know what happened to the other one. There were actually 10 yoga teachers hired because the other one was Jen Brown from the pilot program. She needed one teacher to help cover her school, while she was

frequently overseeing the other 9 teachers and taught one day at the yoga shala for Jois. The district never corrected the judge after he wondered about the 10th teacher, so as to not hurt their own case that Jen Brown was overseeing this program, even as she was still a Jois yoga employee (p. 10, 11).

- The judge states that Jois was not involved with developing the curriculum and that Leslie Wright of EUSD (who had no yoga background) was writing the curriculum. The fact is that most (7) of the yoga teachers had met the advertised criteria of over 3 years Ashtanga teaching experience with Jois yoga, so when they collaborated on Fridays with Leslie, they were developing the Ashtanga curriculum as representatives of Ashtanga yoga. Even if there were modifications, they have the collective experience of Ashtanga, as evidenced by their resumes and websites! (p. 11)

- Then Judge Meyer starts speculating about me for some reason. The judge assumes that somehow I led all these other parents in the district (from all 9 schools at which I didn't know people prior...) to protest about the yoga program. This is humorous given the whole thing was in full swing by October 4th when I got involved, including Broyles leading meetings. Meyer goes on to suggest that my letter to the district didn't have relevant information to the trial, (as if I wrote it for evidence for a trial?) When I wrote that letter to the district in 2012, I had no idea that there would be any trial. Chronologically that decision came later. My intent was to share what concerned me about the yoga program. I didn't have just growing religious issues with Ashtanga yoga; I had many other physical concerns for the children along with contractual concerns on what the District was getting into with Jois Foundation. So, why he thinks I was writing evidence for a trial is a misleading thought he holds about the other parent letters as well. He began stating speculations based on my web address (JenniferSpeaks.com) contained in my letter to the district.

There are comments he made that day that are not included in this written verdict, but like the mandalas, those comments disappeared when the typed verdict came out. I asked the attorney where the judge's comments went, and he said it is the judge's prerogative to revise the verbal verdict in writing. Meyer must have looked up my website for other details he shared. I was surprised at the personal attack, but it didn't matter in the long run because hundreds of us parents were concerned, and no one could have coordinated all the things going on in the district! It was pure fabrication and speculation on his part, and like I said, none of this is about us, nor ever was about our children. The lawsuit just had to have someone stand, and had to put our children in the role that hundreds of other kids could have been on in that same hot seat. Fortunately, we could represent them all, and not have others go through what we did. We were fine to take that place, but I am still shocked Meyer was allowed to create a conspiracy theory of his own making. It's odd listening to someone talk about you when you can't respond at all. However, one thing would later come to pass, that would make me really laugh.

I did, later, become a leader of "information." It just hadn't happened yet. His words would become, well, prophetic if you use that word, foreshadowing, if you prefer that word. In 2014, I would accept the role of organizing people and information for events to educate the public. I was by no means the only one helping, but the hub of information from all over the world seemed to come to the attorney or me, because we were the ones people knew to contact about the trial. My husband's phone numbers are not published, and since my information is publicly available as a speaker, I got the calls to my work line. So, Meyer actually got that right for later, just not in 2012 or 2013! Here was his scaled down written version:

- **MEYER:** "There were – from the very beginning, there were a lot of complaints and questions, and there was kind of a firestorm of protest from the people opted-out. And a lot of the information was conclusory and based on I'm not sure what – based on research and I suspect that there was a lot of – there was a lot of tweeting and there was a lot of Internet work. And I think there was probably coordination by one of the petitioners, Jennifer Sedlock, and she had written a long letter to the board and the superintendent with the tagline "Jennifer Speaks," indicating that she was a professional speaker and author speaking to the head and the heart. So Jennifer spoke, and people listened. And there was a lot that really wasn't connected with religion. And I think Exhibit 10 is her letter to the district and to the superintendent. ...I didn't have to look far to find the Mayo Clinic and the American Yoga Association both saying that Ashtanga yoga is not good for kids and yoga for kids under 16 is not advisable." She then suggests, "Why not offer alternatives for those who would rather do traditional PE? I've taught PE for teachers in the past, and I'm sure there are parents who would volunteer to teach if it is a financial or teaching issue at this point." And then she says, "I am concerned with what this study is trying to do.... In my research, I found many studies encouraging more recess, not silent meditation and stretching for young growing bodies..." (P. 11-14).

- On page 14 the judge again states that based on our not seeing a class that there is no other evidence contradicting. But there was contradicting evidence – parent after parent wrote emails and letters to the district, a few wrote declarations for the judge and he states, "There is no testimony as to what was going on in the classes." There was plenty discussed over and over of what was happening in the classes; Sanskrit, Namaste, lotus, opening sequences, sun salutations, jnana mudra, chanting "om", and all the other things parents said happened in classes in 2012 and 2013. How did he lose sight of all this evidence?
- The judge says it's suspicious that we are concerned about PE minutes when the superintendent is clear that all kids get 200 minutes above and beyond the yoga. What is ironic

is that the judge doesn't see it as suspicious that EUSD all of a sudden claims to give 60 minutes of yoga on top of PE (which is 120 minutes plus 200 minutes of PE every 10 days for a total of 320 minutes)! Which classtime then did the 120 minutes get pulled from? Math or English – that is the suspiciousness the judge never even thinks nor asks about, but that we attempted to clear up after this stretch of district testimony.

The math on that cover-up simply doesn't work! There are 6 school hours and if Carrie Brown couldn't even fit in 60 minutes of yoga for her 4th-6th graders and did 40 per week instead, then how did she come up with the extra 120 per week? It doesn't add up; simple math and the district knows this. Plus, not only is there not a shred of evidence that there was ever given 100 minutes of PE on top of yoga, as Baird said happened. He couldn't prove it, but the *burden of proof* was on us, and we couldn't prove PE minutes beyond the testimonies of all the children opted-out. Some proof was in the existence of emails from the principal as to where our kids would go during yoga, but they claimed to have "changed that" two weeks prior to trial. There was no winning the *burden of proof* unless you work at the school, and no teachers came forward to share the truth for us. It was (in my opinion) too costly for them to do so to put their jobs at risk.

- The video – was produced by Steve Regur (another conflict of interest – Isn't Regur supposed to just be the hiring entity as per Baird?) and was copyrighted by EUSD, but is a promotion for Jois Foundation. More Entanglement the judge doesn't address (p. 16).

So that is the overview of facts and chronology as per the judge…(p. 18).

An observation worth noting

I'll attempt to describe what I as an observer noticed in the courtroom that day – the judge appeared to be pulled in two directions...from the tone of his voice changing to the look on his face, to the sound of his voice, and to the physical changes in his positioning. He went back and forth in what he was saying, as if pulled by two different forces. It was surreal and odd, and that's the best way I can describe it, as I have never seen anything like it before, or since. He would be talking in one demeanor, and all of a sudden shift in his chair, change tones, and go on to say an opposing thought. Watch the video of that day if you can. I know the entire trial was taped, but I just don't know where to find it; perhaps the case archives or the court would know.

I'm no expert on any of this; I've just attempted to document as much as I can and refer you to as much as you want to digest. I'm sure attorneys might delve into the trial court notes, but having just gone through all 1400 pages of them myself, I can't image any person would ever want to spend that time! So congratulations to making it through the condensed version of 250 pages per day, summarized into around 30 pages per chapter. I gave you the insider's perspective, by including as many facts as possible, so you could ponder the verdict and what it means based on the evidence. Now, onto the verdict!

Meyer moving into Verdict

Next he gives his verdict:

- He refers to testimony of Candy Gunther Brown, saying I don't know that you could be a more eminent or qualified scholar on religious studies. He then refers to Malnak vs yoga and Alvarado cases (p. 17, 18). Accordingly, the Court determines that **yoga is religious**. And that brings the Court to the key issue in this case, as the Court sees it. Since yoga and Ashtanga yoga have religious roots and Eastern Hindu and Buddhist metaphysical religious practice, can EUSD yoga be taught in the public school district? (p. 19)

Then he refers to the Lemon versus Kurtzman case, and in the first prong, which is the whether the purpose of the activity is secular, we (both sides agree), that the intent of the district was to do a secular activity (p. 20). The second prong, whether yoga advances or inhibits religion is where the experts disagree. He mentions Silva, the district's witness who stated that after 20 years of yoga she does not think it's religious, and Dr. Singleton in a declaration stating he doesn't think yoga is religious. The judge then *throws out* the entire testimony of Candy Gunther Brown stating that she is biased and seems to be determined to be on a mission against Ashtanga yoga!

This is one place where his demeanor changed a lot before saying this about Dr. Brown. He goes on for a while about how she is qualified to teach, but not to "to fulfill her goal of eliminating yoga in schools" (which is another speculative conspiracy theory on his part, given she researched Ashtanga for this trial, not prior!). Then he goes on that the expert testimony by the Browns (who does he mean – the Brown case, Professor Brown, Principal Brown and/ or Jen Brown?) and petitioners and parent declarations – all thrown out – not relevant he said! (p. 22).

He continues: "Instead of engaging in a," quote, "'battle of experts,'" end quote, "in deciding the establishment clause cases, courts have relied upon assumptions about a hypothetical observer," in this case, a hypothetical child, "to determine whether a government action conveys an endorsement of religion"(p. 22).

What's interesting to me as a lay person not versed in the law is why would they use a child's ability to see it as religious or not, as the foundation of the decision? Aren't fences and laws supposed to protect children from things they don't even know exist? But I'm just a mom; what do I know? Protection of kids seems like it should include things they aren't aware of, like a hot stove before they learn it's hot. Do they really understand there are predators who can abduct them unless we tell them? So if we don't tell children yoga is religious, then it is fine? That's a strange law that seems wrong in its basis. Broyles kept saying the other cases "imputed" the knowledge to a hypothetical child. And the judge kept saying, "I don't think that the average real child would 'see' religion."

MEYER: So then we get to what the courts look at, and that is there a preponderance of credible, competent evidence that a reasonable informed student *in the spring of 2013* would objectively perceive from his or her EUSD yoga classes a message of endorsement of some Eastern religion or some disapproval of Christianity or some Western religion? He refers to Brown and Alvarado cases and Krasner to discuss what advances religion and how much the observer knows.

Then on page 25 Meyer begins to systematically throw out all the parent declarations, saying all of them are *not objective observers* of the classrooms. These parent declarations are posted to the truthaboutyoga.com website, if you would like to read them to determine what you think. I'll summarize some points each make and you can think about whether these seem to pertain to details of the trial or not to you:

- **Parent Eady** – She points to many details covered in the trial about Jois Foundation. For example, the $12 million given to UVA by Jois Foundation, the mission and concerns about Jois yoga as per the Jois family claims found on their websites, the three year research study by USD and UVA for Jois/EUSD yoga, the grant, MOU and Regur contracts, the term "partnership" used several times in documents for Jois and EUSD and even proposing the future partnership, "Jois certified and trained" yoga instructors clearly stated on contract documents, 50 pages of "on-the-mat" curriculum for EUSD, containing all kinds of Ashtanga and Sanskrit with Sun Salutations, Namaste, Lotus and a lot more embedded into the curriculum. She points out things that happened to her son in class and the current embarrassment for him by opting-out of yoga.
- **Parent Hevrin** – This family was at Capri and her letter spells out things covered in court having to do with 8-limb

poster. For instance, the mother was never notified of the biometrics being tested on her children; she visited several yoga classes over time and pointed out the use of Sanskrit and the sun salutations being done to worship deities. She also testifies that her child didn't get state-required PE minutes when opted-out of yoga, and she points out that the board and Baird claimed ignorance of Ashtanga and Jois, but have had ample time to research and continue in their negligence, so how can families now trust the EUSD trustees?

- **Parent Gray** – The Grays had one last child at Capri and verify that Nancy Jois is a teacher there and is the wife of Manju Jois. She points out her child was pulled from math to do yoga biometrics and to watch videos of Ashtanga during math time. Her daughter was taught the warrior pose (Virabhadrasana) and that it means a god (Shiva) slicing off someone's head (Daksha) and replacing it with the head of a goat, from a book they were read in yoga class with Jen Brown. Also, at Capri that year in world history the kids were only taught Hinduism and Buddhism, when the curriculum was supposed to include Judaism and Christianity and they did not cover those. She also presents a study guide of terms sent home with her daughter which contain Sanskrit and yoga words, such as asana, Dristi, Vinyasa, Samastithi, yoga breathing, yogi, and Surya namaskara (Sun Salutations) as words to memorize. She goes on to show various things that happened (lotus, namaste, etc.) and then she pulled her daughter out, who was then not getting the required PE minutes. She includes emails back and forth from Dr. Baird October, 2012 – Dec. 2012.

- **Parent True** – The Trues had 3 children in one of the schools (deleted for privacy) – The Trues visited the yoga class and became alarmed by many things they saw from the 8 limbed tree on the bulletin board (note – this is not the pilot school they discuss in the trial, so this is proof of another school displaying the "8 limbed tree," posted with limbs in Sanskrit. They observed several things kids were doing in yoga they didn't like, so they removed all of their kids from the yoga program and study. They also testify to losing PE minutes during yoga, with no PE alternatives at their school for yoga. They also cover some of the divisiveness that is happening for the children at school. A teacher even called to ask her son not to tell others why he doesn't go to yoga (it is his constitutional right to speak, but over and over these kids were silenced, bullied by adult staff and yoga instructors, into silence. They were even singled-out and embarrassed, by well-meaning teachers doing yoga moves and yoga breathing in the regular classes).

- **Grandparent Nordal** – The Nordals had a grandson at La Costa Heights who is special needs, but was mainstreamed into the regular classes - including yoga. In 2013, they viewed a yoga class and became alarmed at how religious it was, promoting Hinduism and Ashtanga yoga, and then immediately pulled him out. They, too, are concerned their grandson doesn't get enough PE time, but they are willing, as the rest of us were, to forgo the PE time, so "he would not be indoctrinated into this endorsement of Hinduism through Ashtanga yoga".

- **Parent Vigil** – The Vigils had three children over the years go to school at El Camino Creek, and they testify that mandalas were drawn in yoga class (by teacher Christine Reich, teaching art that fall). The mom became concerned when speaking with Reich about the purpose for the art, because Reich was teaching that "everything leads to the center of the world around us and that all in nature has a center." Reich explained to Vigil that she knew mandalas were religious. Mrs. Vigil researched to find they were Hindu and Buddhist sacred traditions, so she went to the principal to complain. All the mandala art, that all the classes of kids at El Camino Creek did that fall, was disposed of after that complaint to Principal Carrie Brown. The Vigils researched the program, voiced their concerns about Jois Foundation, Ashtanga yoga and the religious nature of this program multiple times to the principal, to the board members and superintendent at board meetings in the fall of 2012. They stated that this program directly conflicts with their Christian beliefs. They testified also to not being informed about the biometric data being taken on their children, nor the comprehensiveness of this district-wide program.

- All of that testimony was thrown out by the judge. Dismissed. Deemed not important.

I don't know your thoughts after reading that, but the efforts of those brave parents to report what was happening in our district had been silenced, yet again. Like the children of EUSD not able to voice their opinions or feedback about yoga. Dismissed, quieted, hidden, by the very people who claim they want to help make the programs the best they can be and are following the PE laws of the state. How did Judge Meyer decide to throw out all that testimony?

Surprisingly, Meyer chooses to throw out Professor Brown's entire two day testimony too! He claimed she "would see everything as religious." Ironically, by doing this, he supports the Eastern religions that by definition really do see almost everything as religious; such as cows, tables, statues, and more... to reflect the beliefs of Hindus, and perhaps including a few of the yogis teaching our children.

The judge calls Dr. Brown "not credible" (incredulously, after all his praising of her!). He starts quoting Dr. Brown - she read the declarations and saw the video. "We still see even without that language the same poses and structure and ritual sequence in the order that's done in Ashtanga; the same order, the same opening, the same closing. There is still the emphasis on vital breath. Breath is still very important. Again, this is vital breath, not just breathing. It's coordinated. The declarations and the videos still show the mudras, the mindfulness, the balance, the sound meditation. Many children are still chanting and praying and saying 'om' to a mudra, suggesting that they perceive that this is more than exercise. And it's still yoga, it's still yoking that frames this as something more than an exercise. It is to infuse all of life. It's how to live. You see that, all over the place in the videos, and in the teacher declarations" (p. 27).

The judge disagrees with her and goes over testimony that I covered in this book already, so I won't repeat it here, but he quotes her a lot and then goes on to say that he believes there are people on the "yes it's religious" side that would conclude that a hypothetical objective student would see religious overtones to EUSD yoga (p. 31), then goes on to say that other evidence concludes "no" in the curriculum, which he says is different than when Jen Brown was teaching the pilot. He concludes that none of the things parents are concerned about are happening any longer, and when they are taught, that it's moral teachings that are universal (p. 33).

What's inconsistent is that he *discredits* the parent declarations earlier for being similar and then *credits* the yoga teacher's declarations for being similar (p. 33), Mcklosky, Gerber, Kim Wood and Christian Eady (p. 35, line 11). Did we read that right? Is there really a yoga teacher named Christian Eady, or did the judge just confuse that with the parents who is a Christian and named Mary Eady? With all the double names in this case, it wouldn't surprise me either way.

After 1400 pages of court reporter notes, maybe it boils down to this: 3 Browns, 2 Meyers (judge and a case), 2 Jennifer's (Brown and Sedlock) and one Brown Case, or let me digress a moment in this holiday season:

- 10 yoga instructors
- 9 schools doing yoga
- 8 principals hiring
- 7 Jois-certified yogis
- 6 parent declarations
- 5 golden.... Swings?
- 4 schools starting in January (2013),
- 3 Browns and one case named Brown,
- 2 universities studying
- And a Jois Foundation, in an 8-limbed tree.

Sounds like a Christmas carol, but then, wait, that would be religious....strike that, judge. And a yoga teacher named Christian Eady? I'm still on the floor with laughter once again. If you don't laugh some point during any trial in life, you'll just cry or remain angry, but laughter doesn't mean you aren't taking it seriously. It is serious. Yet, comedy was at its finest – in the Meyer court room.

Yoga is religious!

Meyer concludes that Yoga is religious! We can hardly believe our ears. He just said it is religious. But, then he goes on. He further concluded that the yoga in EUSD was cleaned up enough so didn't *appear* religious (even though he just stated a general blanket that yoga is religious). So the "reasonable child observer" does not objectively see yoga as religious. (p. 37). Well, what does that mean?

But, it's cleaned up enough for ...
the children?

It means, he said EUSD can still do yoga! Even though he called it religious? What? Doesn't that contradict....keep on reading...

- The THIRD Prong to the test is: Does EUSD yoga foster excessive entanglement with religion? – (p. 37).
- **Judge** - in Brown versus Woodland Joint Unified School District, the Court – I'm going to read one final quote. "The Browns claim that the school district's appointment of a curriculum review committee to consider the purported religious content of the impressionist curriculum" – that's the witchcraft curriculum – "demonstrated an excessive administrative entanglement. This one-time review, which was conducted in response to the complaints of, among others, the Browns, clearly does not cause the school district to become entangled with religion. However, even if the review had entangled the school district with religion at the time, this is irrelevant to whether the school district continues to be entangled.

- **MEYER** - The yoga program, the EUSD yoga program, is no different. If the district determined that a particular teacher was infusing something religious, the district could deal with it. It's completely different – different from Lemon.

Judge admits Jois/EUSD relationship is "troublesome"

- **MEYER** – "Let me say, though, that the – a troublesome issue has been the influence of the Jois Foundation. There's been evidence on information and belief. There's been a lot of indirect evidence as to Jois. The opinion of Dr. Brown, as I had read from her testimony, is that the Jois Foundation is on a sinister mind-control conspiracy having a grand design to get these children and yoke them, to get them on a path to become practicing Hindus or Buddhists or Jainists. And it does appear that there – that certainly Jois has a – I guess you could call it a mission to have Ashtanga yoga, at least the physical part of it, taught in the – in the public school."

"And Jen Brown does have a connection with the Jois Foundation. Jen Brown has been to India, has learned Sanskrit, taught at the Jois shala, yoga – she was taught yoga by the wife of Pattabhi Jois (he got that detail wrong too – it was son Sharath she testified to learning under). Her (Sherath's actually) son lives in Encinitas, and his wife Nancy Jois apparently teaches at the district. So that has been a troublesome issue for the Court, probably the most troublesome issue. That's an issue that the Court has thought about a lot. The Court does not believe that the district is in any sort of conspiracy (how about a partnership as the contract states?) with the Jois Foundation. And I suppose, then, the question is, is the district being duped (now your getting somewhere judge…)? I don't think so. So the Court is persuaded by the testimony of the district witnesses, particularly Dr. Brown (that would be Principal Carrie Brown) – Dr. Baird and Dr. Miyashiro, of complete innocence from Jois."

"And as with any other grantor, if somebody wants to give money to a school district to teach something, if Jois doesn't like what the district does as an independent school district with legal obligations, I suppose Jois can do something with its money that doesn't involve the district. But the Court believes that the testimony of the district witnesses is credible, and the Court can't control what the district does in the future. But based on this record, the district – the Court concludes that the district is not teaching any religious component in its health and welfare (does he mean wellness or did court reporter type that wrong – that's funny too) program, which is the cornerstone of which is yoga or Ashtanga yoga."

He then asked Attorney Sleeth to prepare a statement of decision in accordance with the statement of intended decision and a judgment denying the writ of mandate.

Proceedings conclude at 10:40 on July 1, 2013.

Throwing out Professor Brown's testimony

To throw out Professor Brown's entire testimony was very likely *the only way out* for the judge to rule in favor of the district to keep the yoga program. One could not consider her testimony and the parent declarations, and come up with the verdict he did.

However, he did say "yoga is religious," so he did take her testimony into account, while also denouncing it, emerging from the trial with a different opinion than he began with about yoga. But Meyer's addition, "but yoga is cleaned up enough for the children" doesn't match the "yoga is religious" part of verdict. Don't those seem opposite in nature? It seems like it should be if Yoga is Religious = yoga out of schools, or the reverse: Yoga is not religious = yoga can stay in schools. But he states two opposing verdicts which in some respects is a small win for *both sides*. Meyer paved a road for deferred decisions in an appeals or supreme court.

Since Meyer said he thought all of the parent letters sounded too much alike and that probably we all got together and wrote them copying one another – which is so odd he would say this, but a lot of odd things were said, as mentioned. It was strange, sitting in what we thought would be a fairly quick verdict which went on most of the morning. At times, he seemed to lean one direction, stating facts for our side, then to leaning the other direction, stating facts that would support the district. There were multiple "seemingly small" errors of facts that in sum, became a huge problem. I listed about 10, when the judge did a summary on Day 4, that I wrote down and gave to our attorney to point them out to the judge during his closing comments and as you saw, included some above in this chapter. Incorrect facts the judge relied upon in his closing comments, and the verdict indicate that he made decisions based on erroneous information.

Therefore, we began to wonder was this "meant to be" for now, for some facts not be uncovered? There were so many details wrong, yet media, judges, and others still don't know the truth. It was frustrating, but I tried to redirect myself to asking "why did this happen?" Is this so much larger than our district that it needs to move higher? The average person wants to trust the news and judicial system, but as we see all the time – they don't always get it right. We were experiencing "fake news" while reading media reports of the trial and case, long before the term would come about 3 years later. Documents of all this and the appeals are available, and hopefully some of the facts will become clearer through this book and the research others are also publishing. This issue will not be solved in the courts, we would begin to discover. If this is a spiritual battle, and not a physical battle, then it makes sense it will be played out elsewhere.

Our Reaction to the Verdict

The trial ended on July 1st, with the somewhat conflicting verdicts; that Yoga was religious, but it was okay for the EUSD to continue the curriculum in their schools. It was crushing news that EUSD could continue. Not because we thought we would win; it always seemed like such a long shot against public opinion. However, with so many facts stacked up on our side of the court-room, it was surprising. It was unexpected that the judge threw out every bit of testimony by our highly credible (by any of our world standards) expert witness, saying she would see everything as religious. That is about the only way Meyer could have ruled against us. Professor Brown's amazing expertise went well beyond anyone else's in the room on the background, research and any information ever written on the subjects she testified about in the trial. No one in the room, or likely elsewhere, knew more about the topic then she, and yet he dismissed all of it. I recalled the attorney who approached me just a couple months prior who told me how Judge Meyer would rule before the case began in court. He said we didn't have a chance; Meyer will vote popular opinion. He was right. So I quickly shifted to accepting the verdict and wondering what to do next. Do we appeal or do we stop? A few things added fear. And my husband was more down about it than I was that first day. However, remember, he didn't hear the verdict live, and there were no court notes to show him yet.

ADF dinner, July 1, 2013

We were invited that very night to an ADF dinner (Alliance Defending Freedom) where the president and founder "happened" to be in town speaking. We didn't know a lot about ADF, but we did know they supported our case, and sent an Attorney (Brad Abramson) to assist ours who was in court every day. So we decided to show up at that dinner (tail between legs) to slip into a seat and watch. Instead, we were introduced to people who thanked us for standing up against yoga in the schools, and we were even asked to speak about our case for a few minutes. The rest of the time we sat and listened to many other larger and very important cases that ADF was handling across the country, and what the organization does to support the public with its vast amount of specially trained attorneys.

We felt small and barely significant, but we did understand that night that even taking this trial on was a *big deal*, and that losing at this first level was not such a big blow after-all; it was *to be expected*. We were literally just out of the ring that day, bruised and bleeding and feeling the muscle pulls from the fight. But then others gave us the courage to move forward and continue the battle. We were given exactly what we needed; a boost to wake up the next day and walk through the disappointment. We would find we actually needed to help others deal with their disappointment, and to report to them that it was far from over. Others needed us to console them! Although this surprised me, it was preparing me for what would come to pass.

We had an appeal to prepare. There were too many facts on our side, too much cover-up and denial and shiftiness going on from the district to deny, so we knew it was best to lick our wounds, stand up and go back in the ring. Just as each step's timing seemed to draw out, a few months turned somehow into a year. But that was just fine, we were learning patience. And we were learning that there was a lot more than little ol' Encinitas, CA in this battle. There was a lot of other work to be done. There were meetings, educational programs (even educating pastors!), and a non-profit organization to plant soon. There were so many other things ahead that we could not see that day. We took it one day at a time through simple obedience to each next step, with a lot of thought, prayer and questioning along the way as to what to do next, if anything. There was more to come, moving forward. Even one day this book about the whole thing! After the book, I have no idea what's next, but I suspect it won't be over then either. It may be a new beginning to something. At times, we have felt very alone, and writing this book has been one of those times. In reality, we have always been surrounded by others in this same battle, by encouragement we received from others, and by faith. Please know that we are forever grateful. Thank you for the prayers, the calls of support, and the needed grace through this journey, not knowing where it was headed. This road wasn't the easy one.

Media Response to Verdict

https://www.nbcsandiego.com/news/local/Yoga-Lawsuit-Encinitas-Judgment-Ruling-School-Class-Controversy-213853341.html#ixzz2XrSK81Zt2

- See videos of verdict and reaction on both sides (although media lacks accurate facts on verdict): http://www.nbcsandiego.com/news/local/Yoga-Lawsuit-Encinitas-Judgment-Ruling-School-Class-Controversy-213853341.html#ixzz2XrSK81Zt[2]

- India's response to the trial: http://www.indiawest.com/news/global_indian/yoga-poses-new-questions-for-st-century-practitioners/article_3d4cd8c0-72ce-11e5-895f-17a2ef13b575.html[3]

- Press Release post trial, July 1, 2013: http://www.nclplaw.org/wp-content/uploads/2011/12/Post-Trial-Press-Release-FINAL1.pdf[4]

- Press Release post trial, July 9, 2013: http://www.nclplaw.org/wp-content/uploads/2011/12/Post-Trial-Press-Release-CONFLUENCE-FINAL.pdf[5]

- Huffington Post on yoga and the Church vs. State Battle in Encinitas: http://www.huffingtonpost.com/news/encinitas-yoga-trial/[6]

- What Makes the Encinitas Yoga Religious, Huffington Post: http://www.huffingtonpost.com/candy-gunther-brown-phd/encinitas-yoga-lawsuit_b_3570850.html[7]

- LA Times—Objections to yoga curriculum in public schools: http://www.latimes.com/local/lanow/la-me-ln-religious-objections-yoga-public-schools-20130701-story.html[8]

CHAPTER FOURTEEN

To Appeal or Not to Appeal ...

Decision to Appeal

Many layers of consideration go into a decision to appeal. The first part of the verdict by Judge Meyers that *Yoga is Religious,* laid a foundation for more discussion at the appellate level. The potential pool of judges available for an appeal, in the California courts, was a factor of concern. Many other personal and professional decisions needed to be considered, as well, such as the financial commitment.

ADF Backs Out

Alliance Defending Freedom (ADF) financially supported the first level of the trial. Dean Broyles is an ADF trained attorney and the organization paid for some of his expenses. However, a new board for ADF took over at the turn of the year, and they decided to have an external group determine which trials to support. Ours hit the chopping block. ADF was out. My husband and I learned this right after making the decision to appeal. ADF pulling out was a devastating blow. Fortunately, that sort of thing doesn't make the news, so we had time to consider our options. The reasoning we were given from ADF was that they are trying to get freedoms and rights back into the schools, while our case was about getting Hinduism practices out. So going forward, finances to cover attorney expenses looked different and were unknown.

Financial Decisions

The Encinitas Union School District and Coast Law Group ("push in" attorney) billed us for their expenses to the tune of about $6000 which is what the winning side can legally request. We reasoned through some of the facts. If we stop here, we have to pay that bill. If we appeal, the expenses will only become higher, and we might be liable for even more financially. Do we want to take that risk? In the beginning of this trial, we knew that Dean Broyles, the attorney that met with parents and district for months, would be working Pro Bono for the case. That only pertained to fees. His expenses, [for filing court documents and travel for expert witness, etc.] obviously needed to be met. He, nor any of us, ever expected the amount of hours he would end up putting into this case, taking away hundreds of hours to work for his "paying clients."

At one point anxiety came to a head when bills got tight, and we (those closest to the case) experienced internal disagreements. Although we knew *spiritual warfare* was definitely alive and present throughout this case, we were all in a very stressful spot making big decisions. Up to that point, this trial had not cost us financially, beyond our time. Donations were needed to cover costs, and although many people supported the trial, a new test of our faith appeared. Would we be willing to dig into our own pockets risking the move forward, knowing we might be on the line for around $10,000 without a safety net? This is another point in time that it became clear to me why perhaps it was better only one family bear the burden of this trial. A group may have battled over money and fear, while making tough decisions. A couple can make decisions more easily, since we already make so many life decisions together. It may appear it would be more of a burden on only one couple. But that *burden* forgets one big factor:

Fear vs Faith?

Our *tipping point* was faith. Malcolm Gladwell so eloquently illuminates these shifts in thinking with stories in his book *Tipping*

284

Point. For us, it became faith that something would work out for the financial needs if we lost an appeal. Faith, that the trial might end the yoga program in school after an appeal. Faith, that no matter what happened, we would be okay. A great deal of faith was required for David to go up against Goliath. We were continuing to learn how vast the group supporting this yoga program was, with several rich and famous people such as Chopra and Oprah with deep pockets of money and influence. We were at the same crossroads as six months prior when deciding whether to file in the first place. Yet, the stakes kept rising. Fear or Faith? Which will win? Logic and absolutes were available, but there were still a lot of unknown factors. The ridicule from people faded away as we understood by then that most people didn't know what the case was really all about. Even simple facts were buried, causing reporters and readers to assume all kinds of erroneous tangents. Ironically, one of my women's event programs is titled "Moving Forward in Faith" and that is what we did. We moved *through the fear* and decided to appeal the case.

To Appeal

Filing the appeal was one thing, but waiting almost two years for the appellate trial was another. Yoga was still in full swing in the Encinitas Union School District schools and our child was still not getting her legally required 100 minutes of PE each week. The first level of the trial ended in July 2013, but now we had to make a decision that summer whether to return to the same school, or change schools to another within the district. Don't miss the fact that in order to file or appeal against EUSD, our child had to be enrolled in the district. We were in a quandary. The small bit of harassment we got from some parents was not the final straw. We now had to wonder if the principal who testified against our children, would actually be making the best decisions for our daughter going forward (our middle son graduated out of district that year) when she really hadn't for our son, for years.

We had already spent the past six years attempting to get academic help to address dyslexia. The El Camino Creek principal was one of the key decision makers during committee decisions when she denied the needed curriculum... We were forced to go outside the school, paying thousands of dollars for a program that sat unavailable to him, in the special education resource room at ECC. The dyslexia curriculum at the schools is only available for a much smaller pool of kids than have the need for it. My concern went far beyond my child, to those who cannot afford to get the programs needed. So, Carrie Brown's testimony at the trial where she subverted the truth about our kids receiving the state required physical education time per week, and, under her leadership teachers were clearly told to avoid us (confirmed by teachers), which was the *straw that broke the camel's back*. We were done trusting her. She clearly did not have the best interest of our kids in mind. How could we leave our then 8-year old in her care? However, we had to keep our daughter enrolled in the district, in order to appeal. Fortunately, another school in the district was half a mile the other direction from our home.

Personal Trials

I walked the cement pathways and willingly volunteered nearly weekly at El Camino Creek Elementary for the nine years prior. Both our sons completed K-6th grade there, and our friendships with parents and teachers ran deep. We would miss many wonderful teachers and friends. Our daughter had been there three years, and already had enjoyed having some of the same teachers as her brothers from previous years. She was looking forward to the teachers she might get in upper grades. We did our best to explain to her why we needed to move her, and, even through 8-year-old eyes, she could see some reasons. She had seen the changes in how many of the teachers and parents treated us. She had seen anger from other parents expressed toward us, and some of the other kids opted-out of yoga. We didn't need four more years of that principal making decisions for our daughter and she understood some of the reasons why.

We hoped a school move would help others treat her like a normal kid. Had I known how traumatic it would become for her with friends, we might not have chosen to move schools. One of her closest friends cried for two weeks and begged her mom to move her to the same school. Our daughter cried for months and clinginess emerged, covering up the confident little girl we had known. Sometimes not knowing what lies ahead is best. Second grade girls are apparently a lot more connected to their friends than boys seem to be at that age. It was heartbreaking that the choices we made impacted her in this way. Yet, in the long run, we knew she was a strong and resilient little girl. She would soon show us that resilience.

Flying "under the radar"

When we moved over to our new school, La Costa Heights, that summer of 2013, we thought we would enter quietly and "fly under the radar." However, shortly after we arrived at the school, a meeting was held in which many moms figured out who I was, and started asking questions. For the next few weeks, a string of moms approached me as I walked into school, asking if they could get a few minutes of my time about yoga and the trial. I stood on the sidewalks of La Costa Heights (LCH) and answered a lot of questions that fall. The previous principal for LCH, Leighangela Brady, had reportedly shamed all the parents into keeping their kids in yoga with comments at PTA meetings such as: "We aren't going to be like those other schools getting divisive over yoga." She was very close with Superintendent Baird and took Miyashiro's assistant superintendent spot that year (for which incidentally, both she and Carrie Brown interviewed for that summer at the district office). Thus, LCH had a brand new principal. She relocated from Fallbrook, and knew very little about the yoga trial. She likely didn't know that our family was entering the same school. However, what she must have known is that a bright new yoga studio had been built on the LCH campus. Who funded the new yoga studio?

This is how some moms found out who I was at the beginning of the year. At a private meeting in a home with about 15 moms (a moms in prayer meeting), one sat back on a couch and stretched and said "Okay we have to talk about this yoga because I'm going to pull my (3) kids out this year." Other moms started commenting back and forth, positively and negatively about yoga and these were all good friends, but it was getting heated quickly. After a few minutes, and being new, I knew I had to reveal who I was or forever regret that I didn't, and lose their trust that I hadn't said anything. So, I gave my last name and two women gasped. Then, the questions began. One mom was mad at the attorney for some things she had heard. This room of moms, like the schools, was split on the issue. People were confused. Some were not sure how they felt. But one thing I left knowing … I was not able to hide or fly under the radar in this school or anywhere for long.

However, we actually did, for the most part, spend the next three years there, quietly going about our own business of elementary school events. Most people never knew who I was, only that our family was there at their school somewhere. Or if they did know, they ignored us and kept their distance. I felt a strong sense of Godly protection at most times without really understanding when and where we would need it most. I walked my daughter in every morning as any other 3rd grade parent would do at our school, and she eventually made new friends and was pretty much harassment-free at that school and clinginess subsided. She loved her teachers, but fitting in at a new school wasn't easy. She showed her resilience and understanding of the problems with yoga at times, too. One example is the first day of 4th grade her new teacher happened to do yoga moves and yoga breathing during regular class. She marched right up to me after school and said "we need to go talk to my teacher." We did and fortunately, yoga moves didn't happen again in that 4th grade class.

Although she was young, she learned there was something unique about herself, through strangers who thanked her for her role in standing up against yoga in schools. People told her how important what she was doing was, even though she might not understand right now. When person after person stopped to give her a big smile or hug and say similar things to her, she may not have fully understood why, but she knew her role was important and people were grateful.

So, while she was now walking the pathways around La Costa Heights elementary school, we were in the midst of waiting on an appeal.

The Appeal

I don't have a lot to say about the appeal beyond what press releases and written judges' decisions can show you. There was nothing more we needed to prepare as a family. The attorney filed the documents; you can read about why we appealed, but you know the reasons from the previous chapters.

Probably, the most interesting thing to note about the appeal that you wouldn't otherwise know is that there were three judges slotted for this case, and it was fairly apparent one might be more open to our case, while the others likely would not. For some reason, that judge ended up being replaced that morning with another. Four judge names appear on the document written two weeks later. All I know is that our Attorney said it was not good. Our one hope was gone. It was a very belligerent questioning of our attorney at the appellate review, and Dean Broyles appeared to be the firing target. I remember how twisted the appellate attorney questions were, and the facts seemed to twist further from the truth. It was, again, surreal. How can the truth not make it through? It was frustrating to watch the facts get trampled and misunderstood. It was crystal clear that day what way the judges were leaning, even down to their choice of how to ask the questions and the standard (#4 below) they would use to review the case.

If you read the decision of the Appellate Judges, you find that many of the facts they base their decisions on are, once again, information that was skewed by the district testimonies so the true facts aren't clear to these judges. Examples below show you the highlights. The full decision is here: https://truthaboutyoga.files. wordpress.com/2015/01/appeal-court-decision.pdf.[1]

1. The judges refer to court (Meyer) where he stated at one point; there is "no evidence Jois Foundation is a religious organization" (p. 6). (Throws out a lot of testimony).

2. The appellate judges erroneously leave out Russell Case as one of the three who did the workshop training of twenty-two yoga instructors and whittling down to ten yoga teachers for EUSD. They state Miyashiro and Regur were the only ones there, missing the entire point that Russell Case, from Jois Foundation, was involved in hiring, training and certifying these ten instructors (pp. 8, 9).

3. The judges were led to believe there was no input from Jois Foundation in the development of the curriculum for the children (p. 9). Every Ashtanga trained yoga instructor in the room who had three years of Ashtanga teaching experience represent exactly what Jois Foundation wanted in the curriculum written for them to take nationally. The lead teacher, Jen Brown, would be enough proof, given she worked for both Jois and EUSD.

4. We submitted for De novo review of the facts (taking into account historical facts established be reviewed—such as what happened in prior steps of the yoga introduction, not just "as it stands today"). The district submitted for an independent standard of review, only including facts that have substantial evidence being admitted. The judges chose the district's standard of review, further hurting our case and eliminating many facts in court (p. 12).

5. The judges apply the Lemon test and decide that for the first prong that the district is not advancing Ashtanga yoga. For the second prong, they stated that we as petitioners did not contest that the district's "intent" was to have a secular program. For the third prong, the judges decide that EUSD is not endorsing Ashtanga, not advancing it, nor prohibiting another religion by doing it (pp. 15, 16, 17).

6. The judges address the fact that this decision will consider the ages of children "Courts ... have considered the more

vulnerable nature of school-age children when analyzing the primary effect of state actions" ... But then they use a 'reasonable observer' standard as to whether someone watching a given class 'would see religion.' Of course they wouldn't see any without knowledge, *but does that standard protect children?"* (p. 17, 18).

7. Humorously, they judge that there is no evidence that the children were taught jnana mudra (even though the kids are clearly doing it in the video—"maybe they learned it elsewhere," but the teachers claim they don't teach it, so that is what all these judges believe). Sure, "the kids came up with it themselves" they suppose ... (p. 19).

8. The judges don't see the religious mission of Jois Foundation as relevant to EUSD (even though Jois Foundation hired EUSD to develop curriculum for them). The Jois Foundation website was not submitted *in evidence*, so no proof considered (p. 21).

9. They use "[A] practice's mere consistency with or coincidental resemblance to a religious practice does not have the primary effect of advancing religion." To argue that Ashtanga yoga "coincidentally" resembles EUSD yoga. My input: Okay, right judge, with all the evidence of Ashtanga teachers and Jois Foundation, it's a "coincidence" (p. 23, 24)? Seriously? How can you live with that statement? There is *no coincidence* when the whole trial was based on this matter of "coincidence!"

10. The judges then point to "advancing" religion as needing to be direct and immediate (not future) even when performing religious rituals and poses in reference to Brown's testimony that yoga leads the children on a path to acceptance of this spiritual path when done in schools with the endorsement of government (p. 25).

11. They decide the school's program is not inherently religious (p. 27) and go on to state a lot of inaccurate facts on which they base the decision of entanglement (like the district *promptly* taking down posters which were up for a year ... and forgetting that after the complaints the Ashtanga trees

started popping up in the schools, *not before*) and so on. The judges conclude that the district was not entangled with Jois, or religion enough (to a degree is allowed, it has to be excessive) and attempts were made by EUSD to clean it up, so the program is not endorsing Ashtanga yoga any longer to them, nor anything they see as religious (pp. 31-33).

12. Furthermore, entanglement has to have "sustained and detailed interaction." Soon Baird would appear on the Board of Jois Foundation, seen on their website (now Sonima) and other "relational interests that cross over," such as that his daughter was working for Jois/Sonima, and Baird being in promotional videos and speaking at programs for Sonima. None of that may be "enough" entanglement or "detailed" enough, but none of that was in evidence at that time (p. 34).

13. The judges state there is no evidence that Jen Brown worked for Jois, so there is no *evidence* of any ongoing connection to Jois (p. 35). Now, 2013 tax forms are proof.

14. Finally, the judges also contend that since the district began offering that families could "opt-out," that this lessens the argument of increasing the program's constitutionality or coercion into religion and thus violating the establishment clause (p. 31). Opting-out is a lot different than choosing electives or having a PE option. It's not even close to being similar.

Press Release for Appellate Trial — March 11, 2015

NCLP's founder and chief counsel, Dean Broyles, argued that "no court in the past fifty years has allowed state officials to teach formal religious rituals [like prayer, meditation, devotional Bible reading, or Hindu Pujahs to young children with impressionable consciences] in our public schools, and the trial court erred as a matter of law by failing to find the District's Ashtanga yoga program violates the Establishment Clause." We believe that the important American principle of religious freedom allocates to families, religious groups, and individual conscience the important job of teaching and understanding religious beliefs and practices, not to the state," declared Dean Broyles.

Broyles contends that "The District completely ignores the inconvenient truth that its' students are bowing to, praying to, and worshipping the Hindu sun god in yoga classes, by being led through the Surya Namaskara. Both in their briefs, and before the court today, the District had no explanation whatsoever as to why worshipping the sun god and lotus meditation are not formal Hindu Liturgies; how the District purportedly metaphysically stripped them of religion; or how these continuing Hindu ritual religious practices do not violate the Establishment Clause."

"The thrust of our argument today was that, because the trial court failed to find that teaching children of a young age with tender consciences, formal religious rituals in school-sponsored classes violates the Establishment clause, it erred as a matter of law and the appellate court is bound by well-established legal precedents to reverse and find the District's yoga program is unconstitutional."

And as you know ... that is not what happened. The full press release is referenced first in the media for this chapter.

Media

Here is a list of media and then our reactions to the Appellate level loss.

March 11, 2015—Press Release: Oral Arguments before a "Hot Bench" http://www.nclplaw.org/wp-content/uploads/2011/12/Appeal-Press-Release-3-11-15-.pdf [2]

April 3, 2015— Decision of Appellate Judges https://truthaboutyoga.files.wordpress.com/2015/01/appeal-court-decision.pdf[3]

April 3, 2015—Press Release in response to Appellate judges decision http://www.nclplaw.org/wp-content/uploads/2011/12/Appeal-Press-Release-4-03-15-FINAL.pdf[4]

DEAN BROYLES: "No other court in the past 50 years has allowed public school officials to lead children in formal religious rituals like the Hindu liturgy of praying to, bowing to, and worshipping the sun god. We are disappointed with the decision and are carefully considering our options."

- Encinitas parent group Narrative summary about the lawsuit here https://truthaboutyoga.files.wordpress.com/2015/01/lawsuit-in-encinitas.pdf[5]

April 29, 2015 - After appeal - Finally, after 3 years, erupts an article where a reporter is starting to scratch below the surface to see the connections:

- Is Yoga a religion? Courts say it is, but Encinitas schools have scrubbed their yoga programs clean http://www.sandiegoreader.com/news/2015/apr/29/citylights-yoga-religion/#[6]

Press Release - June 11, 2015 - NCLP will not Pursue Appeal Challenging Encinitas' Ashtanga Yoga Program *(Sedlock vs. Baird)*.

- Press Release Appeal, June 11, 2015, http://www.nclplaw.org/wp-content/uploads/2011/12/Appeal-Press-Release-6-11-15-FINAL.pdf[7]

June 13, 2015 - Parents opposing yoga for kids take campaign public with website and links to information. *This reporter has also figured out there is so much more to this case!*

- Parents opposing yoga for kids take campaign public (beyond the trial) http://www.wnd.com/2015/06/parents-opposing-yoga-for-kidstake-campaign-public/[8]

October 15, 2015—India West interviewed us after the case

- Indian courts considering yoga in response to our case. India West reports about yoga throughout trial http://www. indiawest.com/news/global_indian/yoga-poses-new- questions-for-st-century-practitioners/article_3d4cd8c0- 72ce-11e5-895f-17a2ef13b575.html.[9]

After Appellate level loss

This loss was different. Note that the appellate trial was March 11, 2015, and the appellate judge decision filing was April 3, 2015. All along we discussed that our goal was to take the case to Supreme Court if needed, but after the loss of the appeal, the conversations from my husband and the attorney shifted. After much thought and discussion, the attorney pointed to the fact that we had filed in the State system as a Writ Mandate for good reasons (to get the program out quickly), but that at this point, it would be better to file a new lawsuit in the Federal Court. Going to the next level in a liberal state system might only help Jois Foundation in their ability to spread the Ashtanga yoga even faster. Jois Foundation yoga was already in at least five states. They would have more leverage if EUSD won in the California Supreme Court. By moving it to Federal, there could be a jury, more evidence, and many more legal reasons I cannot even begin to explain. Also, we weren't sure *we* should be the couple to take it to the next level. It was suggested that it might be better with a new couple or potentially with a team of families.

After two months of contemplating moving forward, we all decided it was best to not file. Pursing the next level, after what happened in the appeal, didn't seem wise. In that time frame, it also became clear that this *battle* was perhaps not to be won in courts, nor in the court of public opinion. We realized in order to have people learn the facts of the case, the information would have to be revealed through other avenues.

Where are the pastors?

We learned by looking back, that each of us parents had come to this realization about yoga in schools, one by one. None of us was swayed by any one thing, but each of us experienced an evolution of awakening to the problems and issues with yoga in schools. And, although it would appear that the most ideal people to speak out against yoga in schools would be pastors, who impact many families in their own congregations, what we found was that most pastors are just as confused on the issue as the rest of the general public. Pastors didn't have foundational knowledge about yoga either. Yoga was still fairly new the past few decades to most Americans. Some pastors have never even considered the topic, and once they see how divisive it is, many don't want to get involved, nor speak about it in their own churches. However, a few pastors did get involved, and we found some were already speaking out a lot against yoga and idol worship. Through this case, we have met and seen many pastors who understand the magnitude of the impact of yoga. Yoga leans toward New Age religious practices, and people don't realize it is a religion, making it even easier to spread. Many consider yoga a *trojan horse* galloping into the churches, (or rather - slithering in like a serpent idol). Many Christians are not hesitating to do yoga, thinking it is just physical, while others seek to fill a spiritual void, they claim. If yoga creates a path toward a belief opposite of the Christian faith (such as Hindu beliefs of multiple deities and lives), would Christians want to know that?

Just suppose for a moment that yoga does lead toward the deities worshiped in Hindu and Buddhist religions. Perhaps that could be why Bible-reading Christians were clearest on the conflict with their own religious beliefs and yoga in schools. Unless you read and understand about idol worship (in say Deuteronomy) and the pathway of diversions away through the book of Revelation, you might not see it at all. Therein lies part of the challenge of this battle: it's an unseen battle, masquerading in a healthy, appealing activity, seemingly healthy and good. If you knew the Bible teaches that *the enemy will masquerade as good and as the light*, this is

296

a reminder to not be deceived by something that just seems good, but to be alert, and to make sure.

Although you may not agree with me on theology, you must be able to see that yoga is not as innocent as volleyball. There is no *Holy Volleyball,* because there is no need to call it holy. Yoga is not innocent. Even though you may have been to a yoga class that seems to be all-exercise, you as an adult can choose to do yoga, and that is your choice. But for children to be forced by into participating through a yoga curriculum, crosses a line of forcing choices not all parents want for their children due to the spiritual roots and practices known in yoga.

TheTruthaboutYoga.com

Everything you might want to read about the details of the trial can be found on our Truth about Yoga Website on the following page: http://truthaboutyoga.com/law_suit-in-encinitas-2/[10]

You will find these same court documents, press releases and the news surrounding the actual timing of the trial to click onto easily. More news after the trial is continually added to the News and Media page: http://truthaboutyoga.com/news-media/.[11]

These last few chapters were more of an "inside the courtroom look" of the trial and condensed facts presented. There is so much more about the media frenzy. We did not speak to the media as per the instruction of our attorney. And for our protection we waited. Until now. Now, it's time to expose what really happened and explain what is sweeping our nation.

For the latest media, visit the website and sign up to receive newsletters of updates. New groups of parents in the EUSD district are now waking up to some of the *covering-up* about yoga and the relationships promoting the program. For the newest developments, such as occurred when Sonima pulled funding from EUSD (2016), after four years and $4 million, see the "Latest in EUSD" chapter 23. A new set of parents became involved; we sat back to watch the fireworks.

During and after the trial, there were a lot of unintended consequences that began to occur in Encinitas in the schools and across the nation in yoga. The following chapters will give you several foundational concerns fueling the fire for us to continue throughout the lawsuit.

Section Three—Fallout from Yoga Replacing PE in Elementary Schools

P BS did a show on the benefits of yoga taught in schools for PE. These next few chapters display the unintended consequences to children when PE is replaced with yoga. These topics give you a glimpse of a few reasons that yoga is *not* a good idea to be forced upon young children in America. We maintain yoga is fine as an optional choice for families outside of school, and would hope they seek enough information about it to consider their beliefs, but not to replace the physical education that American children have enjoyed for years involving more cardiovascular exercise, coordination, healthy competition and team-building lessons. Even for those kids who don't enjoy physical activity, PE is vital to their growth and development. Through PE, children learn a variety of sports, dancing and fitness that they would never learn, if not for PE in schools.

There is a big difference between yoga and stretching and this article shows you that difference: http://www.differencebetween.net/science/health/difference-between-yoga-and-stretching/#ixzz2BeonizBx.[1] Starting with the basic definition that stretching is a basic of life, where all animals stretch to lengthen muscles, but that yoga requires deeper breathing – so only humans can perform yoga. Definitions of yoga and the origins explain how yoga is focused on the mental and physical, not just physical. The loss of freedom of choice for kids is too great when PE is replaced with yoga philosophies, poses and meditation in schools. Add in yoga-specific youth injuries and the picture deteriorates further.

CHAPTER FIFTEEN

Yoga Injuries and Warnings
for Children

The very first time I sat down to research about yoga in the elementary schools, I ran into two very important pieces of information that were the first red flags for physical problems associated with yoga, especially for children. Young girl's hips are the largest concern.

American Yoga Association and Mayo Clinic

The American Yoga Association[1] does not recommend yoga for children under age 16. Due to the potential for injuries and impaired growth, yoga, as you can see in the following box, is not a good idea for children. You can read more on their website on the link.

According to the American Yoga Association (AYA): "Yoga exercises are not recommended for children under 16 because their bodies' nervous and glandular systems are still growing, and the effect of Yoga exercises on these systems may interfere with natural growth". (http://www.americanyogaassociation.org/general.html[1]

Experience and Knowledge

Second, the Mayo Clinic[2] warned against children doing two specific yogas: Ashtanga and Bickram. Ashtanga was the yoga EUSD contracted to be implemented into all nine Encinitas schools for a student's seven years at the elementary level. Given my background in the fitness industry, this was enough for me to be concerned right away.

Mayo Clinic: Are there styles of yoga that aren't recommended for children? There are many different styles of yoga. Two styles inappropriate for children include:

Ashtanga. This type of yoga, also called power yoga, focuses on strength and flexibility training and rapid movements. Practicing Ashtanga requires excellent physical condition.

Bikram. Commonly called hot yoga, Bikram involves doing vigorous poses in a room heated to 100 to 110 F (38 to 43 C). Practicing Bikram also requires excellent physical condition. http://www.yogaforkidsportland.com/yoga-for-kids-a-good-idea-by-mayo-clinic-staff.html[2]

We gave the Encinitas District this information from AYA and Mayo Clinic in the fall of 2012, and AYA has not changed their recommendation against yoga for youth to date (2018).

Medical Doctors Concerns over Yoga

Let's look at the research of four different doctors and their reports on the impact of yoga. From spine specialists to orthopedic surgeons to OB/GYNs, there are numerous accounts.

First, from a spine specialist:

Can Yoga Wreck Your Body? Dr. Jennifer Solomon, a physiatrist in the Women's Sports Medicine Center at the Hospital for Special Surgery states: "As a spine specialist and a sports medicine specialist I see a ton of yoga injuries." (https://www.hss.edu/newsroom_jennifer-solomon-preventing-yoga-injuries.asp#.VU_ekTnn9lY)[3]

Second, An OB/GYN on female warnings:

> **Eden G. Fromberg, DO,** Holistic **obstetrician/gynecologist** at SOHO OB/GYN has commented in a recent Huff Post article: "I have observed in my own gynecological practice that classical or contemporary yoga can contribute to symptoms of chronic vulvar pain and sexual dysfunction via painful ligamentous instability, hip injuries or herniated discs, overstimulation of already-stressed sympathetic nervous systems, and pelvic floor muscle spasms." http://www.huffingtonpost.com/eden-g-fromberg-do/yoga_b_1202465.html.[4]

American orthopedic surgeons are seeing a marked increase in yoga injuries since the rise in Americans doing yoga. In the last half of a decade, recommendations to practice yoga have exploded and the amount of people practicing has grown exponentially.

The injuries are astounding … and hidden.

Third, the Orthopedic Surgeons:

> *Bad Karma: When Yoga Harms Instead of Heals* "In my practice, I've seen a significant increase in yoga injuries in the past five years," says **orthopedic surgeon Jeffrey Halbrecht, M.D.**, medical director for the Institute for Arthroscopy and Sports Medicine in San Francisco and a specialist in knee and hip problems. http://www.nbcnews.com/id/25400799/#.V1_7Wo-cGhd.[5]

More on Yoga Injuries

Women's flexibility is an issue, according to *New York Times*.

1. http://www.nytimes.com/2013/11/03/sunday-review/womens-flexibility-is-a-liability-in-yoga.html?_r=1.[6]

"To my astonishment, some of the nation's top surgeons declared the trouble to be real — so real that hundreds of women who did yoga were showing up in their offices with unbearable pain and undergoing costly operations to mend or even replace their hips." -William J Broad.

"It's a relatively high incidence of injury," Jon Hyman, an orthopedic surgeon in Atlanta, told me. "People don't come in often saying I was doing Zumba or tai chi" when they experienced serious hip pain, he said. "But yoga is common."

Dr. Hyman said his typical yoga patient was a middle-aged woman, adding that he saw up to ten a month — or roughly 100 a year. "People need to be aware," he said. "If they're doing things like yoga and have pain in the hips, they shouldn't blow it off."

Bryan T. Kelly, an orthopedic surgeon at the Hospital for Special Surgery in Manhattan, echoed the warning, saying yoga postures were well known for throwing hips into extremes. "If that's done without an understanding of the mechanical limitations of the joint, it can mean trouble," he said in an interview.

Yoga Dangers

Dangers of Yoga.com

2..Dangers of Yoga

http://dangersofyoga.blogspot.com/2010/02/yoga-contraindications-of-yoga.html.[7]

"The danger in working with an untrained yoga teacher lies in the unrecognized power of the practices to bring about the uncontrolled release of fears, illnesses, sexual attachment and terrifying archetypal formations from the unconscious, just like the opening of Pandora's Box." (This is just one of the many comments on this website by gurus.)

Kapalbhati Benefits and Dangers. (http://yogayoutube.org/kapalbhati-benefits-and-dangers/752)[8]

Yoga side effects. Yoga DVD guru. (http://www.yogadvdguru.com/yoga-side-effects.shtml)[9]

Yoga Injury Prevention

- Here is one website on injury prevention by the American Academy of Orthopedic Surgeons (AAOS) on Ortho info: http://orthoinfo.aaos.org/topic.cfm?topic=A00063.[10]

- Another website (the organization I was certified through years ago)—Idea Health and Fitness Association http://www.ideafit.com/fitness-library/injury-prevention-yoga-class-take-out[11] on common yoga injuries to the spine, ligaments, cartilage, muscles and tendons.

- The most common yoga injuries and how to prevent them: http://greatist.com/fitness/common-yoga-injuries-prevention-treatment.[12]

- How to prevent *common* yoga injuries: http://www.sheknows.com/health-and-wellness/articles/1025219/how-to-prevent-common-yoga-injuries.[13]

- Yoga can lead to hip injuries and hip replacements: http://www.cbc.ca/news/health/yoga-can-lead-to-hip-injuries-1.2427134[14]

- Injury Prevention in Alignment: http://yogalign.com/yoga-injuries-2/[15]

- 7 Steps to Preventing Injury at Yoga Class: https://www.verywell.com/preventing-injury-at-yoga-class-3567225[16]

- 4 common Yoga Mistakes that Can Cause Knee Pain and Damage: http://blog.gaiam.com/4-yoga-poses-mistakes-that-can-cause-knee-pain/[17]

Yoga Can Wreck Your Body

Studies show that years of yoga actually tear down the body. Yoga over time attacks the very frame of the human bone and ligament structure that was created to hold us up, as was reported on NBC News http://www.nbcnews.com/id/25400799/#.VvBEHI-cFul.[18] There are many yogis who have shared about their injuries—here is one with hip and knee injuries *that are hidden*: https://www.youtube.com/watch?v=BLVb0klaris)[19] and are indicators that fifteen to twenty years of yoga are very damaging to our bodies. The New York Times featured the breakdown effects to your body in an article called "How Yoga Can Wreck Your Body" (http://www.nytimes.com/2012/01/08/magazine/how-yoga-can-wreck-your-body.html).[20]

Background in Fitness

For years, I was a certified aerobics instructor through IDEA Health and Fitness Association. I spent years teaching classes through gyms such as Nautilus in Oregon, Family Fitness in San Diego, and Corporate Fitness of San Diego. Corporate Fitness sent me into different companies each week. At one point, I taught for five organizations, and I taught multiple classes a day working around my professional career in management and training. So, I spent a lot of time on fitness and learning the industry. How to prevent injuries for clients was a critical consideration. After a decade in management, I became self-employed, so when the opportunities to volunteer and help in the schools with needs such as PE arose, I was able to help fill some of those needs just like many other parents in the district. When I taught PE in 2010 in the Encinitas School, El Camino Creek, the underlying foundation was similar in that a lesson takes preparation, concern for each child to prevent injuries, and helping the children learn about their bodies with minimal negative experiences for the ones who are less capable of the activity. Teaching children is very different than teaching adults—whether it's a physical activity or not.

When yoga entered the scene full scale in Encinitas schools, I was no longer teaching in gyms but instead was focused on my own three children, my business, and pouring my time into coaching, working and volunteering at the schools. Anyone who knows me wouldn't think I would have time to get involved in all this, least of all spend seven years in this "battle" and write a book about it, but I couldn't ignore what would happen to these innocent children. So when yoga entered the schools via this highly religious organization from India—twice weekly in the curriculum, replacing PE—I became concerned for what this would do to children physically as well as spiritually.

Glenn Black, a noted teacher of yoga for four decades, has come to believe that "the vast majority of people" should give up yoga altogether. It's simply too likely to cause harm. **How Yoga Can Wreck Your Body— NYTimes.com**. This article by William Broad rocked the yoga world and caused yogis to lose their peace . . .(https://www.nytimes.com/2012/01/08/magazine/how-yoga-can-wreck-your-body.html?_r=2)[20]

Yoga teacher testifying about yoga injuries. Charlotte Bell wrote an article warning yoga teachers about joint problems: http://www.elephantjournal.com/2013/09/yogis-be-careful-with-your-joints-charlotte-bell/.[21] Hip and knee replacements are a huge problem in yoga. But hush, hush in the yoga community. **Yoga Teacher Testifying on yoga injuries to educate people on risks.** "Pop Pop in yoga is muscle tearing from bone." She wound up with hip surgery as well as what she talks about here: https://www.youtube.com/watch?v=BLVb0klaris.[22]

A Huge Concern, On Many Levels

Most PE teachers would agree that a variety of physical activities is important for young children for many reasons. One single activity isn't a better choice, no matter which one. The goal of exposing children to multiple physical activities produces many positive results, such as giving the child opportunity to explore interests, build different physical skills, and learn teamwork. Strength, muscular development, endurance and flexibility grow through physical skills. Playing fair with others, building dedication when something is challenging, learning to be a good leader and a good follower, playing by rules, graciously winning or losing—are all good skills one learns through a variety of sports. Choose just one, and the losers are the children. So that was a huge concern. Second, cardiovascular exercise is needed to combat the obesity problem. Yoga is clearly not going to match other sports in that area, even though that was a purported benefit of this yoga program. The results of the study did not support the district's claims for better physical results. Third, let's not forget that PE is mandated by legislation.

In business, experts will say that you become an expert at something if you study it just seven years. If kids study yoga for seven years in elementary school, kindergarten through sixth, could it perhaps become a lifetime of practice for many of them? Would this *change the face of American culture?* (If Jois Foundation is successful getting into every elementary school for an hour of yoga replacing PE – will we eventually become much more complacent and accommodating—not competitive, lack of free markets, perhaps something more like … Socialism?). Is this the direction we want our country to head? Do we see success in yoga when we look at the countries that have practiced it much longer? Do we want our success in yoga and economy to match that of India for example? This isn't just exercise, the folks from India tell us. Change the children, change the culture, and you change the country. It's not far-fetched, and it's slithering its way in quickly. In the last few years, yoga has seen staggering growth in the United States. Here is the most recent study on the growth of yoga titled *"Namaste Nation"—New 2016 Study Shows Staggering Growth in Yoga in America! This came out in April of 2016,* (http://www.lighthousetrailsresearch.com/blog/?p=19095).[23]

Hip Injury in Young Girls

The most concerning injury, by far, is in the hips of young girls. The growth plates and hips of young girls are fluid and the movement and growth in them from ages ten to sixteen is a time of vulnerability to injury, higher than the rest of their lives. However, once I began to research through doctors and previous yogis (yogis that are exposing the hip and knee surgeries of other yogis), I realized the problem was an epidemic among yoga practitioners. It was a "dirty little secret" being hidden amongst yogis. The literature reveals people exposing the injuries are being shunned in the yoga communities. Other yogis are actively trying to keep them quiet.

Michaelle Edwards

One such person is Michaelle Edwards in Kauai, Hawaii. Edwards attempted to contact me via Linked-In social media after we filed the lawsuit and before the trial. She said she could help us in the trial. I didn't respond to her because 1. We had our one expert witness identified already (the trial was set up to have one on each side) and 2. The name of her company was YogAlign. With what you learned in Chapter Two about the number of angry wackos and yoga promoters contacting us, you can imagine I was very careful who I allowed into my social network. During the appeal stage of the trial, I ran across her offer again and this time I was curious "How did she think she could help?"

Edwards practiced yoga for forty-five years, has been a licensed massage therapist and yoga teacher for thirty years. She was injured doing yoga after fifteen years and set about to create a yoga that was based on stabilizing rather than stretching the joints. Edwards realized that attaining good posture made more anatomical sense than trying to contort the body into linear yoga poses. She created YogAlign where "align the body, don't contort it" has become her motto. She educates yoga practitioners about injuries and provides information on how to be safe and beneficial.

Edwards also saw that yoga injuries were going to continue to grow and people needed resources for injury prevention and research, so she created https://yogalign.com/yoga-injuries-2/ in 2008. Teaching yoga has no government regulation, or licensing, therefore, there are no reliable statistics on yoga injuries. Injury

310

rates are likely much higher than what is being reported and she feels that the emphasis on stretching and pose performance in yoga is feeding a glamorization of flexibility that is putting our young people at risk.

Miraculously, everyone involved in this whole trial seems to "find us" or "show up" for their roles when needed. For example, the expert witness saw the filing and called us from her sabbatical in England. When I started researching injuries in yoga, a man who had been researching yoga injuries for a decade offered a lot of the research with doctors concerned about yoga you just read above. Others just seemed to "show up" for their various roles when it was the right timing. Some became researchers, some media representatives, some helped by offering meeting places, or connections, even editing this book, and so much more. None of us had a solid plan, nor expected half of what transpired. Each of us took on our role for the season, or reason it was needed. Edwards entered when injuries began in the District.

Life continues and Connections happen

Today (written June 27, 2015), I am writing in Kauai, while here for my middle son's basketball tournament. His club team traveled to Hawaii to play against island teams and a few lucky ones from the states (Maui, Big Island and yesterday a Nebraska team). I have spent a great deal of time for the past ten years on basketball benches, scoring, filming and rooting for my boy's teams. A trip to Kauai is rare for any team in the US, and the "coincidence" to proximity to Michaelle Edwards seemed to me to be no accident.

Fast forward to 2017, as my oldest son just signed on with a college to play basketball; the joy of competition and sport goes on while fighting this battle of yoga. (See, I'm just a mom making sandwiches and breakfast every morning for the kids, driving carpools all over town, and taking kids to tournaments and activities). All of us involved have walked our daily lives while each day communicating about yoga in schools, in the midst of our own errands and work.

Injuries *and* **Inappropriate advances common in yoga**

Yesterday, since we happened to be in Kauai for the tournament, I drove to Princeville with my son to meet Edwards. She has a studio on her property where she runs her company YogAlign. As a yoga teacher, she took Ashtanga yoga when it came to the island with K.P. Jois himself, the founder of Ashtanga yoga (as in EUSD), over twenty years ago. She walked out of the workshop within three days she reported to me: disappointed, inappropriately touched by him, concerned about the methods of Ashtanga yoga, and the intentions of Jois himself. However, injuries were her chief concern.

Michaelle Edwards's has made a new life of healing yoga injuries by helping others to align their posture. She can clearly see the dangers in yoga, in particular the over-stretching that she says leads to ligament laxity in the spine and hip joints. The best athletes are agile and strong, not hyper-mobile which is what happens to people who do yoga. Too much stretching or too far can actually weaken muscles and damage joint tissue. There are studies showing that static stretching, as is done in yoga, is harmful to the body. Static stretching harms the muscles, nerves and joint structures. This article is called "Static Stretching can reduce Muscle Strength and Force: https://breakingmuscle.com/fitness/static-stretching-reduces-muscle-strength-and-force.[24]

Muscles and fascia store elastic energy that helps to propel us forward. When people stretch, the recoiling action of the elastic energy is reduced by as much as 30 percent. This next article talks about how contrary to what you may think, stretching prior to working out, could reduce athletic performance: https://www.unlv.edu/news/article/stretching-truth.[25]

Edwards goes on to say that stretching is a socio/cultural phenomenon and not a natural human movement. Animals do something called pandiculation, which people call stretching, but in reality it is a 'reset' for the nervous system and recruitment of

312

muscles. No animal holds static body positions with joints in hyper-flexion or hyperextension like humans do in stretching.

Growth Plates in Children

Children do not have fully formed growth plates in the bones. Girl's bones mature at about age fourteen or sixteen, but for boys, it can be up to age sixteen to eighteen. Static stretching as in yoga can damage the growth plates because they have not yet solidified into solid bone. This makes static yoga stretching contraindicated for elementary and junior high students.

Growth plate injuries: https://www.niams.nih.gov/health_info/Growth_Plate_Injuries/default.asp[26]

Risks of and Techniques to Avoid Growth Plate Injuries in Young Athletes: http://uncwellness.com/2015/02/risks-of-and-techniques-to-avoid-growth-plate-injuries-in-young-athletes/[27] "The Dangers of Overtraining Athletes" covers growth plate issues as well: http://www.active.com/soccer/articles/the-dangers-of-overtraining-youth-876660[28]

Edwards is somewhat of a threat to the yoga community because she has questioned the safety and benefits of traditional yoga poses or asana. Yoga is big business, and her views could damage the billion-dollar industry. There are a number of famous yoga teachers who have had to undergo hip replacement surgery including PT Judith Lasater and Power Yoga Star Beryl Bender. Also Dr. Larry Payne who founded the IYTA or International Yoga Therapy Association underwent a hip and knee replacement. Some of the teachers with hip replacements make the claim that yoga had nothing to do with their hip damage, but are claiming many benefits to yoga to protect their businesses.

Meanwhile, Edwards has many clients who have compressed and flattened the natural lumbar and cervical curves of their spine doing yoga poses such as straight leg forward bends. Our spinal curves are supposed to create shock absorption during movement and Michaelle is seeing yoga practitioners with no spine curves, hyper-mobile joints, and chronic pain.

Chair sitting is also causing much of the back pain and misalignment that plagues our society. She discusses that ergonomic desks that keep the spine aligned would be more of a benefit to the Encinitas school children than yoga. According to Michaelle, a huge percentage of yoga poses require one to get their body in linear, right angle shape, akin to sitting in chairs. Edwards used to believe that yoga poses were old and therefore time tested, but after reading Mark Singleton's book entitled *Yoga Body*, she became aware that most yoga poses originated in the last 100 years from Westernized military drills, contortion and Danish women's gymnastics.

https://www.amazon.com/Yoga-Body-Origins-Posture-Practice/dp/0195395344/ref=sr_1_1?keywords=yoga+body+-origins&qid=1564399520&s=gateway&sr=8-1.[29]

In New York Times science journalist William Broad's 2012 book *The Science of Yoga: Risks and Rewards*, he covers yoga injuries in an entire chapter, as well as concludes that yoga poses have not been researched enough, even though he offers benefits of yoga in the book. This is a copy of the Broad's entire book *The Science of Yoga*: https://thaingwizard.files.wordpress.com/2013/03/the-science-of-yoga-the-risks-the-rewards.pdf.[30]

Yoga Injury Survey

Edwards is conducting a survey for people injured by yoga. Over 500 people have participated. Her goal is to get a baseline of information to see how and why yoga injuries are occurring. Results will be published. These results could be revealing and here is the location to check in the future: http://yogalign.com/yoga-injury-survey/.[31]

As with most professionals, after you do something a while, you can simplify it down to the essentials, and you glide with ease through it, making it seem simple for others when in fact it required years of training. Like watching Michael Jordan dunk a ball, it looks so easy, when in reality there are many moving parts to the skill and it needs to be learned. Feet, ankles, how and when to move is executed, along with the angle to jump and shift, and then the arms—the lift with one and placement of the other, where the eyes are focused and reaction to other players and reassessment in the air and much, much more. It can look smooth—but was it really? And did you see the taped fingers after the skin splits and tears from repetitive tries as the skin rubs on the rim after releasing your fingers? Maybe even "hang on the rim" moments stir the roar of the crowd, but no one thinks about the blisters forming. My sons have walked with those fingers taped, many a day, given they can now dunk a basketball after years of preparation and practice. So there is an ease in the application, but a lot of sweat in getting there.

Edwards isn't looking for the roar of a crowd but to help others heal from moving the body in ways that do more hurt than help. She would tell you that what she does is postural re-alignment, *not* traditional yoga. Some of the clients she works with are those injured from yoga and some are yoga teachers who realize that yoga is hurting them. They are desperate to find a yoga style that will heal and not hurt. Many people are unaware that yoga can be dangerous, and that there is a serious lack of research on the effects of yoga poses. The yoga industry is claiming that yoga can cure just about anything, and yet, there is no real proof or accountability in yoga because there is no government regulation.

Edwards is very interested in participating in research with doctors to find the sources and solutions to the physical problems created by yoga and stretching—primarily the weakening of the joints, which hold up our structures. She has compiled information on her website yoga injuries on this page of her website http:// yogalign.com/yoga-injuries-2/.[32] The most recent addition is the following article where a yogi had an injury for years but didn't realize it was from yoga: https://www.tuneupfitness. com/blog/2017/10/23/surprise-surprise-you-need-a-total-hip-replacement-or-living-with-chronic-pain-without-knowing-youre-living-with-chronic-pain/.[33] For those who do yoga, twenty years down the road looks a lot different on the body than two years. This is not consistent with the advertisements in America. The bodies of those who have done many other sports are touted as "yoga bodies"—when in reality those results are not actually from yoga. The deception runs deep in yoga advertising. However, put a cute animal or baby in it or a sexy woman, and American consumers flock to those products. Marketing professionals knows this. You know this. Do we still fall for it, though? Of course we do. But we need to wake up here. It's the children who are being harmed in the long run for injuries.

In 2012, I read about these challenges to young girls' hips and the softening of joints around the knees, hips and other ligaments in yoga. I became concerned and yoga just didn't make sense for all young children to be doing as a main physical activity in school. We took this information on hip and knee injuries to the District in 2012, and unfortunately, two years later, we learned of the first yoga injury to a young EUSD girl.

Twelve-year-old girl injured hips from EUSD yoga

Within six months of yoga in the Encinitas District, 6th grader Katie Prince, age twelve, developed hip impingements on both hips, and found herself in and out of the doctors trying to figure out what was wrong. She couldn't do any sports. Her hips would pop out of socket. Finally, the doctors found out she had done yoga, and that was the problem. Katie's story was covered during her 8th grade, when she decided to go public with her injury.

Katie Prince, with permission from her parents, NBC news: https://www.nbcsandiego.com/news/local/Encinitas-School-Yoga-Student-Pain-Prince–296736721.html

She wanted to personally tell the EUSD board and superintendent about her injury so that perhaps they would see the impact yoga had on her life. She expressed her sadness that they were ignoring her parents about the injury, let alone the time and expense of doctors and testing. She didn't want this to happen to other kids, which became her driving reason for sharing her yoga injury to the board and Baird at the March 2015, district meeting.

Surprisingly, as she spoke, the board wouldn't even look up at her. The news media even used a clip from another part of the meeting to show Baird looking forward, but he was not. I know because I was there watching her speak to them. They did not respond to her at all. Obviously, they had a plan to remain silent, because how could adults who are listening to a child share about her injury not care enough to look her in the eyes or respond? I felt awful for her, for her parents, angry at these adults on the school board, and concerned for other children's potential for injury. These are people who have taken positions to represent and choose the best for our students. She is one of their clients. Yet they would not give her the courtesy of a response. Obvious to all in the room; they were acting under the influence of something said in meetings closed to the public, perhaps influenced by the superintendent, but we can't be sure when parts of the board meetings are closed. The News covered her story pretty well here: http://www.nbcsandiego.com/news/local/Encinitas-School-Yoga-Student-Pain-Prince–296736721.html.[34] The local Union Tribune newspaper also ran a story on Katie's injury: http://www.sandiegouniontribune.com/news/2015/mar/17/yoga-critics-in-encinitas-raise-health-concerns/[35] titled "Yoga critics in Encinitas Raise Health Concerns."

Immediately other families were negative toward Katie and began attacking her and her family on social media, as if she were making it up or the injury was from another sport. This is just another example of bullying that surrounds yoga. Seriously folks, why would a fourteen-year old girl stand before a board, giving her story if it wasn't true, when she has nothing to gain personally? Most parents are afraid to speak to a board; think this through. She was not the only child injured, but many others did not want to come forward, given how she was treated and the overall fear of the public controversy surrounding yoga. Her parents did not even want her to talk to EUSD—that was all her decision. I personally talked with five families with injured children who pulled their kids from yoga, but didn't want to go public with the injuries. One family was even bullied enough by a principal to put their kid back in yoga, and then she re-injured and was pulled out for good. Sadly, yoga had become very divisive in the schools, even over injuries! And the teachers are caught in the middle without a voice too, if they value their jobs.

Lack of Variety, Inexperience and Discipline Issues

Earlier, it was mentioned that a variety of sports is good for youth. The only other activity my kids were going to get at El Camino Creek was karate! This "outside program" of karate was purchased by the school PTA dollars without a vote of the parents who raised all the money. Instead it was a decision by the principal,

Carrie Brown. She told me "it was a great deal." Was it now? Or was it "relief" to the regular classroom teachers who have to teach PE? (*All* of the teachers at our schools *had to teach PE due to cut-backs*). Mind you, these are not qualified PE teachers like many of you still have throughout some US public schools.

Layer in this fact: most of the yoga teachers had no experience teaching young children, nor large groups. Most yoga settings are one-on-one or involve a small group of adult students for each yogi. A lot of feedback on posturing is common, and the small group is needed for many reasons, safety only being one of them. This was alarming. In 2012, I researched where you could do "kid" yoga. There wasn't much. Just four years later, the advertising grew tremendously and was being introduced everywhere from the local YMCA to sports in school to churches and beyond. It was everywhere in just a few short years. You can't drive five miles without seeing yoga advertised everywhere in San Diego. It's grown exponentially.

Most of these young Jois Ashtanga Encinitas yogis didn't know how to "discipline" young children either. This isn't surprising since they didn't need to have standard teaching credentials. [EUSD solved this by paying them through Regur, a third party and friend of the superintendent who established this Regur Development *specifically for* EUSD yoga teachers in 2011, according to the Regur Website (http://www.rdgsolutions.com/).[36] When you click that website, you actually get this one: http://forhealthyhabits.com/ [36] which is all about the Sonima programs. And because Sonima keeps moving their websites around, you may have to google to find this!] Disciplinary action became an issue in most of the schools right away, and the yoga teachers told some of our group that it was a "lost cause" because there were too many kids in each yoga class. Boys were put in the corner to sit and watch or sent out of the room to where they would simply run down to the playground and play alone, or with another boy who was in trouble too. Word caught on and others "misbehaved," just so they could get out of yoga too!

I digressed off yoga injuries, but you can see the problems overlap, right? Behavioral issues are another matter, but it's interesting to note that the district claims reports of bullying have gone down. Perhaps by "their measure" it has, but the amount of bullying that goes on *in and about yoga* is much more than they ever expected or are willing to pay attention to, let alone report. Boys make fun of everything at the ages we are talking about (especially third through sixth grade). If you are around boys that age, you know exactly what I am talking about. The jokes, the names they give one another, and others. Nothing gets past them, and yoga provides these young boys a great source by which to ridicule one another further!

Perhaps physical suspensions have gone down according to some results that Superintendent Baird posted, but even those results are being questioned right now by parents in the District. And how can that *statistic only be attributed to yoga?* What is the real litmus test for bullying surrounding yoga? Ask the children! Children are honest and have the answers to these questions. And don't just survey them. Sit down with a group of kids and ask the questions. They will warm up and tell you the truth more quickly than you expect. We've suggested that, but to date, the board has not asked the children.

Remember, I am telling this story because I firmly believe that someone needs to speak up for the children. So I'm talking about the five to twelve-year-old children who *have no choice or voice* whether they get to do EUSD yoga beyond opting-out, which would be like opting-out of math. It is curriculum. The yoga was not after school, not during free time, no choice, but part of the written curriculum for the day. The EUSD district will not even call yoga by the name yoga. They call it "health and wellness" and call the teachers "health and wellness teachers" to camouflage. Please keep asking, *why?* Who do you know who needs to see this book?

Yoga is not for everyone, nor every age. Just like basketball isn't for everyone. All kids dribble a ball and shoot, but some just don't continue to build the skill or love it, over time. These facts have been given to you to begin to open your eyes to the problems with forcing yoga into the curriculum at elementary schools. Go watch both PE at an elementary school and yoga at others. What do the kids report on their faces? PE used to be a kid's favorite class. While some do like yoga, and perhaps are even swayed by their parents who love yoga, the majority of kids would benefit from having an option to do a variety of cardiovascular forms of PE. And, although one can get injured in any sport, there are serious issues that can be avoided with many of them, and with yoga there are inherent problems with long term consequences.

Do Your Homework!

You can search the Internet for many examples of yoga causing physical injury. Do your homework, to find there are a great number of doctors, surgeons and health professionals seeing the injuries coming from yoga, and the majority of what the media reports about yoga *is the opposite*. The media tells us that it *helps* with some of these problems, rather than advertising that the root of many of these problems comes from yoga! Yet, clearly, from the rise in hip and knee replacements by Americans doing yoga, there is a trend that needs attention. And these injuries are suffered by adults with a choice and regulation over their own bodies. Children in yoga classes at school cannot monitor their own bodies as well as adults.

As I'm working on edits to this book, a new study emerged:

Negative Experiences in Yoga Practice: What do Practitioners Report?

https://www.yoganatomy.com/negative-experiences-in-yoga-practice-survey-results/.[37]

In this research, they use a sample size of 2613 and it appears that more people (61%) report negative experiences in yoga with physical injuries than not. Knees, shoulders, lower back and hips are the main areas of injury. Many of them report a *healing* in those same areas (from those injuries one can assume), and the primary solution was to modify what they were doing (rather than quit altogether). More research will continue to grow in this area. It is important to note that these were adults, *not children*.

CHAPTER SIXTEEN

Impact on Competition in America

Competition is in the foundation and fabric of America. The ability to compete and have freedom in the marketplace, sports and in education is what makes our country what it is today. Competition is the basis of our democracy. But, all of that is in jeopardy when we replace PE with yoga in American schools, raising children with a completely different foundation.

Let's take a look from a sports perspective. Competition among athletes and teams creates a higher level of performance. A healthy competition within boundaries, creates individuals and teams with the ability to excel to heights and goals they would not achieve on their own. Athletes push themselves and one another as they compete and prepare for competitions.

Every summer there is a four-day national youth basketball tournament in Las Vegas, Nevada that our two boys play in annually. During these four days, multiple games are played by hopeful teens at multiple venues with college coaches on the sidelines watching. Coaches are recruiting, so they carefully watch the kids compete and most of the student-athletes at this tournament would love to play in college. Not all will have what it takes to get recruited and get a scholarship. Most have the ability to play on a college team, yet some do not, for various reasons. The fact that they are being watched helps them play to their best ability.

Don't get me wrong; they all have the skills it takes to play, or they wouldn't be there. But they might not have what it takes *mentally* to fight for a college spot. They may give up due to not having the support or resources to figure out how to make playing college ball work. Or, they may not find the college program into which they fit. Some kids will choose other priorities. Some will just not have the confidence or drive to keep striving for that goal or dream they might have had at an earlier time. Or, they just might get more motivated at the Vegas Tourney watching all the others, and try even harder. Division 17U (seventeen years old and under) are the kids that are entering their senior year. Coaches are focused on this age, while keeping their eyes on the 16U and 15U Divisions as they plan for the future.

Strategic coaches will *scout* students at every age and venue possible because they know that they may find some real super-stars, but even the superstars need other students *to play with and against*. There are hundreds of teams, and every one of them has a best player and every one of them needs all the other players too, or that kid has no game to play either. So competition and role models foster the dynamic nature of the games. Winning and losing is part of the equation, even though growth and improvement are the overarching benefits. This translates directly to our business, education, politics and roles in leadership.

Teamwork is Essential in Youth Development

As a youth in this country, being part of a team matters. Improving as an individual matters as well. When playing as a team, getting better as an individual and being *your* best helps the whole team. Not *the* best but *your* best. We can all be our *own best* and that is the real goal. Then, *we all win*. And being "the best" is usually the motivator to being *our* best. So having stars with higher levels of skill to strive toward is important in most every sport. All the young boys and girls are watching closely every move they make, every shoe they produce, what socks and shirt and shoes they wear, and so on. Young boys and girls are consumed with these things when they love a sport.

But yoga, by contrast, is very individual. It's internal. It's a turning one's self inward to explore its own self. It's centering on self. Yoga encourages its followers to become more centered within themselves, to look within, *for peace,* is one of the stated goals. Yoga is only competitive if you strive *within* yourself to be better *for* yourself. Stretch a little further, push a little harder. And the more centered you become on yourself, the more *self-centered* you become. Perhaps also hyper focused on the shape and curves of their own bodies, which can be a downward frustrating spiral for many a girl in yoga. Is that what we want as a society?

Self-*Centered?*

Look a bit farther into this self-centered practice. Yoga promotes peace, but ultimately many ex-yogis tell of the turmoil that they endured. Listen to them, read their books and stories and blogs and websites. They did not get the peace and what they thought they would out of yoga. They got so much worse than they ever bargained for, or dreamed could transpire. Yoga advertises an inner peace and centering. Instead, these ex-yogis to whom we've linked you to, talk about how it tore up their lives eventually. Some had to fight their way back to a "normal" life, and are willing to help others see what can happen. And these aren't kids at vulnerable ages.

How Is Healthy Competition Fostered?

So, if the competitive spirit of America is not built starting in public schools in the PE games and on playgrounds, then where will it be fostered? How will a spirit of healthy competition be built? Or will it? I'm just asking the questions to be aware of where choices lead us. It's important to ask. If our kids are doing yoga for PE in school, these five to twelve year olds are learning the following:

- Complacency vs competition
- Following vs leading
- Being dormant vs striving
- Forced breathing vs deep breathing,
- stretching vs sweating

- Flexibility vs cardiovascular large muscle exercise
- Sitting quietly after six hours of sitting and writing already!

All kindergarten kids learn right away to line up like ducks to follow their teacher, and do what the teacher does or asks. Everything our teachers do, or endorse, is an example and role model to our children. Good or bad. We all are capable of both. We all make mistakes. Is mandating yoga for all children as weekly curriculum a mistake? Is it a right? Is it a privilege as EUSD wanted us parents to believe?

Blind Trust

We cannot continue to blindly trust that every decision the school district makes for our children as an aggregate is what's best for each child. We cannot continue to put our heads in the sand, thinking that everything the district decides is good for all the children. We should *expect* that they *question and examine* any decisions they made *when hundreds of parents come forward in concern*. It's easy to "not get involved" with district level issues beyond voting for candidates that we think would make good decisions. But children everywhere need us to be awake and aware of what is happening. Other districts want to know how to react to incoming yoga.

Why Pick Just One?

So why would we mandate an exercise that is proven dangerous for some developing bodies, according to the experts at even the American Yoga Association itself? Doctors and ex-yogis have seen and had bad experiences. We are still *early* in the stages of mainstream yoga in the United States. Children have been doing yoga for less than a decade. Think about the far-reaching effects in twenty years. Although we don't know the impact with certainty, we can do the research and find that there are many injuries specific to the loosening of the ligaments around the muscles, as we saw in the last chapter. The frame that holds us up *is* in *harm's way*. Knee and hip joints have been damaged at early ages and are in need of hip and knee replacements. Well-rounded kids seem to grow healthy bodies and frames from a variety of PE over the years, according to the research, so that is why so many parents were frustrated with the yoga at EUSD and wouldn't have been if yoga were rotating with other sports or if any choice were offered.

Is it Subjective?

At the heart of this matter is this big question that the court grappled with: Is yoga religious? It seems obvious to some that it is, and obvious it is not to others. So therein lies a big problem. Does the apple appear red or pink to you? It doesn't matter what we call "it", or how we articulate it, the fact is - it is something, regardless of our opinion. If the yoga teacher knows, but hides the spiritual aspect, does that make it fine when yoga in the next class might have greater influence during, say, a more advanced class?

What someone is using something for doesn't change the item's intended use. We can take a knife and pick a lock, or use it to screw in a bolt, but it doesn't change that it is a knife. It is meant to cut, meant to spread and meant for specific purposes … but usable for other purposes. So even if we were only teaching children the stretching and breathing parts of yoga, the program as a whole is setting kids up for a much different society than what we have previously built for previous generations with the foundation of sports in school. If we plan to change all that by requiring just one type of exercise for most of the week for all of the elementary years, we need to be prepared for the consequences ahead. The kids at EUSD who entered 6th grade in the fall of 2017 will have practiced predominantly yoga for PE for all of their elementary years. Good thing we can afford after-school-sports around here. Many families and communities, however, cannot. What will happen to the children who would have been able to use their athletic skills to earn a sports scholarship for college? And to those who would have gone further to become a professional athlete allowing their family to get out of poverty? Yoga replacing PE closes a lot of doors to the future for many kids. We need to consider these types of consequences when placing such vast programs into schools and replacing what has been a base of activities for our country.

Ask the Kids!

It's worth repeating. After 6 hours of sitting to read and write and learn, does the average elementary kid want and need to jump and run and play or to sit and relax? Do they really need to work on flexibility at age six? Do their large muscles need some exertion or do they need to sit and stretch them out? Ask the kids if they like and want yoga over other sports? In one short year, the kids won't be able to answer that in EUSD because they won't have had anything any different. Even now, the 6th graders likely barely remember not having yoga as part of their every week at school that first year in kindergarten.

Concern over the children should be at the top of the list of priorities. One priority at this age is kids learning how to use their bodies. See this recent report on a Texas district checking into "more recess" and productivity levels: http://www.sunnyskyz.com/good-news/1475/A-Texas-School-Started-Giving-Kids-4-Recess-Breaks-A-Day-And-The-Results-Have-Been-Wonderful.[1] Ask the kids what they want and like? Ask them if yoga provides less bullying, or if they care to sit and stretch or would they prefer to run and play with these same classmates? I know that just because they prefer something doesn't make it better (say chocolate cake over a sandwich for lunch) but in this case—what is healthier for the kids? Our sports teams will change to individual focus on ourselves. Our physical activities will change to sedentary. Longer term, overall health will change for the worse if we change these habits so young.

The "Wussification of America"

"The Wussification of America" was a news story a few years back. Covered in one article were the top 10 things that will lead to decline in America. #10 was "Yoga for Children" http://www.alternet.org/10-things-fox-decided-will-lead-decline-american-values-2013.[2]

Larry Winget, an outspoken, well-known professional speaker, slams parents for taking their kids to yoga classes and points out that yoga is a supplement, not a sport. His style is "in your face" on all topics, so he is not trying to draw out "yoga Nazi's," as he states in the article (but I'm certain he did, given what I've experienced). Winget was asked about soccer and hockey parent sideline over-reactions and he responded "You know, that's just stupid parents." He continues "Sports teach us winning and losing, and life is about winning and losing. It's competitive. And we need to teach those things at a very young age with a real sport. And a real sport usually involves a ball of some type." He claims, "if no one is keeping score, it's not a sport." He goes on to say that sports teach interaction, socialization and working as a team and that getting knocked down and getting back up are good lessons, as opposed to just focusing on yourself. He claims the downward dog isn't going to replace "touchdown" or "you're out." He points to the valuable life lessons of learning to win with humility, and lose with dignity: https://www.opposingviews.com/health/video-motivational-speaker-larry-winget-slams-stupid-parents-who-take-kids-yoga.[3] *Who Hi-jacked our Country?* There was a lot of press about this one interview. Winget is willing to say what others are only willing to think. Others can attempt to shoot the messenger, but many back his basic opinions on needing competitive sports for children. When asked, "What about the sports where kids get cut and lose?" He responds, "Isn't that some of the best lessons in life?" We all lose at something sometime, so help your kids learn how in a lower risk situation early in life in sports: https://www.mediamatters.org/blog/2013/01/03/fox-asks-if-children-doing-yoga-is-leading-to-t/191994.[4]

Dodgeball anyone?

Ironically, a joke during this whole journey amongst many parents has been "what happened to dodgeball?" Many parents are against dodgeball, or had a bad experience when they were kids, and it epitomizes a rough sport. I haven't seen dodgeball in years (in the Encinitas schools) and just recently when we moved schools to a new district, we saw "dodgeball night" advertised. You can bet we laughed about that one! Good ol' American schools are still around! And one day our daughter came home beaming with a bruise and a smile from guess what? Dodgeball. *Dodgeball anyone?*

Competition in America

Competition starts with the education in our homes, our schools, and our sports. If we choose to shift how we compete at the beginning levels, then we need to be ready for the outcomes and consequences. Thus, the choice to have yoga as weekly PE in elementary schools, impacts how business and politics of the future are being shaped. Many people are not thinking about those effects. But more concerning, some are and are trying to impact our culture with those decisions. Consider the literature, because I have barely touched the surface here on how some would like to change our culture through the changes begun in elementary schools. Yoga in schools is a choice that will impact many future decisions and leaders. We need to choose wisely and not just allow anything into our schools.

CHAPTER SEVENTEEN

Former Yoga Teachers Warn of Dangers in Yoga

When former yoga teachers contacted us with bold warnings to get yoga away from children, we listened to understand why. Concern increased when we heard from parents with adult children doing yoga who were depressed, withdrawn and becoming more and more self-centered. Then the worst reports were those whose children had committed suicide over yoga. We were stunned at these reports and investigated further.

According to many ex-yogis, yoga "invites spirits in" and "opens you up" to these spirits as you clear out your mind. Okay what? They warned that if these children do the Ashtanga worship poses repeatedly, the children will unknowingly invite the thousands of gods and evil spirits into themselves. Now I know how odd that sounds. But we began to hear and read this over and over with many documented reports. Patterns emerged and one must consider these past yogi's experiences, especially with young innocent children involved with yoga entering schools at this great a level of practice twice weekly for years. I read a few of their books, blogs, websites and testimonies. I went to meet and listen to some of them. Their warnings suggested these children were in much more danger than we originally conceived. The warnings encouraged us to keep fighting for yoga removal in schools long after we might have.

Wake-up-Call and Warning to the Dangers of Yoga

Most former yogis call yoga a *cult* or *the occult*. They shared that demonization happens through years of yoga practice. They claim that spirits will eventually torment the children. Hmmm … this is all sounding a bit crazy, I first thought … *until this began in children in Encinitas*. We began getting reports of tormented children from unsuspecting parents who reached out to us during the lawsuit, not knowing where else to go. First, I'll give you the resources of some yogis, and then more details of what happened in Encinitas with children's behaviors and reported experiences.

Former Yoga Practitioners who will never practice again

In this book are a few examples, but you can google to find many more sharing their stories and concerns to warn others through you-tube videos and websites. Many former yogis are publishing books, but due to the highly controversial subject of yoga, and spiritual warfare along with it, many do not want to "go public" with their demonic experiences. However, plenty are sharing what happened, so if you choose to, you can readily find many more than offered here.

Rabi Maharaj

The book *Death of a Guru* by Rabi Maharaj, displays his biographical story of how he grew up in the highest caste of India with a father who was a Brahman Guru. His father had followers from all around that would come to worship him. His father fell into a meditative trance about the time Rabi was born, and for almost seven years, he never heard his father speak. Finally, his father passed away (when they cut his hair while in the trance, and it broke a vow he had made—he fell over dead!), still in the trance, locked in an *in- between* world. People came from all around to pay respect to his father, and then after his death they came to see Rabi—as the new top Guru—and he was only sixteen! He tells his story of how he woke up to the lies (for one example when a cow he was worshipping started chasing him around) and then how he eventually woke up to the full truth.

He has been educating people about the harmful effects of yoga for forty years in Europe and over two decades here in the United States. He knows and came from the roots of yoga. In this video, he explains much of the issue to help Americans understand Hindu culture and reasoning for creating yoga to worship and pray out the evil spirits, the anger and destruction of men after hours in meditative prayers that were supposed to cause peace. https://www.bing.com/videos/search?q=rabi+maharaj&view=detail&mid=61C2E08A1F023282402461C2E08A1F0232824024&FORM=VIRE.[1] He explains why westerners are confused about yoga. This best-selling book is over forty years old and explains exactly the problems with what yoga delivers. A quick read well worth your time:

https://www.amazon.com/gp/product/0890814341?ref%5F=sr%5F1%5F1&qid=1468505164&sr=8-1&keywords=death%20of%20a%20guru&pldnSite=1.[2]

Jessica Smith

Another former yogi we met was Jessica Smith. She spent many years pursuing practices such as Reiki, Ashtanga yoga, Hatha yoga, and many other forms in an effort to deepen her own spiritual growth and to "help others" to do the same. After years of practice and teaching, however, the once carefree and happy young woman began having detached thoughts of ending her life, convinced by the spiritual realm that death would be more peaceful than life.

She tells her story for others to be warned not to follow a similar path toward destruction. She describes that she thought she was on a path of truth and peace, and taught yoga under the assumption she was helping people. Far from it, she would learn. After more than a decade of practice, she would fall into a trance from which she could not easily return.

She paints a very disturbing picture in her story, and if you met her, you would never expect what she had been through. A spirit nearly convinced her it would be better to end her life. While in some of the trances, the path after death looked so peaceful, so wonderful, and so attractive. If not for her boyfriend at the time, she may not have come out of the last trance. As she lay unresponsive for hours, he *called her back*. She could not physically respond. She lay unable to move her body parts even though she could hear him. Once she made the "decision" to *come back* and chose the will to live, she was able to focus on each body part, one at a time, and with all her might, to regain the use of just that part. A few *demons* left her body during this episode and she willfully stopped them after a few, because she was terrified they would somehow overtake her on their way out. Overwhelmed with the convulsions that preceded each spirit "going out" and this experience, Jessica immediately contacted a Christian counselor couple who she knew could help. She and her boyfriend traveled to their ranch, and many *demons* left Jessica's body through their help. She tells of the spirits leaving her body with a deep, throaty hiss "much like the Ujjay breath" she had learned in yoga. As they left her, a sound would announce what it was, such as; A*shtanga yoga, reiki, cocaine, Hatha yoga*, etc. As she experienced these spirits rising, a Bible verse she remembered from her childhood popped to mind, "Satan masquerades as an angel of light." And she knew in an instant the Bible was the only real source of spiritual truth. Her story matches many others for the spirits naming themselves on the *way out*.

This is a beautiful young woman who had no previous suicidal thoughts or tendencies before she began to walk this spiritual path. Fortunately for her, she had a mother praying for her for over a decade while Jessica s*earched for truth* through a lot of avenues. Also fortunately, her boyfriend was nearby when the near-death experience occurred, and vehemently *called her back*. Can you imagine what he experienced trying to help her?

The Shattering

Jessica Smith's book *The Shattering: An Encounter with Truth* shares her dramatic testimony of how spirits associated with these practices "of love and light" manifested in their true, terrifyingly dark form from within her after she began to pursue reading the Bible and "working with Jesus." available on Amazon https://smile.amazon. com/Shattering-Encounter-Truth-Jessica-Smith/dp/0942507193/ ref=sr_1_1?ie=UTF8&qid=1468505441&sr=8-1&keywords=the+ shattering%2C+jessica+smith.[3] Also see her website called "Truth Behind Yoga" http://www.truthbehindyoga.com/.[4]

Two Days in Oregon

I personally flew to Oregon to watch Jessica tell her story for two days. There were fifty women at the Applegate Christian Retreat Center, and we were all riveted by her talk. Women arrived who were involved in all stages of yoga. One said she'd been doing it for twenty years, one had just started a few days prior, and a friend encouraged her to come to the retreat instead. One woman said yoga was now a mandatory class in a son's freshman year in college. Another woman said she worked in a preschool and they were starting yoga, and she was asked to learn it to teach the kids. The stories went on and on with the women's variety of experiences with yoga.

After listening to Jessica, these women not only planned to toss their yoga mats in the trash, but prepared for all kinds of battles with friends, family, and loved ones with whom they knew the discussion would be necessary, but not easy. Most of us are ill-equipped to have this type of discussion with loved ones. I've been studying the subject for seven years now, but I still feel ill-equipped to talk about it fully. Jessica's story only increased my concern for the children.

Corinna Craft

Another former yogi that we met during the lawsuit was Corinna Craft, M.A., and J.D.

Her website (https://whatsthematterwithyoga.wordpress.com/)[5] and book "What's The Matter With Yoga?," is another source of someone who started yoga and spent years thinking that it was fine, only to end up in terrifying torment she did not expect. She was "demonized" and led toward suicide, and has seen others around her impacted the same. She wants to help others avoid the same traps. She, too, voiced concerns for the children of Encinitas. On this page of her website, you can see her question and answers to:

Can a Christian be demonized?
https://whatsthematterwithyoga.wordpress.com/demonization-2/.[6]

These stories match many more we ran across: patterns of a slow, demonic, luring, toward suicide. Looking at a few of their stories will support the comments in this book. Corinna has six new videos on "What's The Matter with Yoga?" and why she will never do yoga again. Find them at the following YouTube location: https://www.youtube.com/playlist?list=PLz77njjHxb01SX6Vc j8Zm6M_lt4_L2R31.[7]

Many of the experiences we ran across were told by parents and friends of those who did commit suicide from what they think was linked to yoga. At some of the events we have held, parents showed up that have lost their kids to "a world of yoga" having moved to India and now will not stay in contact with them. Story after story adds up to the same spiritual pathways resulting from yoga practice.

Spiritual goal of yoga the forced breathing moving up the chakras to the point of "third eye" bliss

Mike Shreve

Mike Shreve was a Kundalini Yoga teacher in 1970 with about 400 students attending his classes at four Florida universities; and he also ran a yoga ashram. Today, he is teaching what he calls the spiritual deceptions of yoga that he learned first-hand. You can find out his story and warnings here in this video: <u>https://vimeo.com/125830500</u>.[8] He has many resources, and one of them is a small booklet that discusses the effects of yoga candidly called "Seven Reasons I No Longer Practice Hatha Yoga" found on his website: <u>www.shreveministries.org</u>.[9]

Seven Reasons I No Longer Practice Hatha Yoga by Mike Shreve

1. Spiritual Roots

2. Spiritual Perspective

3. Spiritual Deception

4. Spiritual Transfer

5. Spiritual Intrigue

6. Spiritual Endorsement

7. Spiritual Compromise

In Mike Shreve's booklet "Seven Reasons I no longer practice Hatha Yoga:" https://www.amazon.com/Seven-Reasons-Longer-Practice-Hatha/dp/0942507614,[10] three of the reasons are Spiritual Deception, Spiritual Transfer and Spiritual Compromise. He writes about what happens after years of practicing. He quotes Hindu leaders' assertions that "There is no Yoga without Hinduism and no Hinduism without Yoga" and covers the topic of whether Christians can practice this far eastern practice of yoga and not be "yoking" to something opposing Christian beliefs.

Leslie Marshall

Marshall studied Transcendental Meditation (TM) and Yoga taught by Maharishi Mahesh Yogi (1916-2008). She graduated from Maharishi's University (Fairfield, IA) in 1979. Her four years of academics were thoroughly interspersed with Hindu teachings, i.e., mantra meditation, hatha yoga, siddha yoga (Patanjali's yoga super powers), study of Ayurveda (Hindu medicine), Jyotish (Hindu astrology), study of Rig Veda (Hindu scriptures), and Bhagavad Gita (*Mahabharata*, the Hindu epic).

After spending over twenty-five years practicing yoga and meditation (inextricably linked, she quotes) she found that the results promised by her yoga leaders never came to fruition. And worse, yoga and TM led to New Age religion, Eastern philosophy, and Paganism. She presents programs called "It's Not New Age, it's Ancient," "YOGAmerica," and "From Maharishi to Jesus." She, too, points to the Beatles popularizing TM in the late 1960s and today. Also, pertinent to this book, the David Lynch Foundation (Himilstein connection) finances a TM/Yoga Program in Public Schools (with helpful support from Oprah Winfrey, Russell Simmons, Paul McCartney, Ellen DeGeneres, Ringo Starr, Dr. Oz, Jerry Seinfeld, et al.).

One difference to note is that, while Marshall is against yoga, she teaches a form of Christian stretching that many would say is an attempt to Christianize yoga. Founder Laurette Willis created "Praise Moves" as an alternative to replace yoga. She has hundreds of Christian followers that teach her program. Many Christians believe that all yoga is "yoking" and others believe opposingly, that doing what mirrors yoga poses while reciting "verses" or listening to "praise music" make it fine. Stretching is altogether something different. There is a fine line that Christians are contemplating and references are in the next chapter.

Yoga Dangers

Another former Kundalini yogi has been warning about the dangers of yoga, Kundalini and TM for over a decade: http://www.yogadangers.com/.[11] One article you can find on his website, is called "Yoga and the Occult—A Former Witch Speaks Out." The author of that article has a website called "The Other Side of Darkness." Follow one site and you find more. A recent post for Yoga Danger was *Holy Flying Yoga* where participants are upside down off the ground. He also addresses the dangers of *mindfulness meditation* at the conclusion of yoga practice which is another program pushing into elementary schools as a stand-alone program.

Yet another former Hindu yogi warns about the Dangers of Kundalini yoga, and a "clearing the mind" in a presentation: https://www.youtube.com/watch?v=6DZ7oz_fIq8.[12] She states you cannot separate yoga from its source being Hinduism. She says they are one and the same (like so many other people from India report). She goes on to say that after deep meditation an "overcoming of the personality" occurs where the person becomes a "vessel" for a deity or spirit to *take over,* and the person "will lose some self-awareness" for a period of time. *What? Is this why people say or do things which they are not aware of, and can't recall?* Yikes!

These are just a few examples from the many former yoga instructors that we were exposed to during the lawsuit, and in the time frame of education on what yoga in schools might bring to the children. Each provides a vast amount of information on their websites.

Support from Hindu Organizations

In addition to ex-yogis, former Hindu followers and Hindu organizations came forward to further evidence to us that this may be indoctrination and a highly spiritual path. *In fact, Ashtanga, they warned, was one of the most spiritual types of yoga!* Some of these organizations supported the trial by writing documents for the lawsuit. Others wrote, called and asked how they could help. Some of this detail was given in Chapter 3, but worth noting here, because Hindus are more familiar with the source and history of yoga, and they are very concerned about what's happening with yoga in America, as evidenced by their comments, formation of organizations to combat yoga penetration, and articles attempting to educate purposes of yoga.

The Children of EUSD

What we didn't know back when former yogis were warning us, was, that in two short years, the very dangers these former yoga experts described would soon begin to be reported in EUSD. We thought it would take many more years based on the timeline the yogis gave. The first reporting were two children in a school in our district by their mother who was not sure what to do. So she called us—the truth-about-yoga website parent group. She had just pulled two of her children from yoga at school because one was uncomfortable during the meditation part of the yoga class and saw "a little red man with a pitchfork" and visions that disturbed him. The other child was also very uncomfortable with what the teacher was saying during the meditation portion of his class, which was a different grade. He gave details I cannot disclose here, because it would expose which teacher and that is not our intent. Another child at that school was also having "emotional disturbances" from yoga according to the mom.

One young girl in another school threw herself against the wall (at home) saying things in a deep guttural voice, not her own, and using words not usual to her vocabulary. Another youth experienced evil and suicidal thoughts (5th grade!) who had not suffered from such thoughts prior to Ashtanga yoga.

Another family had similar emotional disturbances with their child at a fourth school that they would like to keep private, so I won't be able to share the details. Sadly, it would make them a target in their own school. At a fifth school in Encinitas, La Costa Heights, the principal formed a "group" to help children with "anxiety problems." Many third and fourth graders that year were beginning to have separation anxiety from their parents.

Going back to the beginning of the placement of yoga in schools weekly, many children were sensitive enough to yoga from the very first classes to alert their parents they didn't want to go back or be with "that teacher." These families in which their children expressed concerns were among the first who became concerned about yoga. And it wasn't just one yoga teacher, it was many. Increasingly, parents grew concerned from their children's reports.

Children could not make stories up matching yogi warnings!

Now that we have heard reporting of these odd occurrences happening to innocent children in our district, what do we do? Who will believe us, (us being the families that are against yoga)? The school board who already doesn't believe us? How can we help these parents who are too afraid to go public with these problems? Are children more vulnerable to these spirits (that the ex-yogi's are referring to), given they are so open and willing and being led in meditations? We are no experts on this. Where do we send them? To contact the EUSD board was my best answer at the time. Call them, write them, and tell them what is happening to your kids. But did they? I doubt it, because fear is and was a huge factor. Fear and spiritual warfare swim more around yoga than anything else I've ever encountered in fifty years. What would you do? How would you help these parents? How do you report these children's scary occurrences to a school board? The Hindus supporting us understand it all too well. They are reportedly, in fact, surprised that America would even perform yoga. They claim to do yoga to pray away the 300,000 evil spirits and are puzzled anyone thinks it exercise.

One Mother's Helplessness

It broke my heart to sit with one mother who felt helpless, listening to her story and trying to make sense of it all. All I could think was *this didn't have to happen.* Our district made a grave mistake placing yoga into schools, and people were too afraid to tell them these things! How do we even begin to "explain" some of this odd stuff, when as parents they hardly understood it themselves, and it seems like private information, since it is coming through their own kids? Who wants to expose *THIS?* The judgmental nature of people surrounding yoga was too risky to expose their children on top of the strange things happening. Some went to doctors. Some asked for prayer. Many are still silent. Many moved out of the district.

Tantric Yoga: For Children, It's Absurd!

Photo credit to Sema Institute of Yoga, Ashby, Muata, 2003,
available on Amazon

Another related occurrence in one school matched what yogis warned. Tantric yoga should be banned from schools! Tantric yoga is two-person yoga where you are doing movements together and touching one another. Here are just two websites explaining the practice: http://healing.about.com/od/sexualhealing/a/tantricsex. htm[13] and http://www.mindbodygreen.com/0-5910/4-Tantric-Yoga-Poses-for-Partners-Who-Want-a-Deeper-Connection.html.[14] It appears to be sexual and for adult couples. In the spring of 2014, a teacher reported passing the yoga room that the children at OPE (Olivenhein Pioneer Elementary) were lying on top of one another during yoga class in a dark room, very crowded with over 40 children and mats. Boys on boys, girls on girls, and girls were on boys, reportedly. Now that is simply outrageous, right? But the teacher who saw it said nothing that day! She felt she couldn't, for fear of losing her own job (for reasons I cannot share). Under normal circumstances, an adult walking by a room with lights out and kids lying on top of one another would march directly into the room and flip on the lights and ask the young yogi, "what are you doing?" Or, go directly to the principal. But this teacher did not feel she could.

The teacher did, however, call one of us. And when I heard about this from that person called, I was for the first time fuming due to our inability to do anything to expose this. How could this happen? But once again the question remained; what could we even do with this information? Our hands were tied at so many junctures like this. The OPE principal, well known to be pro-yoga and in the pocket of the superintendent, praised Tudor Jones and Ashtanga yoga during her tours of the school for prospective students. Reporting this occurrence to this principal would only have gotten *covered up*. We couldn't tell the board; they wouldn't believe us. Write an anonymous letter to her? It probably wouldn't matter. This is the first time I became *angry* over what they had invited into our district, and it gave me more fuel to fight for these children who have *no voice*. Even the teachers had no voice in all of this. So what could we say? We began to simply pray that the children would go home and tell their parents. Some did. But nothing ever seemed to get revealed to the OPE school that made any difference. I'm certain they were silenced if they did. And as you probably guessed, that teacher who saw that room has left the school district. She left quietly, unfortunately. On a tour a few weeks later a parent took photos of the dark room, with about 40 kids close, but side by side on the mats this time. At that point, the kids weren't touching, but even the room being that dark, cramped and hot, seemed odd for elementary students at mid-day in sunny California (for PE). The principal was cheerfully describing the yoga program while passing by the dark room. I wish I could put the photos here, but for the faces of the children and their privacy, I will not.

I don't think many of the yoga teachers even know what they are promoting. Yoga instructors agree to standards as per Yoga Alliance, if they are accredited yoga instructors (https://www.yogaalliance.org/),[15] and yet, do they really know what they are subjecting these children to every week? This is more of the deception. Look into the backers, look into the program, and look into who benefits from *what*. Then you begin to see a clear picture of a deception that each individual might not even see for themselves. There is no denying yoga is spiritual, if you've read about yoga at all by folks who create and promote yoga. You cannot look online and miss how many yogis are clear about the spiritual base and goals of yoga, whether you intend yoga to be spiritual or not. So just by doing the stretches in the sequences provided, there is enough of a chance these kids are worshipping something without knowing it, that we should not have yoga even near the public schools.

Sexual Harassment and Oppression ... **in yoga**

A very concerning part of our research uncovered the oppression of women and sexual harassment occurring inside yoga in other countries and spreading to ours. Sexual harassment is common in yoga and you can find many of the documented allegations online of abuse by gurus and yoga instructors. A recent one included a young male instructor and a child in a school. I won't spend a lot of space here showing all the evidence but it is easily available to you.

Rabi Maharaj speaks of the physical violence from yoga as well, in his book, *Death of a Guru,* and how yoga, prayer, and meditation do center you ... on yourself! This self-centeredness and anger, surprise the very people who spend hours in yoga meditation to avoid such behavior. One can end even up in a trance, he discusses, sort of caught between the world we know and a spiritual world where we cannot reach the person any longer, even though they sit in a room right next to you, as his father did for years. There are many more examples of these near suicide victims of yoga who are willing to share their stories and how they were duped into thinking a reverse of what transpired.

Are We Asleep?

Yoga may not be on your list of things to study either, but you picked up this book, so I'm assuming you cared enough to get this far. I encourage you to keep looking and keep asking questions about yoga and its impact. The trouble is most people think its fine and quit looking. But I hope that you at least by now have considered that yoga is a lot more than stretching.

I resolved to make time to be a *voice for the children*. I walk among innocent children every day. Therefore, I added writing and compiling data into my day for 30 to 60 minute increments just like anyone would add anything to an already busy daily schedule. It hasn't been easy. But I know how much others needed to know what happened in California, and is now seeping into public schools in other parts of the Country. Can you now see the importance? What do you do with stuff like kids lying on top of other kids in yoga class when those in authority think its fine? Last week I got a call that they were teaching kids how to hiss with a squeezed-up-face like a snake in yoga classes in Rancho Bernardo and slither on the floor. Say what? Seriously, I couldn't make this stuff up! What in the world is that teacher thinking? It's no coincidence it's a snake since Kundalini yoga is about the serpent going up the spine of chakras as former yogis explain (see video #2 on education events page of website).

Yoga for all elementary schools could change our nation in just one decade. Yoga changes how PE has formed our sports programs. It will become more about controlling the mind than the body. Yoga won't support our competitive marketplace; it will change it. Thus, we have to question why some are pushing so hard for this young generation to do yoga.

Meditation and Mind Control

Just imagine for a moment, if you wanted to control someone's mind and actions how would you do it? Would meditation help in that? Would yoga? How would one go about it if they wanted to control the minds and decisions of many people, say this next generation? You see, mediation and mind control have been inching their way into the public schools for years at all levels— from collegiate to elementary, and has been called many things over the years like *transcendental meditation* and more recently *mindfulness meditation*. I am not a scholar in this area, but Candy Gunther Brown, Harvard PhD has devoted her life to the subject area and is a leading scholar on meditation and related religious studies. You can start with this website for her credentials and information, if you hadn't looked earlier in the book, then to the information about meditation http://indiana.edu/~relstud/people/profiles/brown_candy[16] in her articles. She has a book available on Amazon titled: *Healing Gods: Complementary and Alternative Medicine in Christian America* by Candy Gunther Brown (Oxford University Press, 2013). Chapter two and sections of the conclusion are on yoga, including discussion of "Christian yoga" https://www.amazon.com/Healing-Gods-Complementary-Alternative-Christian/dp/0199985782?ie=UTF8&*Version*=1&*entries*=0.[17] Brown's new book, *Debating Yoga and Mindfulness in Public Schools: Reforming Secular Education or Reestablishing Religion?* available here, https://www.amazon.com/Debating-Yoga-Mindfulness-Public-Schools/dp/1469648482/ref=nav_ya_signin?crid=1OFSPX9V4PDR2&keywords=candy+gunther+brown&qid=1558984309&s=gateway&sprefix=candy+gunther+browns+books%2Caps%2C319&sr=8-1&[18] includes several chapters about yoga, this trial, and meditation, as referenced on the cover of this book in the endorsements.

So, let's follow some logic here. If you want to change an entire generation of people, how would you do it? If we can get the children to *think differently,* we can get them to follow a leader to *do something differently*, right? Clearly, there are good and bad examples of this in history. Look to cult examples and politics, and you'll see that a bit of charisma can lead many folks to follow just by the skillfully-crafted words of a leader. Even some of history's darkest days of slavery, the Holocaust and cult leaders who have led others to take their own lives. More recently, we see countless young people being indoctrinated into terrorist groups, taught to kill others and themselves. And they do! Why?

I recognize that yoga in public schools was not meant to hurt anyone. But, does it? Could children be led to dark places by well-meaning people and for well-meaning reasons? Can it be possible we have been duped? Led astray? We need to be awake and vigilant about this. We need to realize this can and has happened. We need to have a rude awakening in this country or all will be lost in one decade or very shortly by the actions starting with placing every student in this country under the direction of *yogis*.

The Raising up of the Yogis

And how long did it take to *raise up* all those yogis? Think about it. When yoga first entered the country could it have spread into the schools? No. There would not be enough teachers unless there were other people from other countries to teach yoga. And would that have entered the public schools? Not a chance. So yoga had to infiltrate our adults first—namely, women who would become practitioners of yoga. This makes me cringe because I could have easily, at some point along the way, being in the fitness industry, have become a yoga instructor. Thankfully, I did not.

American consumerism is always about wanting more. *It's the same with yoga.* Most people want yoga for health and peace and for good altruistic reasons. We want better health; we want to look good; we want to look like that model in the ad. Compare real people who have been devoted, lifetime yogis and what do you see? You will see the reality of twenty years or a lifetime of yoga on a body, and it's significantly different than what the yoga ads in America show. A lifetime of yoga results in hip and knee replacements. And after twenty years of yoga you will be more centered on yourself and your own "uni-verse" than ever before.

The Practice of Yoga ... Takes Effort and Practice

To stay on top of yoga requires commitment and dedication to the practice. For the majority of people, exercise is a choice. Yoga is different. Most people practicing yoga will tell you they started off two times a week and quickly wanted to do "more," and for most, it becomes a daily ritual within a short period of time. So then you have to ask, why? Why does one need to do more and more— like an alcoholic to a drink—who just can't stop at one drink, yet think they are still in control? We have noticed this same pattern with people who practice yoga—they just want more and more hours of doing yoga and meditation. It may become meditation for hours. Some will keep it to one session a day, but some will experience a health crisis like the many videos of testimonies. Others will give it up like any other exercise. *But most will not give it up because it's not like any other exercise.*

Yoga has a *spiritual attraction* that is naked to the eye and senses at first. Yoga lures you in, and you don't even know what it is, until it is too late. The relaxation of it grows and falling into a *trance* or *meditative state* progresses to being quicker and quicker. According to many ex-yogis, after a few years, the process becomes fairly quick to fall into trances that practitioners eventually cannot easily pull themselves out of. They fall into a *different realm* is the explanation they would give. A realm that eventually pulls them toward considering death as more appealing than returning to their current lives! These so called *gods and spirits* tell them they will take care of them, and share positive feelings to get them moving toward where these spirits want to take them. But the spirits lure them to a place of fear and *negative scary forces* and then toward suicide eventually. Some of what the kids reported mirrored this.

There are many positive benefits, at first, in yoga, which cause people to want *more*. Like the boiling frog who starts off in pleasant, or what it thinks are peaceful, waters. When the frog realizes that it is getting hotter and hotter, it is too late. *For many yogis it is too late.* Ex-yogis tell of the demonic but very attractive luring toward the worst reported: suicide and death. This is what they tell in their dramatic and very parallel stories particularly about friends and family they've lost to yoga. They are speaking up in an attempt to warn you.

Spiritual Warfare

Dating back centuries when you look into the depths of this yoga battle, there is so much at stake on both sides of yoga, and many see it as a war over good and evil. I'd studied a little about spiritual warfare over the past fifteen years, but I had not experienced any firsthand and so I was still skeptical. Maybe you are too. Now I've seen some firsthand, so I understand it on a different level. When you experience something personally, you understand it more in-depth than just intellectually knowing it. Until you step forward into a position of "stepping out in faith," you may not feel the forces that suddenly work against you. It's as if we aren't enough of a threat to be bothered with previously. It's not until taking action on a stand, like we did in the yoga battle, that some threat causes warfare to attempt to prevail. I don't know what the battle is for you, but taking action in it, will likely bring on some warfare. However, a calm and protection can miraculously cover you through it all.

You could say our family received a new education. One for which we will get no diploma, no awards, and certainly we didn't even pay tuition beyond the firestorm we have endured. For the most part, I think our own children will one day be surprised at a lot that went on as they were shielded from unnecessary details for their ages. One day they can read this book and the website and learn more about the bigger picture of which they were a part. They are simply kids trying to be kids, growing up. Although, they were aware of many *odd things happening,* and of course, they were not immune. Our daughter will remember having to move schools in 3rd grade even if she doesn't remember the details of why. They may recall some of the *strange and unexplainable things* that happened along the way—like the lady plowing into us in her car

349

after a basketball game, which also *happened to be* the evening after we educated 100 pastors on the concerns over yoga. It would seem coincidence if a flood and hospitalization hadn't happened to two other speakers from that day. Then there was the coach who loved our son until one day asking him not to show up for the final championship game, which fell on the day before the trial ... so is it all coincidence? Over and over these odd and extreme reactions or incidents would occur, in tandem with something in the trial or education of yoga also occurred.

When other "odd occurrences" began—like no teacher would look us in the eye any longer at a school after nine years—one realizes this isn't a coincidence, this was a direction from the district superintendent. But was something driving that superintendent that even he doesn't understand? The kids have already looked back and understood why some things happened. We were called to do this, prepared and protected all along the way, and it just was part of our story.

Five years ago, I would never have written about spiritual warfare. I would never have thought about warfare and spiritual battles. I know many people who will read and understand those words better than I. And then there are those that will use them in judgement. I wouldn't wish this battle on anyone. It's not what I want or wanted to spend my time on the past few years. I wish I had never heard the term Ashtanga yoga, but that is silly, because it is now in the fabric of EUSD. And my children happened to go there at just the right timing. We just happened to have kids in the public school in Encinitas. And my daughter just happened to be at the right age for a lawsuit that would linger on for years beyond when other families' kids would have aged out of the district. (None of us even considered that we needed a younger child to be the plaintiff). But her (God-given) name is also pertinent. I had other names in mind, and so did her father, but in the end it was obvious she was to be called this name: Faith.

Seven years later, we would learn just why we were led to name her Faith. An innocent seven year old, at the center of an internationally watched trial and controversy over worshipping idols in yoga, and her name is Faith? Is this perhaps more about faith than *yoga*?

Chapter Eighteen

Sun and Idol Worship

As we pointed out to the district, one of our chief concerns was religious entanglement as it pertains to yoga in the public schools. Regardless your beliefs, Ashtanga yoga involves worshipping the sun, so an important issue in schools doing yoga becomes: does it matter if these kids don't know what are doing? Unfortunately, many adults perform the rituals of worshipping the sun through yoga *not even knowing what they are doing*. They think they are following a *set of stretches*; yet, in reality they are performing a sequence that mirrors the sun salutations, unaware of what they are potentially inviting in, by holding hands in prayer position, palm to palm, bowing and facing east. Children simply follow their teacher.

Sun Salutations

The series of opening sequences that make up the sun salutations are mandatory in Ashtanga yoga. That is why EUSD did not alter that part of the Ashtanga series even after we pointed that out to them. You cannot, according to the founder of Ashtanga yoga, change the opening and closing sequences. You *can change* what is in between the opening and closing sequences. And that is what EUSD has done to claim the kids are not doing Ashtanga *per se*. But they are still practicing Ashtanga, even if they think they aren't, because Jois Yoga defines Ashtanga by the opening and closing sequences (http://joisyoga.com/).[1] As a parent would you want to know if your child was *worshipping* the sun? Maybe not or you think it's no big deal, but some of us did. Sun worship is an ancient

351

pagan ritual as articulated in this article: http://paganwiccan.about.
com/od/lithathesummersolstice/p/SunWorship.htm.[2]

In our school district, children were led to *worship* at least twice weekly for the last six years. The text box here is part of the handout you can see at this linked location online or at the

---

*Sun Salutations (Surya Namaskara A/B) aka Opening Sequence A/B are symbolic rituals of devotion developed as a salute or prayer to the sun god Surya (Sanskrit for Supreme Light). Surya is worshipped at dawn by most Hindus and has temples dedicated to him across India. The devotee adopts a praying hands position (anjalimudra), reaches up toward the sun in praise and petition; bows in surrender and worship; and rises up remembering the true sun is within. P.K. Jois gave two reasons for starting practice with Sun Salutations: the physical reason is to warm up the body; the more important spiritual reason is to "pray to the sun god."

*The lotus position (sitting with feet crossed above or beneath the knees, depending on one's flexibility) symbolizes spiritual purity and enlightenment and is believed to aid the flow of spiritual energy Qtrana), facilitating meditation and ultimately samadhi, or union with God.

*The corpse (shavasana), or resting, pose (lying on one's back relaxing every muscle) symbolizes death of ego and promise of awakening to an enlightened state of consciousness. Thinking about one's death gives a sense of purpose and inspires good use of remaining time.

*Sanskrit is viewed by Hindus as a sacred language (much as Muslims view Arabic as a sacred language). Because it is believed that each Sanskrit letter has a specific sound frequency and each word is encoded with consciousness, teaching Sanskrit names for poses is thought to create a spiritual connection to the poses.

*The purpose of deep, focused breathing Qtranayama) is to "let the prana flow." Prana, or vital breath, is believed to be an external manifestation of Atman, or universal spirit.

> *Yoga flows (vinyasas) of postures and breathing are religious rituals (symbolic actions) that create religious moods and motivations by confirming a worldview (overall picture of reality) and instilling an ethos (life philosophy of how one should live). Yoga sequences, such as Sun Salutations (Surya Namaskara A/B) that open class, and lotus and corpse poses that close class, are to be performed in the same manner and order each time-like a liturgical order of service or interpretive dance-because repetition of rituals communicates meaning even without words.
>
> *Postures and breathing are believed to move Kundalini (female serpent energy, or a goddess, symbolized by the cobra pose) through nonmaterial energy streams (nadis), joined at spinning vortexes (chakras). Yoga awakens Kundalini, so that she uncoils and travels up the spine, opening chakras, until she reaches her male lover, Shiva, in the crown chakra. When Kundalini and Shiva unite, one attains samadhi (union with God) or moksha (liberation from reincarnation).

back of the book, for the full document which reveals what the sun salutation and some of the poses mean. http://www.nclplaw.org/wp-content/uploads/2013/07/Yoga-Fact-Sheet-Rev..pdf.[3]

Intentions

"Does it matter if you *intend to worship* in yoga or not?"

"If I don't intend to worship, then what does it matter?"

"Does it still harm a child if they go through the motions but don't intend to worship?"

Many questions have been asked by many parents trying to figure out where to draw the line.

Some parents don't want their children taught yoga in gym class. No big deal you might say, for various reasons and from your viewpoint, but the vastness of the program is the problem. This is a foundation starting at age five being set, when done twice weekly for seven years. It becomes indoctrination when done repetitively for years as a physical action, not *just a lesson being taught*—it's a habit being formed. And there is a reason behind forming this habit.

Religion and Public Schools

Yoga uses your body to do the *worship* in movements, not just cerebral learning. This worship is ritualistic and rooted in religious background to its founders. The reason our nation chose to keep religion out of the public school system was to promote respect for differing beliefs. To study different religions as we do in schools is fine, but to partake in them as a mandatory part of school is what many found unacceptable. That's not to say that it couldn't be optional and offered as an elective. However, if it were an elective, then we would also need to offer a worship of other religions. But then we are back to the same place ... either religious-based activities shouldn't be in schools, or should all be allowed equally.

Do you see how subtle the undertones are? When you think it is only exercise and you think it's simply just PE, then you don't see the problem. Even as people across our country and from other countries are speaking up to tell you *it's not just exercise*. It wasn't designed for that, it isn't just that, and can't be just that long term, even when you try. So the world watches as America experiments with yoga, in studios, in gyms, in homes and now in schools and churches.

A Yoga Trance... is like a Drug?

Along the trail of research we found that the trance one can experience during yoga meditation is much like being on hallucinogenic drugs! What? The research studies revealed that practicing yoga and taking mind-altering drugs lead to the same place. Seriously? Those people who tried hallucinogenic drugs in the 1960s found the same *high* while doing yoga and found that they *went to the same place*. So it's somewhere in the mind? A documented movement away from drugs and into yoga happened as a result, given yoga was a healthier alternative (or so some thought!). The Beatles helped usher yoga in and gurus moved into the United States. Most of the country still didn't touch yoga and thought it strange and foreign at that time. The sources here will give you the examples and facts that back up those statements, so I invite you to research further through many sources that discuss how the Beatles influenced yoga into the US. I'll include a couple here and you have some from an earlier chapter, but these will lead you to many others if you start with these sources. http://people.howstuffworks.com/beatles-yoga.htm, and https://www.elephantjournal.com/2014/04/the-beatles-yoga-jessie-blackledge/.[4]

Yoga Uncoiled

In Chapter three I mentioned "Yoga Uncoiled" found at http://yogauncoiled.com/[5] as a video that answers the question of whether yoga can separate the physical from the spiritual teachings by asking the experts who created yoga. This author, Caryl Mastriciana, has been researching the New Age development for decades. This video addresses the question of whether one can practice yoga postures, breathing and focusing techniques devoid of yoga's spirituality, when not knowing that yoga is an inherent part of Hindu philosophy, teaching that man and nature are one with divinity. If you haven't checked it out by now, I suggest you get the video and watch it. Mastriciana too, shows the links of yoga to the Beatles, drugs, and New Age Movement in "Wide is the gate": https://www.youtube.com/watch?v=bDBoBhIqfwQ.[6] This video (and longer version is six videos) is a look into how all these pieces fit together and why many might be leading yoga, meditation and earth worship into our society.

Death of a Guru book, mentioned previously, walks through the drug culture discoveries of yoga taking people to the same place as heroin and psychedelics. Drugs are, sadly feeding our children lies, and specifically targeted at our children. So, is it *all in the mind*? Let's suppose for a moment here that the former yogis are correct and that spiritual *demons* can attack your thoughts. I know that sounds wild, but yogis report over and over that demons can impact you *in your mind*. What? Well, if "demons" are real and kids become accessible through drugs and through yoga, which is inviting them in by clearing out the mind, then concern for the children grows exponentially! Reportedly, they just need an open path to you through worship of idols and trance to *clear the path* to get to you. Former yogis share that you *go deeper* each time you meditate and that after a while you can *fall into a trance* very quickly. Many have locked into a trance, not being able to *get back,* and die. The ones who get stuck for a while in the trance, and then *come back* report that there was a force or an evil spirit that looked very enticing trying to show them how they would be better off leaving this life and moving on to the next through suicide or just letting go further into the trance (leading to crossing over to death). They report being led to specific types of suicide. How can this happen if yoga and meditation is "only exercise?" or "only peaceful meditation?" It's important to ask how? As crazy as all that sounded, I continued to push to be open-minded and to research further.

One day it happened. It happened to someone I know well. A 13 year old girl was basically "taken over" by something outside of herself telling her nothing besides *you want to kill yourself*. She repeated this over and over all day to her school, to her parents, to her friends, all she wanted to do was find a way to kill herself that wouldn't hurt too bad or too long. It's all the young girl could talk about for her waking hours. Her mother prayed over her and touched her, and put her down to bed on her own pillow that night and watched and prayed and slept in the little girl's room. Then, the next morning it was gone. The girl claimed an angel visited her -*returning to her* - in a dream that night. Holy Canoli – what was all that? Demonic presence is no joke. No fairy tale. The experiences so many ex-yogi's report are too similar to be fabrications.

EUSD and Idol Worship

Perhaps when the EUSD superintendent changed some things in the yoga curriculum they thought they were "taking the religious parts of yoga out." But what they didn't seem to understand, is that they could never change *enough* because *we knew then as we know now, that yoga isn't solely for the purpose of exercise.* We didn't make that up—*we found it.* We found it from the creators and from the world of yogis ... from the very makers of the Jois yoga that Timothy Baird and EUSD chose. We also find it from the sources about idol worship and the yoga studios themselves. Almost every yoga studio has a small statue placed somewhere— why? An idol is not like a flag we would place for "representing" something—it is to be worshipped by those who understand. Our flag isn't worshipped. It's respected; it's understood what it stands for, but it's a representation, not an idol. Whether you bow to the statue in the yoga studio or not—it is there. Although you probably don't find idols in the schools, there were photos displayed containing idols. And where will the children *practice* once they graduate elementary?

Biblical Warnings on Idol Worship

The Bible, has a lot to say about worshipping idols, so some of that information was gathered together for educating others when researching yoga. Over and over, in many books of the Bible are warnings about idol worship. Some of strongest passages are found in the following: Genesis, Deuteronomy, Exodus, Daniel, Psalms, Isaiah, Joshua, Micah, Matthew, Mark, Romans, 1 Corinthians, 2 Corinthians, Ephesians, 1Timothy, 1 John, and Revelation. See the handout on our Educational Events page for the exact locations in the Bible on this link and provided here in the inset box below: (https://truthaboutyoga.files.wordpress.com/2015/01/biblical-talking-points.pdf).[7]

Regardless your beliefs about the Bible, it is a historical record. So why, historically, was it made so clear in the Old Testament about not worshipping the sun and worshipping idols? Why adamantly against idol worship? Towns went through destruction when they fell from worshipping God to worshipping idols. When they turned away from Him, everyone was destroyed, except the few who didn't turn away. Repeatedly, we see this pattern. God gave us free will, and in the Old Testament we see the choices of free will and the consequences that would come, if not immediately, then over the generations in a family or city. God would only allow so much destruction. There was a huge problem that needed to be solved. A bridge to God was needed. People had blown every chance of repenting and repentance is one of the hardest things for people. The bridge came in the new covenant, his Son. One scripture says: "Tell them 'This is what the Lord God says,' whether they listen or refuse to listen" (Ezek. 3:11). What does idol worship include is important to ask as well. Are we worshipping our bodies and selves in yoga as well?

The text box below was created by the attorney on the case as he prepared for the talk in October of 2013. As he searched for a biblical basis, there was so much more written than expected on the topic.

Can Christians Practice Yoga?

- We are intentionally designed and created in God's image. As created beings we are distinct from our Creator. While God's Holy Spirit does dwell in us, it is
- Unbiblical idolatry to say that individuals are "divine" or are ourselves "gods"
- (Gen. 1:27; Gen. 5:1-2; Rom. 1:25; Matt. 19:4; Mark 10:6).
- Christians should love, worship, bow down to, and obey only the God of the Bible
- (Exod. 20:1-7; Deut. 6:1; Matt. 4:9-10, 22:37; Rom. 1:19-21, 25).
- Christians should not worship, bow down to, or even mention other gods
- (Exod. 20:3, 20:23, 23:13, 23:24; Matt. 4: 9-10; Rom. 1:19-21; Gal. 4:8).

- Christians should not worship or bow down to *idols*; the Bible teaches that idols are connected with demonic activity (Exod. 20:4-5; Ps. 81:9; Isa. 2:8; 44:19; Micah 5:13; Rom. 1:22-23,25; Acts 7:43; 1 Cor. 10:20-21; 2 Cor. 6:16; 1 Tim. 4:1; 1 John 5:21; Rev. 9:20).

- NOTE: Yoga asanas (or poses) inherently acknowledge and depict the worship of Hindu gods and myths. See "Information for Parents: The EUSD/JOIS Foundation Yoga Program" on Educational events page of website.

- Christian *meditation* involves focusing on scripture and thoughts about God, not

- emptying your mind as yoga meditation and Hinduism promote.

- (Josh. 1:8; Ps. 119:15, 23, 48).

- The spiritual realm (angels & demons), although unseen, is very *real* (Mark 16:9; Rom. 8:28; Eph. 2:1-3, 6:10-20; 1 Tim. 4:1).

- As Christians, our battle is not just against the physical/ material realm but is also in the spiritual realm (Eph. 2:1-3; Eph. 6:10-20).

- Christians must refuse to submit to the government when it attempts to force them to violate their religious beliefs (*See* Dan. 3:1-18 (Shadrach, Meshach, & Abednego refuse to bow to the King's idol); Acts 5:29 ("We must obey God rather than men!").

Video explaining yoga and idol worship

In the video, https://vimeo.com/86794950 [8] you find the topic "Is Yoga Religious?" covering idol worship and what Ashtanga Yoga includes. Explained is a serpent traveling up the spine, releasing chakras along the path, and ending in a "third eye" experience of bliss at the top of the head with a sexual energy being released. This description concerned us deeply as to why children would be led to start a pathway like this, knowing where the creators intend this to take people. You would expect a pastor or former yoga teacher to teach what is on this video, but instead you find it was the attorney on the case who researched and reveals the teachings.

Ignorance Is Not an Excuse, not for Long

One of the key problems with not understanding the worship of idols, is then not knowing if, or when, your children are performing it in yoga class. And unfortunately, no action (doing nothing) by parents, meant support of the yoga program at EUSD. Due to the opt-out nature, inaction from parents, on issues with the yoga program, end up looking like support of continuation of mandatory yoga curriculum in the schools. Unfortunately, a *non-vote is a positive vote for yoga in our district, because if you just go along with it silently, the district thinks you support it*. If we as parents simply had been given a choice of traditional PE or yoga, then the votes would have been cast very differently. But the district refused to offer that option. Most people just didn't want to say anything to be "politically correct" or "don't want to make waves." Some of those came to us later for support, when their kids developed issues, but were still unwilling to be public.

It's Creepy, Say Some Kids

Some of those kids that asked to opt-out of yoga said that *creepy things* were said during meditation. Now EUSD said in court in 2013 there was and would be no meditating in the EUSD yoga — just stretching and breathing. Yet, kids were lying on the floor at the end of class and last I checked, no one had to teach anyone *how to breathe*. Forced breathing done in yoga is for a purpose. It means something spiritually, and impacts your body. *The breathing taught in yoga matters* to the *yoga meditation*. It matters for the *trance*

360

process in order to slow your thinking, your body, and to *conform* to a new: peace?

EUSD still claims it isn't doing meditation, but if you go to a yoga class at one of the schools you will probably find kids falling asleep (*in PE, mind you*) when they are lying in what is called in yoga, the "corpse pose" at the end of the session. This is when the teachers will do "guided imagery" - which is meditation. A similar "cool down" time occurred in aerobics, but this is different and goes beyond stretching at the end of class. It wasn't meant for sleeping or meditating. But once again, the children report odd things said by yoga teachers during those end-of-session minutes.

Kids reported to their parents all kinds of concerning phrases. I will give you a few examples, but if you are a parent with kids in yoga right now in your schools —ask them. Ask your kids all about their yoga experiences. Phrases EUSD kids reported such as "we are going to go on a journey now and you can leave behind your thoughts ... just let them go and listen ... my heart loves your heart more than others, so trust me ... " Most children in elementary aren't going to lie, so ask. When no one but the yoga teacher and the children are in the room, the school district, the principals, the teachers who, theoretically, love their classrooms of children, really don't know what is being said to the children. I don't know if yoga teachers are out to intentionally hurt any child—many are just doing what they were taught. They may never see their impact. They may even think that they are *helping* the children.

Just like Jessica thought she was helping people.
Just like Mike thought he was helping people.
Just like Corinna thought she was helping people.
Just like hundreds of yogis thought, until they eventually learned otherwise ...
One major difference was: *None were working with children.*

What they all claim to have learned is that what they were doing actually harmed others and led them down pathways of spirituality they didn't expect.

361

Elementary-age children are the future of this nation. What have we allowed in to guide them? *Seven years of yoga will have its consequences*. It will change our nation dramatically, if it spreads to every school in the United States.

The children need us.

CHAPTER NINETEEN

Has America been Duped?

Have you ever been duped? Fooled? Tricked? Temporarily deceived into thinking something was one way when it was really another. Surprised? Teased? Taken off track for a moment? A week? A year? A decade? Consider the possibility of deception for a few moments while reading this chapter. Deception can come in many forms – advertising, injuries, demonic, oppression, sexual harassment, and is it possible, the seducing of America into yoga?

Ga-Ga For yoga

Clearly America has gone ga-ga for yoga in the past decade as shown in earlier chapters. As a former fitness instructor and now a coach, I have seen many varieties of exercise come and go such as kick boxing and step aerobics. But yoga is different, and it is sweeping the nation in a very different way than Pilates, Spin classes or other forms of modern group exercise in gyms.

What are U.S. Consumers *led* to Believe about Yoga?

Consumers are being told yoga is a solution for almost every need they have these days – such as more energy, focus, flexibility, spiritual awakening, peace, less stress, healing, better health, better sex and the list goes on and on in magazines. And some of those things happen for some people for a while, but the advertising and claims have far surpassed reality. For example America hypes yoga as something it is not, as evidenced by photos of dogs doing yoga, babies doing yoga and cats in yoga positions for photos. Reality, or is this just advertising? My dog likes to run, fetch, eat a treat and be petted, but yoga? No, not reality people, wake up to the advertising all around you. And you know that already, but the photos still move you one direction or another.

Dog photo - compliments of Inspired Living products: http://www. inspiredliving.com/relaxation-products/inner-peace.htm

Cat photo - promotional photos on cards, credits: Avanti press greeting cards

Most people probably think the animal and baby photos are funny but American advertising has driven people into paying more for workout wear than ever before. An article in Bloomberg News points to consumers paying *$400 for a pair of yoga pants*: http:// www.bloomberg.com/news/articles/2015-05-13/-400-yoga-pants-are-just-the-beginning.[1] That's more than a car payment for most people! Clearly many Americans have taken the bait and are gaga for yoga. Retail jumped on the bandwagon and yoga pants are now a term almost as common as jeans. In fact, lately I've run into people who can't even remember the name of them prior to yoga. If you are struggling to remember too, stop and think a moment to try to remember. I'll give some names to you within the next paragraph, but take a moment to test yourself: what were they called before yoga pants?

Photo for Brown Trout Calendars, available on Amazon:

https://www.amazon.com/Yoga-Babies-18-Month-Calendar-Multilingual/
dp/1465018204

Advertising

Yoga pants have taken on a new and fresh "look" to change your vision of what yoga looks like in other countries. The "yoga butt" on that model was probably sculpted by other physical activities long before yoga, if the model even does yoga! Remember, not many kids, if any, went to do yoga at studios prior to yoga entering the schools in our area. Now you can see kid yoga "advertised" everywhere…but *kids in America doing yoga* is a new phenomenon in this decade fueled by advertising. Sweat pants, running tights, leggings, spandex, and many more names were around long before the term "yoga" pants. Full length, calf cut, gymnast length, biker short length and volleyball short shorts are all other options and as we specialize more and more into each sport with our clothing. So we shift as the world shifts around us and advertising has played a huge role in women flocking to yoga classes seeking the purported benefits.

Has Yoga impacted the beliefs of Celebrities?

If yoga is a gateway toward Hinduism and Eastern religions with multiple deities and a belief in reincarnation, then yoga is moving you *away from belief in one God* and *toward a belief in multiple gods*. As in physics, we are moving in one direction or another. Examples are all around us of Americans who have moved toward Eastern religions through actions in their lives of yoga. One example is Julia Roberts who went public with becoming a practicing Hindu as the New York Times reported in August of 2010. http://www.nydailynews.com/entertainment/gossip/julia-roberts-practicing-hindu-actress-converts-religion-filming-eat-pray-love-article-1.201002.[2]

Gweneth Paltrow and Madonna are Ashtanga Yogis, http://www.dietsinreview.com/diet_column/10/ashtanga-yoga-a-favorite-for-madonna-and-gwyneth/.[3] Many more examples can be found and below is just one article. Ten famous celebrities and their favorite form of yoga are in an article dated June of 2011, including Gwenneth and Madonna and the following 8 others: http://www.ecorazzi.com/2011/06/22/10-sexy-celebs-that-rock-the-yoga-scene/.[4] They are:

Jennifer Aniston, Hatha Yoga

George Clooney, Bikram Yoga

Giselle Bundchen (Victoria Secret model), Anusara Yoga

Miranda Kerr, (super model) Hatha

Russell Simmons (hip hop pioneer), Hatha Yoga

Christy Turlington, (model) Kundalini Yoga

Sting, Ashtanga and Jivamukti Yoga

Ricky Martin, Hatha Yoga

The question becomes - *Have any of their faiths changed due to yoga?* Many visible changes make it appear that is probable.

Miranda claims to listen to Deepok Chopra during flights, Russel Simmons and others have gone vegan and he focuses on chanting and liberation of the soul. Ricky Martin is gaining "inner peace and connection." And this is just one article about a few of the celebrities that are jumping on the mat to do yoga and the impact is apparent.

Yoga Has a Hook

So why don't people look farther into the origins of yoga? Because they want to just keep on doing yoga. They love it. *They are hooked*. It's a subtle addiction. When you first start out, it's for a couple days a week. Not unlike many forms of "exercise" you quickly you find you want *more*. You like what you feel and see. You watch the ads, you buy some yoga wear, you want to look and feel better and *you buy the lie*. You buy more and more of the lie, until you are clearing out time *every* day to do yoga. So you sit and meditate, and perhaps you *lose* your mind to another space. It's to relax, you say. It's to get away without getting away, many express. It's to empty your mind, you might offer. But to fill it with *what*, others have asked? To pray into yourself the spirits *over and over* is to *invite* in what you don't even know is coming.

This is our concern for the children. They know the "prayer hands" indicates prayer, but they don't know that the guided imagery exercise that their young yogi is (remember, the ones leading the yoga classes here in schools and across the country are mostly not credentialed teachers for regular classrooms) leading them on a journey away from their own independent thinking. It's a slow lure away from their current life and world view.

Why are so many people oblivious to the unintended negative effects of yoga? Only in recent decades have a portion of our country looked at yoga as only exercise. The answers are readily at our fingertips these days. Most yogis that don't have an agenda to cover up the spiritual nature and foundation of yoga are clear to say it is spiritual, and yet, we believe what we want to believe. The initial effects of yoga stretching and breathing are positive. Therefore, like many other things, many think "more" is better. It's quite easy to do most other sports or activities just a couple or few times a week and be "satisfied." However some extreme athletes want more such as many runners need that "runners high" or they aren't quite settled with themselves. Yoga has a similar "euphoria" created through forced breathing, which is very attractive for a while.

The euphoria in Yoga appears to be consuming where you cannot then just pursue yoga 2-3 days per week, the desire grows quickly to want to do yoga daily. Call it stretching, or worshipping, or meditating, or chanting, or whatever that "time" is - but somehow the desire grows to want it more and more and feel a need to have to have it daily. When people come out of that time, they report feeling one of two things. 1. An elation or euphoria (particularly when doing the forced breathing "through the shakras" which could last all day (sharks is the only spellcheck available by the way). Or 2nd - Angry and aggressive shortly after, surprising even them. Former yogis claim they are more on edge and frustrated after long hours of meditation and didn't understanding why. They resisted for years that there was any real problem. For a while, ex-yogis said that they felt "better" and "looser" and "more in control of my body and mind." They said they didn't want to believe it wasn't all good until it clearly wasn't. Most say it took 15-20 years of practice before they realized the deception and negative consequences due to the subtlety. A deception and very attractive luring appears to happen and may be sustained a while, but the long term results are not the intended effect. Hmm, back to that mind control.

The choice to do yoga is made to look good in advertising and until one experiences this type of extreme internal strife on their own, likely won't believe it exists. You may be defensive to this chapter right now and it's because you don't want to believe there is any problem. We understand that is a pattern, and you are not alone. Many yogis have stayed in yoga long after the warning signs, and even died in these "trances." Today there are even arguments over some guru's as to whether these folks are dead or in a full trance. One yogi is in the news right now with the followers want to preserve him, while his wife and son want to bury him. (We can't make this stuff up if we tried!!!). He is still on ice awaiting trial over whether he is to be preserved or buried! How crazy is that when you aren't involved in the deception of it? It is nuts! And there are many, many stories like that you can find. India is fraught with sexual oppression, physical abuse and if you look at yogis bodies after 20 years- of practicing it looks *nothing* like the false American advertising that you are buying on your way into lulu lemon stores. It's a big fat lie! And like sheep being led to the slaughter, people are buying, buying, buying, the lies, the outerwear and the lie of the results. Thus, the purchasing of $400 yoga pants...

What's the Matter with Yoga?

If you take a little deeper look into what these former yogis are telling everyone it is this: There is the spiritual, demonic side of inviting in many "gods" and evil spirits through the specific poses developed to invite them in while you follow yoga moves. Through meditation and clearing of the mind, other spirits are fair game to fill that space in your mind, especially when invited! One example a former yogi speaks about clearing the mind is in a presentation located here: https://www.youtube.com/watch?v=6DZ7oz_fIq8 .[5] She states you cannot separate yoga from its source and its source being Hinduism. She says they are one and the same (like so many other people from India report). She goes on to say that after deep meditation an "overcoming of the personality" where the person becomes a "vessel" for a deity or spirit to *take over* and "will lose some self-awareness" for a period of time. This is why people say and do things they are not later aware of and/or can't recall. This is demonization. You can see many, many, more examples of this on a simple search of the internet, and we have posted a few on our Truth about Yoga site. A website I referred to a couple chapters ago https://whatsthematterwithyoga.wordpress.com/demonization-2/ [6] gives one ex-yogi's account of the demonization she experienced. These experiences, documented in her own words, reflect how she was deceived for a long time. Many now not only feel duped, but don't want others to end up in the same place. Their goal is for the public to learn more from their stories to help others avoid the experience. . And, the spiritual warfare against them speaking out is unbearable to the others who haven't, yet many are brave enough to share the truth. We would be wise to listen and realize the pattern of their stories.

Are potential injuries to bodies, minds, spirit and soul what we want for innocent, impressionable young children who have been forced into yoga as a replacement for physical education in schools?

Have we been duped?

*Sexual Harassment and Oppression...***in yoga**

A very concerning part of our research uncovered the oppression of women and sexual harassment occurring inside yoga in other countries. Harassment has also happened here in the U.S., but it is common in other countries practicing yoga. Physical abuse occurring at the hands of Hindu men after spending hours in prayer is documented in various books, videos and articles.

Yoga, or sexual harassment?

Compliments of Blogspot (anonymous), photo of Pattabhi Jois teaching Ashtanga yoga

(Yes, the founder of the Ashtanga yoga placed into EUSD)

Yoga is full of sexual harassment and oppression of women particularly in India, and the videos depict the claims of many women. The abuse by men in India that claim to do yoga to "center themselves," is unbelievable by our standards. They would all be in jail if the women were able to do anything about it. Women victims are helpless in many situations and this is just the "way of life" as they know it according to those who will have moved out of those countries and are willing to speak out about the problems. Rabi Maharaj speaks of this in his book "Death of a Guru" and how he couldn't stand the violence that even he saw in himself toward his own mother, after hours of being in yoga prayer and meditation. Yoga, prayer and meditation do center you... on yourself! As in becoming just that: *self-centered*. This self-centeredness is the potential downfall of this generation, and this nation.

Numbers of Guru's have been accused of rape and fondling of numerous women is in all different stages of multiple lawsuits. Too many to count, are being outed for injuries, abuse, and fraud. Yoga is a billion dollar industry in America. Yoga studio owners came out December 2012 to our EUSD district meeting to speak up for yoga and yoga underground chat rooms are full trying to strategize how to continue their influence here.

Oppression and Abuse

But many still don't see the oppression and abuse yet. That is why so many people don't understand what the problem with yoga is, and can't see it yet. It's not invisible though. The results are available when you talk to ex-yogis or look into what is really going on behind the scenes in countries that have practiced yoga for years. The oppression is apparent. There are problems with sexual promiscuity and abuse. Multiple yogis have been caught abusing students. One high profile example of this is the leader of Bikram yoga accused of sexual assault in San Diego. http://www.nytimes. com/2015/02/24/us/cracks-show-in-bikram-yoga-empire-amid-claims-of-rape-and-assault.html?ref=topics&_r=0.[7] Unfortunately, there are many more of these types of stories documented on news sites. Simply search the keywords yoga and assault and you will find these horrific stories. The physical and spiritual problems are all on the news and in reach of your eyes. It's available to find yet so easy to miss if you don't given our information overload society. The rapes and litigation of numerous women are widespread.

Reports contain photos in less-than-appropriate positions with women in classes while gurus are "adjusting" them or showing them a move. "Why does he need to put his private parts onto theirs while they are flipped upside down or bending over?" These photos, stories and more are linked on the truth website too. It's disgusting, disgraceful and oppressive in our culture viewpoint, but it has taken years for women in India to begin to speak out, and most have not. That is why these former America yogis and others around the world (people who practiced for years and are now speaking out about their negative experiences) are documenting in video, photos and websites for you to see the dangers. My effort to show you here is that these former yogis exist and I want to help educate you to avoid this path for the children here. The intent is not to scare, but to prepare. To wake us up, is the intent, to the realities surrounding yoga, and to take some action to protect our children.

How disturbing it was to hear the ex-yogis claims of suicidal thoughts? How frightening that is to affect a child's impressionable mind and spirit. Ex-yogis have claimed that spirits draw you to a place of wanting to "go on to another place" and not stay in the world, to the point of taking their own lives as shared in another chapter. Family members of those people share publicly that their loved one was led to suicide in yoga. Rabi Maharaj speaks about this very topic as well, and how one can end up in a trance, sort of caught between the world we know and a spiritual world where we cannot reach the person any longer, even though they sit in a room right next to you as his father did for years. There are many more examples of these near suicide victims of yoga as mentioned that are willing to share their stories and how they were duped into thinking a reverse of what transpired.

Did *Jois Foundation* (now Sonima) dupe us?

Bravo to Jois - crafty plans!

Jois Foundation fooled the district and public along the way. Or did they? Haven't they been quite upfront about their spreading Ashtanga yoga goals? EUSD received over $4 Million dollars before Sonima cut their financial support, and walked away with the curriculum Sonima needed for their strategic plans. Remember in Chapter 4, I said, follow the money for the truth of the matter. Follow whose hands the money goes through and to, and who is on the board. Most of that money is going to "Jois Yoga" instructors and some to supplies in the districts. Genius Jois Foundation! You found a way to take part-time yoga instructors and give them a full time 40 hour a week job, *creating stronger followers of Ashtanga yoga*. Their devotion to Ashtanga yoga is now as full time instructors, and their authoring of curriculum, while spreading their "gospel," unbeknownst to most kids and parents. Bravo Jois. It was Genius. A smart plan to spread your brand of yoga! That is why this isn't about EUSD. It's about a much larger agenda into our schools and it's not just Jois/Sonima either. Other yoga groups will pop into schools spreading and Jois is like McDonalds as simply a leader. Now we have burger joints of all varieties. Yoga of all varieties will attempt to enter the schools, and Sonima is trying to beat them there with a "standard" curriculum. Stand back and watch it grow. Or, stand up and help stop this in any way you are led to get involved in your community.

Intentions vs Outcomes

Even if the Encinitas District did not "intend" to spread Ashtanga yoga (as they claim), they clearly hired Ashtanga yoga teachers through Regur Development, had Jen Brown working at both Jois Foundation and for EUSD (through Regur) developing curriculum and leading all the other teachers. Intent isn't the issue when the results are the reality and hurting others. Just like if a kid picks up his father's gun and accidentally kills a friend. He didn't intend to, but did he have a warning? The Superintendent and board were warned over and over for months that this type of yoga was highly spiritual and crossed the religious beliefs of many families in their district. There was no vagueness about hundreds of families being concerned. Children had no voice and neither did their parents as evidenced by the board meetings, trial and public outcry. They chose to ignore the warnings. In Austria, it took one parent to complain, and yoga was sent out the door packing. Article here: http://www.upi.com/Odd_News/2014/10/09/Austrian-school-bans-yoga-for-religious-reasons/9621412879176/.[8] If it were any other religion then Christianity speaking up about a program, it would be out the door so fast from the American schools. For some baffling reason, atheists and other religions didn't seem to make the connection to the religious nature of yoga as quickly as Christians who saw the biblical problems of pagan worship of idols, sun and multiple deities. But one thing we could all agree upon is that children shouldn't be made to do any one "sport" for years on end, just because a grant for it was given. And now that parents might have to pay for it, there seems to be a whole new understanding growing of some of the other problems surrounding yoga in schools. Meanwhile, many other districts across the country to date have already accepted their .5 million dollar initial implementation grants from Sonima.

The children have no knowledge of the consequences of the path they are being led down. And many adults don't have time to look into it creating a vast doorway for yoga to enter. We didn't either. But we did anyway. We put aside time in our jobs, in our school volunteering (I used to spend 80 hours a year heading up and planning and executing the Jogathon at El Camino Creek for over 75 volunteers and making in excess of $25,000 for the schools biggest fundraiser). Now instead, I feel it is wasting valuable time asking them over and over to remove yoga – but it is well worth the time invested for the future of these children. We spent the time because something greater than ourselves led us to "take a deeper look" at what is being advertised to us through the district, the media, and the shifting culture. Let's look at some studies vs. advertising.

Research Studies on Yoga

The studies show that years of yoga actually tear down the body. Yoga over time attacks the very frame of the human bone and ligament structure that was created to hold us up, as was reported on NBC News. http://www.nbcnews.com/id/25400799/#.VvBEHI-cFuI.[9] There are yogis who have shared about their injuries - https://www.youtube.com/watch?v=BLVb0klaris).[10] The hip and knee injuries *that are hidden* are indicators that 15 of 20 years of yoga are very damaging to our bodies. Many examples of folks who have had medical issues are on the internet for you to see. The New York Times featured the breakdown effects to your body in an article called "How Yoga Can Wreck Your Body" and others as we went more in-depth into in Chapter 6. http://www.nytimes.com/2012/01/08/magazine/how-yoga-can-wreck-your-body.html?_r=2.[11] Many examples were given in the previous chapters, and studies are available on the spiritual effect of yoga https://truthaboutyoga.com/spiritual-effects-of-practicing-yoga/[12] which are based on conducted research studies that report statistical significance of a "shift" in spiritual development as opposed to being "purely physical."

Is Yoga the Solution?

Yoga is not the solution for obesity.
Yoga is not the solution for peace.
Yoga is not the solution for replacing drugs.
Yoga is not the solution for every exercise program.
Yoga meditation is not the replacement for spiritual needs for everyone
Yoga is not for American elementary schools
Yoga is a very dangerous slippery slope into Idol Worship.

The warnings are all around. Through reading you have now been warned. Now you can research for more truth. Don't just accept or reject this and walk away. You'll be duped. Be alert and be aware. There is *no shame* in being duped. It becomes figuring it out and getting back on a path that matters, not that you got duped in the first place. Look around, so is most everyone else! It's understandable. It's treatable. Just ask questions and look. The answers are there. But be aware of deception and ask for discernment as you search.

So if yoga is not what it appears....
Now *what do we do*?
Drop Your Yoga Mat and *Run!*

CHAPTER TWENTY

Becoming a Yoga Nation

J ust as yoga advertising *covers* and *masks* the very dangers that
lurk in yoga, attractive outfits focus on body and health, to make
yoga appealing and language of "scientific" aid in the draw to yoga.
The leap is quick from "if it's good for us" to "it must be good for
our kids".

The Spiritual cover up

Many yoga teachers have reported that they "don't share the
spiritual part with most of my classes." Thus the deception among
yoga teachers, as to their own spiritual journeys and injuries, are
only *beginning clues* that our children are perhaps not as safe as
at first glance of a seemingly healthy activity. We have looked at
various elements making up how we are becoming a yoga nation.

Why are people oblivious to the unintended negative effects of
yoga? Only in recent decades has part of our country looked at yoga
as just exercise. The answers are readily at our fingertips. Most
yogis (those who don't have an agenda to cover up the spiritual
nature and foundation of yoga) clearly explain that and how, it is
spiritual. The initial effects of yoga stretching and *forced breathing*,
are positive. Therefore, many people think "more" is better. The
euphoria in yoga appears to be consuming – as if you cannot just
pursue yoga two to three days a week; the desire grows quickly
to every day. Call it stretching, worshipping, meditating, chanting,
or whatever that "time" is—but somehow the desire gravitates to
yearning for more.

When people emerge from a long session in yoga meditation, they reported feeling one of two things. First, an elation or euphoria (particularly when doing the forced breathing "through the shakras" which is a feeling that could last all day. And second, *angry and aggressive* shortly after, surprising even themselves of their own thoughts and reactions. Former yogis claim they were more *on edge* and *frustrated* after long hours of meditation and didn't understanding why. They resisted for years that there was any real problem. Ex-yogis said that they felt "better" and "looser" for a while, and "more in control of my body and mind." They didn't want to believe it wasn't "all good" until clearly it wasn't. Most say it took fifteen to twenty years of practicing yoga before they realized the deception, injuries and negative consequences, due to the subtlety of the problems. Deception and very attractive luring happens and may be sustained a while, but the long term results were not the intended effect, they reported.

The choice to do yoga is made to look good in advertising, and until one experiences this type of extreme internal strife on their own, most likely won't believe it exists. Many yogis have stayed in yoga long after the warning signs, and even died in these "trances." India is fraught with sexual oppression, physical abuse and if you look at yogis bodies after twenty years of practicing, they look *nothing* like the false American advertising being bought on the way into lulu lemon stores. It's a big fat lie! And like sheep being led to the slaughter, people are buying, buying, buying, the lies, the outerwear and the lie of the results. Thus, the purchasing of $400 yoga pants. Hmm, back to that mind control and why it's so important to yogis.

Meditation

Former yogis are most concerned with the meditation portions of yoga classes. Pagan worship of hundreds of deities has been seeping into America with many new followers through these practices including yoga and meditation. You don't have to look far for examples of celebrities that are now following various Eastern religions after doing yoga. Focusing on the meditation you find constantly evolving titles of programs, such as Transcendental Meditation (TM) and more recently, *mindfulness meditation*. Some say it is a continuing path toward the *new age, one-world-religion*. Some reference Agenda 21 and United Nations furthering this through what appears as a *unity of religions*. The worldview that "all roads lead to the same place" is purported by many celebrities today.

The yoga mission

International attention to the trial made its point, starting with phone calls after filing, underground yogi communications on the internet about the case, displaying why the pro yoga side *needed* to win. The research catapults you into why the people backing yoga (politically, spiritually, and economically) are fighting so hard to spread it. The mission includes moving away from the previous worldview many Americans professed to believe. Yoga appears to be supported by the highest levels of our own government as evidenced by The White House starting "yoga on the lawn" and adding yoga into the traditional "eggroll on the lawn" event for "Easter" which was a huge public endorsement. Two articles (among many) are *Yoga Rolls out on White House Lawn, April, 2013*. https://www.yogajournal.com/blog/yoga-rolls-white-house-lawn#![1] And *White House Easter Egg Party to include a "yoga garden." April, 2013*. http://www.washingtonexaminer.com/white-house-easter-egg-roll-party-to-include-a-yoga-garden/article/2525784.[2]

You will run into many political reasons by merely researching *yoga,* but for the purposes of this book I will not spend much time on that issue. However, political and religious views cannot be ignored as reasons for importance to place yoga into schools to condition children. Look for the connections right here in this book, tying Oprah through Stedman Graham's leadership training with the Jois's, and you easily link her with the top political people in our country and why they are pushing yoga. You'll find a lot written publicly about the few comments here.

Yoga and Going Green at School, the Truth Behind the Lies

Esther Watchmen's book includes the Encinitas Union School District Trial and its connections to a larger movement. The author came to our second public education event and handed me the book afterwards telling me she wrote it because yoga is tied to a much larger agenda, and to read it to understand the connections. The book connects yoga to Going Green by *saving our planet,* and to actions of the United Nations. As I turned each page, I knew the path we were on to protect the children was so much more important than I'd ever considered. This was much more than a brief trial. Yoga goes back centuries and forward to the future. This is more vast, far, and wide than we could wrap our heads around.

Photo cover approved by Author: Yoga and Going Green at School: The Truth Behind the Lies

http://www.amazon.com/Yoga-Going-Green-at-School/dp/1493520385/
ref=sr_1_fkmr0_1?ie=UTF8&qid=1459441344&sr=8-1-fkmr0&keywords=g
oing+green+and+yoga+in+the+schools+%2C+books [3]

In the book, Watchmen explained why EUSD would implement such a program. Watchman was an outside observer to the trial, had no children in the district, didn't live near Encinitas, but was in the greater San Diego area. On page 10 you find: "Unbeknownst to the general population, yoga and 'going green' represent a return to an ancient, pagan religion that has marked world history with supreme disaster each time it has reared its ugly head." On page 11: "While yoga has been cloaked as healthy physical exercise, its mind-clearing meditation component has received much less publicity leaving people to wonder why a group of parents would seek court relief for their children who are being forced to participate via their state schools and its compulsory attendance laws." Then, on page 13, they start to define some of the meditation issues: "*The New York Times* reporter observed: A circle of six to seven-year-olds contorted their frames, making monkey noises while repeating *confidence boosting mantras."* *Confidence boosting mantras* are defined as "A mystical formula of invocation or incantation (as in Hinduism)." Could the experts have been any clearer, she asks?

Yoga part of a *broader program*

The NYT article ("Yoga Class Draws Religious Protest" on Dec 15, 2012) said "the yoga classes are only 'part of a comprehensive program' and that Timothy Baird, the schools superintendent, 'defended the yoga classes as merely another element of a broader program' which means there is more to the story" (page 14). Well, yes, there is a lot more to the story! Yes, included elements in the Encinitas schools are not only the asanas, but changing eating habits, going green and meditation; clearly mirroring the four areas of Hinduism. On page 15, she shows more connections: "In one of the photos featured in the *New York Times* article, the classroom teacher stood up before her trusting little captives holding up the *ABC's of Yoga for Kids* by Teresa Anne Power. The school insisted there weren't religious implications in the yoga instruction, but a simple glance at the cover tells the reader, that's a big, fat, lie."

Deepak Chopra's Spiritual Involvement

Watchmen continues on, to expose "Prominently displayed on the back of the school's yoga book appears a quote from David Simon, who is identified as the Medical Director for Deepak Chopra's Center for Wellbeing and author of *The Seven Spiritual Laws of Yoga*. That's *not* vague, and it's *not* hidden. It's right there on the back cover of the book for everyone to see. Simon's published cover quote says the book 'lovingly connects our next generation of yogis to their bodies and their world.' Jumping jacks never connected anyone to 'the world'. Of course, there was no book on the *seven spiritual laws of jumping jacks* either. Simon also revealed that establishing the connection between children's lives and the world gives him 'hope for our planet.'" She goes on to show more about why and how yoga targets the mind, body, and soul. *She gets it*. She understands more about why we were standing up against this program than we did! Many others *got it* decades before us and came out of the woodwork to show us, support us and encourage us to keep fighting in this massive battle for the souls of our future generation. That's a tall order and sounded so outrageous at first. But we grew to understand and take one step forward at a time.

Note: Deepak Chopra is on Sonima's website as a board of directors member for the foundation. His deep roots and connection reveal more truth about the program that Baird claims "isn't spiritual." Also important to note is the location of Deepak Chopra's base in the La Costa Spa, which is right in the heart of Encinitas Schools covered in this book. The spa is also just a few miles from the famous "Self Realization Center," so locations are important to see the relevance of why yoga in schools started in Encinitas, and who pursued it, and why.

Watchmen's book goes on to make many other connections to this seemingly innocent yoga program for children linking it to many national concerns—consider reading this 95 page book packed full of insights and overlooked (deception covering it up), yet blatant plans toward influencing our children to shift their thinking and the future.

Two Years Later

A couple years later, we (from the parents group) contacted Watchmen to ask if we could use the same photo on her book for our postcards to educate the public. The photo (kid facing tree) connected visually the message of the innocence of children and how parents might be putting their heads in the sand, to hide from seeing the truth. Watchmen also discovered much of what was going on around Cajon Valley schools in 2014 when they began the same Ashtanga Yoga with a familiar grant by Sonima Foundation, for the same amount of money ($500,000). David Miyashiro was their new superintendent, and as a reminder, he was the Assistant

Superintendent in Encinitas who implemented the contracted yoga in EUSD, prior to leaving the day after the first level trial ended in July, 2013. It appeared some deal was made for him to testify, and then leave the district the following day.

Watchmen makes many more religious and political connections in another one of her books: "Understanding Yoga: It's Origin and Purpose." This one takes you into Agenda 21, (google for what this is as a governmental focus of about 115 programs implemented from summit meetings and the United Nations connections to this issue).

Photo cover approved by Author: Understanding Yoga: It's Origin and Purpose

Understanding Yoga: It's Origin and Purpose

http://www.amazon.com/Understanding-Yoga-Its-Origin-Purpose/ dp/1512228303?ie=UTF8&psc=1&redirect=true&ref_=oh_aui_ detailpage_o09_s00 [4]

An Awakening

Agenda 21 which is alive and at play, and most Americans probably haven't heard of (google it but here is one other source http://www.cfact.org/2014/04/15/agenda-21-what-agenda-21/) is at play here in yoga. For most people, a sudden awakening to a problem with yoga hits them. I've watched this happen to person after person, family after family. They come to a point where they feel they've been "asleep at the wheel" and caught off guard. Each parent I've asked has had that *ah-ha* moment and *is* surprised. It can be a gradual realization, but it still hits you at a "moment" and you almost feel foolish (like the duped feeling). One minute yoga seems fine, then you begin to question it, then perhaps *there is something credible* to these the concerns others share, to the leap of "wow, there is something wrong with yoga." While yoga is fine for those who choose to follow the beliefs and religion of yoga, but not for those duped, mesmerized, and conditioned into it. That is why this mandate for children in schools to perform yoga weekly is *not okay.*

Why the Anger?

Why is it that the people who are standing against yoga in the schools don't express anger to others but the yoga-loving folks show a great deal of defensive anger over the subject? When you first mention the spiritual component of yoga to someone, there are various reactions and they fall into about four categories: 1. Some people are curious but skeptical. 2. Some just agree, already knowing its origins are spiritual. 3. Some avoid the topic and choose not to discuss it at all because they want so badly to believe yoga is fine (usually because they are practicing yoga themselves and like it). 4. The last group is the group that is already hooked on practicing yoga, and they are not only adamantly against what you say, but their response is *angry and defensive* to the point of caustic. Why all this anger over supposedly peaceful, *yoga?*

Is it Taboo **to Talk About?**

It was disarming and surprising at first. We, the concerned parents (group) would be talking about it (individually) with our friends and become quickly aware of how taboo the subject yoga is and the power it contains. People who we had known and loved for years were downright vicious over yoga! It was unbelievable at first. Today, we know the claim that the power and spirits that can dwell inside others, but it still seems surreal at times. Spirits invited in by innocent people who have no idea even of the wrath that comes out of them at times. They don't understand it is from the *ugly underbelly* of yoga. They might not see it at all, or just not understand their own reactions. I don't know any to date who have ever apologized for their lashing out, so I wonder if they just don't see it.

It's a hard leap at first. We concerned parents all understand that and learned patience. Yoga looks so innocent. Yoga seems so good. And if you believe the advertising, it will fix everything that is wrong in your life: from healing your body to healing your mind, to peace and flexibility. Yoga will make you fashionable, fit, and well. It's permeating our society from every angle—fashion, famous people, medical, sports, churches—and now schools. It *looks* like it *could* be good for anyone, but it's a deceptive path many have warned us about through all types of media, but is not on your radar until the day you "wake up" to it. Then you see it so clearly.

Two Competing Worldviews

If you begin with understanding the frame of two opposing worldviews, you can better understand the yoga confusion. One worldview worships God as the Creator and as a separate being. The other worldview worships *creation* as all equal with no supreme being. Many who believe this second worldview *also believe that we are, in ourselves, all gods*. If you start with these two opposing views, you can begin to see that all religions could fall into one of the two worldviews and that many of the movements that call themselves "not religious," (perhaps including atheism, *actually* are of the second worldview, focusing more on the earth as the central equalizing force.)

Dr. Peter Jones of Truthxhange (https://truthxchange.com/)[7] has labeled this Oneism (worshiping creation and the belief we are all gods or can become "one," joining the universe) and Twoism (God is creator and a separate being to be worshipped). You can view his video and details on the education page of the truth about yoga website.

Is Yoga a Gateway to Hinduism and Buddhism?

Of course, recycling and eating better are great. But when you peek behind the curtain, you start to find that the EUSD programs rely heavily on changing the four areas that make up Hinduism and they are the very curriculum that Superintendent Baird is pushing. Baird's defense of yoga being "just an element of a much broader program" is exactly what our concern became and what we were trying to demonstrate. *Somehow* the health and wellness program in EUSD *happened* to get revised to match the four areas of Hinduism—yoga (asanas), revised eating (no meat days), recycling and focus on earth, and the do's and dont's (vedas) in our elementary school. So much for teaching "Character Counts"—that campaign was tossed out of public schools in Encinitas. Character is now being wrapped in the clothing of *"mind-ful meditative followers,"* who are taught to open their mind, dump it all out in the yoga room. Pick up your shoes, and then follow us to the next part of the day. Stay in line, don't question anything, just relax and breathe deeply. Now let's do that for seven years and the kids will be equipped for emptying their minds and following. But following whom? And, why?

Buddhism, Hinduism, and other eastern religions are the opposite of Christianity at their base. Belief in one God as a *supreme being* and *creator* opposes the beliefs of multiple gods and worshiping the sun, the cows, and all the other things that are worshipped in these religions. Many Americans have chosen this kind of worship: worshipping the Earth, Mother Earth, and all its *creation*, as opposed to choosing to worship the *Creator*. As adults, our beliefs are all our own choices in a society of freedom, but what we place into the schools and "push" (advertise, do as adults, promote, picture, pass along, recommend as doctors, coaches, teachers, staff, videos and accepted trainings) makes a vast difference on where our society heads. And those in charge know this better than most of us.

Do You See A Problem?

There's no question that yoga has infiltrated our schools, churches, sports and anywhere that will agree to add yoga. You may see no problem with this, or you may see a huge problem based on your worldview. As it relates to our schools, let's suggest for a minute that we might be completely wrong about yoga and that *"it's just physical exercise."* Great ... then there would be no issue. And there would probably be no controversy. But what if it is spiritual? What if the hundreds of supporters in Encinitas and countless others internationally battling this are *right*? Then, we have a huge mess on our hands. *And, yoga is coming to a school district near you.*

As Watchmen called it, "Encinitas was Ground Zero for yoga entering the US." Before we knew it, district-wide yoga was implemented, a yoga studio built at our elementary school; while the plan for many more years of yoga was apparent right away. Funded and fast. Initially, yoga was funded with outside grants from the Jois Foundation/Sonima to start the program. Now, local taxpayers are on the hook to keep the yoga program going, competing for budget dollars with core curriculum, such as, math and science. Yoga has the potential power to change our schools and our nation quickly. Are we half-way there as Encinitas schools they start the eighth year of yoga curriculum this fall, 2019. Have you seen rapid growth of yoga in your city?

Section Four—Looking back, (History); *Looking ahead*, (Future)

CHAPTER TWENTY ONE

Prepared for *this* Battle *and I didn't even know it!*

Foreshadowing in movies is very similar to what God does with us in our lives. God's plan for us unfolds and, while we may have been struggling through situations and decisions, we look back and realize the Divine touch of God in each situation. For years prior to this yoga debacle, I was being prepared for this battle and I did not know it at the time. Now, I look back and see things over the last fifteen years that led to my role in The Yoga Trial. I would never have been able to connect the dots, but sometimes things are clearer in the rear view mirror. The following will show a little of how we were being prepared.

Forest Home

Forest Home Family Camp, August 2015

Today I'm sitting at a fire pit above the walking path with mountains as a backdrop before and behind me. It is August 5, 2015 and the cold air awakens me. It's early and not much is stirring. The coffee pot is set out at the main dining hall down the hill, and I have already been down there to fill my thermos. With a blanket over my legs, and my computer fired up, my fingers are cold, but ready. I'm ready to record more of what happened with yoga in our schools. More of my thoughts about it to help you discover a side of yoga you may not have considered. I first typed on the island of

Kauai last month for my middle son's basketball team tournament. There was warmth near the shore. Today is cold and mountains.

Forest Home Family camp has become a special place to us and this is their 77th year in operation. The camp is located close to city life, yet feels far away. In just a couple hours you can get there from San Diego and Los Angeles. It's very close to Big Bear Lake and other favorite vacation spots in Southern California. In the summer of 2012 we came here as a family for the first time. We had no idea what a treat our family was in for that week. We hiked and swam, fished and sang, explored and zip lined, and competed at the family Olympics at the swim hole. We learned what the "blob" was at the swimming hole: a big inflated rectangular "blob" that one person jumps from up high on a diving board, to drop on one end of the big blob, catapulting the other person into the air from the other end. Both ends are fun and after you jump to the blob, you crawl to the end and it's your turn to soar. It was a week full of family fun, great lessons and insights away from daily life, and a deep rest from our busy lives.

Clue

There is a theme every year at camp and that year it was "Uncover the Mystery." One night we played a family game called "Clue" only it was a live version where you went from building to building to find who did the murder, with what and where (remember the old *Clue* board game?). It was a blast and we had no idea that "uncover the mystery" was foreshadowing for what we were about to encounter beginning a few weeks later with the beginning of yoga in Encinitas. We only knew something special had happened here. To our family; to our kids; something bonded our family, in a new and deeper tie. Although we would return to our lives down the hill, I would look back years later on this week and realize we were being prepared, and positioned. We had no idea what was about to transpire. We couldn't have.

Uncover The Mystery

Uncover The Mystery

Forest Home family camp prepared us for this battle. Looking backward we saw the *clues*. The last evening of camp we wrote notes to ourselves about the lessons we learned that week and these notes would be mailed back to us in 6 months. I wrote various things that I did not know would be foundational to the battle we were about to be called to enter. We would *stick out* in the front lines of this; to lead and encourage others to research the truth. All along I knew I was never the expert in any of this journey. This is The Lord's battle. This is a battle that has been going on for years, decades and with century-old belief's that we had no idea about during the summer of 2012. No idea the role we would play. No idea the souls at stake. The divisiveness of a religious program put into the schools. No idea we would have to move schools for our daughter's protection soon. No idea we would be the ones to say yes to *suing* the school district (*who does that?*). That never crossed our minds up until the very month we had to decide as a group whether to take legal action or not. We had no idea the Superintendent and board would not respond to our collective words of concern. Never had a clue it would end up *just us;* our family. Eventually it would be clear that it was best for only one family to bear the burden of the attacks and outrage. I wouldn't wish any of that on anyone else, and some marriages might not have survived. We were prepared, positioned and protected.

A Growing Mystery

Fortunately, I was created to be curious and love a good mystery. I will hang on to the end of the movie, game or mystery to try to figure it out or ask others to find out their view of the mystery to piece it together. Many of us had to discuss for years to figure this yoga issue out. *That is an understatement.* There has been a huge amount of data and information to comb through to understand and digest. But we started to see the divisiveness if we barely brought up the word "yoga" among anyone who practiced yoga. They became defensive and offensive. They either mocked or filled in the gaps of what they did not know about the case or the issues. It was an interesting process just watching human behavior and how rapidly people's demeanors can change. By only the grace of God, we didn't get too ruffled to move forward.

Later, we would learn so much more about those responses that would uncover a huge piece of the mystery. I was shocked after spending a lifetime of people pleasing and never really having anyone attack me like they have over yoga. Vicious comments from other Christians! And not just one, but a lot of them, who knew us for years... *Why?* Somehow we were shown that it wasn't about us. We knew it had to be from yoga, but, why? And how does yoga gain this power over people? For them to "lose control" when they don't in other areas of their lives? Some power over them emerged. They claimed yoga is peaceful and centering, but that isn't what they display in conversations. *It was a mystery indeed.*

Foreshadowing

About 18 years ago when my second son was born, I began studying the bible every morning and going to bible studies. I didn't grow up going to church learning about the bible, until I was an older teen. I wanted to understand more in the bible, and not just to understand the stories, lessons and truths I would find in its pages, but to know God himself. I wanted to understand why God did some things, particularly in the historical accounts told in the

Old Testament portion of the bible. And in the New Testament, why did God help those in need sometimes and not in other times, when people were obviously in need. I was still skeptical of some aspects of Christian beliefs, even though I went to church every week and believed in most of what I had heard. I needed to know more.

I love books where investigators work to piece together all the evidence to reach their conclusion. So, take a look at each piece of this journey to help you understand how I ended up in the midst of this firestorm.

Organizations that Strengthened the Foundation of My Faith

About fifteen years ago I began to serve in AWANA (Approved Workers Are Not Ashamed – from 2 Timothy 2:15), a Christian nonprofit that seeks to give children a firm foundation in the Bible. AWANA was a great source of learning scriptures on a child's level. The irony is that adult volunteers typically learn more than the kids they help! With my three kids and their age span of 7 years, I continued to serve in AWANA for ten years. Almost, in every position from secretary to teaching, to leading groups and even as overall leader, the Commander, of the three clubs would become my various roles when volunteering. When I was pregnant with my third child, our second son was in the Cubbie group (for 3-4 year-olds) and one night I literally could not get off the couch exhausted from the pregnancy, so my husband filled in for me to lead a group of wiry 3 and 4 year-old kids.

After that night, he saw the value of the AWANA program too. He decided the following year that our entire family of five would attend weekly and he began to volunteer! Now given that he follows a different church denomination altogether (Catholic), this was a big deal, and later we would understand why. But for that time, my husband would take his new Sparky group (kindergarteners through second graders) of boys almost all the way through TnT (Truth in Training), which is third through sixth graders, before his volunteer years in AWANA ended. We have every color leader shirt since we never knew where we would fill in or be working from year to year: yellow for Commander, green for TnT, red for Sparky and blue for Cubbie.

In the midst of those years, I became involved in the Good News Club, which is a weekly interdenominational Christian-based program for 5 to 12-year-old children featuring a Bible lesson, songs, memory verses, and games. It is a little bit similar to AWANA. I helped start a club at El Camino Creek (as an after-school program). I taught lessons and led small groups. We did service projects for the homeless and led the kids to serve one another. Why am I sharing all this? Because these programs were foundational to why I ended up helping in the schools Jog-a-thon to achieve record donations because in mirroring AWANA prizes for verses, I implemented prizes for kids at school, if they reached $100 donations raised, they got a prize ($3-$5). This raised our average donation from $30 to $100 that year at ECC. That is why the princiapal Carrie Brown *used* to like me before this who trial ordeal. I also taught PE at ECC one year for a pregnant teacher who needed a break... all leading to knowledge foundational for this trial!

A Calling to be Commander

About a year after having my third child I was sitting in a hotel away from home for a speaking event and praying if or where I should serve next in my church, when I sensed a "calling" to Commander of AWANA. I knew this had to be from God because it wasn't something that had even crossed my mind. I didn't even know it was open, or what the job entailed, and I had a one-year-old girl and two little boys. I was busy! I knew from experience with the first two to stay home the first year and get the family in balance before taking on work and volunteering again. My speaking job was flexible for that reason, and stepping back in to AWANA as a secretary would have been easy. Except they were about to cancel AWANA at my church because they had no commander!!!

What does the commander do? I asked the gal when trying to sign up my boys for AWANA with a call from that hotel room. It was the summer of 2006 and she explained the "job duties" which happened to match the odd "dreams" I'd been having for the two weeks prior. I prayed and God was clear when I heard the description, but there were some roadblocks.

My thoughts were racing and I asked: "how in the world can I take on such a big position with a baby that will likely cry in the daycare and need me?" I heard an answer: *trust me* and *I'll take care of that part.* Is this in my head, or is this actually a message? My husband's first thoughts were that I shouldn't take the position because he was interviewing for a new job. But we discussed it a few days and then he said "Let's all go – I will lead, the boys go to club and our baby can go into the daycare." I started to see miracles happen, including the fact that my daughter never cried enough once to interrupt my serving in AWANA nights for 2 years! One woman, Jean, is to thank for that too. She held our baby weekly in the daycare; but I know beyond a shadow of a doubt – it was God's hand in it through hers. He took care of that need. I enjoyed the job, learned a lot, and I grew more in my knowledge of the Bible. So if you are someone doing a job like holding a baby and not thinking it is all that important – you might be impacting an entire program to run smoothly and not have any idea how important your role is to hundreds of others! In addition, of course Steve was soaking in a lot of Bible verses himself. Somewhere in those years he also started studying daily in the mornings. We were both now seeking God's word, guidance and path for our family, daily. Every Saturday night after club we were so exhausted from all the noise and kids we would make Top Ramen and have a glass of wine (milk for the kids!). Cheers to some good years in our little budding family. Miss those "easier" days when most of the cares centered around busy loud kids.

Approved Workmen Are Not Ashamed (2 Tim 2:15)

A Call to Speak

Meanwhile, during all those years I was also going to Bible studies for women weekly.

In 2007, after four years of feeling the "call to speak in women's ministry events" (and not wanting to have that responsibility) I finally launched a page on my professional speaking website (I'd been speaking since 1995) and "surrendered" to that call. I had already given seven programs in churches across Southern and Northern California while still *not* calling myself a women's ministry speaker. In 2008, the following year, faith-based women's events became half of my booked speaking events. *This would become important later, but it was a foreshadowing of what I needed for the battle. Being from "business world" I needed to understand: women!*

Although I didn't know why at the time, I needed experience in women's ministry with positive topics before one day perhaps speaking on a controversial one. I needed to know how retreats operate and how women need refreshment, growth and encouragement for their lives as single women, moms and wives. I wasn't oblivious to the fact that perhaps God called a speaker to be one of the petitioners in the trail to one day utilize those skills to spread the word. At first I dreaded that, then I surrendered to it, and now the journey is unknown, but the willing vessel awaits whatever the adventure becomes.

Moms In Prayer

In 2010 when my last child entered elementary school, I started praying with a group of moms for our school for Moms in Prayer, International. Formerly named Moms in Touch, Moms in Prayer meets and prays weekly in groups for the schools, kids, teachers, staff, and community. This would become important as you read in Chapter one, but my involvement in Moms in Prayer was further foreshadowing and especially in praying for protection for children. Years later when we would pray over the Encinitas campuses for protection of children inside doing yoga, it became crystal clear why a great deal of the people who "saw through yoga" first, were parents who spent time in the bible and in prayer. Those listening closely to God heard the warnings. We didn't know all we would learn, but we were listening, and then hearing. Now in my ninth year and fifth school praying, I see how many school issues and programs are supported through MIP as we cover it all in prayer and sometimes actions to help.

He moved me!

On April 5, 2011 in one fell swoop in *one* day a situation at my home church happened and I had to leave. I had been there nine years. I was way too loyal to leave under any normal circumstances. The first ministry I was involved with ever, was the *mommy and me* ministry in 2002. After a few months of attendance, I was asked to be the leader. A few months later in 2003, and from that group morphing, another mom and I launched the women's ministry Bible study for the church (that still meets today). Over the years I was in or co-led small groups within the women's ministry. In 2004, I started helping in AWANA, as mentioned above and became the commander in 2006-2008 - so I knew over 80 families from that program alone, let alone all the others I'd met through other events and groups involved within the church.

However, that day in April 2011 it was clear, I was to go, and it was a shock. I heard loud and crystal clear message, *do not defend yourself* as I was being accused of things I did not say, or feel. I felt ambushed and I was weak from a surgery just days prior. I felt a sense of peace and calm enter the room though, and it distracted me to even look up and see that I was not to worry about anything being said. As I walked down steps that I'd just helped pay for during months of a capital fund campaign, I knew I was walking down them for the last time as a member of that church. I could hardly drive off in the parking lot, not from the pain of surgery, while I wasn't supposed to be driving, but from the pain of loss and shock of what just transpired. I knew God was telling me "it's time to go child" and I had *no idea* why or where. With tears in my eyes, I wandered over to look at the rock that is still there today cemented into the ground where the founding pastor, Dan Grider, had us all put our last names painted or written on rocks. The Sedlock rock remains as part of the foundation of that church where my family did some growing up. I was momentarily devastated.

Guidance that day!

I wouldn't have more than a few hours for a pity-party because my mother in law – "grandma" reminded me I needed to take her to the mall (doesn't she see that I'm in tears – well yes, grandma's have a deeper knowledge to divert us, rather than ask at times). Later that day a dear sister in Christ gave me the book "Life Interrupted" (by Pricilla Shirer) which is all about God calling Jonah to something and he went the opposite direction. Was I seeing signs to leave and not responding? Yes, I knew right away there were some signs. AWANA had already been cancelled from my church, by the new leadership and new pastor, and I was now serving in another church for that program, and taking my kids there on Wednesdays. I was in two bible studies not tied to my church ... and just 4 months prior I had a sense that something big was going to change. I was so clear on a change that I approached our old pastor (at a funeral!) for advice in preparing for a "change." He directed me to two books that would be great sources over the next few years. (And since you'll wonder if I don't list them – they are "My Utmost For His Highest" by Oswald Chambers – which is a daily reader - and "Communicating for a Change" by Andy Stanley and Lane Jones). That was it. The only advice I got. So, I read the daily reader for the next 2-3 years and I've read the second book thrice so far.

Another safety net that was in place was that four close friends were praying for, and with me, about a problem and potential change. So, the moment this day came, they were all in touch right away to support and show me clarity that I could not see at the moment in how we had prepared for this day. One told jokes that made me laugh through the pain. Have you ever laughed in pain? It's a deep sigh of relief for an aching heart. "Is she drinking the kool-aid too?" she asked of a mutual friend and leader at the church? One came over till well past midnight and we called our primary women's ministry leader who was then a missionary in South Africa. Her words were salve to my wounds. She responded after learning very little of the basics - "God is calling you somewhere. Leave and don't look back. Don't email or call anyone. Just go." "No one" I asked in shock? But these are my friends. These are people I've spent nine years with. Go where? For what? So signs and "safety nets" were right there - But where Lord? And why? And why like this?

Soon I would learn. Soon I learned that, like Jonah, God was calling me away to do something else. I would later learn I needed some seriously thick skin to go through the fire one day to stand firm against something so confusing and deceptive that most will not understand. God needed to move me for *this yoga trial* and ministry. Ugh.

Moved for Ministry

Since my next assignment needed to be elsewhere, I visited several churches over the next two months to figure out where. There was only one church where I didn't hear a *"not here"*. I didn't hear a *yes* either, but I didn't hear a *no*. And don't get me wrong, I wasn't really accustomed to God speaking to me, but I'd started to learn to look for the signs. It was not about "finding a right fit" because I really wanted to go to a specific church at that time. I thought that church would have been perfect – closer to my house, all the right programming for my kids, great music, great preaching, a really great newly-built church with tons of people we knew. It was a lively growing church. But there was one big problem. I visited three times over that two months, and fell asleep the minute the pastor spoke. I was not tired. I go to church well rested, coffee-d up and ready to learn. Three times I fell asleep, once with coffee in hand! That was a clear *no!* And just to prove more foreshadowing, that very pastor would end up working against us for a while in the lawsuit several years later. Hmmmm… it can be very insightful, looking into rear view mirrors!

I was learning *trust* without all the understanding and worldly clarity we would like. Where next then? How about going to the only church where I hadn't heard a "no" yet.

Daily Devotional book by Pastor Bob Botsford – Face to Faith, His Way for Every Day

It had to be Horizon, And Pastor Bob Botsford!

A few weeks after I started going to Horizon (with my "not a no and maybe a yes" in mind), I walked into the women's ministry room and sat down and I heard a loud YES ring in my ear. *You have arrived where I want you.* And that was that. I've been at Horizon ever since. However, it would be a full year before I would begin to understand just *why* I was there. Pastor Bob Botsford is one of the most outspoken pastors on idol worship and yoga over the last decade than any other pastor in the area, according to some of the regular attenders at Horizon. I had no idea. I didn't even notice that in that first year, at all. Or, wait, now I seemed to recall him smashing idols on stage, which at the time, I didn't connect with yoga. Pastor Bob was the one selected for what would come to pass. It had to be him. Later I would even learn that he had grown up at Forest Home and knew the Graham Family from there because as the story goes, Billy Graham made a decision right there at Forest Home to follow whatever God had for him, and what followed was the first large crusade in LA launching a future of these for a lifetime. That's some holy ground our family was led to walk then! Wow. Keep going (for you keep reading) but for me it was *keep going*…Uncover the mystery…

Yoga entering EUSD

When yoga entered the 9 elementary schools in Encinitas in 2012, I had been at Horizon over a year, and I was the Moms in Prayer leader that year for our school, El Camino Creek. Because of my leadership position, several moms came to me with their concerns about yoga, as mentioned earlier in Chapter 1. At the time, I didn't see what the big deal was, and I still didn't stop to "look into it." Over the course of several weeks I had various people warn me and ask me to please read a little about it. I was receiving information via email for my review. And, finally, I was invited to a "concerned parent meeting" consisting of parents from all over the District. I decided to go check it out, given I was the leader and felt that it was the responsible thing to do. I may have ignored it further, if I had not been in that role. Clearly I was supposed to be there, but I didn't have any clue as to what the future would hold.

Wide Awake Now

I walked away from the *Concerned Parents* meeting that night in October of 2012 with the distinct impression that *God meant business and didn't want yoga in the schools or churches*. I didn't even know yoga was entering any churches. But I heard that loud and clear. What I would learn over the next few weeks would be not only very concerning but baffling as well. The district staff and board would react so oddly to parent concerns. Something else was going on in our midst. We couldn't put our finger on why they were so resistant and why the topic caused such hot tempers and wild reactions of otherwise calm people. It would take months to figure out. Some of you will never understand even as I spell it out. Some simply won't believe it. But many of us have walked through this and seen with our own eyes how people have behaved so strangely and gone to great lengths to avoid the subject at all.

The manner in which people have responded is truly unbelievable. But put our culture in context, look at the busy pace of our society now, and in our particular geographic locale, and it starts to make sense that this program would slip right into the public school system. We would sense a *blinding - to yoga*, that hardly makes sense to us who see it, with a demonic force that seems to erupt from otherwise nice people. Why? What's up with *this behavior?*

Faith and Frustrations

One day this whole topic on yoga may be clearer to more people (and maybe not). That is not ours to hang our hat on, because our role is as messengers with a message, but the outcomes are not our responsibility – that is all up to God. We keep meeting more and more people who have been in this battle for decades! It is so fascinating and frustrating, if not for hundreds of others, who also see the truth. As yoga has been rising, I see anger rising... is it connected?

There is a great song by Justin Unger called "Strangers"

"Strangers" by Justin Unger

The lyrics begin like this:

What does it mean when you are out there alone

And you're standing for something the worlds never known?

And you choose to love anyway …

You're a stranger in this place …

How does it feel when your friends turn away,

and they don't understand, and you can't make them change?

And you choose to love anyway.

You're a stranger in this place.

Ooohoo Stranger in this world.

Ooohoo Stranger in this world.

He was the first, who would take all the shame,

and would carry our sin, and suffer our blame …

and He chose to love anyway.

He's a stranger in this place …

Lyric credits to Justin Unger – this song on his cd titled: Some Good Advice

(I think he could retitle it to *Some GREAT Advice*!)

Thank you Justin!!!!

Songs can really speak to us at times. During this trial this one helped me carry on even when others didn't understand. Actually, this entire CD has been played more in my car than any other person alive could have listened to it, I'm pretty certain. I am so grateful to Justin's music and he has no idea. When you go through any trial where your faith is questioned, and you can see clearly what others cannot, it is not easy. Faith is personal, yet so global. Justin captured just the right words for *walking through the fire in faith* and *loving others regardless how they treat you*. Incidentally (or not?), I first heard him at Forest Home camp in 2015. I happened to buy this CD of his and two others. I've never listened to the others!

"Forgive them father, for they know not what they say" from the Bible now means a lot more to me than when I first read those words from Jesus.

God knew I needed to learn a lot more about faith for *this* ministry. No one (self included) would choose *this!*

Ultimately, the Goal *Is* Love

We can relate through music and readings and even those reading this book will each potentially interpret this so differently. I write for those with eyes to see and ears to hear the message of Love and acceptance and taking a firm stand when needed. It's those that make all the critics worthwhile. Hurtful words will pass and deflect off me now. Not by my strength, not by my knowledge, or my shield, but with God that all becomes possible through His armor (Ephesian 6:10-20). That is why, when you take a stand, and put on the armor of God, you can take anything thrown at you when you could never handle any of it on your own. Luckily we don't have to because with God standing with us, what can stand against?

My people pleasing days are over. I do not need to please anyone else but God who called me to this. This is a crazy yet fascinating "ministry" to help others see how yoga and other idol worship is pulling people away from belief in a Sovereign God. I asked for the cup to pass me, but it did not. It was designed for me.

It was prepared for me, I was prepared for this. When you walk in obedience into the plan God has for you, it is unbelievably peaceful. I know this is right and yet to the world, it looks upside down. It is not. It is clearly where God led me – painfully at times, trimming branches of me that had to go, but the branch remaining in the vine will flourish, it will grow, it will need maintenance and pruning again (John 15:2). It will blossom again. Just wait for it. Just trust. Just walk the path intended for you. Then you experience peace beyond all understanding. You can stand firm in the chaos around you and become a peaceful presence during that chaos. You might even unknowingly show others how to handle their trials.

Chaos, I know Chaos

My life is full of chaos with three competitive kids, a competitive husband, and well, yours truly, too. We compete for airtime at dinner, we compete for food (the boys are 17 and 15 and literally eating us out of house and home – thank you Costco)! (note: I wrote this part three years ago when they were those ages – this book took 4 years to write!). I'm thankful for the lower prices of gas in Southern California now too. Yes, I digress. "Squirrel" we yell in our house when someone goes off topic, which is just about every day as we try to get our words in edgewise.

Yes, patience is a rare thing in our home, not a gift we were born with but have had to learn. I laugh when my mother-in-law, or a friend tells me that I have a lot of patience. I just give the glory to God, because it is *not* my nature. My nature is to move too fast, to get the information and *run* with it as fast as I can to the destination. I get ahead of God and myself and others who don't know why I just sprinted by, and I have to learn over and over, to slow down. Any patience I have is out of obedience to God. It's from Him, and it is not me. And therein lies some proof of the existence of God; when we see all the great qualities in others and ourselves that we *know* are truly not our own nature.

408

Surrender brings Peace

Surrender is an interesting thing. Once you surrender, there is a peacefulness and freedom – like you'd been struggling and fighting for, that you would never achieve on your own. It's free, it's available and yet, so hard to "let go" and fall into with trust. And when you do, you wonder why you wasted so much time struggling? So many years… So many questions… We want to *know* first, rather than accept it on *faith*. Gratefulness takes over when you realize how easy the yoke becomes. Grateful even for the hard times! They create who we are today. Tough experiences move us to where we need to be. Hard times are when we turn to someone or something or eventually God, when we become clear we cannot do it on our own.

Approved resources written by Pricilla Shirer, Armor of God womens bible study workbook, and FerVent book, based on movie: War Room

I am grateful for the many studies I was led to do over the course of this battle at multiple different churches, when I was open to listen and be led to them. The study of *Gideon* came right as I needed to get out of hiding and organize the team and direction of our mission. When I walked through the door of that church (North Coast Vista, Carlsbad Campus), I would learn that pastor had been praying for my family for two years! I knew very few women when I went to a retreat, and was placed to room with the pastors mother! Coincidence? No. Not even a thought for me anymore. Too obvious I was to meet him.

Armor of God study, came just as I needed to solidify putting on the armor daily to fight this battle. *FerVent* helped me to pray strategically and specifically against the enemy and his schemes. And many more studies that directly related to the path I was taking. Pricilla Shirer happens to have written all three of the books I just mentioned. Her obedience to write and teach has impacted this journey. She has helped me to handle many things that are *Unseen* and yet mighty and powerful forces against us in this journey. *Unseen* is the name of Shirer's daily reader *for teen boys* that my friend in Ohio bought for *me* to read… (was that a mistake, or a plan she didn't know about?). Later I would coach teen boys – we didn't know then, but I would even end up giving that very book title to graduating seniors. So much is *unseen,* but that doesn't mean it's not there. Air and love and warfare have that in common. You can see signs, you can feel them, but you can't see the actual thing itself.

Grateful for it all.

Grateful you read this far.

Grateful for the blessings you will encounter soon.

Grateful to write and think and be free in this great country.

We all have a lot to be grateful for, even in the midst of storms and chaos.

I recently learned a new focus from Lisa TerKeurst's study, *Uninvited,* that is – "Miracles in the Mess." Life gets messy, but even in the midst of the mess, we can choose to look at the mess or at the miracles. I'm choosing to see the miracles while cleaning up the messes of today.

Role of the Sun

As I sit here again on a chair at the fire pit at 6am, it is very cold and I am shivering with coffee in hand to write and observe the morning begin here at camp. Some people walk or jog by while many are still sleeping in before the 8:30 breakfast. The sun just burst over the mountain, with warmth I haven't felt since yesterday. My right shoulder is warming up while my left is in the shade and cold. Amazing how warm it can become the second the sun hits us. Yesterday sitting at the pool, there was a drastic difference when the clouds moved across the sky. One minute it would be warm and pleasant and the next it would be chilly and dark. Sun is the main warmth in our lives. And yet, being thankful for it is a far different thing than worshipping the sun, as we are observing in the yoga religions.

Why was God so clear in the Old Testament about not worshipping the sun and worshipping idols? He was adamantly against idol worship. Towns went through destruction when they fell from worshipping God to begin worshipping idols and the sun, which caused them to turn away from Him who created them. Over and over we see this pattern. God gave us free will and we see the choices of free will in the Old Testament, and the consequences that would come either right away, or over the generations in a family or city. God would only allow so much. There was a huge problem that needed to be solved. We needed a bridge to God.

People had blown every chance of repenting. Repentance is one of the hardest things for people. Surrender and repentance are seen as negative words to reluctant believers and non-believers. Knowing something and doing something are different. Feeling something and knowing something are also very different. Believing only our own experiences will not get us very far in the faith.

Jesus became the bridge for us to God, as told all about in the New Testament. The Holy Spirit became our gift – for daily connection to God to answer our most vital questions.

411

Truth

Truth is not dependent on our opinion of it. Truth just is. Finding truth for ourselves is a popular phrase today. Whether we find truth or truth finds us, or neither; it is still there. It's not just our own realities or perspective. Our choice to pursue truth, leave it, ignore it, or simply decide we don't think it is true is all free will and choice. Of all the scholars that argue one side or another about faith, all have faith. all of us have faith every day that certain things will happen - like the sun will come up, the ocean will bring the tide in, the house will heat up, or faith in our daily products and devices that we use. We have a great deal of faith in a lot of things. Where we place our faith, is up to us to choose. Seeking the Truth is an important journey.

Photo credit, Irving's Journey: http://www.irvingsjourney.com/wp-content/ uploads/2013/10/seek-truth.jpg

August 9, 2015

The Sun just peeked over the mountain this morning, once again, and gave warmth right away, just as the day before. I will miss my little spot by the fire pit with a nice armed chair for sitting and typing and reading and writing. The view is incredible here. When I put on the glasses that have close up lenses I can see the words, and the mountains go out of focus. When I put on the distance lens glasses I see the mountains, and the words go out of focus. The balance of lenses with mono-vision contacts, help me to see both at once when I have those in my eyes. When we look hard at something, we begin to see more. More detail and more of what is there. Things start to come into focus and sharpen our understanding like the focus feature on our camera. If I hadn't looked closer into yoga, I wouldn't see what I see today.

Thank you Forest Home Family Camp, for being here for families like ours. We will remember you in our lives. We thank you for the lessons, the learning, the serving and the fun. You are a blessing. You are forever in our hearts.

Yoga is in the fabric of our faith story now— so much that it turned our lives upside down a while and became a full-time job for me the past few years, starting with research, the trial, then the organizing for education events, the public and private team updates, the website, the meetings and demonstrations, and now this book. Not a job I would have sought. Not a job that pays me money. Not a job that has any glory, but plenty of ridicule. And still, I find it an assignment worth doing and a mission about which I feel that God has called me to do my unique part. Many have been called to do different parts. My part has been organizing this information from others and spreading the love of God while warning about a path away from God that has for some reason been revealed to me so clearly.

Why it's clear to some and not others is still a mystery to unfold. But clearly, my main focus was to be on protecting the children and awakening parents of those children, from having no choice about doing yoga at school. Anyone who has talked to me about yoga in the past 7 years would agree that I have calmly walked this journey with an open mind, heart and obedience to what to do with the information I was presented at each step. I had no idea what "Uncover the Mystery" would mean for the past few years. But it is clear to me now; I was prepared for this battle. I have been protected along the way, and provided for at every turn. I've learned to stop to pray, ask, listen and wait on the Lord for His guidance.

I will never forget that first meeting in 2012 when I heard *I want yoga out of the schools and churches* (inside my own head) and now it is clear to me why. I pray this book has shown you why. This isn't about me or us as a family, but I shared the stories about us so that you would know a little bit more about our love and devotion to help children, and why this family would actually oppose yoga in Encinitas schools and sue their own district to try to get it removed. Although we haven't been successful in the actual lawsuit, we know this is a much larger issue than our district. Some things need to be taken out at the roots, not the tops – like a weed, it will just keep on growing deeper. Yoga in schools is rapidly growing. Over 1000 schools already. We are in need of more hands in garden gloves to help get the roots up and out.

How are you at gardening?

CHAPTER TWENTY-TWO

Messengers, with Information

As you now know, the trial was three days in May, and three days in June of 2013. The appellate trial was very short - just the morning of March 11, 2015. However, a tremendous amount of activity transpired behind the scenes between those two trials and three years. Yoga continued in Encinitas schools, doubling the yoga teachers to 18. Yoga grew in other states, and it was growing all around us; new studios popping up around town, advertising for yoga increasing, and most notably, *yoga for children* grew exponentially in the timeframe from 2012 – 2018. All the while, the concerned parent group was very busy compiling information, educating the public on what was transpiring, and as fast as they could find information, they created avenues to share the information, and those looking for it across the country responded.

Why Education Events?

Most of early 2013, some of the parent group prepared for trial, yet, many continued to research yoga and communicate findings. Before, during and after the trial, there were blogs, documentation written by people in and near the district, and even a book written by a distant community member about the trial (unbeknownst to any of us that were deepest in the trenches of this controversy – it was the book shown by Esther Watchmen in an earlier chapter). After the trial, many still recorded concerns going on in the district, with Jois/Sonima, and with yoga entering schools in other states. The group of parents connected for updates and alerts to continuing changing decisions at EUSD. At times, we jumped to do an activity

415

to help (such as flyers on cars, meetings, helping create the web-site, prayer and strategic monthly meetings, responding to moves by EUSD like the library yoga promotion, etc.). We attempted to educate those unaware of the controversial aspects of the program, since the whole trial focused on *religion* and not all the other issues straddling this *new curriculum.*

After the May/June 2013 trial, there were a barrage of com-plaints and mocking by people about our "losing the trial." But remember, in the courtroom it appeared the evidence was leaning very far our direction up until the judge's verdict, even with his own words warning the district the day before verdict that they better pull something out of their hat! We remained cautiously optimistic, given what was happening in the culture all around us, and the amount of social pressure on this judge's decision. Popular opinion was clearly on the opposite side of where we stood. But, that was expected, and we knew that our stand would not be popular. We never *expected* to win at the first level, but *hoped* to get yoga out of the schools eventually and 8 years later our mission is the same. We were akin to David fighting Goliath - up against a lot of money, power and influence from Sonima and their famous connections. We understood some reasons for the loss, and that to continue was critical. Perhaps the battle was not over our EUSD issues. Perhaps the international attention this trial received indicated that this rip-ples way beyond *yoga.*

Parents Have a Right to Know

What we knew, was that most parents in our own district had no idea what was happening right under their noses. They didn't know about Jois Foundation, the contracts, the injuries and warn-ings for kids about yoga, and they didn't know about sun saluta-tions, idol worship of Shiva *(the destroyer),* or anything about the deceptions and cover up that were occurring surrounding yoga and the trial. The slick words and lines of cover up coming from the EUSD Superintendent, to camouflage what was being infused into our kids' weekly schedules, was not apparent to all. Since many parents in our district were unaware of so many facts, and what was being implemented, we held an educational event in November of 2013. One month prior, an event would set all this in motion.

Dean's Presentation about Yoga

October of 2013 Dean Broyles, Attorney on the case, was asked to speak for a Salt and Light group about the yoga trial. The talk that he would even claim "prepared itself in some ways," was an eye opener to the concerns about yoga, and the whole spiritual journey toward Shiva and the third eye bliss (the goal of Kundalini yoga). The few of us from our group that attended that meeting knew *it was a turnkey presentation* that would be the foundation of what needed to be shared with the public. It clearly explained the deception of yoga. Broyles should be commended for this program, as it really could have been prepared by pastors. But sometimes, the most unlikely people are used, and he would also realize that he had been specifically and uniquely prepared for years prior for his role in this foundational trial.

Over the next month, eight (8) documents were created to educate parents about the yoga program in EUSD. They are included in this chapter's references and listed below in the chapter. Although well-advertised, only a small few EUSD parents attended the program, however, many highly concerned "others" from the community flocked to this meeting in support. After Dean's highly informative presentation (On DVD and linked on website), a panel of us answered questions. These "other concerned folks" encouraged us to pursue this and "organize" ourselves better to get this word out beyond EUSD. One was a pastor from Horizon who would surprise us all in a new direction.

An Encouragement to Lead and Organize

We didn't offer any more events to the parents of EUSD, because it became clear that night in November, through a pastor what the next step should be: He (no need for his identity) stood up that night and said "We need to take this to the pastors. You need to present this to pastors in the area." He took the information back to his head pastor, Bob Botsford, and recommended that Horizon Church educate other pastors with our information. Just two months later, we did just that. Sometimes a swift shift in direction is needed, even when it isn't what you expect. Letting go of our own agenda surrenders us to a better plan than we might ever dream up ourselves.

On that note, a woman pulled me aside after the November meeting and told me that she had been in court, and she had some words of encouragement for me. Mind you, this is now four months after court. She spoke a whole list of things *to me* that I knew were true the minute she verbalized them. She was confirming what I'd been "hearing," but wasn't fully on board with yet. Like Jonah not wanting to go to Ninevah – I wanted to run from all this. But, alas, who needs to end up in a fish! I knew where this was heading, so I grabbed a piece of paper to write down all that she was saying. She said I was to organize and lead a "ministry" to educate people on the dangers. What? That is the last thing I wanted to do! Can't someone else take the lead? Why me? Haven't I done enough already? Oh my, isn't this exactly what the judge said, or rather predicted? Hmmm. Those were *my thoughts* as I obediently scribbled notes onto the piece of paper. It would take one more phone call, from yet a third encouragement a week later, that would further confirm – I was being called to carry the organizing piece of this group into the future. Ugh. Seriously? When Jonah was spit out of the whale, he knew what to do. So did I.

Educating Pastors?

The last thing any of us parents ever considered to be doing was educating pastors on anything, let alone yoga! (But then, I never expected to sue a school district either!). My parents are public college educators! I was in full support of those public schools, *until yoga came along*.

Nearly 100 pastors from all over San Diego County attended our first event in January of 2014, called "Yoga – Purely Physical or is it Religious?" The strange realization after invitations went out to the entire county of pastors in San Diego was that only two Encinitas and Carlsbad pastors would attend. For some odd reason, there were only two churches represented from the very area where most EUSD parents lived! It was as if a veil of sorts covered the area. We questioned why, but just kept moving forward with who did attend, and the room was packed.

Spiritual warfare was working against us. Some might just call it coincidence, but over and over negative things would happen at just the moment we were doing something important. Three of the speaker's families would experience injury that day. The wife of Dr. Jones went to the emergency room while he was speaking. The wife of Dean Broyles had an emergency in their family that day, and third, my family (Sedlocks) went to a basketball game for our middle son that evening and we were hit full speed while stopped on the on-ramp waiting for a green light. The driver rammed into us at more than 35 mph because the back hatch of my Odyssey van would not open, due to the force of the hit. She said she *didn't notice us*, and then when she did, her brake pedal didn't work. Hmmm. Why? Our daughter (8) was sitting in the far back seat screaming for minutes after impact. The lady then tried to take photos of my kids *inside* our van. I shielded them and asked her to step away from my van. What an odd need for protection, but foreshadowed the need from aggressors in the near future...

At every step, it was important to ask the question: why? We knew this was all so much bigger than what we could figure out, so we learned to listen and proceed only with what we were each led (by God) to do at the time (and no more!). Even this book has been *delayed* at times – as it was mostly written by 2016! Its now 2019! Many pastors from that first event in 2014 were very concerned, and took the DVD to train their churches. The problem is, none was in the area of EUSD parents! Many pastors were enlightened that day as the subject was fairly new to them, but most would not be willing to warn their congregations. Fear of public opinion led in this issue of yoga. And as you saw in previous chapters, the subject of yoga is very divisive, and no pastor wants to divide his members. It's a very sticky, tricky subject. Even though pastors have an opinion on controversial topics, many are not spoken about from the pulpit. Yoga was shaping up to be just as divisive and taboo a subject. And for good reason!

Not for Pastor Bob Though!

Pastor Bob never shied away from the topic and has spoken truth about idols and yoga for years. We would begin to understand more fully why the move to Horizon as a home church – as Pastor Bob would not only understand and support, but lead the charge on educating other pastors about yoga. Pastor Bob opened that event by asking if anyone left their homes unlocked that morning when they left? Would you leave your home unlocked purposely most days? Why not? Some places in the US might still be able to do that, but for San Diego and most citizens, we choose to lock our homes. He likened yoga to leaving the door open, for anyone who wanted to enter. Yoga is a *gateway to spirits* and unknowingly invites them into your children's lives. Meditation from eastern mysticism is like opening your windows and doors wide open to your children, he would wisely share. That was only the beginning of the days information.

Most of the pastors walked out aware and concerned, and needing more tools. Some asked what we had to educate teens, women's groups, and schools. Not much more than what they had in their hands already, but the questions raised the needs, and they didn't go unnoticed by me. I knew they were asking so that they would have tools and methods to spread the knowledge in groups within the churches that needed it most. I knew then what I know now – it's the women bringing yoga into churches... but schools was our first priority of this book, and yet I always think in the bigger picture of what's the next step, the next need, and where else is this insidiously creeping into and why (sports, medicine, retreats, etc. etc).

More Education Events

We also held a Women's Ministry educational event that same month on January 27, 2014, at Calvary Chapel Carlsbad. This time it brought a lot of women in the Encinitas and Carlsbad area into the fold of knowledge. A few men even attended. A couple shared that night that their son got involved with yoga, it quickly progressed to quitting college and moving to India. They now had little to no contact with him. Story after story came from these audiences, growing our concerns further and further.

In June of 2014, another pastor event was held in East San Diego County at Skyline Church with Pastor Jim Garlow. About 60 people were in attendance for "What's up with yoga?" The school board at Cajon Valley called Pastor Garlow multiple times trying to stop the event, but he would not be swayed by a school board... David Miyashiro, (then the new Superintendent at Cajon Valley schools remember – leaving EUSD), even incredulously asked attorney Dean Broyles that morning if he could speak at our event! Dean politely said, "no, but you are welcome to stay." Miyashiro and two board members did stay to watch the event. He departed after two hours, and shortly after his leaving the two board members raised their hands to ask multiple questions and shared their own concerns with the yoga that had entered their schools, just 6 months prior through Miyashiro and Sonima.

Pastor Garlow experienced someone creating a "fake Facebook" page representing him just days prior to the event. Links were sent out fraudulently to his entire contact base, as if he sent a recommendation to look at whatever it was. There were more things that happened to him right at that time that I won't disclose, but suffice it to say that the warfare in this journey has been intense for all of us. This is an ancient battle of good and evil. There is nothing new, when it comes to stepping out in faith, being opposed by one side, and rewarded by the other.

Many pastors have stood in the knowledge and concern, while watching yoga take people away from their faith and churches – slowly and deceptively. Many now see the clear movement away from faith in God transpire over time. While some are lured away by a spiritual need and attraction to the promises from yoga, unsuspecting believers drift in a *New Age* direction away from their very foundation of faith. I'm not great at explaining all this – better to read the experts to make sense of what I am saying. I am a messenger to try to get you to look further into this yoga phenomenon going on and ask more why questions. There are videos captured by many better informants from each of the events to solidify the danger warned against by previous yoga instructors.

Yoga: Purely Physical or is it Religious?

On this link you can find four (4) video segments available from the Yoga Conference held at Horizon Christian Fellowship January 14, 2014 called "Yoga – Purely Physical or is it Religious? The program is available on DVD. https://truthaboutyoga.com/education-events/. [1] The most helpful video to see is video #2 in the series, which defines Ashtanga Yoga and contains the "meat" of the information. If you can only watch one, start there.

Video #1 – Pastor Bob Botsford - overview and Sedlock introduction.

Video #2 – Dean Broyles on yoga and Ashtanga yoga

Video #3 – "Q and A" panel of 7 people including Author and Guru in Highest Caste in India (Death of a Guru) Rabi Maharaj and Dr. Peter Jones, 4 parents in the district, and Dean Broyles, all answering questions from the audience.

Video #4 – Dr. Peter Jones with a message for pastors about putting the yoga issue into a larger perspective with Oneism vs. Twoism (worshipping Creation vs. worshipping Creator).

Another Messenger

Found on the panel above and in some of the interviews, you will also see that author Mary Eady, wrote a pamphlet for talking about yoga to a friend titled "Letter to a Friend."

Booklet by Mary Eady, photo credit: TruthXchange²

Skyline Church in June of 2014 created another 4 videos that are also linked on the education events page of truthaboutyoga website. Rabi Maharaj, a former Hindu, this time spoke about Hinduism, Buddhism, Yoga and Christianity – a not to miss video! The second video is Mr. Broyles giving another overview of Yoga and Hinduism. The third video is me (Jennifer Sedlock) talking a few minutes about yoga in elementary schools, and the fourth video is the *Q and A* session (120 min) concluding the event. The schedule was for 30 minutes of questions, but lasted 2 hours. This happened at event after event – people had so many questions, and they chose to stay until we had absolutely had to conclude the events. These *Q and A* sessions answer many general questions the public had (and still have) about yoga and were videotaped for you.

Educational Documents

Below is essentially what the Education events page of the website looks like when you go to this page <u>https://truthaboutyoga. com/education-events/</u>.³ The documents that appear on the links are all included as references here in the book as well.

Handouts:

Timeline for Yoga in Encinitas[4]
Links to Articles[5]
The 5 Myths of Encinitas EUSD Yoga[6]
Yoga-Fact-Sheet[7]
Yoga Opt-out form[8]
Biblical Talking Points[9]
Jois Family Quotes [10]
EUSD Information on Yoga[11]
Frequently Asked Questions-Ashtanga Yoga[12]

Included is another document that is not online, but one that we used to encourage parents to think deeper about the issues: *Critical Thinking Questions to Consider.*[13] Over the past few years we have been asked if we have curriculum for high school students or women. A womens study is being written, and perhaps one for students will follow. The first place on which anything will be available is on www.truthaboutyoga.com,[14] so check there for updated news, resources and studies.

CHAPTER TWENTY-THREE

After the Trial ... News of EUSD, Sonima and Ashtanga yoga

(A summary of Chapter topics is included for easy reference)

In this Chapter:

> Protest of EUSD yoga demonstration at Encinitas Library, January, 2016
> Giving the children a voice *with "I miss PE" t-shirts*
> 10th family (at least) to leave the district over yoga, May, 2016
> Sonima drops support, 400K district funding as "bridge year," May, 2016
> Protest over $800K for yoga in EUSD 2016/2017 budget, May, 2016
> New (different) parent group - website and evidence made public, May, 2016
> Coast News uncovers evidence, June, 2016
> $400 K slid into budget for 2017/18 school year at board meeting, May, 2017.
> CEPAL yoga study "results" May 2013, January, 2014
> EUSD and Sonima current news

Yoga at the Encinitas Public Library

During January of 2016, EUSD sent out a flyer to all parents inviting children from each of the nine elementary schools to participate in a demonstration of yoga at the Encinitas library, and parents to watch. The invitation divided the demonstrations into three times on Saturday, and gave suggested times for each of three of the nine schools to participate in each. Our group responded swiftly by moving into action. We made signs for the event to show the public that not everyone loves yoga in the elementary schools. Some of the signs were professionally made, with the website on one side, and a photo of a child looking into a tree on the other, mirroring our business cards and postcards. The line under the child says "The Children of Encinitas K-6 Need Your Help!" Additional signs were handwritten by the children protesting the program. The kids wore their bright yellow "I miss PE" shirts with three balls on the back representing the sports they miss in PE.

Photos by author

Giving the Children a Voice

The t-shirts were originally made for kids in 2014, to wear during the school day so they could have a voice in the yoga matter. Prior to that, no one seemed to listen or care about the kids concerns. Staff and even teachers, not only ignored what any of the kids had to say about not liking yoga, but quieted them also with shaming comments. A few brave children chose to wear the shirts and the results were appalling. The days the children wore the shirts they were "shut down" at all schools. Principals and yoga teachers asked them to take the shirts off. The kids were shamed by yoga teachers with comments such as this "hurts my feelings." What about the children's feelings? What about the fact that no one would listen to them? Why weren't staff and teachers willing to ask "why are you so concerned that you would wear this shirt?" or "Tell me more about missing PE." Where was the support for the kid's *feelings*?

Photo by author

Note that the shirts are not negative about yoga. We worked hard to create positive messaging, because that was important to focus on what the kids wanted and were missing, not criticize yoga. Only the children who wanted to participate wore the shirts. Not every family against yoga had kids that chose to wear the shirts. If a child felt strongly enough to wear that shirt, it was a message that they were being affected and wanted PE back. The principals were panicked, and the district was contacted immediately. Stories grew, like Pinocchio's nose, to be much larger than the few kids that were wearing them. Our principal at La Costa Heights told someone that over twenty-five kids were wearing shirts, when in reality it was less than ten at our school that day! She personally questioned one kindergartener pressuring her on where she got the shirt (as per her mother). That wonderful family left the district, after Kindergarten! Many were shamed right out of their shirts! But some kids wouldn't take them off and that didn't go well. Other kids begged to get a shirt and each child carried five more shirts in their backpacks to share, along with a scroll note for parents of how their child got the shirt, and what it represented to give the children a voice about missing PE. After that, the shirts were worn at various events over the next couple years. Opportunities would arise where the shirts could be worn to show a consistent message. I still have a box of the extras in my garage!

Photo by author, at library protest

I Miss PE

Therefore, at the library, the kids donned the shirts and walked with signs. No words were needed. As they paraded around the yoga mats, I wondered what the superintendent felt, if anything, for *these* children. He looked a bit rough that day, having been called by the library to tell him we were there. He came right over apparently, and by the looks of it, he was visibly flustered with us.

Photos by author, EUSD kids made handwritten posterboard signs

He attempted to get the library to ask us to leave, this "private health and wellness event"—but the law was on our side this time. The district had invited all of us to be there on a flyer; therefore, it became "a public event" due to district actions. It didn't matter that the library planned it as a *private event*. EUSD overstepped their boundaries once again, so they were stuck with us for the day.

Superintendent Baird on right of far right photo, photos by author

For a moment, consider the children on the mats and the children in the t-shirts circling the mats—they are in schools together. They all have feelings and a youthful understanding of why they have this separation now between them. The kids on the mats love yoga, or they wouldn't be in a demonstration. The kids circling had been impacted by being treated differently at school for opting-out of yoga. In years to come they will understand more, but for these types of divisions, for which the school would blame us for, we hold them accountable for creating the situations. EUSD generated the divisive environment by keeping a yoga program that clearly caused animosity across the district schools for parents, teachers, and most importantly, children.

The short-term money they would receive would not be worth the long term impact. Families have left the district over yoga and lack of response to parental concerns, displaying one consequence of divisiveness. For your insight into the children who opted-out— they are happy to be out of yoga. Most kids clearly understand why their parents pulled them out. Many requested to be out of yoga long before their parents even noticed a problem! Some of the children knew it was wrong for them to be in yoga and are strong about their convictions to not do yoga while their parents weren't even sure. Some of the youngest simply trust their parents choices, but for the most part, the kids have been involved (even kindergarteners), and actively glad to be out of yoga. So, don't feel sorry for these kids, (as some people have expressed in media comments). These kids are fine. It's the ones *in* yoga that you might want to be concerned for instead! Last reported, 940 schools and growing according to a school yoga study done in 2015, by Butzer et al., called "School-Based Yoga!"[1] The kids are the reason we continue in this battle. Our kids are safe from the effects of yoga.

The children had the freedom to participate or not, for events like this one at the library. Each parent allowed them to be exposed to as much, or as little, as they wanted to what we parents were doing. No child was forced to wear a shirt or show up at any meetings or protests. They had the freedom to choose. Just like Katie, who wanted to share about her own injury. Her parents weren't thrilled about the potential negative exposure. Katie instigated going public with her injury by speaking to the board. She felt called to share her experience (Ch. 15) so that other girls might not end up hurt like her. Her dad was reluctant at first, then said "yes." The kids at the library were a small, but mighty, group. It felt like we had more people in that over-packed room, but in reality, it was a tiny *army*. Each event drew just the right amount of support, for our purposes. Too big a crowd would have created problems, given the tight room at the library.

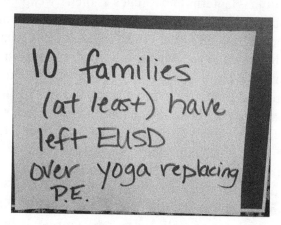

Photo by author

We gave out many cards and post cards that day to people walking through the demonstration. They wanted to know more about yoga and the controversy in the Encinitas schools. One had a child that was just about to enter kindergarten in Encinitas and stopped to see what was going on with yoga. He became very concerned. Another man quickly scooted his four-year-old daughter off the mat and out the door with our card in hand. Another mom was a teacher in a nearby district who was following the story; she was very concerned sharing her support for us speaking out against yoga. And many more ...

Adults want "I miss PE" shirts?

Surprisingly, in 2015, adults started requesting the shirts the kids were wearing! Adults that weren't even in the district wanted to support our cause by wearing them to raise awareness. For example, a teacher at a school in different district (without yoga) wears the shirt. As a result, kids or parents ask him what it is about and the door opens for discussion. The shirts became a conversation starter. A junior high ministry leader wore one on some

Sundays to promote discussion. This interesting use of the shirts reminds us of Gideon. In the Bible, Gideon was surprised by the use of odd tools—lanterns and torches as their "weapons" in battle. Our weapons for battling lack of communication became t-shirts! How unexpected, yet effective. And, Gideon's army was similar to ours. Whittled down to just what was needed; so much smaller than their opponent. What was necessary for Gideon was to trust God and lean into God's courage to grow his own. I was learning to lean more, so that when my courage ran out the door, there was a much more courageous option sitting right in front of my face. Other adults have worn those same shirts around town, and strangers ask about them. Some have heard "just a little in the news" about yoga in the schools and are curious.

Many events and tools like these grew out of our battle, and what we would come to realize along the journey is that this was becoming a *ministry*. Not a trial, but a ministry to spread the deception that comes along with yoga. Not our plan. But it became a path we could not deny we needed to walk forward into—all of us became girded with the knowledge and got questioned by those curious. We continue to share if and when asked. Usually, it's one-on-one conversations in a relationship where the other person wants and is ready to hear the information. Why? None of us is sure where it heads from here, as it almost feels like a rollercoaster ride at times without the ability to see the climbing and descending in advance. What we do see is a common concern; a need and calling to share from our own perspectives what happened in EUSD with yoga, and why it is important and impacting so many other elementary schools and states already. We are messengers in a battle we didn't ask for, serving in a capacity that is not from our own strength.

Postcards made for communicating to EUSD parents, photos by author

Jois / Sonima Foundation Pulls Funding

Late in the spring of 2016, some teachers in EUSD were gathered together and informed by Superintendent Baird that Sonima Foundation was not going to fund "*EUSD yoga*" any longer. The program expense was about $800K annually, and the Superintendent *somehow found* extra money in the budget to fund all $800K to keep the program going. No parents or children were told this, only the teachers. However, unhappy teachers leaked it to some parents to take some action on this budgeted money going toward yoga. What Baird probably didn't expect is the onslaught of new parents against *funding* yoga, over core and supplemental subjects. Parents have been funding these *other subjects* for years, supplementing science, math, music and PE. Parental pockets are not endless.

Other parents from the district were quick to follow this new set of parents, who began to uncover that there was "so much more to this program and the relationships" once you started to look. *Well, yes!* That was always the point! And once you see a little, you find there are more and more questionable decisions to uncover. Start peeling the onion, and it stinks. For one more example, (you'll see in more detail below): one parent at EUSD found the $800K for yoga in the EUSD budget for 2016/17 listed under "*books for library!!!*" *We simply can't make this stuff up!* Why would yoga be listed erroneously as library books, in a district budget, if not trying to hide it? If yoga is fine, why hide the funding under *library expenses*?

Picketing EUSD with Signs, Wearing Red

The May 2016, EUSD board meeting was held at the El Camino Creek School. Several parents shared their concerns over paying $800K for yoga from the EUSD budget. These were parents who were not previously against yoga in schools, but now didn't want yoga at the expense of other programs. Nor did they want to pay for it out of our taxpaying or parental pockets. This group began to uncover the same concerns we had, and by the next board meeting in June, websites had been formed; parent meetings and plans had been made, and picketing began on social media. Further picketing was live before the board meeting in June of 2016, on the street corner of Encinitas Blvd and Rancho Santa Fe where the Encinitas school district is located. The photos tell part of the story http://www.cbs8.com/story/32277906/encinitas-school-board-approves-student-yoga-classes.[2]

Protest prior to May 2016 EUSD board meeting, photos by author

For a couple hours prior to the meeting there were around 50-60 parents and children picketing, mostly wearing red, holding signs and shouting in unison toward cars when at stoplights. Messages such as … .

"Fund Math and Science first"

"Books before yoga mats"

"Property taxes for academics"

"Science before yoga"

"Math before yoga"

"Make parents pay for yoga"

"$800,000 for yoga???"

"Baird is a fraud"

"Parents for responsible spending"

"Our kids want science"

"Music before yoga"

"Yoga does not equal PE" (an = sign crossed out)

"Science B4 yoga"

"Power to the "pupil"

"I love yoga ... when it's free"

"Math books B4 yoga mats"

"Art before yoga" (this sign done artistically by a student)

Protest prior to May 2016 EUSD board meeting, photos by author

My personal favorite being chanted was "Baird has to go." You can see photos of the signs, and hear on several videos in the news section of the *chanting* about Baird http://fox5sandiego.com/2016/06/21/group-calls-for-encinitas-schools-to-deny-yoga-program-spending/.[3] The investigating parents asked for the resignation of the superintendent at the June 7, 2016, EUSD board meeting. More new evidence has been found by these lawyers able to dig further info tax records and documents of concern, proving some of the same concerns we had. The evidence continues to build in this case. But most of the facts being revealed in the relationships and ties have been denied by Baird, since the trial in 2013. The evidence was turned over to the police after the meeting http://www.10news.com/news/encinitas-union-school-districts-yoga-proposal-meets-opposition-062116.[4]

"Baird Has to Go" Chanted (not a Sanskrit chant)

Follow the Money … So, in spring of 2016, when Superintendent Baird attempted to imbed $800K in the district budget for yoga for the 2016-17 school year, parents started to notice some of the other things we had been sharing; such as EUSD won't even call it yoga! They use "health and wellness" in place of yoga in every instance of communication about yoga, as well as the instructors, for the past five years. This new group of parents are digging up evidence for a lot of the connections to who is getting paid for what. Things we knew and simply couldn't prove early on, in 2013. For example, payments to Chandler Hill, which is Scott Himelstein, http://encinitasparents4truth.com/wp-content/uploads/2016/06/Screen-Shot-2016-06-06-at-8.58.08-PM.png ,[5] and he was found on a cruise together with Baird (no entanglement?)

Baird was also flying to nice destinations with Himelstein (also pictured), and others from Jois, on someone's bill for "meetings." Both the taxpayers, and Sonima, footed most of his bills for travel, revealed by Baird himself to a reporter for Coast News article, posted in text box #21.

Baird at social events and travel with Jois Foundation leaders

See a better version online of the photos below on http://encinitasparents4truth.com/.

June 2016, Mr. Baird stated he hadn't worked with Sonima for18 months. This picture was taken 10 months prior.

Some of the comments from the June 2016 board media, article in the Coast News:

"The superintendent colluded with the Sonima Foundation and Scott Himelstein at the University of San Diego to falsify research about the yoga program to induce the district to implement and continue this yoga program," said Anna Hysell, an immigration attorney who has children in the district.

"Because you colluded to defraud the district with false research, and your role in the Sonima Foundation as a board member, you are in violation of California fraud and conflict-of-interest laws, as well as the federal False Claims Act and you are subject to prosecution," she said to Baird.

Hysell said she is handing over all the evidence she has gathered to the Office of the Inspector General at the US Department of Education, the California Audits and Investigation Unit and the San Diego Civil Grand Jury.

"The district attorney here in San Diego has been notified," she added. "All are very interested in my information. I move for Mr. Baird's termination. If the board does not remove him within 30 days of today's date, I will see to it that a recall petition be started for a special election to remove you all."

(Channel 10 news referenced above shows parts of this).

Timothy Baird, Exposed

As you can see, Timothy Baird, Superintendent EUSD, shown on left as an Advisory Board member in lowest photo on left. In the latest version on right, he is taken down. Notice Salima Ruffin top middle is deleted from board as well at this snapshot in time (she was an original co-founder!). Note Scott Himelstein was taken down from Board page as well. See Stedman Graham in both photos.

The New Group *for Responsible Spending - No* to funding Yoga

The media available will tell you so much more than I can present here, but it's all posted for you with ongoing developments. A picture can be worth a thousand words, so I'll save the words and you look at the photos. Beyond the twitter, Facebook and the media page we have provided (www.truthaboutyoga.com, facebook.com/

factsaboutyoga, https://twitter.com/truthaboutyoga),[6] this new group of parents have locations to follow media and developments as well, such as this website: http://encinitasparents4truth.com/,[7] and Facebook page called Parents for responsible spending: https://www.facebook.com/encinitasparents/ and a twitter page: https://twitter.com/Pres_Encinitas?ref_src=twsrc%5Etfw,[7]

@Pres_Encinitas. The history of these postings and websites give you great insight into where the money traveled, the cover-ups and relationships that go beyond entanglement, and into close working relationships on various projects, current and past.

June 2016, EUSD Board meeting, parents protesting $800K budget for yoga, photo by author

Best EUSD Board Meeting Ever

I, as you can imagine, could hardly contain my smile, while beaming at that June 2016 EUSD board meeting, while silently seated in the midst of the crowd. I could hardly believe my ears! I was so thankful that I heard about the meeting (through the upset teachers and parents) and was able to be there to just be a fly on the wall. We moved out of the district one month prior, so I was in the midst of boxes and unpacking daily. I had no idea what was unfolding and being said, but I was excited to hear the new parents speak with more factual evidence to unravel what was transpiring in EUSD.

Finally, *money speaks,* to many parents who thought yoga was fine, *as a gift.* But now, as taxpaying citizens, they did not want to pay for yoga. We knew Somina wouldn't pay for the yoga forever. Did these parents not realize this too… a few years ago? Most just simply didn't think about it, I suspect. When EUSD made such a big deal about renaming yoga with their own name (EUSD yoga), did parents somehow miss the strong alliance and connection the district would have to the program? EUSD spent years creating the yoga curriculum on paper, defending and fighting for *this yoga* in court, so would they really drop it when Sonima pulled the funds? Hardly a thought, if you took more than a moment to think about those facts. Baird had too many eggs in this basket, and too many perks and connections, to end this program. Not without a good fight would he ever let go of this. This would be apparent to all in attendance at the board meeting. He would make a deal, and I was surprised he even gave up ½ the funds, and ½ the yoga time, but he did to save it. One yoga class per week, per school, would now be the new minimum yoga curriculum required. What did schools each choose for their second "enrichment" session for the week?

May 2016, outdoor protest, then inside board meeting, photos by author

Decision for 2016/17 School Year Budget

As you can see in the Media reports—the parents were only able to talk the district down to $416K to budget for yoga, and the ability to choose at each school site whether to have a second yoga session, or another PE session each week. All the schools chose yoga only *once* per week, according to my sources. By the way, parent yoga is offered at most of the schools weekly also, and if you are a taxpayer in Encinitas you are paying for that. Some parent classes are outside school hours with the same yoga instructors. Ah, so many issues, so little time ...

Follow the Money

The following documents expose the relationships that were claimed in court by EUSD to not be co-mingled, yet our Attorney claimed were "entanglement on steroids." These links are available on the truthaboutyoga.com website, as well, in case the other parent group chooses to take theirs down one day. If you click on this (Ebook) and it says it contains viruses—these pdf documents don't, that just happens on wordpress documents, but you can always just go to the page https://truthaboutyoga.com/san-diego-county/[8] and click on each of the links from there as well. There is more than one way to (skin a cat, or) find the same documents!

1. EUSD-RDG-MOU-for-2015-16 Memo of Understanding Contracting Regur. (https://truthaboutyoga.files.wordpress.com/2018/01/eusd-rdg-mou-for-2015-16.pdf)

2. EUSD Travel Report 2012-13 ($9,900 Baird expenses, $2500 over budget) https://truthaboutyoga.files.wordpress.com/2018/01/fy2012-13districtoffice_travelconfreport-1.pdf

3. EUSD Travel Report 2013-14 ($14,700 Baird—$7,981 over budget) https://truthaboutyoga.files.wordpress.com/2018/01/fy2013-14districtoffice_travelconfreport.pdf

4. EUSD Travel Report 2014-15 ($23,000 Baird—4x the travel expense prior to yoga in schools) (https://truthaboutyoga.files.wordpress.com/2018/01/fy2014-15districtoffice_travelconfreport.pdf)

5. Sample Approval of Out of State Travel Funding for Timothy Baird https://truthaboutyoga.files.wordpress.com/2018/01/skmbt_c35316060118000.pdf

6. 3 Payments in 2014 to Scott Himelsteins's companies:
   1. To Chandler Hill—$481,000 (Himelstein). See page 8 of 2014 Sonima Tax Return
   2. To Portico—$60,000 (Himelstein). See 2014 tax return.
   3. To UCSD Center for Ed Policy and Law—$377,000 (Himelstein). See tax return.

7. Sonima Foundation 2012 Tax Return (https://truthaboutyoga.files.wordpress.com/2018/01/sonimafoundation2012taxreturns.pdf)

8. Sonima Foundation 2013 Tax Return (https://truthaboutyoga.files.wordpress.com/2018/01/sonimafoundation2013taxreturn.pdf)

9. Sonima-2014 Tax Return Sonima (https://truthaboutyoga.files.wordpress.com/2018/01/sonima-2014taxreturn.pdf)

(all of these are in resource section back of book in detail, but ebook can click on link).

Let's focus on the 2014 Tax return alone.

1. Eugene Ruffin was paid $170,000 as Executive Director of Sonima.
2. "Executives" expense totaled $342,062—his $170,000 = so $172,062 to other unnamed executive(s)?
3. "Management Expenses—$697,974 (Who? How many?).
4. "Other /salaries"—$149,500 (remember yoga teachers paid by Regur, not Sonima, so these are "other" people).
5. Travel Expenses for 2014 on taxes—$104,450.
6. Vacation and Healthcare—$13,385.
7. Legal—$50,000 (was during lawsuit, 2013-2015).

8. Accounting—$8,500.
9. Payment to Sonia Ruffin's "Creations" travel agency—$88,723.
10. Baird's buddy Himelstein made a whopping $918,000 (2014) from the three payments to Portico, Chandler Hill and UCSD department, that Himelstein is recipient and head of all three.
11. Find all these details in 1-10 on the Tax Return Linked above and here. Sonima-2014 Tax Return Sonima / https:// truthaboutyoga.files.wordpress.com/2018/01/sonima-2014taxreturn.pdf.

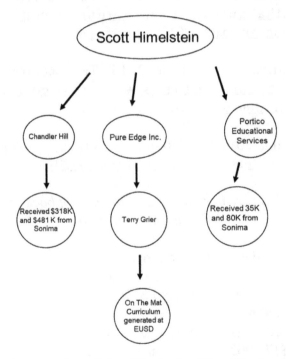

Sonima website now has a link to Himelsteins "Pure Edge" website for the Jois/Sonoma/Pure Edge/EUSD yoga curriculum. (Note: After publication of this book "on the mat" will likely move and you'll need to google to search for it as they have moved it several times, but it's available for schools despite where Sonima and Himelstein "shift" the location. This is the same curriculum discussed at trial.

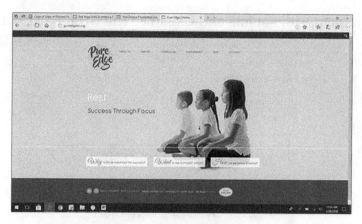

This is the current yoga-in-schools curriculum location:
http://pureedgeinc.org/ [9]

Chandler Hill Group - **$481,000**

Taxes 2014 (page 8) for Sonima payment to **Chandler Hill Group—$481,00**

Agreement with Sonima and Chandler Hill Group—$104,167

Statement to Form 990
Page 8, Part VII, Section B (cont'd)

(A) Name and Business Address

Chandler Hill Group
Director of Public Policy
8278 Chandler Hill CT
San Diego, CA 92127

(B) Description of Services

— Develop a partnership with the University of San Diego or University of California
San Diego to research and report on the results of the Encinitas program
implementation.

— Plan, manage and execute with the Foundation, designated public relations firm and
Encinitas school district a "Kick Off Campaign" for the Encinitas program initiative.

— Research opportunities with Community Colleges as well as Private and Public
Universities to develop post-secondary certification and/or degrees for educators in
health and wellness best practices (yoga, meditation and nutrition).

— Support required public relation/public policy changes on the state and local levels
to make health and wellness best practices (yoga, meditation and nutrition) an
integrated component of the public education system, including the education of
members of the legislative and local school boards, also the benefits of health and
wellness programs in public schools, working with the Curriculum Commission to
gain support for the Jois Self Mastery programs as part of school curriculum.

(C) Compensation

$104,167.00

Agreement with Sonima and Chandler Hill Group—
$104,167 found at links in references and above

CEPAL study (Himelstein).

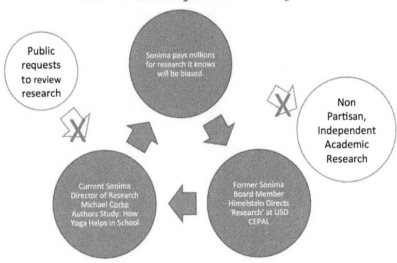

Finally! Two local reporters dig deeper in 2016!

It took reporters years to finally see that there were problems far beyond the media hype about religious issues with the yoga placed into the Encinitas District. Follow the money and you find the other problems, but no reporter took the time any sooner to do the research. The following are the only two reports in the four years in which I saw reporters come close to scratching under the surface of the potential fraud and concerning relationships behind the program being developed for our nation's children.

The first article you can go to the link to read. The second one is the best, so I will include it in a text box following a few comments.

April, 2015: Is yoga a religion?

Court said it was, but Encinitas schools have *scrubbed their yoga programs clean* http://www.sandiegoreader.com/news/2015/apr/29/citylights-yoga-religion/[10]

June, 2016: Ties between EUSD yoga program, foundation and school raise concerns:

https://www.thecoastnews.com/ties-between-eusd-yoga-program-foundation-and-school-raise-concerns/[11]

Quote from second article:

It says "... a complex web of payments from the Sonima Foundation to the director of the USD center that conducted the survey, raising conflict of interest concerns among parents and experts."

If you read the comments after the article, you could see that the writer took a lot of ridicule for asking the questions and digging up dirt on this program. Why? Again, we have to continue to ask the question why—if yoga isn't religious and has no connections to spiritual pathways—why all the fuss and viciousness of folks *over yoga, when people claim it is peaceful?* As evidenced by the behaviors, it does not calm everyone … in fact, a lot of folks are all twisted up about it. A good chuckle about this is necessary at times, but don't miss the serious messages where this reporter is starting to get to the reality of the situation. There are a few more miles to go, and hopefully this book helps more investigations into the truth about what is transpiring still today in Encinitas schools, and with Sonima yoga spreading nationwide and internationally.

Note—notice in this photo from the article, showing that the three organizations shared office space on Highway 101 in Encinitas: Jois Yoga for the foundation (Sonia Tudor Jones and Salima Ruffin), Creations World Concierge (Salima Ruffin), and Ed Futures (Eugene Ruffin) from 2011 – 2016. With that pointed out, now read the full news article, understanding some of the *entanglement* when Baird claimed *no connections.* It's the closest any reporter has uncovered thus far, and will separately show evidence for some of the serious and solid concerns we had during the trial.

Photo by author, 2016. Marque for office space still shared by Salima Ruffin's Creations Travel Agency, Eugene Ruffin's Ed Futures, and Jois Yoga.

Ties between EUSD yoga program, foundation and school raise concerns: http://www.thecoastnews.com/2016/06/23/ties-between-eusd-yoga-program-foundation-and-school-raise-concerns/[11] Find at this link, but it was so good, I had to print the whole thing here for you in the book.

Photo of door to empty office space in Encinitas, by author, 2016

Proof of the three organizations in one location from 2011-2016: Eugene Ruffin's Ed Futures, Salima Ruffin's Creations Travel Agency, and Jois Yoga.

ENCINITAS — Encinitas Union School District officials have long touted its yoga program and its benefits to students, and they have pointed to a study by the University of San Diego to bolster its claims.

The yoga program has recently become the center of a controversy after the school district tentatively agreed in April to use $800,000 of taxpayer dollars to keep it going after the foundation that has given the district millions in grant dollars to start it and maintain it, the Sonima Foundation, announced it would no longer provide the funding. The district has since scaled back the amount to just over $400,000.

In the defense to parents who have questioned whether the district should use the funds to maintain the program, school Superintendent Tim Baird again touted the USD report.

"Research conducted by USD and the District shows there is a cor-relation with the program and increased attendance, decreased behavior issues, and improved physical health and skills," School Superintendent Tim Baird wrote in a recent document answering questions about the yoga program. "This program has been pop-ular with students, parents, and staff. In focus group data gathering and surveys, approximately 2/3 of all respondents or more have expressed that they value the program."

But an investigation by The Coast News into the financial records of the Sonima Foundation reveal, among other things, a complex web of payments from the Sonima Foundation to the director of the USD center that conducted the survey, raising conflict of interest concerns among parents and experts.

The Coast News also found that the very report the district has used to advance the yoga program calls into question its effectiveness, but that Baird, USD and the Sonima Foundation — which is primarily funded by several billionaire hedge fund investors — have high-lighted only the positive aspects of the report.

In addition, Baird's own daughter appears to have been employed by the Sonima Foundation at the height of the partnership, raising further concerns about the relationship between Baird and the foundation.

Baird and Scott Himelstein, the director of the University of San Diego Center for Education Policy and Law, the school at the center of the controversy, both defended their roles in relationship and denied any allegations of conflict of interest, calling any such alle-gations "a red herring."

"There is definitely a legitimate and healthy discussion that should be happening, and is happening, dealing with what our budget pri-orities should be," Baird said. "But when it devolves to these accu-sations and name-calling, this is where I have to say no, this is not healthy discourse."

The Coast News reached out to Sonima Foundation officials for the story, including former Executive Director Eugene Ruffin and current Executive Director Terry Grier, who formerly served as superintendent of the San Diego Unified School District. Ruffin declined comment and Grier did not respond to numerous calls, emails and messages for comment.

Complex web of payments

The Coast News reviewed the IRS 990 tax returns from 2012, 2013 and 2014 from the Sonima Foundation, which coincides with the start and height of the EUSD yoga program. Tax returns for the 2015 calendar year are not available through publicly available websites such as Guidestar and the state Attorney General's charity database.

The Sonima Foundation, previously known as the Jois Foundation, awarded USD Center for Education Policy and Law, known as CEPAL, nearly $500,000 in grant funds to research the foundation's yoga programs between 2012 and 2014, including the Encinitas program. This included $90,000 in 2012 and a $377,000 grant in 2014, as the program had expanded to several other districts across the country.

Beginning in 2012, the Sonima Foundation also began contracting with two educational-based companies—The Chandler Hill Group Inc. and Portico Educational Services, LLC.

The Chandler Hill Group first received a $104,000 contract in 2012, and the amount escalated to $318,000 and $481,000 in 2013 and 2014 respectively. According to the tax returns, the company was to, among other things, "develop a partnership with the University of San Diego ... to research and report on the results of the Sonima programs," as well as to "support required public relation/public policy changes on the state and local levels to make health and wellness best practices an integrated component of the public education system."

Portico Educational Services received payments of $35,000 in 2013 and $80,000 in 2014 to perform data collection at the various sites, including Encinitas.

Business records show that both the Chandler Hill Group and Portico Education are companies owned by Scott Himelstein, who currently serves as the director of CEPAL—the center that performed the Encinitas yoga research study.

At the same time as Himelstein's companies received more than $1 million from the foundation, he also served on the Sonima Foundation as an advisory board member, listed alongside Baird, who was listed as an advisory board member until earlier this month.

Himelstein also said that he requested to be removed from the advisory board after he "reconsidered" his participation. Baird was also recently removed from the advisory board section, work, he said, that he hadn't done in more than 18 months.

USD produced two reports that exclusively focused on Encinitas yoga during its early stages. One of those reports was authored by Michael Corke, who was listed at the time as the interim research director at CEPAL. Corke is now the Sonima Foundation's director of research.

Parents have questioned whether the funding from the Sonima Foundation and the ties that it had with USD could have created an incentive that could be construed as a conflict of interest that calls into question the veracity of the study and its reported findings.

The parents have created a website, encinitasparents4truth.com, which details many of the same findings made by The Coast News. It also lists several conclusions that the parents drew from their findings.

"USD CEPAL research is not independent and produces misleading, biased research conclusions complicit with the missions of its wealthy founders," according to the website. "Backed by multi-millionaires, these Foundations influence school policy by providing hidden massive monetary incentives to USD Research Director Scott Himelstein and directly compensate other researchers."

"The relationship between these parties is intentionally hidden from the public through the use (of) complex payment schemes to 3rd party entities," the website continues.

Two experts in nonprofit research said that the financial connections between the foundation, Himelstein and USD Center were "unusual."

"It is not normal as far as I know," said James Ferris, a professor at the University of Southern California school of Public Policy and Development. "There are a number of questions/issues the facts as noted raise ... both from the Foundation side, as well as potential conflicts on the USD side."

Mark Hager, an associate professor of Philanthropic Studies in the School of Community Resources & Development at Arizona State University, echoed Ferris' sentiments.

"I think you can call those things into question, and it raises some interesting questions," Hager said. "It could be that they have a legit-imate reason, or they could be just investing in their friends to tell them what they want to hear and tout the good results."

Encinitas Union School District board members, who have supported the yoga program, were unaware of the many of the details of the district's partnership with Sonima and USD. One board member who spoke to The Coast News said the allegations raised by parents in recent weeks and the information uncovered by The Coast News was surprising, though they believed it isn't relevant to the current decision — whether the district should be funding yoga with tax-payer dollars.

"The issue on the table is budget and yoga," Board President Emily Andrade said. "That is where my focus and priorities are, is this something the district should fund. If there was something illegal going on, that would be my job, and at this time I am not aware of anything suspicious or illegal being done by Tim Baird."

A rosy report

In 2013, a year after the foundation had launched its yoga initiative at Encinitas schools, USD released its first report on the Yoga Program, "Implementing Yoga in Public Schools: Evidence from the Encinitas Union School District's Pilot Yoga Program 2012–2013." This report outlined findings of the challenges found during the pilot's implementations and recommendations to make the program run smoother.

Two months later, USD released its data-driven report that showed some preliminary findings about the impact yoga was having on the students and the schools. This report, entitled "Yoga in Public Schools: Evidence from the Encinitas Union School District's Yoga Program 2012–2013," collected data from parents, teachers, students and instructors about the program and made findings based on that data.

Two of the chief findings that the school district immediately seized onto were that students like the yoga program and that students' emotional wellness had improved since the implementation of yoga.

The report, however, also details other less than enthusiastic findings, including that teachers at schools that had the yoga program the full year reported more instances of bullying and disruptive behavior than schools who had it for half of the year, and that students at full-year yoga programs performed worse on certain fitness benchmarks, such as for upper body strength, than their half-year counterparts.

Baird, in an interview with The Coast News, acknowledged the reports' findings were mixed, but said that its findings were consistent with the district's own focus group studies, which showed that students, parents and teachers saw benefit from the yoga program.

Parents who have been opposed to the proposed expenditure, however, argue that Baird is now retreating from his previous enthusiasm towards the report findings, and that he misled parents by not mentioning the mixed or negative aspects of the report.

Baird said that he had always informed Sonima about his reservations with the research studies they wanted to perform, because he was skeptical they would yield a one-to-one relationship between yoga and improved student performance, which he believed the Sonima Foundation was looking for.

"They wanted to see the Holy Grail, and I said that it was going to be a very hard thing to find," Baird said. "What we were looking for in the research was to see if students valued the yoga program. Our studies and our teacher and student focus groups have been in favor of it."

Baird said that his decisions regarding the yoga program were not based solely on the USD studies, and that frankly the results didn't matter.

"We were seeing enough good things in this program that we felt it should continue," Baird said. "The report was more for the funders of Sonima, not for us."

As for the appearance that the research could be compromised by the Sonima Foundation's payments to Himelstein and later by Corke taking a job with the foundation, Baird said he believed the argument was a "red herring."

"These are professional independent researchers, they are not going to jeopardize their professional roles as researchers by saying what the foundation wants to say," he said. "And when Sonima went to hire a researcher, it makes sense they would look to someone with whom they had a relationship. This is about people knowing people and quality work, and you go to the people you know and they know what you are doing."

Himelstein echoed those sentiments.

"More than a year ago the foundation requested to consider and interview the author of the Encinitas study for a newly created position in their organization and I was pleased to provide him with the opportunity to do so," he said about Corke.

Hager said that the fact that the report did contain both positive and negative information about the program eases the appearance of impropriety by the researchers. Once the research is complete, however, the foundation and others could spin the findings to their benefit.

"Why would they do that?" Hager said, "Perhaps because they are more interested in something that results in additional contributions than generating a true program evaluation that results in a more productive direction for the program.

"The second set of motivation is less about the science and the researchers, and more often than not what happens is that the communications wings take over, and they will continue to tout the program," Hager said.

EUSD, Sonima tied from beginning

To understand the earlier ties between the school district and the Sonima Foundation, one must first understand that the foundation was born from the fledgling yoga program introduced at the school district.

The KP Jois Foundation was formed in 2011 by billionaire hedge fund manager Paul Tudor Jones and his wife Sonia with the concept of bringing yoga to and researching its benefits in underserved schools. The first school was Ivy Hawn Charter School for the Arts in Lake Helen, Fla., which received a $40,000 grant and $8,000 to pay for several yoga instructors.

Also involved in the foundation's inception was Carlsbad resident Eugene Ruffin, who served as the executive director.

Later that year, however, the foundation underwent a significant overhaul, focusing its attention on Encinitas Union School District, introducing yoga to students at Capri Elementary School.

Encouraged by the results, in 2012 the organization put together a $533,000 grant for yoga and nutrition at all nine EUSD campuses and rapidly expanded its board and fundraising. The organization's 2012 tax returns show that money coming into the foundation jumped from $125,000 in its first year to $1.3 million the next year.

That year, they awarded USD CEPAL a $90,000 grant, though the tax return doesn't provide an explanation for the grant's purpose.

The foundation also hired the Chandler Hill Group, Himelstein's company. According to the 2012 tax returns, among the company's duties were to, "plan, manage and execute with the Foundation, designated public relations firm and Encinitas school district a 'Kick Off Campaign' for the Encinitas program initiative."

After declining comment on several occasions, Himelstein emailed The Coast News a statement in which he attempted to explain the relationship between his companies, the Foundation and the USD program that he directs.

"The Sonima Foundation provided a donation to support CEPAL to do work in the area of health and wellness in schools. We of course focused our work in Encinitas as the foundation had informed us of their partnership with EUSD. Subsequently thereafter and only after the donation was pledged was my company Chandler Hill asked by the foundation to consult on issues unrelated and not undertaken in the specific work done by CEPAL," Himelstein wrote.

"These included many tasks on the local, state and national levels but did not include arranging for any contractual/partnership agreement with CEPAL.

"CEPAL was the recipient of a donation from the Foundation, interacted and communicated with the Foundation but did not enter into any partnership or contractual relationship with the Sonima Foundation," Himelstein continued.

Baird said his recollection was that Sonima had contacted Himelstein about doing policy work that would promote health and wellness on a national level, and then afterward engaged him about CEPAL studying the Encinitas program.

"Once that (policy contract) was in place, they started talking about, "You (Himelstein) are in charge of one of the best research facilities in the area, can we hire you to do a research evaluation as well," Baird said. "Foundations do this all the time, they evaluate to see if their money is making a difference."

Baird said he had met Himelstein before the yoga program when USD was looking at Encinitas Union School District to launch a pilot mobile learning program.

The partnership between the foundation and Encinitas Union rose dramatically in 2013, when, despite a lawsuit being filed on behalf of a local family claiming the yoga program was indoctrinating Hinduism on the district students, the foundation awarded the school district a $1.4 million grant. This allowed the school district to hire two yoga instructors at each school.

The Foundation's fundraising, once again, exploded, rising from $1.3 million to nearly $3.2 million, with most of the donations coming from two sources: Sonia Jones and the Dalio Family Foundation, which was founded by Ray Dalio, the billionaire businessman who founded the Bridgewater Associates investment firm.

In 2014, the foundation and school district's partnership reached its height. The district again received $1.4 million in grant funding, and the foundation brought in more than $4.4 million in donations.

This allowed the foundation to continue to expand the program to other areas, including Cajon Valley Union School District, whose superintendent is a former Encinitas Union administrator, the Monarch School, which serves homeless teens in San Diego, and Broome Street Academy, a school that serves homeless and foster-care teens in New York City.

During the peak of the partnership between Encinitas, the Foundation and USD's research, Baird attended numerous conferences alongside Himelstein and Sonima representatives where he touted the district's yoga program. One such event was a three-day symposium April 2014 in Lenox, Mass.

Baird said he was not on district time when he went to the symposiums, but said the Sonima Foundation did pay for his travel expenses.

Baird's daughter, Kelsey, also got a job with Sonima, doing public relations work for several months with the foundation. Baird acknowledged that his daughter worked for the foundation but said the employment was only temporary and he did not see any potential conflicts.

"I don't see how there is a quid pro quo here, because I wasn't getting anything out of it, and it wasn't like we were hiring Sonima people at the district," Baird said. "My daughter had been doing volunteer work for them, and there came a time where the foundation really needed help outreaching with reporters and the media, so they brought her on, but it was only for a few months."

By 2015, the relationship between the foundation and Encinitas began to wane. The Foundation's Encinitas office shut its doors, a Wellness Center on Coast Highway 101 that opened early in 2015 shut down and Ruffin had stepped down as the executive director, replaced by Terry Grier, who had recently stepped down as the Houston Independent School District superintendent.

The program began to focus on more at-risk and low-income schools, with the remaining connection between Sonima and Encinitas being the grant funding that it was giving to the school district.

Then, in March of 2016, the foundation abruptly informed the district that the funding would be cut off. Baird said he attempted to work out an arrangement that would have wound down the funding over a course of a year, but did not succeed.

Baird, when speaking to The Coast News, said the foundation had been in the process of changing its business model in 2015, going to a "three years and out" model in which schools would receive funding for three years, and then would be expected to maintain the program on their own.

Since the controversy erupted over the program, however, Baird said he was unable to get board members or executives with the foundation on the phone. He said he was trying to remove his name from the website as a board member, which he succeeded in doing this month.

"At some point in the journey, the foundation went in a new direction that was to serve high-impact districts with high poverty rates, and the focus and the implementation was much more structured than what we were doing here," Baird said. "Our model doesn't look like the other models and I think that is unfortunate because I felt we have a better model.

"In reality, our school district has had very little to do with Sonima and USD for more than a year," he said. "I couldn't even get them on the phone when all of this happened."

Baird said the flaw in the argument, that he somehow benefits from the relationship with Sonima, is the fact that Encinitas is no longer being funded by the foundation.

"The whole line of reasoning is a bit ludicrous because if I was so connected with Sonima, they would be funding my program, which they are not," Baird said. "Sonima is out of the picture. I wish I had some kind of control because they would still be funding it."

Conflicts of Interest

For an "easy to read" version of the conflicts of interest (with visuals) see the PowerPoint from the new parent group in the EUSD district below (I was not involved with this separate research done in 2016). It proves the relationships (financially) we were seeing in 2012, but could not prove in 2013 without tax records and other documentation that would surface later. These relationships and ties, now proven, were adamantly denied in court. The relationships between these parties were intentionally hidden from the public, through the use of a web of payment entities to third parties. With patience and persistent research, the truth comes to light.

Entire Conflict of Interest power point created by other parents in the EUSD District:

http://encinitasparents4truth.com/wp-content/uploads/2016/06/ ConflictofInterestEUSDSonimaUSD.pdf[12]

The following topics are on that parent website

- Players of Interest
- Superintendent Baird's Conflict of Interest
- USD Director of Research, Scott Himelstein's Role
- Sonima Foundation's Hidden Payments to Himelstein
- Sonima: Cushy Jobs for Researchers, School Officials
- The Illusion of Independent Research
- USD "Yoga in Schools" Actual Findings: No Benefits
- Baird's Intentional Misrepresentation of Study Results
- USD CEPAL Research Conclusions: Altered to Meet Sponsor Mission
- How Billionaires Influenced EUSD policy

Jois "Cepal" Study at USD

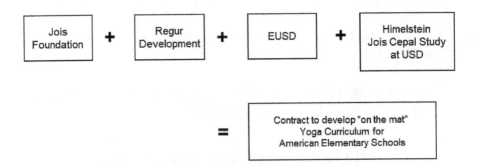

CEPAL Study Results

One big frustration that parents had was that "the University of San Diego 'CEPAL' research was not independent, and thus, produced misleading, biased research conclusions complicit with the missions of its wealthy founders," according to the website above. "Backed by multi-millionaires, these Foundations influence school policy by providing hidden massive monetary incentives to USD Research Director Scott Himelstein and directly compensate other researchers."

Two reports were produced by USD CEPAL:

1. https://truthaboutyoga.files.wordpress.com/2015/01/cepal-report_implementing-yoga_2013-2014.pdf[13]
2. https://truthaboutyoga.files.wordpress.com/2015/01/eusd-yoga-student-effects-2012-13-formattedforwebsite.pdf[13]

This Research indicates that the CEPAL study showed Yoga caused:

- More bullying with yoga, not less.
- More behavioral problems, not less.

- More suspensions and unexcused absences, not less.
- Less academic effort, not more.
- Less endurance and strength, not more.
- No benefit to yoga, and yet Baird expanded the program and claimed its positive findings, intentionally misrepresenting and hiding the above.

  http://encinitasparents4truth.com/ wp-content/uploads/2016/06/ ConflictofInterestEUSDSonimaUSD.pdf[14]

See the facts and his claims hiding negative results!

http://www.sonimafoundation.org/wp-content/ uploads/2015/05/Sonima-2013-AR-050615- FINspreads.pdf [14] and http://encinitasparents4truth.com/ baird-intentionally-misrepresents-study-results/[14]

A financial conflict of interest has a lot of definitions, but here is one: a financial conflict of interest is a significant financial interest that could directly affect the design, conduct, or reporting of externally funded research.

A second one to note is that a financial interest means anything of financial value whether or not the value is readily ascertainable (such as speaking at events, yacht and cruise ship adventures, significant travel paid for by Sonima ... and this is not a complete listing).

Unreasonable doubt?

CEPAL Study Analysis

Analysis of the CEPAL findings is available here (by an anonymous source on our side of the battle lines): https://truthaboutyoga. files.wordpress.com/2015/01/cepal-bulletpoints.pdf.[15]

It begins: *The Sonima Foundation commissioned the Center for Education Policy and Law (CEPAL) at the University of San*

Diego to conduct a three-year study of EUSD's yoga program.
CEPAL published two full reports analyzing data collected during
2012-2013.1

The CEPAL study failed to support the hypothesis that all-year
yoga students (at five EUSD schools) would perform better than
half-year yoga students (at four control-group EUSD schools) in
measures of fitness, behavior, attendance, academic performance,
or emotional well-being. In fact, in some measures it shows the
opposite, that full-year yoga students did worse than half-year
yoga students.

- In tests of 1) resting heart rate, 2) body mass index (BMI),
  3) body composition, 4) aerobic capacity, and 5) abdominal
  strength and endurance, there was not a significant
  difference between all-year and half-year yoga students.
- For the upper body strength and endurance test, all-year
  yoga students scored significantly lower than half-year
  students (91% vs. 82%, $p = .01$), suggesting that yoga
  was less effective than traditional PE in conditioning the
  upper body.
- For the trunk exterior strength test, 99% of all-year yoga
  students passed compared with 97% of half-year yoga
  students, but this result is not statistically significant ($p =$
  .10, whereas the commonly accepted threshold for statistical
  significance is $p < .05$). The CEPAL report asserts that $p =$
  .10 is statistically significant, but few rigorous researchers
  would agree with this claim.
- For the flexibility test, CEPAL reports a pass rate of
  88% for all-year yoga students, compared with 78% of
  half-year students, which is statistically significant, $p =$
  .01. However, in order to report this result, CEPAL had
  to exclude from their analysis one-fifth of the all-yoga
  data. A footnote rationalizes excluding one of five full-
  year yoga schools "due to what appears to be errors in the
  administration of the Flexibility activity." At this school,
  100% of tested students scored "Needs Improvement"
  after a year of yoga, compared with a quarter (23%) and

a third (33%) of students who had done traditional PE during 2010-2011 and 2011-2012 respectively. Contrary to researcher expectations, there may have been a trend toward progressively worsening flexibility — and yoga may have exacerbated rather than reversed this trend. Excluding unwanted data in this particular case with these numbers goes against generally accepted research practice, and it may skew statistical results.

- Students on average like yoga only "a little." On a Likert scale from 1.0 "I don't like it," "2.0 I like it a little," to 3.0 "I like it a lot," students on average reported that they like yoga "a little": 2.28, with boys (2.18), older grade 5 and 6 children (2.18), and more fit children (2.29) giving lower than average scores.

- Survey response rates for teachers and parents were "poor." Teacher response rates ranged from 0%-62.5% per school, averaging 29.2% for all-year schools and 22.8% for half-year schools. Only 7.9% of district parents responded to the first survey, 1.7% to the second survey, and 2.9% to the third survey. Although responses were "almost uniformly positive (94.3%)," low response rates raise questions about the representativeness of the sample; program supporters may have been more likely to take time to complete surveys.

- Even so, both teachers and parents reported student complaints about yoga. Parents commented that some students, "especially upper grade males, were trying to get kicked out of yoga classes on purpose by displaying disruptive behavior." Teachers commented that older students and males described the classes as "boring," "too slow paced," and "lame." Teachers also reported students complaining about yoga replacing PE, stating "'well, that's not PE, that's not what we like to do.' They want to play games."

- Overall, the quantitative data failed to corroborate stakeholder perceptions of yoga's benefits. "Although stakeholders report yoga is improving student behavior, academic performance, and emotional wellness, student results do not corroborate all these sentiments." Indeed, "this disconnect between adult (qualitative) and student (quantitative) findings is intriguing … The positive changes parents, teachers and principals shared may be informed by their class or school-level perspectives while students might be drawing their own conclusions based on peer interactions or other experiences to which adults may not have access."2

- Although school personnel perceived yoga as improving student behavior, both teachers and students reported more behavioral problems at the all-yoga compared with the half yoga schools, including incidents of bullying ($p = .01$) and detentions ($p = .05$).3
- Although school personnel perceived yoga as decreasing absenteeism, quantitative data shows that unexcused absences ($p = .05$) increased more over the course of the year at the all-year than the half-year yoga schools.4
- Although school personnel perceived yoga as motivating students to try harder, students at half-year yoga schools reported "trying harder" than did all-year students ($p = 0.05$).
- Contrary to perceptions by administrators, teachers, and parents that yoga enhanced emotional well-being (for instance by "self-calming"), student survey data showed a slight decline (3.25 to 3.20) in sense of belonging over the course of the school year.
- In sum, the study did not show that yoga caused any observed improvements. "The level of rigor commonly associated with an RCT [randomized controlled trial] could not be achieved. Thus, it would be irresponsible to assert causal inferences related to yoga participation."5

Resources on analysis of CEPAL study:

1 CEPAL, *Yoga in Public Schools: Evidence from the Encinitas Union School District's Yoga Program 2012-2013*, January 30, 2014), retrieved June 1, 2016, https://www.sandiego.

edu/soles/documents/EUSD%20Yoga%20Student%20
Effects%20201213%20Formattedforwebsite.pdf; CEPAL,
*Implementing Yoga in Public Schools: Evidence from the
Encinitas Union School District's Pilot Yoga Program 2012-
2013*, November 8, 2013, retrieved June 1, 2016, http://
www.sandiego.edu/soles/documents/cepal/CEPAL%20
Report_Implementing%20Yoga_2013%20%202014.pdf.

2 CEPAL, *Yoga in Public Schools*, 22, 21.

3 A CEPAL research brief on the 2013-2014 yoga program
isolated a subgroup of 101 (out of 768) fifth graders who
reported "being teased by other kids or feeling left out or
rejected," and found that 57% (58/101) improved their
"ability to self-regulate" and "adapt to" bullying (which did
not seem to decrease) over the course of the school year. As
the investigators acknowledge, "because this analysis did
not include a control group, this finding cannot be directly
attributed to EUSD yoga participation." See *CEPAL,
Encinitas Union School District Health & Wellness Program
2013-14 Research Brief, January 21, 2015*, retrieved June
1, 2016, http://www.sonimafoundation.org/wpcontent/
uploads/2015/01/CEPAL-Y2-Briefing-2015.01.21.pdf.

4 A CEPAL research brief on the 2013-2014 yoga program
sliced up the data to suggest that "students who participated
in highly rated yoga experiences attended school more regularly"—but this seems to be a correlational rather than a
causal finding; in other words, the same types of students
who "liked" yoga more (generally younger girls) may also
have had qualities that made them more likely to attend
school regularly. 5 CEPAL, *Yoga in Public Schools*,

Photos of Baird and Himelstein

Photos of Baird and Himelstein in Venice at a conference called mlearn were posted by Katie Martin, October of 2015. Baird is also in a photo that has surfaced, on the stairs of a large cruise ship with various Sonima folks and others, spotted by these new investigating parents. Back row sixth from right you can see Baird with a big smile and Himelstein.

Baird and Himelstein on a cruise ship, back row, 6th from right

This provides more than enough proof of the personal relationships between EUSD, the Cepal Study and Sonima. Baird admitted knowing Himelstein prior to yoga, in the article you just read, and evidenced by the Ipad introduction into EUSD. Himelstein was the man doing the study at CEPAL for Sonima Foundation, holds the current curriculum for Sonima, and this further links them as "entanglement on steroids" as Dean Broyles mentioned in court. Traveling for Sonima Foundation together to speak about the yoga success in EUSD, is a perk that is now evidence of them together, and both serving on the Sonima board. And these are only two of the many examples. We have several more, but didn't have enough proof back in 2013, nor were many items permissible to the court.

Not a great photo, so look online to find who speaks at events together.
Pictured are Deepak Chopra, Stedman Graham, Terry Grier, Scott Himelstein,
David Miyishiro, Timothy Baird, the same cast of characters ... .

Let's see who's on this panel of speakers? — remember in court—
"entanglement on steroids!"

What Is the Truth Behind the Lies?

No Informed consent from 5600 parents of kids being studied in 2012?

Truth in Advertising?

Truth in Reports about the Cepal Study?

Why won't EUSD call it Ashtanga yoga when it clearly is, by definition?

Why won't EUSD even call it yoga?

Why did Himelstein create at least three organizations all funded by Sonima?

Why did Sonima move their yoga curriculum to a Scott Himelstein website? Since he did the study, doesn't this show *clear* conflict of interest?

And on and on ... When will people see the truth?

EUSD Still using Sound, Vibrations, and Meditating

The District said they pulled Sanskrit and movements out of the yoga program and told yoga teachers not to do certain things such as: We won't draw mandalas, we won't say Namaste. We won't say OM, we won't meditate. But what do the EUSD yoga classes look like today? Are they still cleaned up?

Kids reportedly fall asleep in yoga. How is that possible? (This is supposed to be exercise, right?) The answer is meditation. Guided meditation in use of words from the yoga instructors, leading kids on a pathway into themselves at the "cooldown" part of class "to relax" is the stated purpose. Bells are used in traditional Hindu format to signal what to do next. So, the reality is that what the district promised in court wouldn't happen in yoga, is still happening.

Photos tell the story better. These photos were taken at La Costa Heights Elementary yoga studio. After five years of yoga in the schools and EUSD stating in court it isn't really doing Ashtanga yoga, there still remained the Ashtanga opening sequence on the wall. Photos of the kids doing poses are still posted, including the banned poses in the US for health reasons (straight knee stretches). The worship bells are still in use. Added are now crystals by the doorway in a prominently positioned display. Crystals in the yoga rooms now, one has to ask: Why?

Photos by author at La Costa Heights Elementary, 2015

Sonima continues to spread Ashtanga yoga throughout the country. Here are two examples of their teaching and reaching. They still mean business. EUSD was just the first stop.

News:

1.   Sharath on Tour http://ayny.org/event/sharath-jois-us-tour/[16]

Sharath on Tour, public promotional photos http://ayny.org/event/
sharath-jois-us-tour/

2. Sonima on Tour http://www.sonima.com/about/tour/[17]

Stedman Graham speaking for Sonima with Paul and Sonia Tudor Jones's Daughter teaching kids

3. Government initiatives to make International Yoga Fest a "mass movement," March 2017: https://www.aninews. in/news/national/politics/govt-for-initiatives-to-make-international-yoga-fest-a-039mass-movement039/[18]

4. Paul Tudor Jones purchased a $71 Million dollar estate: http://www.cnbc.com/2015/04/01/paul-tudor-jones-buys-71-million-palm-beach-estate.html[19]

Chopra Foundation speakers listed on website, 2017:

What Next?

For now, we are watching, waiting, writing, and revealing to the public what EUSD and Sonima are up to as a result of continuing yoga in the elementary schools in Encinitas. Sonima has been drastically changing their website, and you can hardly find children on there anymore, unless you dig to deeper pages and take the link over to—oh what's this? We find it is Scott Himelstein's new yoga curriculum site http://pureedgeinc.org/,[20] which, oh, by coincidence, matches the EUSD yoga curriculum "on the mat." Hidden? A new name, a new website: Why? Here is the link above, but by the time you read this book you might need to look at our website instead to find the new link, because they change their links frequently (both EUSD and Sonima), and we have to keep finding them. "A moving target," Broyles once said in court, and that has become an understatement of the truth!

CHAPTER TWENTY-FOUR

Summary

The Children need us to take a look

I would guess most parents simply want to trust our school boards and administrators, and not have to worry about their decisions. Some *might* vote and select them, but most parents stop there. Most parents have never entered a monthly board meeting, nor have any idea what their Superintendent and staff really do on a daily basis. *Safety on campus* and *effective curriculum* are the top concerns for most parents. For the first 9 years of my children's public education, I gave full trust to the board and couldn't even name one board member if asked. I commend those who are active in watching, voting and keeping a check on school boards everywhere. That wasn't me. Only when yoga was introduced for 2/3 of our PE time and Karate was the other 1/3, did I begin to question the decisions of our principal and district. What I found was so appalling, and so much worse than I ever dreamed.

The facts awakened me to keep looking further as shown in this book; to keep digging into what the superintendent selected and the board accepted for our children. Ironically, the "teachings" of yoga have a similar effect to what happens to the parents in "following" district decisions without questioning them. Yoga teaches children to be "followers," to empty their minds and relax more by lying on a mat (in PE, mind you), rather than to question or be alert to the world around them, but to "go inside" and allow guidance through a visual tour by the yoga teacher. Kids started "falling asleep" *on the mat* – during PE!!!

The goal was to "de-stress" through stretching, forced breathing, and meditation rather than traditional activities where kids used to de-stress by running around and doing something a little more active for their hearts. Running, jumping, kicking and traditional PE games gave them the muscle-building and stamina naturally, along with heavy breathing to exert energy as a reaction to their exercising. No need for "forced breathing" or meditating as a technique. Is "one size fits all" really applicable in PE? What if we only did, say softball, 60 minutes a week for 7 years? So religiousness was never the *only* issue with yoga. It was just that *Separation of Church and State* and *mandatory PE minutes* were two of the laws being broken.

PE is fun!

Standing up in this trial was not easy, nor were our actions ever for personal gain. It was not for our children, but for the "other" ~ 5998 children in the district (and all American children potentially, given the Jois Yoga mission). And now it's apparent, that maybe even children in India and other countries watching. Our children were protected. We pulled them out of the curriculum before it started in our school, so our involvement wasn't for our own kids. They lost PE time though, for years. My son went to a computer lab with another class for the lost hour of PE the entire spring semester of 2013. For four years our daughter received less than the state requirement of hours for 200 minutes of biweekly PE. She went into a computer lab that spring with another class, and other years she was given an Ipad by herself in a room, or in another class sitting in the back with basically nothing to do. But, we gladly gave up those hours of PE (knowing our kids would get their exercise outside the school day) *in order to* stand firm on the unfolding issue–allowing a highly religious organization (Jois/Sonima Foundation) to buy into the school district to teach our children "their spiritual programs."

On their website, Sonima was crystal clear that Ashtanga yoga is their religion and plainly stated their objective to evangelize through the US elementary school system. How was this ignored by the Superintendent and EUSD board? We showed them. We warned them. And what did the principals at the schools think about yoga? They dare not speak up on their opinions for fear of job loss. Did thousands of dollars influence the administrator's focus? Why, after dozens, and then hundreds of parents questioning this for four months of board meetings and growing community concerns, (with stacks of information and a petition), did the board not look at these websites and see the truth in the agenda of the Jois Foundation? Instead, the Superintendent began to "scrub" (his words) the yoga and eventually rename it. This reveals that they did see issues, but were they unable to back out by then? Were they in too deep?

Follow Me

"EUSD yoga" (the term they coined in the middle of the trial in June, 2013) is to this day still identical to the mandatory opening sequencing of moves in Ashtanga, the Jois trademark. Children's memorization of weekly sequences (which are sun worship poses to particular gods, whether the children know it or not) and to "empty their minds," all followed the pathway laid out on the Sonima program for Ashtanga yoga. The children were to follow. And they have. Seven years now. Spiritual and physical consequences occurred sooner than the former yogis predicted.

When the former yogis contacted us to boldly warn us, we were surprised. They claimed: "If these children do the Ashtanga worship poses repeatedly, the children will unknowingly invite the spirits in, and spirits *will* come." And they *will* eventually torment children. *And this has unfortunately begun,* as reported in previous chapters: tormented children from unsuspecting parents, who then reached out to us, not knowing where else to go. This was, by far, the part that was beyond my comprehension prior to learning about yoga. When yogi after yogi called to report what happened with them after years of yoga, one cannot deny testimony after testimony of unrelated people, warning us about the potential consequences to the children in the future. After much research, this became a driving force of needing to protect these children beyond what the eye could see. The Ex-yogis warned us to keep fighting this until it is removed from the schools. We will. We are not gone just because the law suit is over. We are a band of people who believe what is happening is wrong and against our freedoms, crossing over the separation of religion and state. But more importantly: potentially dangerous. Does the anger and wrath that has escalated in the world today have anything to do with people doing yoga the past few years? Silent and deceptive as yoga can be for a while – very few have probably considered that option. The only way a "one world religion" could happen is if people don't know it's a religion.

Yoga and Anger

A peek into escalating wrath of people doing yoga – ponder this example: a sister killed her twin and no one probably thought much about this fact, except those of us who have researched yoga—the girls were yoga studio owners together. What drew this woman to kill her own twin sister? Yogis claim that spirits could have led her to this. Here is just one of the articles and most discuss the twins' escalating arguments the longer they had the studio together: http://www.palmbeachpost.com/news/crime-law/bail-denied-for-yoga-studio-owner-accused-sister-death/ZEBtrowNC3DkOFRmTIYoeK/.[1] One stop on google gives you many articles on this twin's case, but I'm pretty sure not *any* make the connection to yoga. Silent and deceptive as yoga can be—very few have probably considered these consequences. "No religious winners" in school is the law, and yet, yoga is winning a spot in the curriculum. Are the children worth our time to seek the truth and defend them?

We explored many of these issues in this book. Provided were some of the basics: the trial, the awakening of parents in the district as problems became evident, the Jois/Sonima Foundation that donated over $4 million to this one district and multiple others already. The contracts between the district, the foundation and their "middleman" formed the way they wanted to "appear" (Regur Development), and many concerns and facts found along the way.

Much has been revealed through our research. We created the website to see the many concerns of hundreds of people around the globe (www.truthaboutyoga.com).[2] People from many countries have contacted us with knowledge, with stories of injury and that yoga can become a path to suicide, and with grave concern. The deaths are a hidden, dirty little secret, until you talk to the friends and families who have experienced losing their loved ones from following yoga. Much more is connected here than you ever dreamed, or cared to consider. But it can no longer be ignored. It's not just a matter of exercise; it can be life and death for some.

Yoga Growing Exponentially

It's been 7 school years of children in Encinitas praying in the yoga style at school, and much is changing in Encinitas. More religious programs are entering the schools with agendas of a similar bent. When reviewing any of these new programs, go directly to the board biographies to see the similarities in what they are promoting in "New Age" religion. Various school districts across the country have jumped on board with Sonima Foundation (formerly Jois) in states such as Virginia, Texas, and New York. Our own EUSD Superintendent who swore under oath that he wasn't comingled with Sonima, actually, in reality; sat on the Sonima board of directors, was in photos on cruises and other "conference" trips, revealing the truth. See the famous other folks sitting on that board and their common interests such as Stedman Graham (Oprah), Deepok Chopra, Scott Himilstein and more. Some of the truth has still not been revealed yet. It was quashed by a judge, himself practicing Bikram yoga, who allowed himself also to be swayed much more by public opinion, than by the facts sitting right in front of him, which he would claim were "troubling." This was a highly publicized case in other countries and across ours. Law schools across the U.S. are analyzing this case, as shown. Health and Wellness seminars across the globe are talking about yoga and the trial and still disagreeing about what it all means.

The subject is here to stay. Therefore, *we are here to stay* to educate people on the deceptions and realities of yoga and the dangerous potential consequences for children to be subject to this as curriculum for all of elementary school, becoming the "norm" in their lives.

Yoga is not "what you see is what you get" in America advertising. If you look for the yogis who have been doing yoga for over 20 years, you'd see the contortionist look with hip and knee replacements and emaciated bodies rather than the healthy photos that are luring Americans to yoga. There are many versions of yoga, and as adults, we can choose to do whatever we want. This book is about children with *no choice and no voice*. This is about farming our children (ages 5 to 12) into a funnel toward an ideology that will shape their "worldview" for life. Yoga will become "second nature," sliding kids toward Hinduism and Buddhism. The fact that teachers, administrators and parents are endorsing it (even by saying nothing and not questioning it in the curriculum), is leading the children straight down a path of acceptance. It has become just "part of the normal day" with all the authority figures in their life accepting it. Why would kids question it? *But they did*. Many kids alerted their parents that something seemed wrong. Many kids spurred their own parents to research yoga. Which kids? Usually Christians, which goes to prove what? Could it be that there is a spiritual battle going on for the souls of our children?

This was not an optional program in Encinitas; this is mandatory with the exception that later you could *opt-out* your children, just like you can opt-out of math if you really want to do so. But there is still harm and there are consequences. Children don't get a PE replacement for yoga at every school. In our daughter's case, she had to do paperwork that is yoga and health-related while sitting in a room by herself or in another classroom where she is "on display" as one of the *opt-outs*. She sat with her Ipad, playing games when she finished what the opted-out kids now call "the packet." In some of the schools, the packet isn't utilized. The standards are not consistent across the 9 schools, something our group of parents would continue to uncover over the months and now years. We communicate as a group across the schools, and we report how the district and each school are operating and what they are implementing either as a whole or per school. There are many other "issues consuming our district (Ipad retinal screening, Common Core math, Ipad insurance money kept by district, Steven Covey *leader in me* program that is secretly also biased in one religion, Sexualized *sex education* , and more...). We have even found websites from previous parents in the district, concerned about other issues that were not responded adequately to, from the district. And to go to the length of making a website is no small task! And yet, yoga was one of the most heated issues, given the *spiritual nature* of yoga.

Yoga Battle over in Encinitas?

Keeping yoga on the front burner of issues, is our job for now, and many of us are committed to getting yoga out of the curriculum of elementary schools. More families keep leaving Encinitas school District (EUSD) and yet are still very active in helping to get yoga out. Length of time the program is in place does not make it right, only accepted...accepted by folks who don't know or don't care enough to research and respond to the warnings. Sadly, inaction is in support of this program. We live in a fast-paced, busy world and many of us are good people who want our kids to "fit in" and "not be embarrassed" or to "go with the flow"– which is fully understandable, but at times like this, faulty and might be dangerous. Once you see what is behind the program and the agendas of the Superintendent and the Sonima Foundation, we hope you are as alarmed and will do whatever you are led to do as a result.

Yoga for kids weekly in school is concerning enough to spend precious time writing this book about what really happened and what is still happening. And it's spreading. Yoga has taken America by storm. It's important to sit back on your mat and ask why? Why are we so crazy for yoga? What is it replacing or doing for us? We needed to be more relaxed? More fit? Do we have some gaping holes in our emotional wellness? We live in an addictive society, and this obsession seems better than many others... (Like workaholism?) and yet, we haven't really looked at where it leads, just at the short-term benefits. While writing this book, I have watched the demise of many older teens to a world of legalizing pot. "The world is going to pot," my grandma used to say, she was prophetic, I suppose. The pros of yoga cannot outweigh being led to places never intended. Innocent kids led astray when thinking they are doing something healthy. Again, the trial and our active efforts focus on the children who cannot choose. This book, however, is for the parents and public citizens making decisions for our children by allowing yoga, choosing it, or by standing aside, saying "I don't have time to look into it." Remember, the fences around schools are to protect. They are built by adults, not children.

We get why people stood by watching yoga enter.

So we did the research for you.

Reading this book and our website for the facts of the case is a start. Our family is not standing alone in all this, and the group will stand firm against yoga in our schools because we know that it is spiritual and not just stretching. So do many others. We may be up against what seems to be bureaucracy and big money and "the systems." What we have gone through personally as a group of parents fighting for our rights and for the children all across the U.S. is small compared to the potential long-term dangerous consequences. We sacrificed our own personal time and agendas to stand up against the larger agenda that is making it's money off converting all these children into followers to come to their studios. Now, we are simply showing you the conflicting and biased agendas, resource links, and perspectives we have located (or stumbled across, at times), just as you could have.

I can see why people think yoga might be "fine". Parents teaching PE is normal here due to school budgets. An occasional yoga class was no problem to most. It was when this India-derived organization offered millions to have access to test our children and teach them their form of yoga, that we had to stop and look at what is happening when an outside organization can buy into a school district. Yoga became regular curriculum over-night, replacing kickball, baseball, and all the PE games kids used to learn in elementary schools here in the US. That has changed here and in at least 7 districts in US (940 schools last reported), as this book is being published. How will America change in its base of competition and economic competition when now the only "sport" taught is yoga in elementary schools?

The advertising of yoga pictured here in the Houston Airport in 2013 causes everyone to begin to feel "yoga is a norm" now… "go to a happy place" was the saying and attempts to normalize kids and a business woman in a suit sitting with eyes closed in spiritual hand positions promoting yoga *in the airport*! Was this a "play" on the busy-ness of an airport?

Photo taken by a friend traveling in Houston, Texas Airport, 2013

We have to wake up and look at yoga as required curriculum in schools, otherwise it will continue to spread quickly to a district near YOU. In 7 short years all the children who do yoga from K-6 will create us into a yoga nation! I wouldn't even want that for, say, basketball, which is not religious at all. There is no term "holy basketball" and yet, we wouldn't want that to be the "chosen sport" weekly for 7 years either, and not *any* one PE activity, would we? This has to stop, and we hoped to stop it before it started to spread nationally, but the train has left the station and we need more people across this country to wake up and stand against what is happening in the public schools. The answer is not to leave the schools, but that is what is happening at an alarming rate. Over 20% of the San Diego Unified School District has left for "Charter Schools" according to the latest news and statistics. This is causing problems for districts losing funds. And the district officials are scratching their heads and don't know *why*...

If we leave, we only help our own children. Our aim is to help *all the children*. That is why you are reading this book. The future lies in your hands.

CHAPTER TWENTY FIVE

Signs of Hope

As I began to pray about how I would wrap up this book I started to see signs. No, literally – everywhere I went I would see signs ... that said "Hope." Sometimes things are all around us, but the moment we are supposed to see them, they come into focus. I'm sure there are always items with the word Hope on them in my path, but I hadn't noticed them prior to seeking the final message of the book. I'd walk into Ross or TJ Maxx and there would be a plaque or trinket with Hope inscribed. You've probably seen them. The word just kept popping out to me. The last straw was when we were house hunting and I peeked over a fence to see the largest HOPE sign I've ever seen. It is a church with HOPE in gigantic letters. This was a clear message to me that the last chapter would be about that, *Hope*.

Not my hope, nor your hope, but the source of Hope. Without hope, we go to dark places. The hopeless are worse off than the homeless. When we lose hope as a human, our lives spiral out of control. We are united by the fact that we need some sort of hope in something to put one foot forward. We are wired for hope. From a newborn who responds to his mother and father's voice and touch, we know there is hope. From people that are barely conscious responding to a person's voice or touch, we recognize hope matters. Hope draws and pushes us forward. Without hope we are lost, aimless, and at worst, destructive.

Hanging on to Hope

I watched my brother spend over 30 years in a nursing home and what kept him going every day, was hope. I have no idea how, but he had hope in a new day and finding something to have hope for each day. With severe Multiple Sclerosis, he couldn't feed himself, he couldn't walk, talk or lift his arms on his own any longer. But he somehow had hope. He was a fighter and he wanted to live to see as much and as long as he could. He met all three of my children and enjoyed any time with us when we visited. He listened to his favorite music from his high school days after he lost the ability to see a TV show. His mom lived there in town near him to bring meals and visit. His father and stepmother visited every quarter for his lifetime. Extended family visited and although his daily life wasn't much on the scale you might have, his life was full. Full of *hope*. Michael passed away in May of 2014 during the appellate trial level. I share this because you can see that our lives marched on as well, with weddings, funerals, kids' sports, schooling, work, travel, family and holidays. We lived through the elections of 2016 just like you. We are watching fake news and protests just like you. Our world is turned upside down when we view that something isn't going how we want. But the reactions we are seeing display a new level of unacceptability and lack of tolerance. Everyone wants hope that everything will be okay. Once you have the peace that it will be okay – you calm down. Sometimes, like in this journey with yoga in schools, you can't see the change yet, but if you continue with hope, you can walk through each day making the difference needed while balancing your own day. I've learned a lot about patience.

One hope I have is that *you* might be more aware with this book about some of the unseen dangers lurking in yoga. If yoga causes anger like many of the former yogi's claim – then maybe we ought to watch the anger levels to measure the impact of yoga. Read the former yogi stories since there are many experts in this topic, not I. I give you the foundation here to spring into many other places to look for the reality and global issues that are happening. Don't take my word for any of it. I can easily say that because I've done a lot of research. I see the connections. I know they exist when you look. I didn't go seeking much in the beginning beyond: what is yoga and why did Jois foundation want all of our children in this three year study so badly that they would give money and require yoga twice weekly in schools? In researching that, I found so much more… as you have read.

Seven years of yoga in elementary – what is the impact?

The answers to that research were alarming from the beginning, starting with what the Jois Foundation claims and mission for the future were on their website. We took them at face value of their words: they wanted to be in every elementary school in the United States.

Why does Jois Foundation want *every child practicing yoga weekly,* in the U.S. in grades K-6th? Seven years of yoga (foundational…). Why? I would learn it was not an accident or coincidence, but a strategy. Every child will walk out of elementary school with the notion that yoga is just a normal part of life. One generation prior very few kids ever did yoga. Supported by our government, supported by our schools, and supported by our parents (because they didn't question it, so in turn are endorsing it) so - why would we expect anything but a yoga nation in one decade? Since we are in the seventh year of that now in Encinitas schools, this year the kids graduating from 6th grade will have done yoga weekly for seven years (minus summers). What impact does that have on these kids – will anyone ask? I bet there's no surveys done by EUSD.

Centered? Peaceful? If only those words were the reality after yoga, that would be wonderful. Self-centered and angry is the true result for many people in yoga, and they don't see it until they stop and reflect on their lives and how it has "shifted." As the ex-yogis spoke and wrote about, their reactions got worse over time. The years of seduction into yoga and the cult-like behaviors of the leaders and followers slowly became apparent to many of them willing to share their stories. Reading their blogs, articles and books you can see years lost to a path they never intended. For those reading this book, if any parents in Encinitas district pick this up, how is your child behaving after 7 years of yoga? Just asking.

Austria bans yoga from school for religious reasons

https://www.upi.com/Odd_News/2014/10/09/ Austrian-school-bans-yoga-for-religious-reasons/9621412879176/

https://www.nbcsandiego.com/news/local/Yoga-Lawsuit-Encinitas-Judgment- Ruling-School-Class-Controversy-213853341.html#ixzz2XrSK81Zt

Why isn't America looking? Why aren't we listening? We're like a teenager with headphones on to tune the world out for a while. Our culture is tuning out. Numbing out. Numbing the pain, and numbing reality. Are we closing our eyes and following a lead without really knowing who we follow?

Shall we cover our eyes and run?

Massive turnout for first International yoga day, India Newsroom, June 2015

488

Or shall we take a look and ask questions?

Most of us have an innate desire to help others to some degree. For some it might only be during an emergency. There are displays of this splashed all over our culture and have nothing to do with the faith we choose. People of no belief in a higher power may even be serving the poor and helping to build homes, etc. The world has needs. Most of us do our part to help anywhere we can regardless of our faith choices. It is innate in most of us, if not impacted otherwise by abuse, drugs, starvation or other extreme intervening issues on a life. We are born with some spiritual needs and desires and we exercise them differently.

How Did We Get Here?

Three problems and likely many more led to yoga in schools. 1. Financial cuts and decisions for schools to not offer full time PE teachers. 2. Obesity and childhood health issues. 3. Spiritual holes in lives of those that see "religion" as too rigid, but have a desire for a spiritual experience. As we've discussed, some states have likely cut more PE than others, but in our schools PE was taught by every teacher vs. trained and qualified teachers which led to further issues of keeping good PE teachers when they weren't paid much nor got many hours. So turnover of PE teachers, parents filling in for PE and teachers who are full time teachers without a passion for PE were teaching physical education. Across the country there are problems in pockets with obesity starting younger and younger and the need to focus on nutrition and exercise is nothing new, but obesity has escalated from previous decades. There are many solutions to obesity and it is being addressed by many, but yoga so far does not appear to be the solution as evidenced by even the very studies Sonima solicited. Stretching and flexibility simply aren't the biggest needs of a 5, 6 and 8 year old on up to 12 years-old. They need to run and jump and climb and be active as our former PE programs supported. Stretching is a good thing *before during, or after exercise*...but it isn't a *main exercise* as noted in many articles linked for you in this book. When financial difficulties meet obesity issues, stretching is not the solution from a physical standpoint. Add in the spiritual component and parents wanting something "less competitive" for their children and of course something like yoga looks more inviting. Who was most interested in their children doing yoga in schools?

It's the women!

Women are doing yoga in record numbers in our country now. I'd guess almost 1/2 of the women in any group setting have either tried or are doing yoga actively each week. When first considering how yoga entered the churches, what popped into my head was "It's the women." Children aren't initiating yoga in schools or churches. Men certainly aren't the ones in churches pursuing a yoga class addition – "it's the women." That thought made me realize yoga would always come into churches through women's efforts and ministry on into the children's.

So what is it that women feel they are missing spiritually to want to add yoga or any exercise into the church walls? Even though this book is primarily about schools, this is an important question to many people with whom I talk to about yoga. They point out a spiritual "hole" is what may be leading many away from "traditional methods" to *shiny new looking* "spirituality." This delves into a whole other research project in itself, but it's something I've thought about a lot along the way since the churches began getting involved with yoga.

Yoga is not only knocking on the door of churches but into youth sports at an alarming rate, professional sports, high schools now adding it as well as preschools and colleges. I have responded to calls from coaches across the US concerned because yoga is being added to many sports without the consent of the immediate coaches, nor the parents. I just talked to a friend yesterday who said she suggested to the head coach to give the day off to the kids as a reward and instead she walked into a gym all set up for yoga the following day by the head coach. Some of the kids walked out and so did she. She's been on this journey too long to even be in the room. There are moments in this battle where retreat without saying a word is needed. Then later we are equipped with exactly how to get a message to the person who needs to hear it, in God's timing, not our own.

Yoga is entering the churches at a staggering rate, too, so it is important to think about this topic for pastors and church leaders. Keep asking why until you see clear answers. I'm hoping to help you with this book, to even to ask the questions and start to see how yoga is infiltrating so many areas of life and consider the answers to: why?

Called to warn others?

Yoga in schools is part of the fabric of our story now. So much that it has turned our lives upside down and become a full time job for me for a while. Not a job I would have sought. Not a job that pays me money. Not a job that has any glory but usually ridicule from others. But a job I ended up finding worth doing and a job in which I know that God has called me to do my part. Many of us have learned just to follow God's lead and do the part given to us. No more and no less. My part is to help warn about the potential dangers and to spread the love of God the best I can to those in my path. I have no idea who will be reading this book, nor is it my business to worry about that. It was clear I was to write it and the rest will take care of itself. That is not the human way of thinking for most of us, but it's a trust beyond understanding today where this is all headed. A trust I have grown into through standing in the fire. A trust I wouldn't have known if I sat on the middle of the fence or jumped to the side of "I don't want to get involved." Nope, that won't get you to the side of trust. I've been there and it was more like regret, missed opportunities and pulling myself out of a pit I'd slipped into somehow. The middle of the fence doesn't seem like an option any longer these days for most people either. Seems one could sit there for years and many still do – but lately the world is changing fast and it would appear to me that there is becoming "forced choice" rather than sitting lukewarm as an ongoing option.

Questions for further consideration

Q: If you do yoga, is the yoga you are doing leading anyone else astray into a yoga that is a problem for them spiritually?

Q: Is yoga taking your thoughts off God and onto yourself?

Q: Are you meditating on things of The Lord or are you concerned with your health, your body, your breathing?

Q: Is there any alternative that could give you the same health benefits, the same or more cardio work to meet your health goals?

Q: Does yoga lead some people away from Christianity?

Q: What do the ex-yogis say yoga did for them?

Q: Why did so many yoga teachers turn to Christianity and start speaking out about yoga as a cult. Occult?

Q: Why is talking about yoga in schools and churches so divisive if it is not spiritual?

Q: Where does the divisiveness come from?

If it were merely physical – like, say, whether to play soccer or not - then the controversy is low. The divisiveness is low. The issue is preference, not morality. Take away the morality issues and there is no argument in the validity of the choice.

Q: When is a form of "exercise" or a spiritual path to Hinduism?

Q: What is Hinduism? If you don't know what Hindu's believe, how do you know you aren't on that path in yoga when you don't know what to look for?

Q: Would you go into a YMCA, sit in a class on Islamic 5 pillars and consider it not religious because it is offered at the Y? No, of course not. Just because the Y offers it, doesn't mean it's void of spirituality...

Q: What is the difference between students studying something and physically acting it out?

Q: Is there a difference to you?

Q: How do we make ourselves as Christians a holy and living sacrifice to The Lord?

Q: What does that mean to you if you are not a Christian? Nothing right? Or does it annoy or anger you a little when you read it?

Q: What does it mean to stay away from things that are not holy?

Q: What does it mean to confess when we touch and choose things that are not holy so we can be back in the presence of God?

Q: What sacrifices do we make for The Lord?

Q: Are they really sacrifices when we see how much better our lives go?

Q: What sacrifice did The Lord make for us?

Q: What sacrifices are made on our behalf from others?

Q: As a parent do you sacrifice your time to teach and take care of your children?

Q: Do you weigh the costs and choose to sacrifice anyway.

We are wired to sacrifice.
We are wired to love and seek truth.
We are wired to want love and thrive on love.
We are wired to want to know.
We are wired to think and figure and count and decipher.
We are wired to grow.
We are wired to avoid pain.
We are wired to avoid death.
We are wired to fix things, clean things up, make things new again or buy new things.
We are wired to worship.

We all worship something

If we don't worship God, we worship something: such as sports, musicians, actors, food, drink or drugs, and, other people. We worship and dance. We love to move. We thrive to move. We are wired to worship. We are given the choice, and the freedom to choose. What to worship? Where to go? What to do? We give our teens a little bit of freedom, but not the freedom The Lord gives us. No we don't trust our teen enough yet, until they prove themselves. We don't want to let the full reigns out yet. But God did. He wants us to trust Him. He trusted us with this decision. He gave us freedom to learn to love Him, rather than demand that we love him. And we can't force a teen to like us while they are trying to separate from us, by nature and timing.

Surrender

A new level of surrender to live fully for Jesus came for me along with the call to stand up against mandatory yoga in the schools. That decision took me off the fence, highlighted that I was a Christian to many folks I'd known for years that most likely didn't know. It was a turning point for being "all in" on God's plans for my life. I had to choose to *surrender* my husband, my children, my job, my daily life, my pride and my plans. My life would change dramatically and our security, privacy and safety would change. But I still knew it was right, even when forces came against us quickly and hard, opposing us and setting us back. That made it clearer we were on the right path, that something wasn't quite right. A lot of people and things gave us insight to knowing it was the right decision.

When former yogis that called to tell us to fight this for the children, that it was evil and demonic, that was new news to us. Yoga-loving-folks came out of the woodwork stabbing comments at us on email, voicemail, on blogs, and even to our faces through friends (doing yoga). The common denominator - already hooked on yoga. The "hook" that draws you in is so very innocent and "healthy-seeming". The deception is effective and the blindness to the issues and problems runs deep for most people caught in the wave of the yoga they so dearly love already. They can't get enough (most sports you can). They want more and more. Claim no spirituality, but it's not like other exercise, it is spiritual, and only when one wants to see it will they be open to look. Truth always surfaces over time. That is why I can say what I'm saying in truth and love. I can rest in the joy of knowing and recognizing that no matter where someone is in their path of yoga, there will be enlightenment one way or another and if warned, then the choice is truly theirs, to live out any consequences, good or bad, of their choices.

In addition, I've been on my knee's, grateful that doing yoga passed by me - I could have *easily* fallen into yoga at various points in my life. I didn't know there was anything wrong with yoga and I almost did it several times in my older years. After 45, yoga looked a lot more attractive than high impact workouts. I am thankful I only did it once. I am thankful that I have been entrusted with this knowledge and can help to alert others who have ears to hear and eyes to see. That is not everyone. Some will read this book and not just disagree, but actually spew hate at me, yet I am not afraid of that any longer. Courage and trust come from The Lord. Fear and confusion are from his fallen angel. I refuse to be afraid of his tactics and schemes. Satan is not the winner, and I am not on his team. I will look to Jesus as my role model of how to live this life, how to love others, how to serve one another (like driving boys to a tournament in Vegas when other parents think I'm way too nice), and how to praise and worship God, even when the world is turning upside down and mocking Him, even when the trend is to hate Christians.

Not Afraid

There are 375 scriptures in the bible telling us "do not fear." Through Christ, I am now not afraid. Not afraid to write this book. If it helps just ONE person, it was worth my time. It wasn't my time anyway - it was the Lords. I am His. I am surrendered to His will for my life and I am at peace and forgiveness and operating as best as I can in His love. I still get frustrated, prideful, sinful in my mind or sometimes actions, say things I shouldn't say to or about someone, get competitive, lose my cool, and give bad advice at times or bad role modeling to my own kids.

However, every day I make the attempt to trade God's courage for my fear, God's love for my anger, God's encouragement for my disappointments, God's forgiveness for my judgements, God's grace and mercy for my condemnation, God's plans for my plans, God's peace for my worries, and God's unconditional love for my weaker love. The "great trade" I heard it called once. If I read His word every morning and study what Jesus came and did for us and the Old Testament of fallen people with God's grace, I can make the great trade for one day. Then the next morning the bible says is a "new start" and I can make the trade again. Every day I get better at dropping my garbage and picking up his sweet bread. But it's not about performance; it's about learning who God is and what He is like. It's about becoming more like Him, while walking with Him. The more like Him I become, the more the others around me think I'm kind, but it isn't me. It is He. I'm the judgmental, scared, worried little girl behind his great cross and cloak. It is He you see in me, if you see anything good. If you see pride, that's me, if you see anger, that's me, if you hear bad words out of my mouth, that's me. But if you hear sweetness and encouragement, that is He. If you hear thoughtfulness and generosity, that is He too. He, replacing parts of me.

The great trade each day is the best I know to do. Each day the manna is provided and it is sour by the next day if we don't make the trade again. Repentance is available, Mercy is there and forgiveness to us when we do. I'm so grateful we can repent and be heard. We can choose Christ anytime, no matter what our sins. Sin separates us from God. Repentance joins us back to God. Wisdom is given after surrender. After the decision, then what is written in the Bible all of a sudden miraculously makes sense, when before, the words were confusing and unmemorable.

No sin is too big. No sinner is too far gone. Satan would have us think that thought - he will jump all over us to keep us down. He will invade your mind with "stinking thinking" as long and as hard as he can. He will use his angels (demons) of depression and suppression, doubt and confusion, guilt and disappointment, fear and worry, insecurity and wonder, anger and disrespect, negative self-talk and disillusionment, attraction to "zoning out" or running away, of leaving your life and giving up. Satan is the master of deception and he is out to steal, kill and destroy. And he is good at it. In "The Case for Grace," by Lee Stroebel, each chapter is about a different person who endured a major story of sin and living caught in lies they did not know they lived in, nor could get out to avoid the sin and the consequences. Satan is good at deception. That is why the bible says over and over, especially for *end times* - "Do not be deceived." Pray not to be deceived and watch what happens!

How do you know if you are being deceived? If you know, then you aren't deceived, right? You know someone is trying, but you aren't deceived by their attempts. However, how do you know if you *are* being deceived? You don't. You don't think you are, and you don't see it. How do you find out or at least "look into it?" Really, *how?*

Some would include private investigators and surveillance, following others to find deception. How does a Christian find out if they are being deceived? Read, pray and ask. Ask to be shown. In one of the chapters of *Case for Grace*, I was reading while in a Las Vegas hotel room (yet another basketball tournament for the boys) very early one Sunday morning. The chapter ended up was about a church in Vegas (do you think that is coincidence?) so I got up and found that the church was just *four miles* away, so I went that morning to meet the man in the chapter. Ironically he was in San Diego that weekend! But, the message from the pastor preaching that day was helpful – for THIS book! No coincidence at all! If we are willing to listen, and go the extra mile (or 4), we are led to exactly where we need to be at times.

When yoga was introduced to EUSD, others knew something was wrong. I did not. Others that I trusted and respected were concerned. I did not know of the deception. I was deceived. But I knew that since others were concerned, I should look into it. I prayed for understanding and over time I began to see the whole picture for what it was and it was so much worse than I could have conceived in the beginning. The small deceptions that the school district would maintain, over and over in meetings were surprising. The deception in not revealing Jois Foundation's real role (contracted for clarity) in our district. Why the lies – why the perjury on the witness stand? Why the cover-up? Why the clarity of the mission on their website and contracts, yet the verbal contradictions of that in person and then in court by the Superintendent and staff? Why the need for covering the facts? I don't think most of the district board even understands what they are really promoting. They didn't look into it and then refused to see so much of what we pointed out to them. They didn't "want" to see it. They "wanted" to be known for implementing a grand program that changes the health of children. That is a good goal. They fall short by not seeing the agenda and realities of Jois Yoga that are even clearly stated on the Jois webpage from the beginning and still to this day.

Many parents didn't want to believe anything was wrong. Many wouldn't take the time to look into even the information given to them. Instead, many simply brushed it aside. "I'm too busy". "I like yoga". "It's healthy." "It's not spiritual." "You must be a Christian."

First International Yoga Day, June 21, 2015, Wikipedia

"International Day of Yoga, or commonly and unofficially referred to as *Yoga Day*, is celebrated annually on 21 June since its inception in 2015. An international day for yoga was declared unanimously by the United Nations General Assembly. Yoga is a physical, mental and spiritual practice originated in India. The Indian Prime Minister Narendra Modi in his UN address suggested the date of 21 June, as it is the longest day of the year in the

Northern Hemisphere and shares a special significance in many parts of the world." *Wikipedia, 2019*

If You See Something, Say Something

"If you see something, say something" is a bumper sticker you may have seen or a slogan that has been used for people to speak up, or point something out. This usually pertains to a negative thing, for feedback, but it can be used for the positive as well. You could see something in others they don't know about themselves. Yet by pointing it out, you help reinforce it in them. It can also be used for praise or compliments when others do something well.

I saw something, so I said something

So if it's not crystal clear by now why I wrote this book, these are the main reasons

Warnings about what can happen as a result of extensive yoga in American schools.

Exposing the trial - from the side not covered accurately in most media.

To provide a "wake-up call" - to protect the children of our nation.

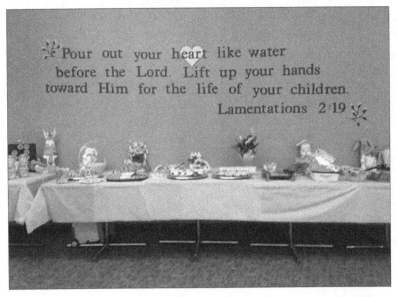

"Moms in Prayer" brunch – Verse on wall at Tri City Christian for years

Acknowledgements

I want to thank so many people surrounding this yoga trial, but I will mention a few and trust that the many others know how much it mattered that they shared their knowledge, experiences, concerns, research and insights with us. For some, I will use first names only for privacy.

I first acknowledge all the parents who awakened to the problems before I did. Many parents at various Encinitas schools were concerned and were consistent in asking others to look into the program promoters and contracts with the district: Mary, Samantha, Silvia, James, Desiree, Lydia, Stephanie, Laura, Jeff, Marcia, and Cindy to name a few. Right after *back to school* nights when the new yoga program was announced district-wide, three different moms invited Attorney Dean Broyles to the newly-forming "concerned parent meetings" along with a couple of pastors. I thank all the parents with initial concerns, and Dean and Pastor Doug for attending meetings to help the parents of Encinitas voice their concerns. I thank all the parents at the EUSD board meetings who shared their concerns, which led me to research more deeply into the subject, leading to my own concerns during the fall of 2012.

I thank the group of parents who continue to this day to spread the concerns, issues and knowledge we have found surrounding the Ashtanga program of yoga in the elementary schools. So many others joined us within the year, both actively and behind the scenes, privately sharing with others. I thank Amanda, Lori, Craig, Sian, Diana, Darryn, Karen, Terri, Patrice, Angie, another Silvia, another Amanda, two Susans, two Sarahs, Leslie, Richard, Pam, Alicia, Rebecca, Kristine, Suzanne, Lisa, Mary Ann, Kym, Kim, Greg, Jen, Janet, Joyce, Heather, Amber, Ed, Ann, and Chris.

Thank you for your insights Anne, Darlene, Dran, Kent, Larry, Stacey, Mike, Jessica, Corinna, Michaelle, Gina, Shawn, David, Gini, Penny, Anne, Sarah, and Nancy.

A huge thank you to our expert witness Dr. Candy Gunther Brown. Without her expert testimony our case would have been easily dismissed rather than grow from a two-day trial to a six-day trial once the judge realized there were legitimate concerns. Brown has been studying, teaching and publishing over twenty years on the very topics this case raised. The judge said she was the brightest and most articulate, educated expert witness he had ever come across in all his years on the bench. And yet, one month later would ignore her entire testimony! Further proving, this was not a normal battle!

Thank you to Dean Broyles from Center for Law and Policy, for standing firm for Equality and Freedom as he appeared to be hand-selected (and not even by us) for this groundbreaking trial that would be one of the most challenging in spiritual warfare of his career. At one point, he realized he was being called "The Yoga Lawyer." Thank you for your tireless hours of research, preparations and time spent for EUSD kids and beyond.

Thank you to attorneys Rob Reynolds and Bradley Abramson, Alliance Defending Freedom (ADF) for all your assistance and prayers.

Thank you to Pastor Bob Botsford and his wife Bonnie of Horizon Church. Bob was the first pastor to stand fully and publicly in agreement with our battle. He held a pastor event to educate pastors in San Diego County on January 16, 2014. Thank you to Pastor Jim Garlow who held the second pastor event in June that year, and to Pastor Roger Moyer who hosted the women's ministry leader event, also in January, 2014.

Thank you to Becky, Alicia, Bill, Patrice, Terri, Desiree, Lisa, Angie, Suzanne, Diana, Richard, Lori, Amanda, and Mary Ann who all kept me going through some of the toughest moments these past few years. Your prayers and encouragement made a big difference along the way. Thank you to the "pit crew" of praying women and all the prayers from around the world that poured in, when needed. Your calls, emails and texts from across all borders made all the threatening ones fade away quickly. We stand not in fear, but in the knowledge of the truth that is on solid ground.

Thank you to Camille Akin for helping with edits and formatting for the first 10 chapters. Dr. Rebecca Melton and Bill Stump for thorough edits to the entire book (twice through for Bill!), and a few others who all edited parts, prior to publisher, Xulon, edits as well. Not an easy task, for anyone given the subject and Sanskrit words, throughout. Like others who touched this whole journey, they all showed up at just the time needed, having been unknowingly prepared for their roles. Thank you to the endorsers of the book: Pastor and Author Bob Botsford, Superintendent Clark Gilbert, and Professor and Author, Candy Gunther Brown. And thank you to the children who professionally posed for the cover, may your futures be full of PE!

Thank you to my father, William Bentz, for standing in to protect the interests of our children, his grandchildren, for the trial. Thank you to the three grandmothers for their unwavering support: Janet Mills, Patricia Bentz, and Mary Sedlock. Your love and encouragement through all of life is, immeasurable.

I want to thank my children, for standing firm in their faith through this battle. And for Faith who at age seven even took the stand in court to tell the truth that she wasn't getting PE time, that the district was claiming she got each week. I am grateful for their understanding as I worked on not only this book, but attending other meetings and projects for this stand, taking me away on occasion from time with them. I hope in reading this book one day, they will understand that the time we all invested was worth every effort. Life marched on, and we had a busy, full, fun and sometimes challenging life, through it all. I will note here on my last edit, that the last few months of completing this manuscript, my three children underwent horrible spiritual attacks that would send most families to the loony bin for good. They endured, hung on to the promises of God, and came out the other end, "just fine," yet, forever aware of spiritual attacks. I can't wait to see what God does with them in their lifetimes! They are strong in Him and have always been on a short leash – for what? I don't know. I can only imagine...

And a big thanks to my husband: My love, my partner in life, through all of life's ups and downs. I am so proud of the man he is, and his strength in the storm of this, along with many other challenges of life. I respect and adore his ability to lean into God and stand firm against injustice. I love you and look forward to holding your hand through the rest of this life we share.

I am forever grateful for the amazing people that surround my life and the new friends that I have met through this journey. I would have never asked for this, and at times would have gladly not followed through, but the spirit moved me to press on, through many miles of rough roads, over obstacles that seemed too large, to the finish line, and now continue to follow where He will lead.

And finally, I thank *you*, the reader, for reading this book and hope that you are enlightened in some way, and refer or pass this to someone else who needs to know:

The truth about yoga

About the Author

Jennifer Sedlock grew up in Columbus, Ohio; Lawrence, Kansas; and Norman, Oklahoma. With two parents as professors, she and her brother lived as Buckeyes, Jayhawks and then Sooners. In her sophomore year of high school, Sedlock won a regional top-five spot in a three mile race to run in the Kinney National Cross Country race in Balboa Park in San Diego (in December in the middle of icy cold Oklahoma weather). It was then, while running the beaches at Coronado Island. lodging at the Hotel Del, and racing in the famous Balboa Park, that she fell in love with California. The University of California at Berkeley, was her choice for what became her undergraduate business degree in Finance and Advertising. During her favorite class, Entrepreneurship, she built and ran her first company, prior to graduating. Fifteen years later she would complete her Masters of Organization Development and Masters Thesis on MBTI Teambuilding, at the University of San Francisco.

Her choice of profession was first retail clothing sales manager, then weight loss management and training with Jenny Craig, and then staffing company management, which grew into a passion for training and development. As a hobby along the way, she taught fitness classes at gyms and corporate training centers for a decade; ran numerous road races and a marathon; and is still involved with athletics through coaching varsity boys and girls high school cross country and track. Jennifer met and married Steve in San Diego, who grew up in Detroit, Michigan. Together, they are raising three children in California, who *happened* to be enrolled in the Encinitas schools, when *Ashtanga yoga* entered their district.

Uncle Mike, Jennifer's brother, passed away during this trial, through complications of lifelong Multiple Sclerosis from age 13. He has been a source of inspiration all her life, first as a big brother, then as a *strong fighter* of his disease living in a nursing home, who never gave up hope for one more day to "live and love in a new

505

way" as found in one of his numerous poems. Those in wheel-chairs who *can't* do all the things that we sometimes doubt we can, is a source of inspiration as Sedlock presses on during the stormy trials of brazen ridicule. With the armor of God through faith, and knowledge of fitness and rights for the children, she is able to offer these pages to you. If you wondered what makes the author tick, you now have part of the answer. Standing for Freedom, Fairness, Unity, Equality, and Protection for Innocence; these are some of the reasons you hold this book and that this trial came to pass.

Resources
Websites, Articles and Documents

Referred to in text of each chapter
*Note: If the resource does not link anymore, many times a
simple search finds the same article or information moved
to another location. Periods at end need to be taken off (a
common error) if cutting and pasting. Also typeset added
dashes and spaces so look closely or just get the Ebook!*

Chapter 1

1. Moms in Prayer International: https://momsinprayer.org/.

2. The California State Board of Education guidelines for PE: https://www.cde.ca.gov/ls/fa/sf/peguideelement.asp.

3. Attorney Dean Broyles, National Center for Law & Policy: http://www.nclplaw.org/.

4. ABC News Radio, *"Parents May Sue Over Yoga Lessons in Public Schools,"* October 23, 2012. http://abcnewsradioonline.com/health-news/parents-may-sue-over-yoga-lessons-in-public-schools.html.

5. Kevin Dolack of ABC News, *"Suit Eyed Over Yoga in Public Schools,"* Yahoo News, October 23, 2012. https://www.yahoo.com/news/suit-eyed-over-yoga-public-schools-184622594--abc-news-topstories.html.

6. California State Board of Education PE requirements http://www.cde.ca.gov/ta/tg/pf/.

7. Several Articles for *"Warnings of physical injuries by doctors for youth doing yoga" here:* https://truthaboutyoga.com/concerns-about-yoga/.

8. Tony Perry, *"Group of Parents in Encinitas view yoga in elementary school as religious indoctrination,"* LA Times, November 12, 2012. http://articles.latimes.com/2012/nov/07/local/la-me-yoga-20121107.

9. Will Carless, *"Yoga Class Draws a Religious Protest,"* New York Times, December 16, 2012. http://www.nytimes.com/2012/12/16/us/school-yoga-class-draws-religious-protest-from-christians.html?_r=1.

10. Petition on *"How you can help" page:* https://truthaboutyoga.com/how-can-you-help/.

11. Homepage of Truth About Yoga: www.truthaboutyoga.com.

12. Debra Cassens Weiss, *"Parents Claim Grade School Yoga Classes Are First Amendment Violation,"* ABA Journal, December 19, 2012. http://www.abajournal.com/news/article/parents_claim_grade_school_yoga_classes_are_first_amendment_violation.

13. Gary Warth, *"Yoga Packs Board Meeting,"* San Diego Union Tribune, Dec, 4, 2012, http://www.sandiegouniontribune.com/sdut-classroom-yoga-topic-packs-board-meeting-2012dec04-story.html.

14. Yoga BlogSpot, *discusses "how to cover up spiritual language in Ashtanga yoga and over 104 comments from public on reactions to yoga in schools," October, 2012.* http://grimmly2007.blogspot.com/2012/10/the-joisyoga-grant-and-yoga-in-schools.html.

15. Movie trailer, *"We Bought a Zoo," (on "20 seconds of courage"),* 1 minute video: https://www.bing.com/videos/search?q=we+bought+a+zoo+20+seconds+of+courage&view=detail&mid=BF4EA8C498890F7265B3BF4EA8C498890F7265B3&FORM=VIRE.

16. Press Release, *"Encinitas adopts Religious Ashtanga Yoga Program to Replace Physical Education,"* National Center for Law and Policy, October 22, 2012. https://www.nclplaw.org/wp-content/uploads/2011/12/NCLPPressRelease20FINAL1.pdf.

17. Information for Parents, *EUSD/Jois Yoga Foundation*, October 3, 2012. https://truthaboutyoga.files.wordpress.com/2014/01/eusd-yoga-information-updated-10-03-12.pdf.

18. The Sedlock letter (and others) to the EUSD District, *Truth About Yoga website*, December, 2012. https://truthaboutyoga.com/about/lawsuit-in-encinitas-2/.

19. Frequently Asked Questions (FAQ) from Concerned Parents Group, 2012. https://truthaboutyoga.com/education-events/ or directly here: https://truthaboutyoga.files.wordpress.com/2015/01/frequently-asked-questions-ashtanga-yoga.pdf.

Resources: Chapter 2

1. Superior Court of the State of California, *Sedlock request for Removal of Jois Foundations Ashtanga Yoga from EUSD*, February 20, 2013. https://truthaboutyoga.files.wordpress.com/2015/01/sedlock-complaint-final.pdf.

2. Ibid, #2 location at: https://truthaboutyoga.com/about/lawsuit-in-encinitas-2/.

3. Press Release for Removal of Yoga, *"EUSD sued for civil rights violations resulting from its inherently and pervasively religious Ashtanga Yoga program,"* Feb. 20, 2013. http://www.nclplaw.org/wp-content/uploads/2011/12/NCLP-Complaint-Press-Release-FINAL.pdf.

4. Larry Mantel, *"Does Yoga have a Place in Public Schools?"* NPR Interview, December 17, 2012. http://www.scpr.org/programs/airtalk/2012/12/17/29724/does-yoga-have-a-place-in-public-schools/.

5. Kyla Calvert, *"Controversy Won't Stall Encinitas Yoga Plans,"* KPBS, January 22, 2013.

    http://www.kpbs.org/news/2013/jan/02/controversy-wont-stall-encinitas-yoga-plans/.

6. Associated Press, *"Yoga programs in Public Schools face Backlash,"* Fox News, December 17, 2012. http://www.foxnews.com/us/2012/12/17/yoga-programs-in-public-schools-face-backlash.html.

7. Victor Chi, "Parents Object to Yoga classes in Schools," The Post Game, October 22, 2012. http://www.thepostgame.com/blog/training-table/201210/parents-object-yoga-classes-schools.

"When you walk through the fire, you will not be burned"
Isaiah 43:2b, NIV

³ Press Release, February 20, 2013:

THE NATIONAL CENTER FOR LAW & POLICY NEWS
RELEASE February 20, 2013—FOR IMMEDIATE RELEASE
CONTACT NCLP MEDIA RELATIONS: (760) 747-4529

EUSD sued for civil rights violations resulting from its inherently
and pervasively religious Ashtanga yoga program.

SAN DIEGO, CA — Attorneys for the National Center For Law
& Policy (NCLP) filed a civil rights lawsuit in San Diego Superior
Court today against the Encinitas Union School District (EUSD).
The lawsuit seeks a writ of mandate and injunctive relief to order
EUSD to comply with the California constitution's religious
freedom provisions and a state education statue requiring EUSD
to provide a mandatory minimum number of physical education
minutes. The NCLP represents petitioners and plaintiffs Stephen
and Jennifer Sedlock and their minor children, who are students
in the district.

The lawsuit is the result of EUSD's decision to accept $533,000
from the Jois Foundation in exchange for providing the religious-
ly-based organization access to its young and impressible students to test and prove the feasibility of Jois' "health and wellness"
Ashtanga yoga curriculum. According to Harvard educated religious studies Professor Candy Gunther Brown, Ph.D., who wrote a
declaration supporting the complaint, EUSD's Ashtanga yoga program is inherently and pervasively religious, having its roots firmly
planted in Hindu, Buddhist, Taoist, and Western Metaphysical religious beliefs and practices. As such, the program violates California
constitutional provisions prohibiting government religious preference and religious discrimination (article I, § 4), prohibiting use
of state resources to support religion (article XVI, § 5), and for-
bidding employing government resources to promote religion in
public schools (article IX, § 8).

"EUSD's Ashtanga yoga program represents a serious breach of the public trust," declared attorney Dean Broyles. "Compliance with the clear requirements of law is not optional or discretionary. This is frankly the clearest case of the state trampling on the religious freedom rights of citizens that I have personally witnessed in my eighteen years of practice as a constitutional attorney. The program is extremely divisive and has unfortunately led to the harassment, discrimination, bullying, and segregation of children who, for good reasons, opt out of the program. EUSD's Ashtanga yoga program represents a prime example of precisely why in America we wisely forbid the government from picking religious winners and losers, especially when you have a captive audience of very young and impressionable children as we do in our public schools." "EUSD's 'model' yoga program sets a very dangerous precedent. No matter how starved our school districts are for money, we must not allow our public servants to 'sell' our precious children to the highest bidder to be used as religious 'guinea pigs' to fulfill the self-serving marketing purposes of a religiously motivated organization. Religious freedom is not for sale. EUSD's improperly cozy relationship with the Jois Foundation has entangled the district in an unnecessary and avoidable religious controversy and has caused considerable damage and negative fallout in the community. EUSD had more than three months of warnings to make the right call and suspend the illegal program voluntarily, yet has negligently failed to act. The EUSD Trustees have persistently closed their eyes to the transparently religious nature of the program, determining to take the money and run with it. They have shown little concern or respect for families who were religiously burdened by the program and appropriately objected to religious beliefs and practices being illegally promoted in the public schools. And the EUSD Trustees and Superintendent have done nothing to solve the major problem that Children who opt out of Ashtanga yoga for religious and other reasons and who are not receiving the state mandated 200 minutes of PE every 10 days. Sadly after learning that the program violated the law, rather than doing the right thing and immediately suspending the program, EUSD's Superintendent and Trustees engaged in months of delay and inaction. Meanwhile,

Superintendent Baird repeated the misleading 'mantra' to the public and the press that EUSD had "stripped" the program of religion or that it was not "religious."

The lawsuit does not seek money damages; but rather seeks to immediately suspend EUSD's divisive Ashtanga yoga program and restore traditional physical education to the district.

Please address all media inquiries to The National Center for Law & Policy. We ask that you respect the privacy of the Sedlock family, whose children's names have been withheld to protect their privacy.

For additional background information, see the October 2012 NCLP press release @ http://www.nclplaw.org/wp-content/uploads/2011/12/NCLPPressRelease20FINAL1.pdf

The National Center for Law & Policy is a non-profit 501(c) (3) legal defense organization dedicated to the protection and promotion of religious freedom, parental rights, and other civil liberties. www.nclplaw.org

For comment, please contact The National Center for Law & Policy at 760-747-4529 or dcarter@nclplaw.org.

Resources: Chapter 3

1. Rabi Maharaj, *Death of a Guru*, (Harvest House, 1977). https://www.amazon.com/Death-Guru-Remarkable-Story-Search/dp/0890814341/ref=sr_1_1?s=books&ie=UTF8&qid=1468246369&sr=1-1&keywords=Death+of+a+Guru.

2. The Hindu American Foundation (HAF), *India Times*, *February, 2013*. (http://economictimes.indiatimes.com/topic/Hindu-American-Foundation).

3. HAF, *"Take Yoga Back,"* 2008 campaign, http://www.hafsite.org/media/pr/takeyogaback.

4. HAF, Facebook site: https://www.facebook.com/
   Hindu-American-Foundation-105243818008/.

5. Pattabhi Jois, *"The essence of yoga is to reach oneness with God,"*
   (Quote by founder of Ashtanga yoga – the yoga placed in Encinitas
   schools), *"Yoga Beyond Asana: Hindu Thought in Practice,"* HAF.
   (http://www.hafsite.org/media/pr/yoga-hindu-origins).

6. Dean Broyles, Attorney for Yoga Case, website with Press
   Releases: http://www.nclplaw.org/news/, (also available at
   truthaboutyoga.com). Ibid, Press Release, Feb 20, 2013. http://
   www.nclplaw.org/wp-content/uploads/2011/12/NCLP-Complaint-
   Press-Release-FINAL.pdf.

7. Nathan Kanter, *"The Future of Religious Choice: Sedlock v.
   Baird and the Establishment Clause,"* Wheaton Undergraduate
   Law Review, (*"How the CA Judge got it Wrong"*), Spring of
   2016. https://wculrcom.files.wordpress.com/2016/04/wculr-vol-
   1-no-1.pdf.

8. Candy Gunther Brown, *"What Makes the Encinitas School Yoga
   Program Religious?"* Huffington Post, July 24, 2013. http://www.
   huffingtonpost.com/candy-gunther-brown-phd/encinitas-yoga-
   lawsuit_b_3570850.html.

9. Contract between the three organizations: *Regur Development,
   EUSD and Jois Foundation,* June 24, 2012. (Note wording:
   "Partnership," "Yoga curriculum," "scalable curriculum,
   transferable.") https://truthaboutyoga.files.wordpress.com/2014/01/
   jois-moufinal.pdf.

10. Anonymous and Various, *Parent testimonial page on website:*
    https://truthaboutyoga.com/testimonials/

11. Caryl Mastrisciana, Video, *"Yoga Uncoiled - The Satanic Roots of
    Yoga."* http://yogauncoiled.com/.

12. Caryl Mastrisciana, Video, *"Wide is the Gate",* Yoga as New Age
    Religion tied to The Emergent Church: https://www.youtube.com/
    watch?v=bDBoBhIqfwQ.

13. Definition of Namaste as per Wikipedia: https://en.wikipedia.org/
    wiki/Namaste.

14. Mary Eady, Letter to District as Testimony, *"Five year olds
    at Paul Ecke were taught Namaste,"* December 2012. https://
    truthaboutyoga.com/lawsuit-in-encinitas-2/).

15. Jennifer Sedlock, "yoga poster in 5th grade classrooms at Back to School Night," Photo taken at La Costa Heights School, August, 2015. Same yoga poster was in every upper classroom (grades 4, 5 and 6) and remained all year after objections.

16. "Om" (Sanskrit for "I am god"): https://en.wikipedia.org/wiki/Om, http://hinduism.about.com/od/omaum/a/meaningofom.htm).

17. Sanskrit, (spiritual language for ceremonies) definition: https://en.wikipedia.org/wiki/Sanskrit).

18. EUSD Website, Board of Directors page: http://www.eusd.org/board_agds.htm.

Resources: Chapter 4

1. Jois Yoga website: http://joisyoga.com/.

2. Ashtanga Yoga, definition (literally means eight-limbed yoga), http://www.ashtanga.com.

3. Ashtanga Yoga, "Yoga Sutras," (as outlined by the Sage, Patanjali). http://www.yogajournal.com/article/yoga-101/beginning-journey/.

4. Ashtanga definition, "eight limbs" in Sanskrit on another website: http://yoga.about.com/od/yogabooks/fr/yogamala.htm.

5. Ann Pizer, "The Meaning of Asana in Yoga," Very Well Fit, November 9, 2018, (Ashtanga Sanskrit 8 limbs). https://www.verywell.com/what-is-asana-3566793)

6. Very Well Fit, "Ashtanga Yoga Sutras of Patanjali" (https://www.verywellfit.com/yoga-beginner-4157112).

7. What is Ashtanga Asana? (https://www.verywell.com/what-is-asana-3566793).

8. Ann Pizer, Ashtanga method of Asana practice as interpreted by T. Krishnamacharya, "the father of modern yoga," Very Well Fit, June 28, 2018. (https://www.verywell.com/krishnamacharya-father-of-modern-yoga-3566898) and Sri K. Pattabhi Jois from an ancient text called the Yoga Korunta.

9. Ashtanga Moon Days: http://ashtanga.com/html/moondays.html .

10. Why you must rest on Moon days: http://ashtangayogacenter.com/moon-days/.

11. Opening or Surya Namaskara A: https://www.verywell.com/surya-namaskara-a-3566700.

12. Closing or Surya Namaskara B: https://www.verywell.com/surya-namaskara-b-3566701.

13. Photos, Surya Namaskara A and B, La Costa Heights Elementary School. Open House 2015. https://truthaboutyoga.com/about/.

14. Chase Sagum, "5 Reasons you shouldn't lock your knees," January 25, 2013. (Banned stretching poses by US doctors promoted here in Ashtanga and EUSD yoga): http://www.memetics.com/5-reasons-you-why-you-shouldnt-lock-your-knees/.

15. Chris Centeno, MD, "Injuries from tendons and ligaments being pulled from the bone come from this type of stretching," December 23, 2015. http://www.regenexx.com/knee-locking-up/.

16. Worship poses created to invite in spirits of the gods - as per Jois: http://joisyoga.com/.

17. Ashtanga yoga is a set series of poses done in a flowing Vinyasa style ("search" on this page for Ashtanga). http://yoga.about.com/od/yogabooks/fr/yogamala.htm).

18. Ann Pizer, Ashtanga Yoga and Founder Pattabhi Jois, May 15, 2018. http://yoga.about.com/od/ashtangayoga/a/ashtangs.htm.

19. In 1958, Pattabhi Jois published his treatise on Ashtanga Yoga, Yoga Mala, Very Well Fit, (https://www.verywell.com/yoga-classics-yoga-mala-by-sri-k-pattabhi-jois-3566934 and (http://yoga.about.com/od/yogabooks/fr/yogamala.htm).

20. Ann Pizer, "How to do the Ocean Breathing (Ujjayi-Pranayama) in yoga," updated March, 10 2019. https://www.verywellfit.com/ocean-breath-ujjayi-pranayama-3566763

21. Ann Pizer, "How to Use Mula Bandha in Yoga," June 22, 2018 (https://www.verywell.com/how-to-use-mula-bandha-in-yoga-3566803),

22. Ann Pizer, "How to Use Uddiyana Bandha in Yoga," updated June 23, 2018. (https://www.verywell.com/uddiyana-bandha-3566811).

23. Ann Pizer, "How understanding Drishti can help your yoga practice," updated May 26, 2019. (https://www.verywell.com/how-understanding-drishti-can-help-your-yoga-practice-3566795).

24. "Ashtanga yoga is a system of yoga recorded by the sage Vamana Rishi in the Yoga Korunta." http://ashtanga.com/html/background.html.

25. Jois Family and Sonia Jones, Grand opening video for the Jois Yoga Shala in Encinitas, Vimeo - 8 minutes: https://vimeo.com/21459292).

26. Bethany Mclean, "Whose Yoga is it Anyway?" March 5, 2012. (Sonia Tudor Jones and famous others devoted to Ashtanga). http://www.vanityfair.com/news/business/2012/04/krishna-pattanbhi-trophy-wife-ashtanga-yoga.

27. Mysore teachings of Pattabhi Jois, R, Sharath Jois, and R, Saraswathi: http://joisyoga.com/about/story/.

28. Jois Yoga Facebook page for postings of happenings in Encinitas: https://www.facebook.com/joisyogaencinitas.

29. Kim Bhasin, "$400 yoga pants are just the beginning," Bloomburg, May 13, 2013. http://www.bloomberg.com/news/articles/2015-05-13/-400-yoga-pants-are-just-the-beginning.

30. What is up with Jois Foundation? Think Body Electric, June 2013. http://www.thinkbodyelectric.com/2013/06/yoga-train-wreck-in-encinitas-or-whats.html.).

31. Aaron Burgin, "The Ties between EUSD and yoga program foundation and schools raises concerns," Coast News, June 23, 2016. https://www.thecoastnews.com/ties-between-eusd-yoga-program-foundation-and-school-raise-concerns/.

32. Jois/Sonima Shala, 2nd year celebration. 3 minute Vimeo: http://joisyoga.com/events/jois-yoga-encinitas-2nd-anniversary/.

33. Yogananda, Self-Realization Fellowship (SRF) in Encinitas (since 1920's). http://www.yogananda-srf.org/About_Self-Realization_Fellowship.aspx#.V4TryI-cGhd.

34. Paramahansa Yogananda, Website of SRF: http://www.yoganandasrf.org/faqs/Frequently_Asked_Questions.aspx#1

35. Website of Parents for Responsible Spending: www.encinitasparents4truth.com.

36. The initial grant information about Jois Foundation is recorded in many places, here is another location at Paul Ecke Central

Elementary School website as of 2016: http://pauleckecentral.com/jois-foundation-grant/.

37. Website of Tim Miller: http://ashtangayogacenter.com/a-brief-history-of-ashtanga-yoga-in-encinitas/.

Resources: Chapter 5

1. Lawsuit page of EUSD parents website containing legal documents, media and press releases. https://truthaboutyoga.com/about/lawsuit-in-encinitas-2/.

2. Court Documents, National Center for Law & Policy: http://www.nclplaw.org/resources/.

3. Writ of Mandate filed, October 20, 2013: https://truthaboutyoga.files.wordpress.com/2015/01/sedlock-complaint-final.pdf. Or https://www.nclplaw.org/wp-content/uploads/2011/12/Sedlock-Complaint-FINAL.pdf.

4. The press release, October 20, 2013: http://www.nclplaw.org/wp-content/uploads/2011/12/NCLP-Complaint-Press-Release-FINAL.pdf.

Media Surrounding Trial

5. Maria Nickias, *"Yoga Lawsuit: Encinitas Union School District in California Sued over Classes,"* ABC News, February 21, 2013. https://abcnews.go.com/US/yoga-lawsuit-encinitas-union-school-district-california-sued/story?id=18561237.

6. Brandon Arnold, *"Encinitas School District Yoga Trial Starts,"* Fox News, May 20, 2013. http://fox5sandiego.com/2013/05/20/encinitas-school-district-yoga-trial-starts/.

7. City New Service, *"Trail Begins in Lawsuit over Yoga in Schools,"* KPBS, May 20, 2013. http://www.kpbs.org/news/2013/may/20/sd-yoga-lawsuit/.

8. Misha Dibono, *"Doctor (Religious Studies Professor) Testifies at Yoga Trial,"* May 21, 2013. http://fox5sandiego.com/2013/05/21/expert-witness-testifies-teaching-yoga-is-a-conspiracy/.

9. Jared Whitlock, *"EUSD Yoga Trial Underway,"* Coast News, May 21, 2013. https://www.thecoastnews.com/eusd-yoga-trial-underway/.

10. Yoga Alliance, *"Questioning the Definition of Religion as the Trial Begins,"* May 21, 2013. https://www.yogaalliance.org/Learn/Articles/Questioning_the_definition_of_religion_as_the_trial_begins.

11. R. Stickney, *"Yoga Lawsuit, Schools Accused of Spreading Gospel,"* NBC News, May 22, 2013. http://www.nbcsandiego.com/news/local/Yoga-Class-Encinitas-Lawsuit-San-Diego-Reglious-208538581.html.

12. Rebecca Klein, *"Encinitas Yoga Trial: Parents Argue School is Violating Separation of Church and State,"* Huffington Post, May 23, 2013. http://www.huffingtonpost.com/2013/05/23/encinitas-yoga-trial-religion-in-school_n_3327247.html.

13. Yoga Alliance, *"Yoga Trial without Resolution,"* *(to resume June 24, 2013)*, May 23, 2013. https://www.yogaalliance.org/Learn/Articles/Yoga_trial_without_resolution.

14. Bob Ponting, *"Trial on Yoga in Schools Resumes,"* Fox News, June 24, 2013. http://fox5sandiego.com/2013/06/24/trial-on-school-yoga-classes-resumes/.

15. Megan Tevrizian and Sarah Greico, *"Parents Testify in Encinitas Yoga Class Trial"* NBC News, June 25, 2013 http://www.nbcsandiego.com/news/local/Parents-Testify-in-Encinitas-Yoga-Class-Trial-212831061.html.

16. Lilly Fowler, RNS, *"Yoga on Trial in San Diego, Religious Lawsuit,"* Charisma News, June 26, 2013. http://www.charismanews.com/us/40019-yoga-on-trial-in-san-diego-religious-lawsuit.

17. Jared Whitlock, *"Attorneys Deliver Closing Arguments in School Yoga Trial,"* Coast News June 26, 2013. https://www.thecoastnews.com/attorneys-deliver-closing-arguments-in-school-yoga-trial/.

18. Kyla Calvert, *"Closing Arguments Begin in Encinitas Trial,"* KPBS, June 25, 2013 http://www.kpbs.org/news/2013/jun/25/closing-arguments-begin-encinitas-yoga-trial/.

19. Eric Yates, *"School Sun Salutations Here to Stay (Encinitas Yoga Case),"* Encinitas Patch, July 12, 2013. https://patch.com/

california/encinitas/candy-gunther-brown-school-sun-salutations-here-to-stay-encinitas-yoga.

20. Candy Gunther Brown contributes: *"Yoga Can Stay in School, Looking More Closely at the Encinitas Yoga Trial Decision,"* Huffington Post, July 2, 2013. http://www.huffingtonpost.com/candy-gunther-brown-phd/what-made-the-encinitas-p_b_3522836.html.

21. *"Yoga and the Church vs. State Battle in Encinitas,"* Huffington Post, June, 2013. http://www.huffingtonpost.com/news/encinitas-yoga-trial/.

22. Candy Gunther Brown, PhD, *"What Makes the Encinitas Yoga Religious,"* Huffington Post, July, 24, 2013. http://www.huffingtonpost.com/candy-gunther-brown-phd/encinitas-yoga-lawsuit_b_3570850.html.

23. Sanskrit, definition: https://www.bing.com/search?q=sanskrit&form=EDGHPC&qs=LS&cvid=864ea0fdac7b481e85831 96209fa5fdd&pq=sanskri

Resources: Chapter 6

1. Jared Whitlock, *"Encinitas School District rolling out IPads into schools for K-2,"* September 13, 2013. http://encinitasparents4truth.com/baird-himelstein/. Also found here: https://www.thecoastnews.com/encinitas-school-district-rolling-out-ipads-for-k-2/.

2. Encinitas Undercover, *"Encinitas Superintendent Tim Baird Sues EUSD,"* (re: Pacific View Property), October 10, 2011. http://encinitasundercover.blogspot.com/2011/10/eusd-superintendent-tim-baird-sues.html.

3. Baird's travel expenses exploded 2012-2015: http://encinitasparents4truth.com/timothy-baird-eusd-board-travel-costs-exploding-higher/.

4. University of Virginias Contemplative Sciences Center: http://www.uvacontemplation.org/.

5. Regur Development website: http://www.rdgsolutions.com/.

6. Steven Regur listed as an "Education Consultant from Newport Beach" and owner of Educators Cooperative: https://educators.coop/.

7. Ibid. Aaron Burgin, June 23, 2016. *The Chandler Hill Group*, Himelstein. https://www.thecoastnews.com/ties-between-eusd-yoga-program-foundation-and-school-raise-concerns/.

8. Encinitas Parents for Responsible Education Spending Himelstein payments tax records: http://encinitasparents4truth.com.

9. Himelstein owner of website with Sonima curriculum for Schools: http://pureedgeinc.org/.

10. Ibid, #3. Sonima Foundation is spreading this curriculum to any school districts they can enter: http://pureedgeinc.org/partnerships/.

11. Himilstein funding/payments from William D Lynch Foundation, CEPAL at USD, Capitol Hill, Portico Educational Services, and perhaps others, such as Pure Edge. https://www.corporationwiki.com/California/San-Diego/scott-b himelstein/42111831.aspx.

12. "Deputy Secretary of Education" in 2005: https://www.linkedin.com/in/shimelstein.

13. Ed Futures, website: http://www.edfutures.org/.

14. Eugene Ruffin listed as Executive Director of Pure Edge, Inc.: https://www.guidestar.org/profile/45-3182571 (Himilstein owner).

15. Rory Devine and R. Sticknew, *"San Diego Judge Okays Yoga in Schools Denies Religious Component,"* (Eugene Ruffin speaks to the media in June after watching trial in court). http://www.nbcsandiego.com/news/local/Yoga-Lawsuit-Encinitas-Judgment-Ruling-School-Class-Controversy-213853341.html#ixzz2XrSK8lZt.

16. Stedman Graham on Sonima Board of Directors: https://www.sonima.com/.

17. Graham working with Ed Futures *as evidenced by claims on the Ed Futures website:* http://www.edfutures.org/.

18. Russell Case named one of the *most influential Ashtanga Yoga Teachers* in the US on Website: http://downtownyogashala.com/apps/mindbody/staff/100000232.

19. Russell Case—a *"Level 2 Ashtanga-yoga instructor"* for Stanford, 2014: http://events.stanford.edu/events/418/41803/ .

20. Case's classes in San Francisco, 2010: https://www.yogagardensf.com/ashtanga-yoga-at-the-garden/.

21. Eddie Stern, Founder of Ashtanga New York: http://ayny.org/.

22. Eddie Stern, *"Downtown New York Guru - for serious yoga students:"* http://tmagazine.blogs.nytimes.com/2012/02/27/pose-posse/.

23. Gwyneth Paltrow on you tube with Eddie Stern: *"I teach Ashtanga Yoga and I run a Hindu temple:"* https://www.youtube.com/watch?v=Xw_6ore09UU.

24. CEPAL Study produced two reports for EUSD: 1. Jan 30, 2014: https://truthaboutyoga.files.wordpress.com/2015/01/eusd-yoga-student-effects-2012-13-formattedforwebsite.pdf. 2. Nov 8, 2013: https://truthaboutyoga.files.wordpress.com/2015/01/cepal-report_implementing-yoga_2013-2014.pdf.

25. Analysis of the CEPAL reports: https://truthaboutyoga.files.wordpress.com/2015/01/cepal-bulletpoints.pdf.

26. Michele Fondin (Vedic Educator), *"What is a Chakra?"* According to the Chopra Center, September 3, 2014. http://www.chopra.com/articles/what-is-a-chakra#sm.01pahbe910lcfc611rw22umdt0y36.

Resources: Chapter 7

1. Sian Welch, Daily updates of trial, May 20, 2013. https://sedlockvseusd.blogspot.com/?spref=fb.

2. Candy Gunther Brown, PhD: books, lectures and information at Indiana University: http://indiana.edu/~relstud/people/profiles/brown_candy.

3. Candy Gunther Brown -The declaration of the expert witness: http://www.nclplaw.org/wp-content/uploads/2011/12/DECLARATION-OF-CANDY-BROWN-FINAL.pdf Also available at: https://truthaboutyoga.files.wordpress.com/2015/01/declaration-of-candy-brown-final.pdf.

Media covering the day

4. Sedlock v. EUSD Trail Transcript Day 1 — May 20, 2013 (Entire Transcript): https://truthaboutyoga.files.wordpress.com/2015/01/13-05-20-part-01-court-notes-day-1.pdf.

5. Brandon Arnold, *"Encinitas School District Yoga Trial Starts,"* Fox News, May 20, 2013. http://fox5sandiego.com/2013/05/20/encinitas-school-district-yoga-trial-starts/.

6. Jared Whitlock, *"EUSD Yoga Trial Underway."* Coast News reported from the Courtroom, May 20, 2013. https://www.thecoastnews.com/eusd-yoga-trial-underway/.

7. Kyla Calvert, *"Trial Begins in Lawsuit over Yoga in Schools,"* KPBS, May 20, 2013. http://www.kpbs.org/news/2013/may/20/sd-yoga-lawsuit/.

Resources: Chapter 8

1. Sedlock v. EUSD Trial Transcript Day 2 - May 21, 2013: https://truthaboutyoga.files.wordpress.com/2015/01/day-2-annotated-court-notes.pdf.

Media covering the day

2. R. Stickney, *"Yoga Lawsuit Schools Accused of Spreading Gospel,"* NBC News of trial, May 22, 2013. http://www.nbcsandiego.com/news/local/Yoga-Class-Encinitas-Lawsuit-San-Diego-Reglious-208538581.html.

3. *Reposted, "EUSD Yoga Trial Underway,"* Coast Law Group News, May 21, 2013. https://www.coastlawgroup.com/eusd-yoga-trial-underway/.

4. *"Definition of Yoga as Religion on Trial,"* Yoga Alliance, May 21, 2013. https://www.yogaalliance.org/Learn/Articles/Questioning the definition of religion as the trial begins.

Candy Gunther-Brown—I received my B.A. (1992 summa cum laude, history and literature), M.A. (1995, history), and Ph.D. (2000, History of American Civilization) at Harvard University and currently serve as an Associate Professor in the Religious Studies department (and as an affiliate with the American Studies department and Liberal Arts and Management program) at Indiana University. At Harvard University (attended 1989-2000), I received broad, interdisciplinary training in American religious history and culture, from the 1600s to the present.

Honors awarded include Hugh O'Brien National Leadership Ambassador (1989); Robert C. Byrd California Honors Scholar (1989); Detur Prize (1990); John Harvard Scholar (1990, 1991, 1992); Elizabeth Cary Agassiz Scholar (1990, 1991, 1992); Phi Beta Kappa [Junior 12] (1991, 1992); Charles Warren Center Thesis Research Fellowship, Harvard University, $2,000 (1991); Houston Public Service Award, Phillips Brooks House Association (1992); Fulbright Graduate Student Fellowship (1992); Lilly Fellowship for Graduate Study (1993, 1994); Mazur Fellowship for Graduate Study (1994); Sarah Bradley Gamble Fellowship for Graduate Study (1995); Sidney E. Mead Article Prize, American Society of Church History, $250 (1995); Graduate Society Travel Grant, Harvard University, $500 (1995); Graduate Society Fellowship for Dissertation Research, Harvard University, $1,000 (1995); John Clive Teaching Prize, Harvard 1789-1880 (Chapel Hill: University of North Carolina Press, 2004); Testing Prayer: Science and Healing (Cambridge, MA: Harvard University Press, 2012); and The Healing Gods of Christian America: Complementary and Alternative Medicine in the Mainstream (New York: Oxford University Press, forthcoming July 2013). I am the editor of Global Pentecostal and Charismatic Healing (New York: Oxford University Press, 2011); co-editor of The Future of Evangelicalism in America (Columbia University Press, under contract). I have published ten peer-reviewed journal articles, eight scholarly book chapters, eight op-eds and blog posts, eighteen teaching-oriented publications, seventeen academic book reviews; delivered fifty-three invited lectures and professional society presentations, and given fifty-one media interviews (listed on c.v.).

8. I have been teaching courses on American religion and culture since 1996. As a Ph.D. candidate (1996-1999), I taught in the Religion and History and Literature programs at Harvard University, and in the Comparative Literature department at Lesley University. After earning my Ph.D., I worked as an assistant professor in the History department at Vanderbilt University from 2000-2001. I was an assistant professor in the American Studies department at Saint Louis University from 2001-2006. I have been employed as an associate professor in the Religious Studies department at Indiana University from 2006 to the present. I have taught a wide variety of courses (usually two courses per semester, with enrollments for each course up to 120 students), including Religion, Illness, and Healing; Religion, Health, and Healthcare Management; Sickness and Health; and Religion and American Culture. I have also advised

twenty-three theses and Ph.D. dissertations. I regularly draw upon my research in my teaching, including my research on yoga, meditation, Hinduism, Buddhism, Taoism, and metaphysics.

Resources: Chapter 9

1. Sedlock v. EUSD Trial Transcript Day 3 - May 22, 2013: https://truthaboutyoga.files.wordpress.com/2015/01/13-05-22-part-03-court-reporter-notes-day-3.pdf.

2. Media of trial day 3, R. Stickney, *"Yoga Lawsuit, Schools Accused of Spreading Gospel,"* NBC News, Updated May 23, 2013. http://www.nbcsandiego.com/news/local/Yoga-Class-Encinitas-Lawsuit-San-Diego-Reglious-208538581.html.

3. Russell Case, Stanford: http://events.stanford.edu/events/418/41803/ .

4. Russell Case, http://downtownyogashala.com/apps/mindbody/staff/100000232 .

5. Russell Case—Yoga classes https://www.yogagardensf.com/ashtanga-yoga-at-the-garden/.

6. Andrea Silver, "Om practice" website http://www.namasteomwinnipeg.com/.

More Media of Day 3

7. Rebecca Klein, *"Encinitas Yoga Trial Parents Argue School is Violating Separation of Church and State,"* Huffington Post, May 23, 2013. http://www.huffingtonpost.com/2013/05/23/encinitas-yoga-trial-religion-in-school_n_3327247.html.

8. Yoga Alliance, *"Trial without Resolution,"* (to resume June 24, 2013), May 23, 2013. https://www.yogaalliance.org/Learn/Articles/Yoga_trial_without_resolution.

Resources: Chapter 10

1. Sedlock v. EUSD Trial Transcript Day 4 - June 24, 2013: https://truthaboutyoga.files.wordpress.com/2015/01/2013-06-24-sedlock-baird-trial.pdf.

2. Jois (now Sonima) Foundation mission: (NOT http://www.
   sonimafoundation.org/). (Note – it is now 2019, I am doing final
   editing and found Sonima changed their domain yet again, to
   http://www.sonima.com/. By the time you read this, you may need
   to google to find them moved yet again). Deepok Chopra is now
   enmeshed into Sonima's programming and if you look on Sonima
   site here: https://www.sonima.com/about/, you find now Pure
   Edge, Inc. holds the kids yoga curriculum. The founder is listed
   as Sonia Jones, while ownership of the Pure Edge website is Scott
   Himelstein. An ongoing puzzle indeed!

Media of Day 4:

3. Megan Tevrizian and Sarah Greico, *"Parents Testify in Encinitas
   Yoga Class Trial,"* NBC News, June 24, 2013. https://www.
   nbclosangeles.com/news/california/Parents-Testify-in-Encinitas-
   Yoga-Class-Trial-213042641.html.

4. Blog site – Sian Welch: http://truthaboutyoga.blogspot.com/

Sian Welch is a parent from the EUSD district that attended court every day in support of removing Yoga from the school curriculum. She wrote a blog daily and this is one of the excerpts from this day:

The first witness today was Carrie Brown, Principal of El Camino Creek Elementary. She testified that from the beginning of the program at her school, spring of 2013, yoga was an elective. CB testified that because of the number of families that opted out of the program at El Camino Creek, she needed to make the decision to change her yoga program so every child would continue to receive the required 200 minutes of PEPE. Yoga, music, technology and "kinder karate" (which were taught at her school with excess funds from PTA) were electives above and over the 200 minutes of required PEPE. The funny thing was when Carrie Brown was cross examined, nowhere in her declaration was the word "elective" used, and that declaration was taken about 30 days prior to today's testimony. Her explanation was "I just didn't use that term." Well I guess it was an oversight??? Come on, it wasn't in the declaration because yoga isn't really an "elective." at least until they decided it needed to be for the trial.

With each and every witness testimony from the district, it is clear that the curriculum, the stipulations the EVERYTHING is being changed to satisfy this case. After I opted Emma out of the program at Capri I was told she would have music class for that period. I went to the school to check it out and I found her and 3 other girls in the back 10x10 storage room with no teacher playing with instruments. The next time I came to the school she was hula-hooping at the back of the quad with a few other kids while the other kids practiced yoga on the grass in front of them.

It didn't get better from there! When Principal Brown was asked why she hired and thought Christina Reich was qualified to be the yoga teacher at her school, she said she hired Reich because she was also a nanny, mom and worked as a part-time art teacher. Qualified????

Cross: Are you aware that Christina Reich says she has committed her life to teaching Ashtanga Yoga?

Brown: No

Cross: Are you aware that she has taken pilgrimages to India to study?"

Brown: No

Cross: Do you have any understanding of the main tenants of Hinduism?

Brown: No

It was interesting, Dr. Baird & Jen Brown testified that all yoga teachers would be certified and chosen in a pool of candidates by the Jois Foundation. Today, according to Principal Brown, there was no certification process, no selecting by the Jois Foundation, complete control and discretion was left up to the principal hiring who said she knows nothing, or very little, about yoga.

Dr. Miyashiro, Assistant Superintendent was called.

I can only sum up this testimony by calling it damage control. Dr. M basically tried to tell the court that nothing that was written in the Jois grant has been followed. The judge asked "Why?" if the grant is agreed upon between Jois and EUSD (yourself & Baird)? Dr. M's response was that they were just too busy to change the MOU.
(Memorandum of Understanding). HA! I truly believe Dr. M went on the stand today to deny all sworn testimony that had been already heard to try to unwind and convince the judge that the Jois Ashtanga Yoga Program funded by the Jois Foundation is not and will not be what the Jois Foundation outlined in the grant MOU.

The judge was very involved with questioning the witnesses today. He warned the district counsel many times that this was a court of law, not a town council meeting. The judge asked Dr. M, "Did you have ANY concern WHATSOEVER that there was ANY religious COMPONENT to Ashtanga Yoga when you signed the Grant to accept this program?
Dr. M: No, none whatsoever.

***earlier Dr. M testified he didn't know anything about yoga before the program came to the district.

Judge: Did you do any research into Ashtanga Yoga before implementing the program?
Dr. M: No
Judge: So it's your personal belief that Ashtanga Yoga is NOT religious
Dr. M: Yes
Judge: So did you hear Candy Brown's testimony that the US Religious Studies Scholar's consensus is that, yoga is religious? Do you agree?
Dr. M: No
Judge: Did you hear her testimony that particularly Ashtanga Yoga is the MOST religious forms of yoga practices in the US today?
Dr. M: (silence)
Judge: If I ask you right now do you agree or not?
Dr. M: I do not have enough knowledge
Judge: Where do you get your opinion, what due diligence did you do?
Dr. M: The few teachers that I have met, doctor friends, colleagues that practice yoga and my personal experience.

Testimony goes on and on . . .

. . . you must see the DECEPTION by the school board and the lack of ANY due diligence or concern of respecting our Establishment Clause of the First Amendment is evident . . .
It is not coincidental that every person who has testified pleads to know NOTHING about Ashtanga yoga, even their expert witness knew NOTHING and she was qualified to teach it!
Our side has no money involved, only justice. Their side . . . just follow the money. The founders of the Jois Foundation are Billionaires and throwing a lot of money at this project in various districts and states now . . .

Resources: Chapter 11

1. Sedlock v. EUSD Trial Transcript Day 5 - June 25, 2013: https://truthaboutyoga.files.wordpress.com/2015/01/13-06-25-part-01final.pdf.

2. EUSD's grant proposal to Jois Foundation, July 24, 2012: https://truthaboutyoga.files.wordpress.com/2015/01/jois-grant-2.pdf.

3. Megan Tevrizian and Sarah Greico, *"Parents Testify in Encinitas Yoga Class Trial,"* NBC News, June 25, 2013. http://www.nbcsandiego.com/news/local/Parents-Testify-in-Encinitas-Yoga-Class-Trial-212831061.html

4. Kyla Calvert, *"Closing Arguments Begin in Encinitas Yoga Trial,"* KPBS, June 25, 2013. http://www.kpbs.org/news/2013/jun/25/closing-arguments-begin-encinitas-yoga-trial/.

Broyles quoting Pattabhi Jois

Broyles said the Jois Foundation has deep roots in Hinduism, tracing back to Pattabhi Jois, an Indian yoga instructor who taught yoga periodically in Encinitas for 20 years beginning in 1975.

"He is very clear: The practice might appear physical, but this is very wrong, it produces a spiritual transformation," Broyles said of Pattabhi Jois.

And Broyles said it's troubling that the grant proposal for the program specifies the Jois Foundation should train and approve the yoga teachers.

The grant proposal, which was drafted July 2012, states that Jois would certify teachers, according to the program's architect, David Miyashiro, who is the assistant superintendent of education services for EUSD. But in reality, the Jois Foundation didn't have a final say on the 10 instructors were hired, he said.

Miyashiro said the grant language should have been "changed," but wasn't amended due to the busyness of preparing for the approaching school year. He added that the Jois Foundation had little influence over the curriculum.

Why then was Eugene Ruffin the Director of Jois Foundation at the Trial? He is the husband of co-founder Salima Ruffin.

Sian Welch's excerpt from blog today at trial reads:

Even though Dean Broyles' closing arguments were scheduled for about a 2 ½ hour presentation, the judge had a lot of communication and questions, so the arguments went all day. This is significant because the facts and the case presented is overwhelmingly in proving yoga is religious and should NOT be taught in public schools. Actually when this case was compared to other cases the court has heard regarding "religion" in public schools this case looks like religion on steroids! It is incredible how the EUSD school district were able to so easily disavow the required state standards and curriculum to just put yoga in the school at all. What state laws allowed this public school district to just rewrite curriculum standards in the first place to allow yoga as their main physical education component? It is obvious and very apparent from the Judges line of questioning, that the judge has a very hard decision to make. There is a lot of "weight" behind this and a decision based on the facts may not be as easy to render a judgment as the overwhelming facts of this case proves. Not only because the decision to remove yoga from the public school curriculum would be hugely unpopular but, not surprisingly, our White House is weighing into this case as well.

WASHINGTON: The White House (https://timesofindia.india-times.com/topic/White-House) has wholeheartedly embraced Yoga as a worthy physical activity at a time some schools in America (https://timesofindia.indiatimes.com/world/us/articlelist/30359486.cms) are railing against the ancient Indian practice, saying it promotes Hinduism.

Resources: Chapter 12

1. Sedlock v. EUSD Trial Transcript Day 6 - June 26, 2013: https://truthaboutyoga.files.wordpress.com/2015/01/13-06-26-part-02final.pdf.

2. Nathan Kanter, "*The Future of Religious Choice: Sedlock v. Baird and the Establishment Clause.*" (How the judge got it wrong), The Wheaton Law Review, Spring, 2016. https://wculrcom.files.wordpress.com/2016/04/wculr-vol-1-no-1.pdf.

3. Jared Whitlock, "*Attorneys Deliver Closing Arguments in School Yoga Trial,*" Coast News, June 26, 2013. https://www.thecoastnews.com/attorneys-deliver-closing-arguments-in-school-yoga-trial/.

4. Lilly Fowler, RNS, "*Yoga on Trial in San Diego, Religious Lawsuit,*" Charisma News, June 26, 2013. http://www.charismanews.com/us/40019-yoga-on-trial-in-san-diego-religious-lawsuit.

Broyles quoted in the article—This "represents the clearest case I have observed of the government advancing, endorsing, or promoting religion," said Dean Broyles, president of the National Center for Law and Policy, a nonprofit based in Escondido, Calif., dedicated to defending religious freedom, traditional marriage and the sanctity of life.

"In America we do not allow the government to pick religious winners and losers, especially when you have a captive audience of very young and impressionable children as we do in our public schools," he said.

Note: The Three prongs:

1. *The government's action **must have a secular legislative purpose;***
2. *The government's action **must not have the primary effect of either advancing or inhibiting religion;***
3. *The government's action **must not result in an "excessive government entanglement" with religion***

Key word "Entanglement"—no matter how you see this case, "entanglement in religion" is impossible to avoid when you are teaching children yoga. The proof of this is the constant revisions of the "religious" parts of the curriculum. If yoga didn't have religious tenets there would be no reason to continually monitor, revise, and remove basic concepts of the yoga practice.

Resources: Chapter 13

1. The Verdict, *court reporter notes*: https://truthaboutyoga.files. wordpress.com/2015/01/statement-of-intended-decision-meyer.pdf.

Media Response to Verdict

2. Rory Devine and J. Stickney, *"San Diego Judge Okays Yoga in Schools, Denies Religious Component,"* July 1, 2013. http:// www.nbcsandiego.com/news/local/Yoga-Lawsuit-Encinitas-Judgment-Ruling-School-Class-Controversy-213853341. html#ixzz2XrSK81Zt. Videos of *verdict and reaction* on both sides (although media lacks accurate facts on verdict), Baird, Broyles and Ruffin, all 3 speak to media after verdict.

3. India's response to the trial: http://www.indiawest.com/news/ global_indian/yoga-poses-new-questions-for-st-century-practitioners/article_3d4cd8c0-72ce-11e5-895f-17a2ef13b575.html.

4. Press Release post trial, July 1, 2013: http://www.nclplaw.org/ wp-content/uploads/2011/12/Post-Trial-Press-Release-FINAL1.pdf.

5. Press Release post trial, July 9, 2013: http://www.nclplaw. org/wp-content/uploads/2011/12/Post-Trial-Press-Release-CONFLUENCE-FINAL.pdf.

6. Huffington Post on yoga and the Church vs. State Battle in Encinitas: http://www.huffingtonpost.com/news/ encinitas-yoga-trial/.

7. Candy Gunther Brown, *"What Makes the Encinitas Yoga Program Religious?"* Huffington Post: http://www.huffingtonpost.com/ candy-gunther-brown-phd/encinitas-yoga-lawsuit_b_3570850.html.

8. Robin Abcarain, *"Yoga in Public Schools is Exercise, Not Religion,"* LA Times, July 1, 2013. http://www.latimes.com/local/lanow/la-me-ln-religious-objections-yoga-public-schools-20130701-story.html.

Resources: Chapter 14

1. The Appellate Decision (37 pages): https://truthaboutyoga.files.wordpress.com/2015/01/appeal-court-decision.pdf.

2. Press Release: *"Oral Arguments before a 'Hot Bench,'"* March 11, 2015. http://www.nclplaw.org/wp-content/uploads/2011/12/Appeal-Press-Release-3-11-15-.pdf.

3. Decision of Appellate Judges, April 3, 2015. https://truthaboutyoga.files.wordpress.com/2015/01/appeal-court-decision.pdf.

4. Press Release in response to Appellate Judges Decision, April 3, 2015. http://www.nclplaw.org/wp-content/uploads/2011/12/Appeal-Press-Release-4-03-15-FINAL.pdf .

5. Encinitas parent group, Narrative summary about the lawsuit: https://truthaboutyoga.files.wordpress.com/2015/01/lawsuit-in-encinitas.pdf.

6. Don Bauder, *"Encinitas Schools have Scrubbed their Yoga Programs Clean. Is Yoga a Religion? Courts say it is,"* The San Diego Reader, April 29, 2015. Finally, (after three years), an article where one reporter is starting to scratch below the surface to see the connections: http://www.sandiegoreader.com/news/2015/apr/29/citylights-yoga-religion/#.

7. Press Release, *"NCLP will not Pursue Appeal Challenging Encinitas' Ashtanga Yoga Program (Sedlock vs. Baird),"* June 11, 2015: http://www.nclplaw.org/wp-content/uploads/2011/12/Appeal-Press-Release-6-11-15-FINAL.pdf.

8. Bob Unruh, *"Parents Opposing Yoga for Kids take Campaign Public,"* WND, June 12, 2015. http://www.wnd.com/2015/06/parents-opposing-yoga-for-kidstake-campaign-public/.

9. Sonia Waraich, *"Yoga Poses New Questions for 21st Century Practitioners,"* India West interviews us after case, October 15, 2015. http://www.indiawest.com/news/global_indian/yoga-poses-new-questions-for-st-century-practitioners/article_3d4cd8c0-72ce-11e5-895f-17a2ef13b575.html.

10. Webpage with court documents, press releases and the news surrounding the actual timing of the trial to click onto easily: https://truthaboutyoga.com/about/lawsuit-in-encinitas-2/.

11. More news after the trial is continually added to the News and Media page: http://truthaboutyoga.com/news-media/.

Section Three

1. Manachu, Kumar, *"What is the Difference Between Stretching and Yoga?"* Difference/Between.net, Nov. 2, 2009. http://www.differencebetween.net/science/health/difference-between-yoga-and-stretching/#ixzz2BeonizBx.

Resources: Chapter 15

1. American Yoga Association (AYA), *"Yoga is not for Children under 16."* http://www.americanyogaassociation.net/.

2. Mayo Clinic, *"Yoga for kids: A good idea?"* Ashtanga Yoga not good for kids, Nov. 17, 2010. http://www.yogaforkidsportland.com/yoga-for-kids-a-good-idea-by-mayo-clinic-staff.html.

3. Dr. Jennifer Solomon, *"Can Yoga Wreck your Body?"* NBC, January 11, 2012. (https://www.hss.edu/newsroom_jennifer-solomon-preventing-yoga-injuries.asp#.VU_ekTnn9lY).

4. Dr. Eden Fromberg, *"Obstetrician/gynecologist on yoga complications to women's health,"* Huffington Post, March 13, 2012. http://www.huffingtonpost.com/eden-g-fromberg-do/yoga_b_1202465.html.

5. Jennifer Wolff Perrine, Orthopedic Surgeon, *"Bad Karma, When Yoga harms instead of heals,"* NBC, July 15, 2008. http://www.nbcnews.com/id/25400799/#.V1_7Wo-cGhd.

6. William J. Broad, *"Women's Flexibility is a Liability (in Yoga),"* New York Times, Nov 2, 2013. http://www.nytimes.

com/2013/11/03/sunday-review/womens-flexibility-is-a-liability-in-yoga.html?_r=1.

7. Marie Carrico, *"Dangers of Yoga"*, IDEA health and Fitness, 1998. http://dangersofyoga.blogspot.com/2010/02/yoga-contraindications-of-yoga.html.

8. Kapalbhati Benefits and Dangers: (https://www.youtube.com/watch?v=itZp-2IsoE4).

9. Yoga Guru, *Side effects of yoga*: http://www.yogadvdguru.com/yoga-side-effects.shtml.

10. American Academy of Orthopedic Surgeons (AAOS) on Ortho info, injury prevention. http://orthoinfo.aaos.org/topic.cfm?topic=A00063.

11. Idea Health and Fitness Association, *"Injury prevention for common yoga injuries to the spine, ligaments, cartilage, muscles and tendons,"* October 4, 2006. http://www.ideafit.com/fitness-library/injury-prevention-yoga-class-take-out.

12. Laura Newcomer, *"The most common yoga injuries and how to prevent them,"* The Greatist, September 10, 2012. http://greatist.com/fitness/common-yoga-injuries-prevention-treatment.

13. Maggie Guiffrida, *"How to prevent common yoga injuries,"* Health and Wellness, February 5, 2014. http://www.sheknows.com/health-and-wellness/articles/1025219/how-to-prevent-common-yoga-injuries.

14. Kim Brunhuber and Marijka Hurko, *"Yoga can lead to hip injuries and hip replacements,"* NBC News, November 15, 2013. http://www.cbc.ca/news/health/yoga-can-lead-to-hip-injuries-1.2427134.

15. Michaele Edwards, *"Injury Prevention in Alignment,"* Website: http://yogalign.com/yoga-injuries-2/.

16. Ann Pizer *"7 Steps to Preventing Injury at Yoga Class."* Updated May 1, 2019. https://www.verywell.com/preventing-injury-at-yoga-class-3567225.

17. Sadie Nardini, *"Four common Yoga Mistakes that Can Cause Knee Pain and Damage,"* Gaiam Website. https://www.gaiam.com/blogs/discover/4-yoga-mistakes-that-can-cause-knee-pain.

18. Jennifer Wolff Perrine, *"Yoga attacks the frame of the human bone and ligament structure,"* NBC News http://www.nbcnews.com/id/25400799/#.VvBEHI-cFul.

19. Diane Bruni *"Yogis share hip and knee injuries"* You Tube, https://www.youtube.com/watch?v=BLVb0klaris).

20. William Broad, *"How Yoga Can Wreck Your Body"*, New York Times, January 5, 2012. http://www.nytimes.com/2012/01/08/magazine/how-yoga-can-wreck-your-body.html?_r=3).

21. Charlotte Bell, *"Yogis Be Careful with Your Joints,"* Elephant Journal, September 11, 2013. http://www.elephantjournal.com/2013/09/yogis-be-careful-with-your-joints-charlotte-bell/.

22. Charlotte Bell, *Yoga teacher goes public and testifies to injuries in yoga,* You Tube: https://www.youtube.com/watch?v=BLVb0klaris.

23. "Namaste Nation," New 2016 Study Shows Staggering Growth in Yoga in America! April, 2016. http://www.lighthousetrailsresearch.com/blog/?p=19095.

24. Joshua Wortman, *"Static Stretching reduces muscle strength and force.* https://breakingmuscle.com/fitness/static-stretching-reduces-muscle-strength-and-force.

25. Tony Allen *"Stretching prior to working out could reduce athletic performance."* July 22, 2009. https://www.unlv.edu/news/article/stretching-truth.

26. What are Growth Plate Injuries? Website: https://www.niams.nih.gov/health_info/Growth_Plate_Injuries/default.asp.

27. Risks of, and Techniques to Avoid Growth Plate Injuries in Young Athletes; http://uncwellness.com/2015/02/risks-of-and-techniques-to-avoid-growth-plate-injuries-in-young-athletes/. Jonathaon Cluett, MD *"Types of Growth Plate Fractures,"* April 24, 2019. https://www.verywell.com/types-of-growth-plate-fractures-2549446?_ga=2.179866663.2023927512.1522678167-498532204.1522678167.

28. Melissa W Sais, *"The Dangers of Overtraining Youth,"* covers growth plate issues as well: http://www.active.com/soccer/articles/the-dangers-of-overtraining-youth-876660.

29. Mark Singleton, Book *"Yoga Body,"* Oxford University Press, 2010. https://www.amazon.com/Yoga-Body-Origins-Posture-Practice/dp/0195395344.

30. William J. Broad, *"The Science of Yoga, Risks and Rewards Science of Yoga,"* 2012. https://thaingwizard.files.wordpress. com/2013/03/the-science-of-yoga-the-risks-the-rewards.pdf.

31. Michaele Edwards, *Yoga Injury Survey*: http://yogalign.com/ yoga-injury-survey/.

32. Michaelle Edwards, *Weakening of Joints, Tendons, Ligaments and Alignment*: http://yogalign.com/yoga-injuries-2/.

33. Jill Miller, *"Yoga Teacher surprised after years to find out her injury was from yoga,"* Tune Up Fitness, October 23, 2017. https://www.tuneupfitness.com/blog/2017/10/23/surprise-surprise-you-need-a-total-hip-replacement-or-living-with-chronic-pain-without-knowing-youre-living-with-chronic-pain/.

34. Katie Prince (14 year old EUSD student), *"Schools Yoga Class Leads to Lifetime of Pain for Student"* Yoga Injury at EUSD on NBC, May 18, 2015. http://www.nbcsandiego.com/news/local/ Encinitas-School-Yoga-Student-Pain-Prince--296736721.html.

35. Dave Summers, *"14 year old Katie Prince, EUSD student on her Yoga Injury"* and *"Yoga critics Raise Health Concerns,"* Union Tribune, May 18, 2015. http://www.sandiegouniontribune.com/ news/2015/mar/17/yoga-critics-in-encinitas-raise-health-concerns/.

36. Regur Development *specifically for* EUSD yoga teachers in 2011: (https://www.rdgsolutions.com/) when you click on the only link on their homepage you are sent to this website: http:// forhealthyhabits.com/ (on this one, go to upper right and hover over curriculum).

37. Survey: *"Negative Experiences in Yoga Practice: What do Practitioners Report?"* Yoga Anatomy, March 21, 2017. https://www.yoganatomy.com/ negative-experiences-in-yoga-practice-survey-results/.

38. CBC, *"Yoga can lead to Hip Injuries,"* November 15, 2013. http://www.cbc.ca/news/health/ yoga-can-lead-to-hip-injuries-1.2427134?cmp=fbtl.

Resources: Chapter 16

1. Sunny Skyz, Study results show that *more recess* improves productivity levels, Jan 10, 2016. http://www.sunnyskyz.com/

good-news/1475/A-Texas-School-Started-Giving-Kids-4-Recess-Breaks-A-Day-And-The-Results-Have-Been-Wonderful.

2. Michelle Leung and Ellie Sandmeyer, *"Fox News - 10 things that will Lead to Decline of American Values"* (# 10 is Yoga), Media Matters, December 21, 2013. https://www.alternet.org/2013/12/10-things-fox-decided-will-lead-decline-american-values-2013/.

3. Michael Allen, *"The Wussification of America"*, Interview of Larry Winget, Opposing Views, January 3, 2013. http://www.opposingviews.com/i/health/fitness/video-motivational-speaker-larry-winget-slams-stupid-parents-who-take-kids-yoga.
    "Who Hi-jacked our Country?" Interview of Larry Winget, January 4, 2013. https://whohijackedourcountry.blogspot.com/2013/01/if-you-want-to-have-sport-you-need-to.html.

4. Fox News asks if children doing yoga is leading to the "Wussification of America?" Fox News, January 3, 2013. Life Lessons on learning to lose and get back in the game. https://www.mediamatters.org/blog/2013/01/03/fox-asks-if-children-doing-yoga-is-leading-to-t/191994.

Resources: Chapter 17

1. Rabi Maharaj—Video to help Americans understand Hindu culture and yoga: https://www.bing.com/videos/search?q=rabi+maharaj&view=detail&mid=61C2E08A1F023282402461C2E08A1F0232824024&FORM=VIRE.

2. Rabi Maharaj, *Death of a Guru*, Lillenas Publishing Co, 1924, renewed 1952. https://smile.amazon.com/Death-Guru-Remarkable-Story-Search/dp/0890814341/ref=sr_1_1?ie=UTF8&qid=1468505164&sr=8-1&keywords=death+of+a+guru.

3. Jessica Smith, *"The Shattering, An Encounter with Truth,"* Deeper Revelation Books, 2015. https://smile.amazon.com/Shattering-Encounter-Truth-Jessica-Smith/dp/0942507193/ref=sr_1_1?ie=UTF8&qid=1468505441&sr=8-1&keywords=the+shattering%2C+jessica+smith.

4. Jessica Smith, website: http://www.truthbehindyoga.com/

5. Corinna Craft, M.A., J.D, website: https://whatsthematterwithyoga. wordpress.com/.

6. Corinna Craft, *"Can a Christian be demonized?"* https:// whatsthematterwithyoga.wordpress.com/demonization-2/.

7. Corinna Craft, six short videos answering *"What's The Matter with Yoga?"* https://www.youtube.com/ playlist?list=PLz77njjHxb01SX6Vcj8Zm6M_lt4_L2R31

8. Mike Shreve—Former Kundalini Yoga teacher on *"Reasons not to practice yoga"* https://vimeo.com/125830500.

9. Mike Shreve's website: www.shreveministries.org.

10. Mike Shreve's booklet, *"Seven Reasons I No Longer Practice Hatha Yoga,"* Deeper Revelation Books, October 1, 2015. https:// www.amazon.com/Seven-Reasons-Longer-Practice-Hatha/ dp/0942507614.

11. Dangers of yoga (website), Kundalini and TM (meditation): http:// www.yogadangers.com/.

12. A former Hindu yogi speaks about *The Dangers of Yoga and Kundalini in clearing the mind and being tricked*: https://www. youtube.com/watch?v=6DZ7oz_fIq8.

13. Tantra Yoga website: http://healing.about.com/od/sexualhealing/a/ tantricsex.htm

14. Another Tantra website: http://www.mindbodygreen.com/0- 5910/4-Tantric-Yoga-Poses-for-Partners-Who-Want-a-Deeper- Connection.html.

15. Yoga Alliance, *(for accredited yoga instructors)*: https://www. yogaalliance.org/.

16. Candy Gunther Brown, PhD. http://indiana.edu/~relstud/people/ profiles/brown_candy

17. Candy Gunther Brown, *"Healing Gods: Complementary and Alternative Medicine in Christian America,"* Oxford University Press, 2013. https://www.amazon.com/ Healing-Gods-Complementary-Alternative-Christian/ dp/0199985782?ie=UTF8&*Version*=1&*entries*=0.

18. Candy Gunther Brown, *"Debating Yoga and Mindfulness in Public Schools, Reforming Secular Education or Reestablishing Religion?"* University of North Carolina Press, 2019. https://www.amazon.com/Debating-Yoga-Mindfulness-Public-Schools/dp/1469648482/ref=nav_ya_signin?crid=1OFSPX9V4PDR2&keywords=candy+gunther+brown&qid=1558984309&s=gateway&sprefix=candy+gunther+browns+books%2Caps%2C319&sr=8-1&.

Resources: Chapter 18

1. Jois Yoga defines Ashtanga by Opening and Closing sequences: http://joisyoga.com/.

2. Patti Wigington, *"Sun Worship"*, Learn Religions, April 22, 2018. http://paganwiccan.about.com/od/lithathesummersolstice/p/SunWorship.htm

3. Biblical locations about idol worship: . http://www.nclplaw.org/wp-content/uploads/2013/07/Yoga-Fact-Sheet-Rev..pdf

4. Janet Chatraw, *"Did the Beatles introduce Yoga to the Western World?"* How Stuff Works, http://people.howstuffworks.com/beatles-yoga.htm, and Jessie Blackridge, *"The Beatles and Yoga," April 20, 2014.* https://www.elephantjournal.com/2014/04/the-beatles-yoga-jessie-blackledge/.

5. Caryl Mastriciana, *"Yoga Uncoiled,"* Website of Research of the New Age and Emergent church development: http://yogauncoiled.com/ .

6. Caryl Mastriciana, records evidence of the New Age Movement in this video, *"Wide is the Gate:"* https://www.youtube.com/watch?v=bDBoBhIqfwQ.

7. Dean Broyles, *"Biblical talking points for idol worship in yoga,"* November, 2013. (https://truthaboutyoga.files.wordpress.com/2015/01/biblical-talking-points.pdf).

8. Dean Broyles, *"Is Yoga Religious?* Video, January 16, 2014. https://vimeo.com/86794950.

Resources: Chapter 19

1. Kim Bhasin, "*$400 yoga pants are just the beginning,*" May 13, 2015. http://www.bloomberg.com/news/articles/2015-05-13/-400-yoga-pants-are-just-the-beginning.

2. Kristina Everett, "*Julia Roberts now a practicing Hindu,*" New York Times, August 6, 2010. https://www.nydailynews.com/entertainment/gossip/julia-roberts-practicing-hindu-actress-converts-religion-filming-eat-pray-love-article-1.201002.

3. Heather, "*Ashtanga Yoga a favorite for Madonna and Gwyneth,*" October 19, 2018. http://www.dietsinreview.com/diet_column/10/ashtanga-yoga-a-favorite-for-madonna-and-gwyneth/.

4. Ali Garfinkel, "*Ten Sexy Celebs that Rock the Yoga Scene,*" June 22, 2011, http://www.ecorazzi.com/2011/06/22/10-sexy-celebs-that-rock-the-yoga-scene/.

5. Martus, "*Think You Can Be a Christian and do Yoga?*" You Tube Presentation, July 3, 2014. https://www.youtube.com/watch?v=6DZ7oz_fIq8.

6. Corinna Craft, "*Can a Christian be Demonized?*" Webpage: https://whatsthematterwithyoga.wordpress.com/demonization-2/ .

7. Jack Healy, "*Schism Emerges in Bikram Yoga Empire Amid Rape Claims,*" (Bikram Choudhury, the leader of Bikram yoga college in India, accused of sexual assault in San Diego), Feb 23, 2015, http://www.nytimes.com/2015/02/24/us/cracks-show-in-bikram-yoga-empire-amid-claims-of-rape-and-assault.html?ref=topics&_r=0.

8. Ben Hooper, "*Austria School Bans Yoga for 'Religious Reasons',*" (one parent complained, and yoga was sent out the door packing in Austria), October 9, 2014. http://www.upi.com/Odd_News/2014/10/09/Austrian-school-bans-yoga-for-religious-reasons/9621412879176/.

9. Jennifer Wolfe Perrine, "*When Yoga Harms instead of Heals,*" NBC News, July 15, 2008. http://www.nbcnews.com/id/25400799/#.VvBEHI-cFul.

10. Diane Bruni, "*I was addicted to yoga practice,*" You Tube of Yogis injuries: https://www.youtube.com/watch?v=BLVb0klaris).

11. William Broad, *"How Yoga Can Wreck Your Body,"* New York Times, January 5, 2012. http://www.nytimes.com/2012/01/08/magazine/how-yoga-can-wreck-your-body.html?_r=2

12. *Four studies on the spiritual effects of practicing yoga*: https://truthaboutyoga.com/spiritual-effects-of-practicing-yoga/

Resources: Chapter 20

1. YJ Editors, *"Yoga Rolls out on White House Lawn,"* April, 2, 2013: https://www.yogajournal.com/blog/yoga-rolls-white-house-lawn#!

2. Charlie Spearing, *"White House Easter Egg Party to include a 'Yoga Garden',"* March 29, 2013: http://www.washingtonexaminer.com/white-house-easter-egg-roll-party-to-include-a-yoga-garden/article/2525784.

3. Esther Watchmen, *"Yoga and Going Green at School, the Truth Behind the Lies,"* 2013. http://www.amazon.com/Yoga-Going-Green-at-School/dp/1493520385/ref=sr_1_fkmr0_1?ie=UTF8&qid=1459441344&sr=8-1-fkmr0&keywords=going+green+and+yoga+in+the+schools+%2C+books.

4. Esther Watchmen, *"Understanding Yoga: Its Origin and Purpose,"* 2015.

http://www.amazon.com/,Understanding-Yoga-Its-Origin-Purpose/dp/1512228303?ie=UTF8&psc=1&redirect=true&ref_=oh_aui_detailpage_o09_s00.

5. Esther Watchmen, *"The Armageddon Movement,"* 2015, (book not listed in chapter) http://www.amazon.com/Armageddon-Movement-Esther-Watchmen/dp/1512226718/ref=sr_1_1?ie=UTF8&qid=1459441691&sr=8-1&keywords=the+Armageddon+movement.

6. Agenda 21, http://www.cfact.org/2014/04/15/agenda-21-what-agenda-21/).

7. Truthxhange (https://truthxchange.com/).

Resources: Chapter 21

None

Resources: Chapter 22

1. *Yoga: Purely Physical or is it Religious?* DVD, YouTube program, https://truthaboutyoga.com/education-events/.

2. Booklet, Mary Eady, *Letter to a Friend*, 2014, TruthXchange.

3. Education Events: https://truthaboutyoga.com/education-events/.

   Each of these are linked (on the ebook) to the website https://truthaboutyoga.com/education-events/ so you can find them there, or the full documents are also here below.

4. Timeline for Yoga in Encinitas

5. Links to Articles

6. The 5 Myths of Encinitas EUSD Yoga

7. Yoga-Fact-Sheet

8. Yoga Opt out form

9. Biblical Talking Points

10. Jois Family Quotes

11. EUSD Information on Yoga

12. Frequently Asked Questions-Ashtanga Yoga

13. *Critical Thinking Questions to Consider*

14. www.truthaboutyoga.com

4. Timeline for Jois Yoga in Encinitas

2011/2012 – Pilot Program, Jois Foundation teaching Ashtanga yoga at Capri in EUSD

June/July 2012 – Recruitment – Invitations on Jois Foundation website eliciting yoga teachers with 3+ years Ashtanga experience (w/adults) to apply for EUSD yoga jobs for 2012/2013 school year.

July 2012 – EUSD District trains around 30 Ashtanga yoga teachers to decide which were the best fit; EUSD hired the top 10. The 9 principals selected one from that pool of 10 for their schools. Jen Brown, the yoga teacher at Capri, oversaw all the yogis. Jen also works for the Jois Foundation. Many of the yoga teachers still work for the Encinitas Jois yoga studio and some go to India annually.

Aug 2012 – 5 of the 9 EUSD schools begin yoga with the other 4 are "test" sites for comparative data and slated to start yoga in January, 2013. A "study" on the 5000+ students began (without parental permission). Back to school nights presented the "$533,000 Grant" given from Jois Foundation for (mandatory??) Ashtanga yoga in the schools. Stated goal is to co-develop Ashtanga yoga curriculum, beta test it on EUSD students, and export nationally to public schools. Several parents from the district independently contacted Christian constitutional attorney Dean Broyles, president of the National Center for Law & Policy.

Sept 2012 – A group of concerned parents met to discuss the religious experiences their children were having in EUSD Ashtanga yoga classes. Dean Broyles, who is a mentee of attorney Jay Sekulow, of American Center for Law and Justice, attended.

Oct 2012 – Concerned parents met on October 4th, then 65 parents attended the October 9th EUSD Board Meeting where 7 parents spoke to the trustees. Parents told the board that the yoga crossed religious boundaries. The Superintendent responded "No it doesn't," while some, not all the board, were sure.

Nov 2012 – Concerned parents met again. 100 parents went to the Board Meeting. Again 6-7 spoke (only 15 min per topic and 2 min per speaker allowed). Board united in dismissing us.

Dec 2012 – Concerned parents met again. About 150-200 at the EUSD district meeting. About ½ were pro-yoga (yoga studio owners, teachers, and parents). About ½ were parents and grandparents opposing yoga. There were 19 speakers. The media was filming. A petition was presented to the board, with 250 taxpayers in the district, asking the board to take the yoga out. The district still claims today that "only a few parents" are against yoga.

Feb 20, 2012 – "Sedlock vs. Baird" Lawsuit filed. Within 24-hours news media from around the world, including Pakistan and India, were calling the homes and offices. Media spread quickly.

May 20, 21 and 22, then June 24, 25, 26 – 6 days of trial.

July 1st – Statement of Intended Decision read in court by Judge Meyer.

August – Another hearing with Judge Meyer, where he conceded on 2 major points, thus helping an appeal.

October 2013 – Appeal is filed. Briefing, oral argument, and decision expected in 2014.

5. Links to start your research

"Yoga Can Stay in School: Looking More Closely at the Encinitas Yoga Trial Decision," Huffington Post, July 2, 2013, http://www. huffingtonpost.com/candy-gunther-brownphd/what-made-the-encinitas-p_b_3522836.html

"What Makes the Encinitas School Yoga Program Religious?", Huffington Post, July 24, 2013, http://www.huffingtonpost.com/ candy-gunther-brown-phd/encinitas-yogalawsuit_b_3570850.html

"Op-ed: School Sun Salutations Here to Stay," Encinitas Patch, July 1, 2013, http://encinitas.patch.com/groups/schools/p/candy-gunther-brown-school-sun-salutationshere-to-stay-encinitas-yoga

"Understanding the Encinitas Public School Yoga Trial," OUPblog, August 6, 2013, http://blog.oup.com/2013/08/ is-yoga-religious-encitas-public-school-trial/

"Controversy Grows Over School Yoga," discussion aired on Huffington Post Live, August 21, 2013, http://live.huffingtonpost.com/r/segment/ school-yogacontroversy/520572f42b8c2a23cc0005d9

The Coast News: Lawyer appeals judge's ruling over yoga in schools https://thecoastnews.com/2013/11/ lawyer-appeals-judges-ruling-over-yoga-in-schools/

Courts in India now questioning if yoga is too religious for their schools http://www.washingtonpost.com/national/on-faith/ is-yoga-religious-an-indian-court-mullsmandatory-school-exercises/2013/10/28/74117ade-3ffc-11e3-b028-de922d7a3f47_ story.html

http://www.wnd.com/2013/10/religious-yoga-in-class-has-some-bent-out-of-shape/

Video on why yoga is not for Christians by an x-yogi http://www.
youtube.com/watch?v=wKwEkXcmEUQ

History of Jois (yet completely changed and scrubbed website from
last year). It was Hindu site last year, now very "Encinitas kid
friendly looking". http://joisyoga.com/about/story/

Will America Become Hindu by the end of the Century? http://
www.yogaforums.com/forums/f33/will-america-become-hindu-
by-the-end-of-thecentury-6266.html

6. 5 Myths/Realities of EUSD Ashtanga Yoga

Myth #1: People think "It's just Exercise!" or "It's just stretching
and breathing."
>   Reality: There is a lot of evidence that yoga is religious. An
>   international discussion is now happening. Judge Meyer
>   ruled, "Yoga is religious" in the Sedlock vs. Baird lawsuit.
>   Research is available online and in our "Yoga Facts Sheet."

Myth #2: Our kids can pray to God while doing yoga and be fine.
>   Reality: Participation in yoga as a Christian is not just about
>   our intent (praying to God while doing it). In Daniel 3,
>   Shadrach, Meshach and Abednego did not bow to pray to
>   the idol of King Nebuchadnezzar (following the 1st & 2nd
>   commandments of not bowing before idols). They stood
>   boldly against idol worship, proclaiming the One, true God.
>   Why didn't they just bow with everyone else and INTEND
>   to pray to God? Because, our physical posture in worship
>   is not just about intent.

Myth #3: My kids are okay because they know who Jesus is and
have accepted Him as savior.
>   Reality: These are innocent children who need protection
>   and guidance. They do not yet have a fully developed sense
>   of spiritual discernment, as adults do. Yoga goes beyond
>   healthy stretching & breathing into the spiritual arena of

false worship. As Christians, we do not want to dance any-where near the boundary of God-ordained protection for our own good.

Myth #4: Yoga must be okay if the school board chose this program and the principals are supporting it.
Reality: Our children are entrusted to the schools for educa-tion. While they are at school, we do not abdicate our rights and responsibilities in caring for our children. Parents should have choice for participating or not.

Myth #5: We have to live among people of all faiths, so keeping our kids in yoga exposes them to interacting with people who believe differently. We do not want to offend others with our choices.
Reality: Jesus hung out with tax collectors, prostitutes and other sinners. He did not sleep with prostitutes, get drunk with these people or take advantage of people lining his own pockets at the poor's expense. As Christ followers, we can love, accept and live life with people who hold different beliefs from us without participating in these activities. In this specific case, we love people and accept their choices, however we choose to not participate in a form of false worship named Yoga.

Questions & Concerns about pulling your kid(s) out of EUSD yoga:
- I/We do not want them separated from their classmates.
- I/We do not want my child(ren) to feel awkward or left out.
- Our child(ren) might miss out on P.E. minutes (state requirement is 100 min/week).
- I/We do not want to be viewed at as "Extremists".
- I/We are concerned about being labeled as "Troublemakers".
- I/We trust the institution of the school; how can I/we question them?
- Are we even allowed to opt out of a class? How would I do that?

7. Yoga fact sheet…please look online for this document.

8. Opt Out Form: Encinitas Union School District

101 S. Rancho Santa Fe Road Encinitas, CA 92024-4349
Phone: (760) 944-4300 FAX: (760) 942-7094
www.eusd.net

I request that my child _____, grade _____ attending _____ not participate in yoga as part of their required 200 minutes of physical education every ten days.

I understand that alternate physical activities will be provided to my child meeting their required 200 minutes and will be scheduled by their classroom teacher.

_____   _____
Signature   Date

9. The Practice of Yoga Violates Clear Biblical Principles:

• We are intentionally designed and created in God's image. As created beings we are distinct from our Creator. While the God's Holy Spirit does dwell in us, it is unbiblical idolatry to say that individuals are "divine" or are ourselves "gods" (Gen. 1:27; Gen. 5:1-2; Romans 1:25; Matt. 19:4; Mark 10:6).

• Christians should love, worship, bow down to, or obey only the God of the Bible (Exodus 20:1-7; Deut. 6:1; Matthew 4:9-10, 22:37; Romans 1:19-21, 25).

• Christians should not worship, bow down to, or even mention other gods (Exodus 20:3, 20:23, 23:13, 23:24; 32:1-28 (golden calf) Matt. 4: 9-10; Rom. 1:19-21; Gal. 4:8).

• Christians should not worship or bow down to idols; the Bible teaches that idols are connected with demonic activity (Exodus 20:4-5; Psalm 81:9; Isaiah 2:8; 44:19; Micah 5:13; Romans 1:22-23, 25; Acts 7:43; 1 Cor. 10:20-21; 2 Cor. 6:16; 1 Tim. 4:1; 1 John 5:21; Rev. 9:20).

• Yoga is NOT a "non-essential" or "debatable" issue for Christians like "meat sacrificed to idols" (See 1 Cor. 8). In yoga, you are the meat — your body is engaging in pagan worship/idolatry. Your intent alone does not control whether yoga is religious.

• Christian meditation involves focusing on scripture and thoughts about God, not emptying your mind as Hinduism promotes (Joshua 1:8; Psalm 119:15, 23, 48).

• The spiritual realm (angels & demons) although unseen is very real (Mark 16:9; Romans 8:28; Eph. 2:1-3, 6:10-20; 1 Tim. 4:1).

- As Christians, our battle is not just against the physical/material realm but is also in the spiritual realm (Eph. 2:1-3; Eph. 6:10-20). We don't fully understand nor can we control this realm.

- Christians must refuse to submit to the government when it attempts to force them to violate their religious beliefs (See Daniel 3:1-18 (Shadrach, Meshach, & Abednego refuse to bow to the King's idol); Acts 5:29 ("We must obey God rather than men!")).

10. Quotes From The Jois Family About Yoga

"The reason we do yoga is to become one with God and to realize Him in our hearts. You can lecture, you can talk about God, but when you practice correctly, you come to experience God inside. Some people start yoga and don't even know of Him, don't even want to know of Him. But for anyone who practices yoga correctly, the love of God will develop. And, after some time, a greater love for God will be theirs, whether they want it or not. It is true and that is why yoga is real. It develops inside you and helps you to realize the inner light of the Self." (Sri K Pattahbi Jois, Founder of Jois Foundation)...From Interview with Three Gurus

"Yoga is to unite. You can unite with yourself whenever you want; there's no set rule. It's not like you have to see the Pope to be a good Catholic. You can see the Pope in a pew (soulself). That's what so-ham means: I am God, I am the Creator. I am the Vishnu, the Preserver; I am the Shiva, the destroyer; and I am the Creator, the Brahma. I am all three, the three is you. What you create is what you see, God is not over there, he is inside of you, he is making you do all these things. We think that someone did something to us, but no, you did it, it's all your own creation. You've got to unite within yourself, then there won't be any more confusion. See, we are having a problem uniting with ourselves, because we have ego, selfishness, jealousy, hate, and mada [intoxication]. We are totally filled with kashmala [filth], so we have to purify all those things.

Then, we can see exactly what it is. That is what yoga is all about. See, we just confuse ourselves with a lot of things." (Manju Jois, son of Guruji, teacher at Jois Foundation)... http://www.kripalu.org/pdfs/manju_jois_article.pdf

"Many people think yoga is like a gym, or like going to a work out, but that is not yoga. Nowadays, it has become a trend to take a yoga course for something like one month, and then you are able to say that you have become a teacher. But that is not yoga. Yoga is spiritual. You should consider it a spiritual practice, not just exercise. Spiritual. Asana (posture) is only one step on the path of yoga. Yoga really means self-consciousness, self-realization — that is the ultimate meaning of yoga. Not just doing postures. This is only one aspect, but it is the foundation for you to realize what you are. To realize the source, what we are inside, that is real yoga.... Yoga is so powerful that even if you practice without thinking or believing anything — you will benefit. If you are thinking that yoga is only exercise — still you receive benefits. But you can also dig deeper, research further, and learn about yoga philosophy, a process that is never ending. You can keep learning your whole lifetime. It also depends upon how you think about yoga. Some people think it is only about asana, exercise and practice. Yet still they receive the benefits to their health. Problems will solve. They become concentrated. Many people have come to me and said, 'I started practicing yoga and my life has been changed.' People can improve their whole lifestyle. Yoga changes your life. It doesn't matter what or how you think. It has already changed so many lives, that's why it is getting more popular." (Sharath Jois, son of Guruji, teacher at Jois Foundation)... http://life.gaiam.com/article/meet-ashtanga-yogi-r-sharath

"Let everything come in its own time. A plant and tree needs proper time to grow under right conditions, why should we human beings be any different. To grow into yoga means growing into life, proper conditions need to be there, but when start to feel it; you'll come to know it is real. Don't look for God or the Goddess outside of you. Learn to listen from within and explore a new energy within you. The constant which always remains, is the clarity and balance that the ashtanga yoga practice gives. The years of practice become a framework for how we live our lives each and every day." (Sarawathi Rangaswamy, daughter of Guruji and teacher at Jois) http://www.saraswathiashtanga.com/insights.html "The Western world has a tendency to focus only on the physical side. This is NOT yoga. You are only practicing yoga and getting the complete benefit when you combine the physical with the spiritual. You can't do one without the other because it causes confusion. If you only practice the physical side you become physically strong but spiritually weak." (Manju Jois) http://theaspiringyogi.wordpress.com/2010/06/05/an-interview-with-manju-jois/

Links for Further Research...

"Practice and All Is Coming, long time students remember his love and wisdom http://www.yogajournal.com/wisdom/2568

"Extracts from 'Guruji', A Portrait of Sri K. Pattabhi Jois Through the Eyes of His Students" http://www.aysnyc.org/index.php?option=com_content&task=view&id=212&Itemid=220

"Ashtanga Yoga. In the tradition of Sri K. Pattabhi Jois" http://www.yogalar.com/sample-page/

"Ashtanga Yoga' means 'eight limbed yoga." It is an ancient system that can lead to liberation and greater awareness of our spiritual potential..... www.joisyoga.com

Ashtanga Vinyasa Yoga http://en.wikipedia.org/wiki/Ashtanga_Vinyasa_Yoga#Eight_Limbs_of_Ashtanga

"Find the Eastern Roots of Yoga in the West" Sharath Jois speaks.... http://life.gaiam.com/article/meet-ashtanga-yogi-r-sharath

11. <u>EUSD Information on Yoga</u>

Information for Parents: The EUSD/JOIS Foundation Yoga Program

The JOIS Foundation has given EUSD a $533K grant to implement a religious form of yoga at all 9 of its school sites.

- The JOIS Foundation is a religious institution that trains people in a very religious form of yoga, known as "Ashtanga" yoga.

- JOIS Foundation classes include physical practice of yoga along with religious instruction like a class called "Yoga Sutras of Patanjali" – literally, a class in the eight spiritual limbs of yoga, systematized in 150 A.D.

- The grant explicitly states that Ashtanga yoga training will be taught to students and provided to staff and families. Many people have been told that the yoga being taught is not religious, but Ashtanga yoga is inherently religious.

- The founder of Jois Yoga, Sri K Pattahbi Jois, the guru of JOIS yoga (a guru is a Hindu religious leader or enlightened master) said, "**It is very important to understand yoga philosophy -- without philosophy, yoga practice is not good, and yoga practice is the starting place for yoga philosophy**. Mixing both is actually best."

- Jois, also known as "guruji" said that Ashtanga yoga *IS* Patanjali yoga, directly designating what he taught, and his institute continues to teach, as religious practice. In fact, in the biography page on the JOIS Foundation site, they state, "Guruji lives on through his teachings {…} and every time we practice as he has taught us."

- Ashtanga literally means "Eight Limbed" and the eight limbs of this religious yoga are based in Hindu spirituality (which is also ancient yoga "philosophy").

- The ultimate (eighth) goal of Ashtanga Yoga practice (which includes *moral* codes, self purification and study, postures, breath control, sense control, concentration, and meditation) is **absorption in the Universal** (Samadhi).

- All steps of the path along the eight limbs, including physical practice, are designed and intended to lead followers to that eighth goal. As Jois said, "Do your practice. All [the Universal] is coming."

- The physical poses of yoga (Asanas) were developed to tell the stories of Hindu gods and events. In a widely acknowledged book called *Myths of the Asanas*, the authors write to yoga teachers and practitioners, "Asana practice's… *philosophical principles encourage spiritual growth…*[that] Asanas can be viewed as a kind of prayer."

- Even according to expert yoga teachers and practitioners, **yoga poses are not ever merely exercise, they are different from other forms of systemized practices *because they are inherently religious.***

- All of the teachers hired by the school district to teach yoga at the school sites must be certified by the JOIS Foundation and should have established Ashtanga practices.

- This literally means that a religious organization is paying the school district to bring teachers with their specific certification into our schools to teach children a religious practice as a major part of their PE program, for a grade, and with no alternative program for children whose beliefs conflict with those of yoga philosophies and practice.

This religiously based yoga program is called a "mind/body" program which includes more than stretching and exercise, though to many parents it has been presented as mere exercise.

- The grant stipulates the development of a "life skills curriculum" which is, in part, based on "key yoga life concepts," and requires the curricular model to include "life skills built around key themes of yoga instruction."

- As stated above, yoga life skills include yoga philosophy, which is **inherently religious** and conflicts with the beliefs of Christians, Muslims, Mormons, Jews and others.

- Students at one school site have already been instructed regarding how to channel energy through a yoga pose to calm anxiety.

Students are required to take these courses and are being graded in participation.

- Parents will not be asked permission to opt their children into this program. It is a compulsory program and all children are participating unless their parents opt them out.

- If you have not already opted your child out of the program, he or she has likely already begun to participate in Ashtanga yoga instruction.

- Students whose religious beliefs conflict with the beliefs taught in Ashtanga yoga are not being offered an alternative course of physical education to replace those minutes of physical education lost as a result of their having to be pulled.

- Other course work is being cut to make room for this curriculum. At one school site, math time has been cut in order to include this curriculum.

The Ashtanga yoga program violates the U.S. Constitution's First Amendment (the "separation of church and state") and California law.

- The EUSD Ashtanga yoga program involves Hindu religious worship and practices and illegally promotes the religion of Hinduism (*See* above).

- The U.S. Constitution's First Amendment states that government "shall make no law respecting **the establishment of religion** . . ." The EUSD yoga program unconstitutionally establishes the Hindu religion as the preferred and favored religion in the district.

- The U.S. Constitution's First Amendment also states that government shall not prohibit the **"free exercise" of religion**. The EUSD yoga program is not religiously neutral and undermines the religious free exercise rights of and discriminates against Christian, Jewish, Muslim, Mormon and other children and parents by offering only participation in religious activities that violate their religious beliefs and practices.

- The federal courts have already ruled that the promotion and practice of **Transcendental Meditation** in New Jersey public schools which, like yoga, is also a Hindu religious practice, is a violation of the First Amendment's prohibition of governmental establishment of religion (*See Malnak v. Yogi*, 1979).

- The California Constitution states that the government may not **"prefer" one religion** over another (Art. I, sec. 4). The EUSD yoga program illegally prefers Hinduism over Christianity, Judaism, Islam, Mormonism and other religions.

- The California Constitution also states that the government may not **engage in religious "discrimination"** (Art. I, sec. 4). The EUSD yoga program is not religiously neutral because it illegally discriminates against and excludes from the physical education program objecting Christian, Jewish, Muslim, and Mormon parents and children as well as those of other religions.

- State law and curriculum guidelines states that "materials on religious subject matters [must] remain **neutral**; do not **advocate one religion over another**; do not include **simulation or role playing** of religious ceremonies or beliefs . . . ." The EUSD yoga program violates these guidelines because it is not religiously neutral, it advocates Hinduism over other religions, and includes simulation and role playing of Hindu religious practices.

- The California Code of Regulations forbids the **separation** of students in public schools **on the basis of religion** as well as other factors (5 CCR Sec. 4940). The EUSD Yoga program is **divisive** and **discriminatory** and violates the law by separating parents and students of other non-Hindu religious beliefs from the parents and students who do not object to Hindu religious beliefs and practices.

- Parents and students who object to the program are left without any P.E. program for their children. This violates California Education Code 5120.1(a)(2) which requires that "[A]ll pupils have access to a high quality, comprehensive, and developmentally appropriate physical education instruction on a regular basis."

The physical education program should not be structured to exclude and harm children.

- P.E. in our public schools should be inclusive, bringing kids from different backgrounds together to engage in unifying *physical* activity, not divisive *religious* activity.

- Students should not be put in a position where they are singled out and treated differently for not being able to participate in a school program which discriminates against their religious beliefs and practices in favor of another system of religious beliefs and practices.

You have rights as a parent or guardian.

- To become fully informed about the Ashtanga yoga program in the district.

- You may ask to observe a yoga class at school and ask to review any texts that are being used to instruct children in this practice.

- You may demand that EUSD board of education suspend this unconstitutional and divisive promotion of the Hindu religion to young and impressionable children.

- You may talk to the principal and teachers at your child's school and explain to them why you object to the yoga program, and your child's participation.

- You may respectfully request that your child be removed from this instruction.

- You may ask for an explanation of where your child will be placed during that time and what instruction he or she will receive instead.

- You may consider taking legal action on behalf of your child to end this unlawful religious practice.

You should be concerned not only for your children participating in this program, but for the precedent that is being set by the agreement between EUSD and JOIS Foundation.

- By allowing EUSD to move forward with this program, our community is implicitly approving a public school district choosing and teaching a religious practice of its preference.

- This approval opens the door for the district to bring in any other religious practice of its choosing based, not on the legality of the decision, but the perceived benefits of the religious practice.

- Allowing EUSD to carry on with this agreement implicitly approves of the District making illegal decisions regarding curriculum development for financial gain from a religious institution.

- Pulling your children from the program without speaking out against the program protects only your children and does not change the inappropriate precedent being set which could embolden the District to make choices like this in the future.

This document was created using, in large part, information from the following sources:

- The EUSD Grant agreement with JOIS

- The MOU between EUSD and JOIS

- The MOU between EUSD and Regur Development Group

- Information found at the JOIS website, http://www. joisyoga.com

- Information found at the website http://www. ashtanga.com

- Information found at the informational site http://www. ashtangayoga.info

- From excerpts of a book called "Myths of the Asanas: The Ancient Origins of Yoga".

12. FREQUENTLY ASKED QUESTIONS

Is Ashtanga yoga good for all children of the Encinitas school district?
Our children are worth your time to seek the facts

Background: The Encinitas Union School District (EUSD) made up of 9 elementary schools is replacing most of Physical Education (P.E.) each week with Ashtanga Yoga following a $533,000 grant given to EUSD by the Jois Foundation, beginning in August, 2012.

Q: Why are parents opposing yoga in the schools?

A: Parents are opposing the specific type of yoga called "Ashtanga Yoga", one of the most religious forms of yoga. In addition, parents are opposing the Jois Foundation itself, and the billionaires, Paul and Sonia Tudor Jones, who funded the startup of a Contemplative Sciences Center at the University of Virginia to study and pro-mulgate Ashtanga yoga. The billionaires also funded the Jois Foundation which then paid EUSD in exchange for classes and subjects for the study (our children). Finally, parents are opposing the Jois Foundations' stated agenda to spread Ashtanga Yoga to the entire West and to children in schools in the USA. Links to all of these details you will find in this document.

Q: What is Ashtanga Yoga?

A: Ashtanga Yoga has deep Hindu spiritual and religious roots and involves recitation of mantras and the assumption of yoga poses. http://www.thevoicemagazine.com/christian-living-christianity/spiritual-warfare/yoga-and-the-kundalini-spirit.html Ashtanga literally means "Eight Limbed". The eight limbs of this religious yoga are Hindu spirituality http://www.ashtanga.com/html/background.html. Also see "The Heart of Yoga Revealed," at http://kpjayi.org/the-practice, the last paragraph of which is particularly disturbing.

Q: What does the founder of the Jois Foundation say about yoga as "just exercise"?

A: This is a video by Sri IK. Pattabhi Jois on Ashtanga Yoga saying that yoga speaks for itself. He says "you cannot separate the "exercise"

from the spiritual worship" and the Kundalini spirit: http://www.
youtube.com/watch?feature=player_embedded&v=uQGRq00xqbI.

Q: What is the difference between yoga and stretching?
A; Read here: http://www.differencebetween.net/science/health/
difference-between-yoga-and-stretching/#ixzz2BeonizBx.

Q: Is Ashtanga yoga or are other types of yoga good for children?
A: The Mayo Clinic reports that two styles of yoga may **be inappropriate for children** including: Ashtanga and Bikram. Risks
and safety for kids include: vomiting, migraines, asthma, etc.
Read more: http://www.mayoclinic.com/health/yoga-for-kids/
MY01401/NSECTIONGROUP=2 .

In addition, many pediatricians cite yoga precautions since children
tend to have looser joints and great enthusiasm; and as a result, they
may be unaware when they are stretching beyond what is safe. They
state: "do not consider yoga to be a substitute for aerobic exercise,
which is a crucial way to combat the childhood obesity." Parents
should be aware of the risks. Read more: http://www.ourkidssake.
org/upload/files/Children-and-Yoga.pdf. Still, the American Yoga
Association states, "Yoga exercises are not recommended for children fewer than 16 because their bodies' nervous and glandular
systems are still growing, and the effect of Yoga exercises on these
systems may interfere with natural growth." Read more: http://
en.wikipedia.org/wiki/Yoga.

Q: What is the Jois Foundation? Although this website has completely transformed since September, you will still find the religious philosophy and foundation here. They've taken the whole
India look out and "westernized" and "modernized" it.
A: See http://www.joisyoga.com/

**Q: Hasn't the District told us they "scrubbed" religious parts
out of the yoga program already?**
A; The sun salutations poses (worshipping the sun) are practiced in our classes, http://4.bp.blogspot.com/-wOjHmeEpOa8/
T6s0NCClqqI/AAAAAAAAADQ/Su6rDIq_BxI/s1600/
surya-namaskara-A1.gif. Eight-limbed posters have been found at
Capri on the wall of the yoga classroom, Sankrit names for limbs
(feet, hands, etc.) were taught to children in several schools, children sitting in a circle and saying "Namaste" to one another was

seen at Park Dale Lane (Literally means I see the gods in you), coloring mandalas have been "art" at El Camino Creek but then mysteriously went away before most parents saw them, and so much more has been witnessed by parents of our District.

Q: How are Jois Foundation, Paul and Sonia Tudor Jones and the University of Virginia linked?

A: Billionaire Paul Tudor Jones and his wife Sonia have been instrumental in funding the Jois Foundation. Tudor Jones also donated $12 million to the University of Virginia in April of 2012 to start the Contemplative Sciences Center ("CSC"). A clear and stated goal of the Jois Foundation is to study and promulgate Ashtanga yoga worldwide. The stated goal of the EUSD grant is to establish an Ashtanga-centered K-6 program; and, if all goes as planned, Ashtanga yoga will go into EUSD in lieu of regular gym class for at least 60 of the 100 required minutes per week. At least one school is doing 90 minutes of yoga. Read more on the **conflict of interest**, http://www.c-ville.com/yoga-u-is-the-contemplative-sciences-center-the-answer-to-uvas-reputation-gap-or-an-expensive-new-age-sideshow/2/#.UHcNRs5cYyA.

Q: Why is Ashtanga yoga mandatory at EUSD and not an option?

A: The $533,000 grant from the Jois Foundation requires mandatory yoga as outlined in the Memorandum of Understanding (MOU) between the Jois Foundation and EUSD and the MOU between EUSD and Regur Development Group. In it Jois has a stipulated right to review all the curriculum developed and have input into it through the Regur Development Group. The MOUs can be obtained from the district upon request. www.eusd.k12.ca.us/

Q: What are the terms of the Jois Foundation grant?

A: The grant gives the funds to EUSD in exchange for a study of approximately 6,000 students participating in yoga classes with data collection of vital signs and other measurements available for the study. These measurements are being completed by yoga instructors and parent volunteers during Math and English time rather than during yoga sessions (as seen by parents volunteering in the schools).

Q: Did parents have to authorize their kids for the study?

565

A: No, our kids were all placed in the study and Ashtanga yoga classes without required parent authorization as a mandatory program. You can choose to opt your child out of the class and/ or study.

Q: Who is responsible for hiring the Ashtanga yoga program instructors and do they have any K-6 teaching experience?

A: EUSD has claimed it had sole responsibility in hiring all teachers for the program, however, the Jois Foundation advertised to its own community of teachers for these positions and requested applications leading to EUSD's selection from this pool. These instructors, now being called district employees, are trained in Ashtanga yoga that is primarily taught to adults. It is unclear as to the specific K-6 instructor experience and/or formal teaching credentials of the recently hired Ashtanga yoga program instructors.

Q: Would the EUSD Board have implemented the Ashtanga yoga program and replace the majority of regular P.E. if there were no grant money provided?

A: Probably not.

Q: What if kids are embarrassed by doing the Yoga movements on the mat in front of their classmates – can they opt out and still get P.E.?

A: Yes, they can opt out, however, no P.E. alternative(s) are currently available even though the district stated in the news that there is an alternative. As of March 28, well into the school year, there is not an option and those children are not getting the 100 required P.E. minutes. Some parents of younger children pick their child up for the 30 minute sessions of yoga; some children go to classrooms or libraries.

Q: Other questions for consideration?

A: Here are a number of other questions for personal consideration:

- Are we setting a precedent for the rest of the nation with an Ashtanga yoga program in the EUSD?
- Do you support all children across the USA doing Ashtanga yoga every week for 6-7 years with a lot less exposure to all the traditional American P.E. sports (for example kickball,

baseball, basketball, soccer, field hockey, flag football, volleyball, etc.)?

- Do you want kids taught any one form of P.E. weekly – all year?
- Should 5th and 6th grade boys and girls be taking yoga together? Is bending over on mats in front of each other causing any sexual ramifications?
- Should there be a Yoga dress code on the two yoga days?
- Have you read the press release from The National Center for Law & Policy? See http://www.nclplaw.org/wp-content/uploads/2011/12/NCLPPressRelease20FINAL1.pdf.

13. **Critical Thinking Questions To Consider**

Ashtanga Yoga, Wellness Study & Grant Monies

1. Why is Ashtanga yoga mandatory – why not an option?
2. Is the $533,000 grant from the Jois Foundation associated with mandatory yoga?
3. Would the board have implemented yoga if there were no grant of money attached?
4. Would the board have ever implemented yoga if they had to pay the same amount for it?
5. Do you know who is funding the Jois Foundation, USD & UVA for this study?
6. Could it be that the Jois Foundation & UVA need large numbers of subjects thereby funding the study?
7. Have you researched Jois Foundation?
8. Have you read the EUSD/Jois Grant/ MOU?
9. Does this study of Yoga aim to replace the variety of PE? Do you know?
10. Do you know the intended study in Encinitas is for 3 years?
11. Do you know what our district has committed to already? Do you feel informed?

Ashtanga Yoga's Roots

1. Have you researched Ashtanga yoga?
2. Have you considered the possibility that the sequence of yoga poses being taught to the kids, are worshipful in nature?
3. Do you know what the sun salutations (worshipping the sun) are and that your kids will do them in class? What will happen if we ask the teacher to change the order?
4. Do you know what the warrior pose and other poses really mean? Do you know it is easy to find these out?

Ashtanga Yoga As Every Child's Exercise

1. Is yoga the ideal exercise for every single child?
2. What happens if some kids don't like yoga? Most kids don't like some forms of PE but it is usually only a unit, not the whole class for the year. Does this pose a problem?
3. What if kids are embarrassed by doing the Yoga movements on the mat in front of their peers?
4. What about the kids who are obese, ADHD, and other physical challenges to standing in poses for long periods?
5. What if kids get made fun of MORE rather than less? Will we know it? (Does yoga decrease bullying as the stated goal or open kids up to more?)
6. Should 5th and 6th grade boys and girls be taking yoga bending over on mats in front of each other? Are there sexual ramifications? Can they really not look at each other even if told not to? (Ask the 6th grade boys to find out!). Should there be a Yoga dress code on yoga days?

Ashtanga Yoga Across The USA

1. Are you aware you can read the stated agenda for the study? It is for yoga to replace all PE for first 7 years of elementary school across the USA.

2. When you think beyond our own school district, do you realize we are setting a precedent for the rest of the nation? Do you support all children across the USA doing yoga every week for 7 years instead of exposure to all the traditional American PE sports (ie: kickball, baseball, basketball, soccer, field hockey, flag football, etc)?

3. Do you want kids taught any ONE form of PE weekly all year?

4. Have you considered that some families cannot afford to pay for extra-curricular activities after school so PE is the only place they learn and practice a variety of sports?

5. Would it be okay if that were say volleyball–one hour per week for 7 years? Wouldn't we become a star "volleyball" nation?

6. If children take yoga for these first 7 years of school, what do you think the result will be in that generation of children? It is important to consider where this could lead and our role.

7. Have you thought about the authority given to the yoga teachers over the kids and what the ramifications of that could be over time? Do their credentials match that of our teachers on how to handle children in classroom?

8. Do you want to be partially responsible (by your participation in the study) for this program of Ashtanga yoga replacing PE across the entire US after the study is done in 3 years?

Ashtanga Yoga vs. Other Options

1. Could yoga be offered as an afterschool option (like many other sports) and still studied?

2. Could yoga be an alternative to regular PE and kids/parents get to choose?

3. Can you do yoga but not be in the study?

4. Do you want to know if your child is being studied and sign off on that?

Going Forward...

1. Have you read the parent information page?
2. Have you read the press release?
3. Are you sure beyond a shadow of a doubt that you are in support of this program now?
4. Do you now have enough concern from these questions to investigate on your own a little bit more?
5. Are our children worth your time seeking some facts?

Resources: Chapter 23

1. Butzer et al., *"School-Based Yoga" Study*, 2015, (reports 940 US schools had yoga). https://www.yogacalm.org/research-tables/ https://www.ncbi.nlm.nih.gov/pmc/articles/PMC4831047/

2. Richard Allen, *"Encinitas School Board Votes Yoga Funds,"* (Picketing in Red, at Encinitas Blvd and Rancho Santa Fe where the Encinitas school district EUSD is located), June 21, 2016. http://www.cbs8.com/story/32277906/encinitas-school-board-approves-student-yoga-classes.

3. Jamie Chambers, *"Encinitas School Board Votes to Keep Yoga Program,"* (Investigating parents asked for the resignation of the Superintendent at the June 7, 2016 EUSD board meeting), June 21, 2016. http://fox5sandiego.com/2016/06/21/group-calls-for-encinitas-schools-to-deny-yoga-program-spending/.

4. Rachel Bianco, *"Encinitas Union School District's yoga plan approved by School Board"* (Chanting of "Baird Has to Go." Replaces Om...), June 21, 2016. http://www.10news.com/news/encinitas-union-school-districts-yoga-proposal-meets-opposition-062116.

5. Sonima payments to Chandler Hill (which is Scott Himelstein); http://encinitasparents4truth.com/wp-content/uploads/2016/06/Screen-Shot-2016-06-06-at-8.58.08-PM.png.

6. Our Facebook and the media pages: (www.truthaboutyoga.com, facebook.com/factsaboutyoga, and https://twitter.com/truthaboutyoga).

7. Another group of parents *Parents for Responsible Spending* website: http://encinitasparents4truth.com/, and media pages: https://www.facebook.com/search/top/?q=parents%20for%20responsible%20education%20spending, https://twitter.com/Pres_Encinitas?ref_src=twsrc%5Etfw, @Pres_Encinitas.

8. All documents available: https://truthaboutyoga.com/san-diego-county/.

9. *This is the current yoga-in-school curriculum location, Himilstein, Pure Edge Inc., http://pureedgeinc.org/.*

10. Don Bauder, *"Encinitas Schools Have Scrubbed their Yoga Programs Clean. Is yoga a Religion? Top of Form Courts Bottom of Formsay it is,"* April 29, 2015. http://www.sandiegoreader.com/news/2015/apr/29/citylights-yoga-religion/.

11. Best Article: Aaron Burgin, *"Ties between EUSD Yoga Program, Foundation and School Raise Concerns,"* June 23, 2016. https://www.thecoastnews.com/ties-between-eusd-yoga-program-foundation-and-school-raise-concerns/.

12. Conflict of Interest power point created by *parents for responsible spending* in EUSD http://encinitasparents4truth.com/wp-content/uploads/2016/06/ConflictofInterestEUSDSonimaUSD.pdf.

13. Two reports produced by Himelstein for USD, CEPAL: November 8, 2013: https://truthaboutyoga.files.wordpress.com/2015/01/cepal-report_implementing-yoga_2013-2014.pdf January 30, 2014: https://truthaboutyoga.files.wordpress.com/2015/01/eusd-yoga-student-effects-2012-13-formattedforwebsite.pdf

14. Conflict of interest power point, Baird intentionally misrepresenting and hiding negative results: http://encinitasparents4truth.com/wp-content/uploads/2016/06/ConflictofInterestEUSDSonimaUSD.pdf and http://www.sonimafoundation.org/wp-content/uploads/2015/05/Sonima-2013-AR-050615-FINspreads.pdf and http://encinitasparents4truth.com/baird-intentionally-misrepresents-study-results/.

15. Analysis of CEPAL Report findings: https://truthaboutyoga.files.wordpress.com/2015/01/cepal-bulletpoints.pdf.

16. Sharath on Tour: http://ayny.org/event/sharath-jois-us-tour/.

17. Sonima on Tour: http://www.sonima.com/about/tour/.

18. Government initiatives to make International Yoga Fest a "mass movement" March 2017: http://www.aninews.in/newsdetail-MTA/MzAzMjE5/govt-for-initiatives-to-make-international-yoga-fest-a-039-mass-movement-039-.html, https://www.oneindia.com/india/yoga-no-religious-activity-a-global-mass-movement-modi-2132798.html.

19. Paul Tudor Jones purchased a $71 Million dollar estate: http://www.cnbc.com/2015/04/01/paul-tudor-jones-buys-71-million-palm-beach-estate.html.

20. Himelstein's website with Sonima curriculum (matching EUSD): http://pureedgeinc.org/.

Not mentioned in chapter, but worth a look:

Religion, Education and Human Rights

March 17, 2017—*Religion, Education and Human Rights* is a book this article presents: http://clrforum.org/tag/education/

This book examines the interconnectedness between religion, education, and human rights from an international perspective using an interdisciplinary approach.

Resources: Chapter 24

1. Twin kills sister, *"Bail Denied for Yoga Studio Owner Accused of Twin Sisters Death"* Yoga studio co-owners: http://www.palmbeachpost.com/news/crime--law/bail-denied-for-yoga-studio-owner-accused-sister-death/ZEBtrowNC3Dk0FRmTIYoeK/

   - https://torontosun.com/news/world/yoga-twin-on-trial-for-sisters-death-murder-or-tragic-accident.
   - https://www.usmagazine.com/celebrity-news/news/yoga-teacher-accused-of-murdering-twin-sister-w209150/.

https://nypost.com/2016/06/09/judge-orders-release-of-twin-accused-of-killing-her-sister.

2. Website: (www.truthaboutyoga.com)

Resources: Chapter 25

1. Wikipedia. *International Yoga Day*, 2015.

CPSIA information can be obtained
at www.ICGtesting.com
Printed in the USA
FSHW011508151219